5G $15⁰⁰P

5G $15⁰⁰P

The
CORONADO
EXPEDITION

1540-1542

Lithographed By McKnight and McKnight Publishing
Bloomington, Illinois

Bound By Stappenbeck Bookbindery, Inc.
Bloomington, Illinois

The
CORONADO EXPEDITION
1540-1542

by

George Parker Winship

The Rio Grande Press Inc.,

1734 East 71st Place, Chicago 49, Illinois

First edition from which this
printing was reproduced
was supplied by
FRED ROSENSTOCK
1228 East Colfax Avenue
Denver, Colorado

A RIO GRANDE CLASSIC
First published in 1896 as part of the
Annual Report of the
Bureau of American Ethnology
of the
SMITHSONIAN INSTITUTION
1892-1893

LIBRARY OF CONGRESS CARD CATALOG NUMBER
64-15130

1964

The Rio Grande Press Inc.,
1734 East 71st Place, Chicago 49, Illinois

INTRODUCTION

Few adventures in the history of earthbound man can surpass, or even equal, the journey of Francisco Vázquez de Coronado from Mexico City to the plains of Cibola (now Kansas). It is an exciting tale of heroic men in search of gold; it is a story to set the blood tingling, and the mind to conjuring up images of armored figures riding horses under a golden sky. It is easy, in imagination, to look down from a New Mexican mesa and see the glittering conquistador and his brave soldiers gradually emerge from the mists of time. The sun glints from their proud lances, and their colorful pennants flutter in the air. The men ride boldly, tall in the saddle, cursing the ubiquitous heat, the thorny desert growth, the shimmering landscape and the unrelenting panorama of empty miles. All men curse when constant vigilance is the price of survival.

A rush of wind from the canyons can destroy the illusion with a whirl of dust. Still, the name of the great explorer can always re-evoke the picture of a handful of men riding boldly into the unknown natural furnace of the Southwestern dry country.

Francisco Vázquez de Coronado was born in Salamanca, Spain, in the year 1510. In the wake of Hernán Cortés, Coronado came to Mexico with Viceroy Antonio de Mendoza. In 1538, Vázquez was appointed governor of the province of Nueva Galicia; in the same year, Friar Marcos de Niza returned from the north with news that he had, with his own eyes, actually seen one of the fabled Seven Golden Cities of Cibola.

Viceroy Mendoza, dazzled at the thought of the legendary wealth of the Seven Cities, organized an elaborate expedition to go and take the land in the name of the king of Spain. He appointed Francisco Vázquez de Coronado to lead it, and named him captain general of the Spanish army overseas. Herbert Bolton states that Coronado's army consisted of 300 soldiers and a large body of friendly Indian allies. The Spanish outpost farthest north in New Spain was the village of Culiaçan (in Sinaloa), and from thence Coronado set forth in the spring of 1540. His trail led across modern Sonora and Southeast Arizona to the Zuñi country of New Mexico, and from there into the plains now called Kansas. None of the Spaniards found splendor or wealth in Cibola—all they found was the squalor and savagery of primitive Indians, and unending herds of wild buffalo.

It was the legend of the gilded man that brought the Spaniards into what is now Central and South America; it was the legend of the Seven Golden Cities of Cibola that led them into New Spain and northward into the dry country of the American Southwest. That legend died forever when Francisco Vázquez de Coronado returned empty-handed to Mexico City. For a Spanish conquistador, failure meant oblivion. Although Coronado resumed his duties as governor of Neuva Galicia, he fell from favor and was no longer as welcome at the royal court in Mexico City. By 1544 he was dismissed from his posts and stripped of his property. He was banned from the society of hidalgos. He died in poverty in Mexico City in the year 1554, and only a few marked the passing of this historic adventurer and soldier. Only the passage of time has elevated his name to the recognition the man deserved, long ago, as the explorer of the great Southwest.

I

The Spaniards were fanatic historians, and contemporary scholars are prone to quip that every Spanish deed in the New World is recorded in some document somewhere. George Parker Winship began his study of the Spanish documentation relating to Coronado at the age of about 21—as a student at Harvard. He dedicated himself to the great task with scrupulous care. Because of the meticulous manner with which he did his research, THE CORONADO EXPEDITION, 1540-1542, was first published in 1896 as part of the Fourteenth Annual Report of the Bureau of American Ethnology of the Smithsonian Institution. Since then, the Winship work has remained as an outstanding English-language translation of a major segment of the Hispanic-American historical records.

Spain's spectacular drama in the exploration of America, as represented by the Coronado expedition, was only a few years removed in time from the great reconquest of Spain. Though the stage setting of this colorful pageant was thousands of miles removed from mother Spain, there was something geographically familiar in the obvious similarities that the explorers of 1540-1542 found in the Southwest. A semi-desert land like the plains of Castile and the valleys of Andalusia evoked many comparisons and resulted in the transfer of many place-names; the Spaniards equated the unknown new land with the known features of old Spain. Only the actors on the stage were different, and yet even here there was some similarity. The Indians in the New World were the heathen, just as had been the Moors on the Iberian peninsula, though the hope of converting the North American aborigenes to Roman Catholic Christianity certainly outran the Hispanic expectation of bringing the Moor to The Faith.

The importance of Vázquez de Coronado's expedition, coupled with the dramatic impact of such a unique adventure, has frequently commanded the attention of the scholar. Some of the most important historians and anthropologists have chosen the Coronado theme for study. They have succeeded in establishing beyond the possibility of eclipse a name for that intrepid explorer that is as well known today as it was little known 75 years ago. A modern freeway, shopping center, national forest, state park, student dormitory and dozens of streets commemorate the name of a man who was born Vázquez, but who by English misusage has come to be known irrevocably as simply Coronado.

Most definitive of the Coronadoists was Herbert Eugene Bolton, who in his 1940 book CORONADO, KNIGHT OF PUEBLOS AND PLAINS (reprinted by the University of New Mexico Press, Albuquerque, 1964), retold the story of the conquistador with brilliant style and grace. A. Grove Day (CORONADO'S QUEST, Berkeley, 1940) and George P. Hammond and Agapito Rey (jointly, NARRATIVES OF THE CORONADO EXPEDITION, 1540-1542, Albuquerque, 1940, a limited edition) have contributed significantly to Coronadiana. Other important writers have been Arthur S. Aiton, Frederick W. Hodge, Frederick S. Dellenbaugh, Lansing B. Bloom, Adolph F. A. Bandelier, Hubert H. Bancroft, Carl O. Sauer and George P. Hammond, writing alone his CORONADO'S SEVEN CITIES (Albuquerque, 1940).

Behind these contributions, and regularly cited by other established authorities, lies the first basic work in English on this theme of early

American history, THE CORONADO EXPEDITION, 1540-1542, by George Parker Winship. This Rio Grande Classic reprint is being published because the Winship work was the initial endeavor in English in its field; because of its continuing usefulness to students of Southwestern history; because of the very nature of the important documents translated by Winship for publication, and finally, because of the continuing popular demand which has brought into print five previous editions of all or of a significant portion of the Winship study.

Hammond and Rey, in the introduction to their independent translation of much of the same documentation, have called Winship's book ". . . the standard work on the subject since its publication in 1896." Bolton rates the Winship original as a ". . . monumental source book containing most of the essential documents at that time known." That subsequent research has uncovered additional material and made corrections in the earlier translations is an obvious fact. Fresh insights into history have also been gained from the new information. The pioneer Coronadian was here and there mistaken in paleography, in the imperfect interpretation of the Spanish idiom, or in minor other matters, but the scholar is particularly interested in the fact that new material has disclosed relatively few major errors in the Winship work.

No attempt has been made here to "correct" the original manuscript, as our purpose is to make available to the public once again the same material that first appeared in the FOURTEENTH ANNUAL REPORT OF THE UNITED STATES BUREAU OF ETHNOLOGY, PART I, PAGE 329-613 (Washington, 1896). With its many illustrations and rare maps, the 1896 edition has a special appeal to scholars (and second guessers) in that both the original Spanish documentation and the English translation is presented at the same time. The outstanding single document in this work is the Castañeda account of the expedition.

Both the Bureau of Ethnology and the Department of History at Harvard University were interested in publishing Winship's work, with the honor finally going to the former. This points up the anthropological significance as well as the historical value of this study. At the time of writing, the author was listed as Assistant in American History at Harvard. It was noted that the work had been done by this youthful scholar as an undergraduate project at that institution, and apparently continued in the seminar of American History. Though Harvard professors Justin Winsor, Henry W. Haynes, J. Walter Fewkes and Edward Channing were instrumental in shaping Winship's study, a larger personal debt was to that dedicated Southwesterner Adolph Bandelier and to early ethnologist Frederick W. Hodge. The latter was to provide an introduction and notes for the two later editions of Winship's CORONADO.

In 1904, a second edition of Winship's work appeared, somewhat less valuable in that it contained only the translated documents rather than both the originals and the translations. Bearing the title THE JOURNEY OF CORONADO, 1540-1542, FROM THE CITY OF MEXICO TO THE GRAND CANYON OF THE COLORADO AND BUFFALO PLAINS OF TEXAS, KANSAS AND NEBRASKA, AS TOLD BY HIMSELF AND

HIS FOLLOWERS, this work appeared as part of The Trail Maker Series published in New York by A. S. Barnes & Co. An identical edition was published in 1922, as part of the American Explorers Series, by the Allerton Book Co. of New York.

The first of two editions in which Hodge participated appeared in 1907 under the title THE NARRATIVE OF THE EXPEDITION OF CORONADO, by Pedro de Castañeda, in SPANISH EXPLORERS IN THE SOUTHERN UNITED STATES, 1528-1543, and included only Castañeda's account. The same work also formed a part of J. Franklin Jameson's series of ORIGINAL NARRATIVES OF EARLY AMERICAN HISTORY, published by Charles Scribner's Sons in New York. Hodge added notes to Winship's original work. In 1933, the Grabhorn Press published a collector's edition limited to 550 copies, and this bears the lengthy title THE JOURNEY OF FRANCISCO VAZQUEZ DE CORONADO, 1540-1542, AS TOLD BY PEDRO DE CASTAÑEDA, FRANCISCO VÁZQUEZ DE CORONADO, AND OTHERS. TRANSLATED AND EDITED BY GEORGE PARKER WINSHIP, WITH ADDITIONAL NOTES AND AN INTRODUCTION BY FREDERICK WEBB HODGE, DIRECTOR OF THE SOUTHWEST MUSEUM AT LOS ANGELES. In this collector's edition, Hodge augmented the notes of his previous edition.

George Parker Winship, whose career as a scholar of the Spanish Southwest seemed so promising with the 1896 publication of his first work, was a mere 25 years of age when his CORONADO appeared. Born on July 29, 1871, in Bridgewater, Mass., Winship received his A.B. and A.M. degrees from Harvard in 1893 and 1894, respectively. From 1893 until 1895, he was Assistant in History at Harvard. The years 1895-1915 found Winship as Librarian of the John Carter Brown Library, which employment determined the remainder of his active career of dedication to the field of professional librarianship.

Between 1915 and 1925, Winship was Librarian of the Widener Collection at Harvard. In 1917, he was honored with a Litt.D. degree from the University of Michigan. From 1926 to 1936, Winship served as Assistant Librarian of Harvard Library, retiring at the age of 65 to become a free lance writer. Winship died on June 22, 1952.

Though never destined to become one of the great Southwestern historians, Winship did produce a lengthy personal bibliography, principally in the field of librarianship. His diverse specialties included, HISTORY OF FINE PRINTING, THE BIBLE IN PRINT, PRESSES, CHAUCER, WILLIAM CAXTON, EARLY MEXICAN PRINTERS, and incunabula. Notwithstanding this outstanding service in librarianship, to the Southwesterner, the name of George Parker Winship will ever be associated with this classic study of the New World's best-known explorer, Francisco Vázquez de Coronado.

DONALD C. CUTTER
Professor of Southwestern History,
University of New Mexico

Albuquerque, 1964

ABOUT THE AUTHOR OF THIS INTRODUCTION

Dr. Donald C. Cutter is presently Professor of Southwestern History at the University of New Mexico in Albuquerque. He was born in Chico, Calif., on Jan. 9, 1922. He took his undergraduate and graduate degrees from the University of California, A.B. (1943), M.A. (1947), Ph.D. (1950). From 1950 to 1951, Dr. Cutter was an Instructor at San Diego State College; from 1951 to 1962 an Assistant Professor and Professor of History at the University of Southern California; since 1962 he has been associated with the faculty of the University of New Mexico.

He heads the New Mexico Historical Review board, and is a member of the editorial boards of ARIZONA AND THE WEST, JOURNAL OF THE WEST, THE AMERICAN WEST, and THE AMERICAS. He has produced an impressive list of distinguished publications:

> MALASPIÑA IN CALIFORNIA (1960)
> THE DIARY OF ENSIGN GABRIEL MORAGA'S EXPEDITION OF
>   DISCOVERY IN THE SACRAMENTO VALLEY, 1808 (1957)
> TADEO HAENKE Y EL FINAL DE UNA VIEJA POLEMICA
>   (in press, Buenos Aires)

He has contributed historical articles to:

> ENCYCLOPEDIA BRITTANICA
> COLLIER'S ENCYCLOPEDIA
> HISPANIC AMERICAN HISTORICAL REVIEW
> CALIFORNIA HISTORICAL SOCIETY QUARTERLY
> REVISTA DE INDIAS
> REVISTA DE HISTORIA MILITAR
> PACIFIC NORTHWEST QUARTERLY
> QUARTERLY OF THE HISTORICAL SOCIETY OF SOUTHERN
>   CALIFORNIA
> (and others)

Dr. Cutter has been a Fellow in Pacific Coast History, of the Native Sons of the Golden West; a Research Training Fellow in the Social Science Research Council; a Del Amo Foundation Fellow in Spain; A Faculty Research Fellow for the Social Science Research Council and a Fulbright Research Fellow in Spain.

The Rio Grande Press is most grateful to Dr. Cutter for his fine introduction to our reprint edition of THE CORONADO EXPEDITION, 1540-1542. We are honored and pleased that he was able to take the time from a very busy schedule to prepare this material, and we consider it a privilege to publish his words.

ROBERT B. McCOY, President
THE RIO GRANDE PRESS, INC.

October, 1964

THE CORONADO EXPEDITION, 1540–1542

BY

GEORGE PARKER WINSHIP

CONTENTS

IX

CONTENTS

CONTENTS

XI

CONTENTS

CONTENTS

XIII

ILLUSTRATIONS

XV

THE CORONADO EXPEDITION, 1540-1542

By George Parker Winship

INTRODUCTORY NOTE

The following historical introduction, with the accompanying translations, is the result of work in the Seminary of American History at Harvard University. Undertaken as a bit of undergraduate study, it has gradually assumed a form which has been considered worthy of publication, chiefly because of the suggestions and assistance which have been given with most generous readiness by all from whom I have had occasion to ask help or advice. To Dr Justin Winsor; to Professor Henry W. Haynes, who opened the way for students of the early Spanish history of the North American southwest; to Dr J. Walter Fewkes, who has freely offered me the many results of his long-continued and minute investigations at Tusayan and Zuñi; and to the careful oversight and aid of Mr F. W. Hodge and the other members of the Bureau of Ethnology, much of the value of this work is due. Mr Augustus Hemenway has kindly permitted the use of the maps and documents deposited in the archives of the Hemenway Southwestern Archeological Expedition by Mr Adolph F. Bandelier. My indebtedness to the researches and writings of Mr Bandelier is evident throughout. Señor Joaquin Garcia Icazbalceta—whose death, in November, 1894, removed the master student of the documentary history of Mexico—most courteously gave me all the information at his command, and with his own hand copied the *Relación postrera de Sívola*, which is now for the first time printed. The Spanish text of Castañeda's narrative, the presentation of which for the first time in its original language affords the best reason for the present publication, has been copied and printed with the consent of the trustees of the Lenox Library in New York, in whose custody is the original manuscript. I am under many obligations to their librarian, Mr Wilberforce Eames, who has always been ready to assist me by whatever means were within his power.

The subject of this research was suggested by Professor Channing of Harvard. If my work has resulted in some contribution to the literature of the history of the Spanish conquest of America, it is because of his constant guidance and inspiration, and his persistent refusal to consent to any abandoning of the work before the results had been expressed in a manner worthy of the university.

Before the completion of the arrangements by which this essay becomes a part of the annual report of the Director of the Bureau of Ethnology, it had been accepted for publication by the Department of History of Harvard University.

GEORGE PARKER WINSHIP

Assistant in American History

in Harvard University.

CAMBRIDGE, MASSACHUSETTS,

February, 1895.

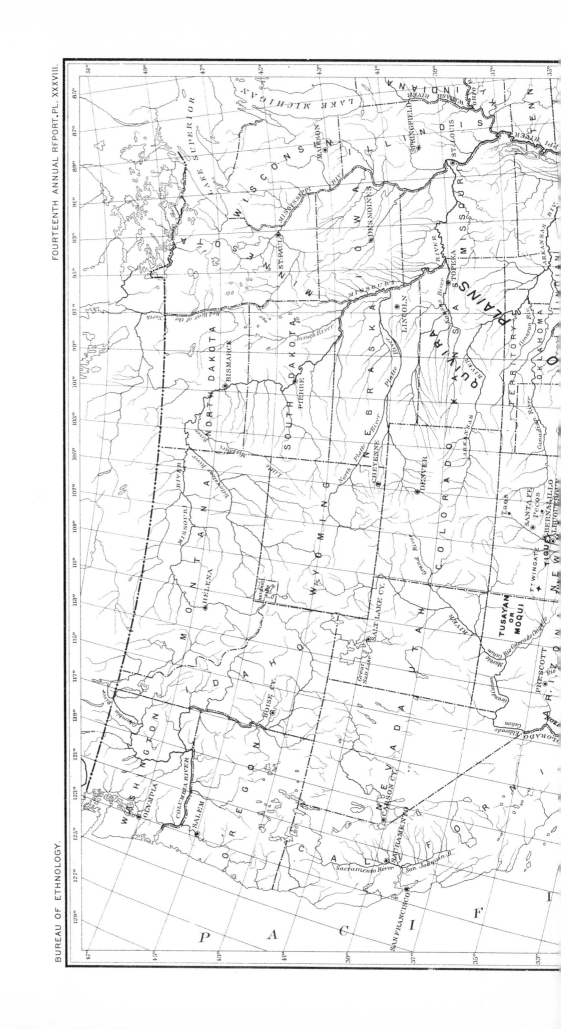

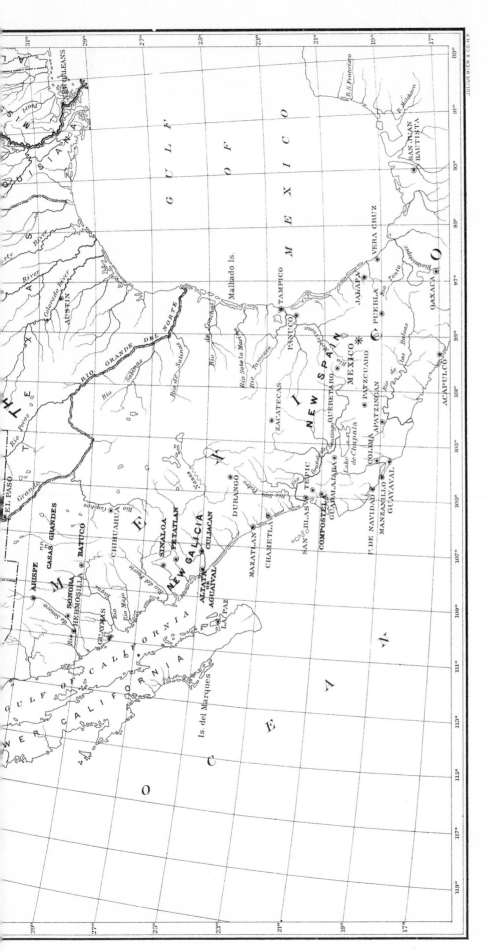

THE NEW SPAIN AND NEW MEXICO COUNTRY.

ITINERARY OF THE CORONADO EXPEDITIONS, 1527–1547

1527

June 17   Narvaez sails from Spain to explore the mainland north of the Gulf of Mexico.

1528

April 15   Narvaez lands in Florida.

Sept. 22   The failure of the Narvaez expedition is assured.

1535

Cortes makes a settlement in Lower California.

Mendoza comes to Mexico as viceroy of New Spain.

1536

April   Cabeza de Vaca and three other survivors of the Narvaez expedition arrive in New Spain.

The Licenciate de la Torre takes the residencia of Nuño de Guzman, who is imprisoned until June 30, 1538.

1537

Franciscan friars labor among the Indian tribes living north of New Spain.

Coronado subdues the revolted miners of Amatepeque.

The proposed expedition under Dorantes comes to naught.

April 20   De Soto receives a grant of the mainland of Florida.

1538

September It is rumored that Coronado has been nominated governor of New Galicia.

1539

Pedro de Alvarado returns from Spain to the New World.

March 7   Friar Marcos de Niza, accompanied by the negro Estevan, starts from Culiacan to find the Seven Cities.

April 18   The appointment of Coronado as governor of New Galicia is confirmed.

May   De Soto sails from Habana.

May 9   Friar Marcos enters the wilderness of Arizona.

May 21   Friar Marcos learns of the death of Estevan.

May 25   De Soto lands on the coast of Florida.

July 8   Ulloa sails from Acapulco nearly to the head of the Gulf of California in command of a fleet furnished by Cortes.

August   Friar Marcos returns from the north and certifies to the truth
Sept. 2   of his report before Mendoza and Coronado.

October   The news of Niza's discoveries spreads through New Spain.

7

November   Mendoza begins to prepare for an expedition to conquer the Seven Cities of Cibola.

Melchior Diaz is sent to verify the reports of Friar Marcos.

De Soto finds the remains of the camp of Narvaez at Bahia de los Cavallos.

Nov. 12   Witnesses in Habana describe the effect of the friar's reports.

1540

Jan. 1   Mendoza celebrates the new year at Pasquaro.

Jan. 9   Coronado at Guadalajara.

Feb. 5   Cortes stops at Habana on his way to Spain.

February   The members of the Cibola expedition assemble at Compostela, where the viceroy finds them on his arrival.

Feb. 22   Review of the army on Sunday.

Feb. 23   The army, under the command of Francisco Vazquez Coronado, starts for Cibola (not on February 1).

Feb. 26   Mendoza returns to Compostela, having left the army two days before, and examines witnesses to discover how many citizens of New Spain have accompanied Coronado. He writes a letter to King Charles V, which has been lost.

March   The army is delayed by the cattle in crossing the rivers.

The death of the army master, Samaniego, at Chiametla.

Return of Melchior Diaz and Juan de Saldivar from Chichilticalli.

March 3   Beginning of litigation in Spain over the right to explore and conquer the Cibola country.

March 28   Reception to the army at Culiacan, on Easter day.

April   The army is entertained by the citizens of Culiacan.

Mendoza receives the report of Melchior Diaz' exploration, perhaps at Jacona.

Coronado writes to Mendoza, giving an account of what has already happened, and of the arrangements which he has made for the rest of the journey. This letter has been lost.

April 17   Mendoza writes to the Emperor Charles V.

April 22   Coronado departs from Culiacan with about seventy-five horsemen and a few footmen.

April   Coronado passes through Petatlan, Cinaloa, Los Cedros,
May   Yaquemi, and other places mentioned by Jaramillo.

May 9   Alarcon sails from Acapulco to cooperate with Coronado.

The army starts from Culiacan and marches toward the Corazones or Hearts valley.

May 26   Coronado leaves the valley of Corazones. He proceeds to Chi-
June   chilticalli, passing Senora or Sonora and Ispa, and thence crosses the Arizona wilderness, fording many rivers.

The army builds the town of San Hieronimo in Corazones valley.

THE ULPIUS GLOBE OF 1542

In Possession of the New York Historical Society

July 7   Coronado reaches Cibola and captures the first city, the
             pueblo of Hawikuh, which he calls Granada.
July 11   The Indians retire to their stronghold on Thunder mountain.
July 15   Pedro de Tovar goes to Tusayan or Moki, returning within
             thirty days.
July 19   Coronado goes to Thunder mountain and returns the same day.
Aug. 3   Coronado writes to Mendoza. He sends Juan Gallego to
             Mexico, and Melchior Diaz to Corazones with orders for
             the army. Friar Marcos accompanies them.
Aug. 25 (?) Lopez de Cardenas starts to find the canyons of Colorado
             river, and is gone about eighty days.
Aug. 26   Alarcon enters the mouth of Colorado river.
Aug. 29   Hernando de Alvarado goes eastward to Tiguex, on the Rio
             Grande, and to the buffalo plains.
             Pedro de Alvarado arrives in New Spain.
Sept. 7   Hernando de Alvarado reaches Tiguex.
             Diaz and Gallego reach Corazones about the middle of Sep-
             tember, and the army starts for Cibola.
             Coronado visits Tutahaco.
September   The army reaches Cibola, and goes thence to Tiguex for its
  to   winter quarters. The natives in the Rio Grande pueblos
January   revolt and are subjugated. The Turk tells the Spaniards
             about Quivira.
October   Diaz starts from Corazones before the end of September,
             with twenty-five men, and explores the country along the
             Gulf of California, going beyond Colorado river.
             Diego de Alcaraz is left in command of the town of San
             Hieronimo.
Nov. 29   Mendoza and Pedro de Alvarado sign an agreement in
             regard to common explorations and conquests.

1541

Jan. 8   Diaz dies on the return from the mouth of the Colorado, and
             his companions return to Corazones valley.
March   Alcaraz, during the spring, moves the village of San Hier-
             onimo from Corazones valley to the valley of Suya river.
April 20   Beginning of the Mixton war in New Galicia.
             Coronado writes a letter to the King from Tiguex, which has
             been lost.
             Tovar and perhaps Gallego return to Mexico
April 23   Coronado starts with all his force from Tiguex to cross the
             buffalo plains to Quivira.
May   The army is divided somewhere on the great plains, perhaps
             on Canadian river. The main body returns to Tiguex,
             arriving there by the middle or last of June.
             De Soto crosses the Mississippi.

June   Coronado, with thirty horsemen, rides north to Quivira, where he arrives forty-two (?) days later.
June 24   Pedro de Alvarado is killed at Nochistlan, in New Galicia.
August   Coronado spends about twenty-five days in the country of Quivira, leaving "the middle or last of August."
Sept. 28   The Indians in New Galicia attack the town of Guadalajara, but are repulsed.
Oct. 2   Coronado returns from Quivira to Tiguex and writes a letter to the King.
November   Cardenas starts to return to Mexico with some other invalids from the army. He finds the village of Suya in ruins and hastily returns to Tiguex.
December   Coronado falls from his horse and is seriously injured.
            The Mixton peñol is surrendered by the revolted Indians during holiday week.

1542

Coronado and his soldiers determine to return to New Spain. They start in the spring, and reach Mexico probably late in the autumn. The general makes his report to the viceroy, who receives him coldly. Coronado not long after resigns his position as governor of New Galicia and retires to his estates.

April 17   De Soto reaches the mouth of Red river, where he dies, May 21.
June 27   Cabrillo starts on his voyage up the California coast. He dies in January, 1543, and the vessels return to New Spain by April, 1544.
Nov. 1   Villalobos starts across the Pacific. His fleet meets with many misfortunes and losses. The survivors, five years or more later, return to Spain.
Nov. 25   Friar Juan de la Cruz is killed at Tiguex, where he remained when the army departed for New Spain. Friar Luis also remained in the new country, at Cicuye, and Friar Juan de Padilla, at Quivira, where he is killed. The companions of Friar Juan de Padilla make their way back to Mexico, arriving before 1552.

1544

Nov. 30   Promulgation of the New Laws for the Indies.
            Sebastian Cabot publishes his map of the New World.

1547

Mendoza, before he leaves New Spain to become viceroy of Peru, answers the charges preferred against him by the officials appointed to investigate his administration.

HISTORICAL INTRODUCTION

THE CAUSES OF THE CORONADO EXPEDITION, 1528–1539

ALVAR NUÑEZ CABEZA DE VACA

The American Indians are always on the move. Tribes shift the location of their homes from season to season and from year to year, while individuals wander at will, hunting, trading or gossiping. This is very largely true today, and when the Europeans first came in contact with the American aborigines, it was a characteristic feature of Indian life. The Shawnees, ·for example, have drifted from Georgia to the great lakes, and part of the way back, during the period since their peregrinations can first be traced. Traders from tribe to tribe, in the days when European commercial ideas were unknown in North America, carried bits of copper dug from the mines in which the aboriginal implements are still found, on the shores of Lake Superior, to the Atlantic coast on the one side and to the Rocky mountains on the other. The Indian gossips of central Mexico, in 1535, described to the Spaniards the villages of New Mexico and Arizona, with their many-storied houses of stone and adobe. The Spanish colonists were always eager to learn about unexplored regions lying outside the limits of the white settlements, and their Indian neighbors and servants in the valley of Mexico told them many tales of the people who lived beyond the mountains which hemmed in New Spain on the north. One of these stories may be found in another part of this memoir, where it is preserved in the narrative of Pedro Castañeda, the historian of the Coronado expedition. Castañeda's hearsay report of the Indian story, which was related by an adventurous trader who had penetrated the country far to the north, compares not unfavorably with the somewhat similar stories which Marco Polo told to entertain his Venetian friends.[1] But whatever may have been known before, the information which led to the expedition of Friar Marcos de Niza and to that of Francisco Vazquez Coronado was brought to New Spain late in the spring of 1536 by Alvar Nuñez Cabeza de Vaca.

In 1520, before Cortes, the conqueror of Motecuhzoma, had made his peace with the Emperor Charles V and with the authorities at Cuba, Panfilo de Narvaez was dispatched to the Mexican mainland, at the

---

[1] The Indian's story is in the first chapter of Castañeda's Narrative. Some additional information is given in Bandelier's Contributions to the History of the Southwest, the first chapter of which is entitled "Sketch of the knowledge which the Spaniards in Mexico possessed of the countries north of the province of New Galicia previous to the return of Cabeza de Vaca." For bibliographic references to this and other works referred to throughout this memoir, see the list at the end of the paper.

head of a considerable force. He was sent to subdue and supersede the conqueror of Mexico, but when they met, Cortes quickly proved that he was a better general than his opponent, and a skillful politician as well. Narvaez was deserted by his soldiers and became a prisoner in the City of Mexico, where he was detained during the two years which followed. Cortes was at the height of his power, and Narvaez must have felt a longing to rival the successes of the conqueror, who had won the wealth of the Mexican empire. After Cortes resumed his dutiful obedience to the Spanish crown, friends at home obtained a royal order which effected the release of Narvaez, who returned to Spain at the earliest opportunity. Almost as soon as he had established himself anew in the favor of the court, he petitioned the King for a license which should permit him to conduct explorations in the New World. After some delay, the desired patent was granted. It authorized Narvaez to explore, conquer, and colonize the country between Florida and the Rio de Palmas, a grant comprising all that portion of North America bordering on the Gulf of Mexico, which is now included within the limits of the United States. Preparations were at once begun for the complete organization of an expedition suitable to the extent of this territory and to the power and dignity of its governor.

On June 17, 1527, Narvaez, governor of Florida, Rio de Palmas and Espiritu Santo—the Rio Grande and the Mississippi on our modern maps—sailed from Spain. He went first to Cuba, where he refitted his fleet and replaced one vessel which had been lost in a hurricane during the voyage. When everything was ready to start for the unexplored mainland, he ordered the pilots to conduct his fleet to the western limits of his jurisdiction—our Texas. They landed him, April 15, 1528, on the coast of the present Florida, at a bay which the Spaniards called Bahia de la Cruz, and which the map of Sebastian Cabot enables us to identify with Apalache bay. The pilots knew that a storm had driven them out of their course toward the east, but they could not calculate on the strong current of the gulf stream. They assured the commander that he was not far from the Rio de Palmas, the desired destination, and so he landed his force of 50 horses and 300 men—just half the number of the soldiers, mechanics, laborers, and priests who had started with him from Spain ten months before. He sent one of his vessels back to Cuba for recruits, and ordered the remaining three to sail along the coast toward the west and to wait for the army at the fine harbor of Panuco, which was reported to be near the mouth of Palmas river. The fate of these vessels is not known.

Narvaez, having completed these arrangements, made ready to lead his army overland to Panuco. The march began April 19. For a while, the Spaniards took a northerly direction, and then they turned toward the west. Progress was slow, for the men knew nothing of the country, and the forests and morasses presented many difficulties to the soldiers unused to woodcraft. Little help could be procured from the Indians, who soon became openly hostile wherever the Spaniards encountered them. Food grew scarce, and no persuasion could induce the natives to reveal hidden stores of corn, or of gold. On May 15, tired and discouraged, the Spaniards reached a large river with a strong current flowing toward the south. They rested here, while Cabeza de Vaca, the royal treasurer accompanying the expedition, took a small party of soldiers and followed the banks of the river down to the sea. The fleet was not waiting for them at the mouth of this stream, nor could anything be learned of the fine harbor for which they were searching. Disappointed anew by the report which Cabeza de Vaca made on his return to the main camp, the Spanish soldiers crossed the river and continued their march toward the west. They plodded on and on, and after awhile turned southward, to follow down the course of another large river which blocked their westward march. On the last day of July they reached a bay of considerable size, at the mouth of the river. They named this Bahia de los Cavallos, perhaps, as has been surmised, because it was here that they killed the last of their horses for food. The Spaniards, long before this, had become thoroughly disheartened. Neither food nor gold could be found. The capital cities, toward which the Indian captives had directed the wandering strangers, when reached, were mere groups of huts, situated in some cases on mounds of earth. Not a sign of anything which would reward their search, and hardly a thing to eat, had been discovered during the months of toilsome marching. The Spaniards determined to leave the country. They constructed forges in their camp near the seashore, and hammered their spurs, stirrups, and other iron implements of warfare into nails and saws and axes, with which to build the boats necessary for their escape from the country. Ropes were made of the tails and manes of the horses, whose hides, pieced out with the shirts of the men, were fashioned into sails. By September 22, five boats were ready, each large enough to hold between 45 and 50 men. In these the soldiers embarked. Scarcely a man among them knew anything of navigation, and they certainly knew nothing about the navigation of this coast. They steered westward, keeping near the land, and stopping occasionally for fresh water. Sometimes they obtained a little food.

Toward the end of October they came to the mouth of a large river which poured forth so strong a current that it drove the boats out to sea. Two, those which contained Narvaez and the friars, were lost. The men in the other three boats were driven ashore by a storm, somewhere on the coast of western Louisiana or eastern Texas.[1] This was

---

[1] The most important source of information regarding the expedition of Narvaez is the Relation written by Cabeza de Vaca. This is best consulted in Buckingham Smith's translation. Mr Smith includes in his volume everything which he could find to supplement the main narration. The best study of the route followed by the survivors of the expedition, after they landed in Texas, is that of Bandelier in the second chapter of his Contributions to the History of the Southwest. In this essay Bandelier has brought together all the documentary evidence, and he writes with the knowledge obtained by traveling through the different portions of the country which Cabeza de Vaca must have

in the winter of 1528-29. Toward the end of April, 1536, Cabeza de Vaca, Alonso del Castillo Maldonado, Andres Dorantes, and a negro named Estevan, met some Spanish slave catchers near the Rio de Peta-tlan, in Sinaloa, west of the mountains which border the Gulf of California. These four men, with a single exception,[1] were the only survivors of the three hundred who had entered the continent with Narvaez eight years before.

Cabeza de Vaca and his companions stayed in Mexico for several months, as the guests of the viceroy, Don Antonio de Mendoza. At first, it was probably the intention of the three Spaniards to return to Spain, in order to claim the due reward for their manifold sufferings. Mendoza says, in a letter dated December 10, 1537,[2] that he purchased the negro Estevan from Dorantes, so that there might be someone left in New Spain who could guide an expedition back into the countries about which the wanderers had heard. An earlier letter from the viceroy, dated February 11, 1537, commends Cabeza de Vaca and *Francisco* Dorantes—he must have meant Andres, and perhaps wrote it so in his original manuscript—as deserving the favor of the Empress. Maldonado is not mentioned in this letter, and no trace of him has been found after the arrival of the four survivors in Mexico. All that we know about him is that his home was in Salamanca.[3]

Cabeza de Vaca and Dorantes started from Vera Cruz for Spain in October, 1536, but their vessel was stranded before it got out of the harbor. This accident obliged them to postpone their departure until the following spring, when Cabeza de Vaca returned home alone. He told the story of his wanderings to the court and the King, and was rewarded, by 1540, with an appointment as adelantado, giving him the command over the recently occupied regions about the Rio de la Plata. The position was one for which he was unfitted, and his subordinates

traversed. Dr J. G. Shea, in his chapter in the Narrative and Critical History of America, vol. ii, p. 286, disagrees in some points with Mr Bandelier's interpretation of the route of Cabeza de Vaca west of Texas, and also with Mr Smith's identifications of the different points in the march of the main army before it embarked from the Bahia de los Cavallos. Other interesting conjectures are given in H. H. Bancroft's North Mexican States, vol. i, p. 63, and map at p. 67.

[1] Buckingham Smith collected in his Letter of Hernando de Soto, pp. 57-61, and in his Narrative of the Career of Hernando de Soto (see index), all that is known in regard to Ortiz, one of the soldiers of Narvaez, who was found among the Indians by De Soto in 1540.

[2] Mendoza to Charles V, 10 Diciembre, 1537. Cabeza de Vaca y Dorantes, . . . despues de haber llegado aquí, determinaron de irse en España, y viendo que si V. M. era servido de enviar aquella tierra alguna gente para saber de cierto lo que era, no quedaba persona que pudiese ir con ella ni dar ninguna razon, compré á Dorantes para este efecto un negro que vino de allá y se halló con ellos en todo, que se llama Estéban, por ser persona de razon. Despues sucedió, como el navio en que Dorantes iba se volvió al puerto, y sabido esto, yo le escribí á la Vera-Cruz, rogándole que viniese aquí; y como llegó á esta ciudad, yo le hablé diciéndole que hubiese por bien de volver á esta tierra con algunos religiosos y gente de caballo, que yo le daria á calalla, y saber de cierto lo que en ella habia. Y él vista mi voluntad, y el servicio que yo le puse delante que hacia con ello á Dios y á V. M., me respondió que holgaba dello, y así estoy determinado de envialle allá con la gente de caballo y religiosos que digo. Pienso que ha de redundar dello gran servicio á Dios y á V. M.—From the text printed in Pacheco y Cardenas, Docs. de Indias, ii, 206.

[3] Some recent writers have been misled by a chance comma inserted by the copyist or printer in one of the old narratives, which divides the name of Maldonado—Alonso del Castillo, Maldonado—making it appear as if there were five instead of four survivors of the Narvaez expedition who made their way to Mexico.

sent him back to Spain. The complaints against him were investigated by the Council for the Indies, but the judgment, if any was given, has never been published. He certainly was not punished, and soon settled down in Seville, where he was still living, apparently, twenty years later.[1]

While Dorantes was stopping at Vera Cruz during the winter of 1536–37, he received a letter from Mendoza, asking him to return to the City of Mexico. After several interviews, the viceroy induced Dorantes to remain in New Spain, agreeing to provide him with a party of horsemen and friars, in order to explore more thoroughly the country through which he had wandered. Mendoza explains the details of his plans in the letter written in December, 1537, and declares that he expected many advantages would be derived from this expedition which would redound to the glory of God and to the profit of His Majesty the King. The viceroy was prepared to expend a large sum—3,500 or 4,000 pesos—to insure a successful undertaking, but he promised to raise the whole amount, without taking a single maravedi from the royal treasury, by means of a more careful collection of dues, and especially by enforcing the payment of overdue sums, the collection of which hitherto had been considered impossible. This reform in the collection of rents and other royal exactions and the careful attention to all the details of the fiscal administration were among the most valuable of the many services rendered by Mendoza as viceroy. The expedition under Dorantes never started, though why nothing came of all the preparations, wrote Mendoza in his next letter to the King, "I never could find out."[2]

The three Spaniards wrote several narratives of their experiences on the expedition of Narvaez, and of their adventurous journey from the gulf coast of Texas to the Pacific coast of Mexico.[3] These travelers, who had lived a savage life for so long that they could wear no clothes, and were unable to sleep except upon the bare ground, had a strange tale to tell. The story of their eight years of wandering must have been often repeated—of their slavery, their buffalo-hunting expeditions, of the escape from their Indian masters, and their career as traders and as medicine men. These were wonderful and strange expe-

---

[1] Besides the general historians, we have Cabeza de Vaca's own account of his career in Paraguay in his Comentarios, reprinted in Vedia, Historiadores Primitivos, vol. i. Ternaux translated this narrative into French for his Voyages, part vi.

[2] The Spanish text of this letter has not been seen since Ramusio used it in making the translation for his Viaggi, vol. iii, fol. 355, ed. 1556. There is no date to the letter as Ramusio gives it. Ternaux-Compans translated it from Ramusio for his Cibola volume (Voyages, vol. ix, p. 287). It is usually cited from Ternaux's title as the "Première lettre de Mendoza." I quote from the French text the portion of the letter which explains my narrative: ". . . Andrès Dorantès, un de ceux qui firent partie de l'armée de Pamphilo Narvaez, vint près de moi. J'eus de fréquents entretiens avec lui; je pensai qu'il pouvait rendre un grand service à votre majesté; si je l'expédiais avec quarante ou cinquante chevaux et tous les objets nécessaires pour découvrir ce pays. Je dépensai beaucoup d'argent pour l'expédition, mais je ne sais pas comment il se fit que l'affaire n'eut pas de suite. De tous les préparatifs que j'avais faits, il ne me resta qu'un nègre qui est venu avec Dorantès, quelques esclaves que j'avais achetés, et des Indiens, naturels de ce pays, que j'avais fait rassembler."

[3] Two of these are extant—the Relacion of Cabeza de Vaca and Oviedo's version of an account signed by the three Spaniards and sent to the Real Audiencia at Santo Domingo, in his Historia General de las Indias, lib. xxxv, vol. iii, p. 582, ed. 1853.

riences, but the story contained little to arouse the eager interest of the colonists in New Spain, whose minds had been stirred by the accounts which came from Peru telling of the untold wealth of the Incas. A few things, however, had been seen and heard by the wanderers which suggested the possibility of lands worth conquering. "A copper hawks-bell, thick and large, figured with a face," had been given to Cabeza de Vaca, soon after he started on his journey toward Mexico. The natives who gave this to him said that they had received it from other Indians, "who had brought it from the north, where there was much copper, which was highly esteemed." After the travelers had crossed the Rio Grande, they showed this bell to some other Indians, who said that "there were many plates of this same metal buried in the ground in the place whence it had come, and that it was a thing which they esteemed highly, and that there were fixed habitations where it came from."[1] This was all the treasure which Cabeza de Vaca could say that he had seen. He had heard, however, of a better region than any he saw, for the Indians told him "that there are pearls and great riches on the coast of the South sea (the Pacific), and all the best and most opulent countries are near there." We may be sure that none of this was omitted whenever he told the Spanish colonists the story of the years of his residence in Texas and of the months of his journey across northern Mexico.[2]

THE GOVERNORS OF NEW SPAIN, 1530–1537

Don Antonio de Mendoza, "the good viceroy," had been at the head of the government of New Spain for two years when Cabeza de Vaca arrived in Mexico. The effects of his careful and intelligent administration were already beginning to appear in the increasing prosperity of the province and the improved condition of the colonists and of their lands. The authority of the viceroy was ample and extensive, although he was limited to some extent by the audiencia, the members of which had administered the government of the province since the retirement of Cortes. The viceroy was the president of this court, which had resumed more strictly judicial functions after his arrival, and he was officially advised by his instructions from the King to consult with his fellow members on all matters of importance.

Nuño de Guzman departed for New Spain in 1528, and became the head of the first audiencia. Within a year he had made himself so deservedly unpopular that when he heard that Cortes was coming back to Mexico from Spain, with the new title of marquis and fresh grants of power from the King, he thought it best to get out of the way of his rival. Without relinquishing the title to his position in the capital

---

[1] See Buckingham Smith's translation of Cabeza de Vaca's Narrative, p. 150.

[2] The effect of the stories told by Cabeza de Vaca, and later by Friar Marcos, is considered in a paper printed in the Proceedings of the American Historical Association at Washington, 1894, "Why Coronado went to New Mexico in 1540."

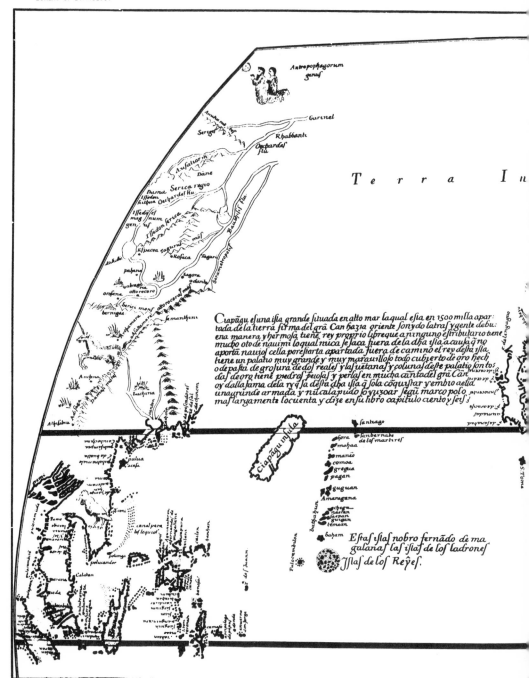

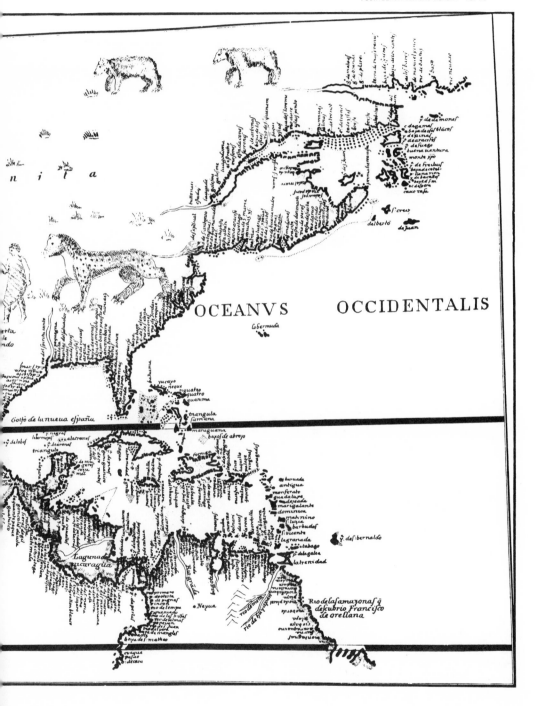

city, Guzman collected a considerable force and marched away toward
the west and north, determined to win honor and security by new conquests. He explored and subdued the country for a considerable distance along the eastern shores of the Gulf of California, but he could
find nothing there to rival the Mexico of Motecuhzoma. Meanwhile
reports reached Charles V of the manner in which Guzman had been
treating the Indians and the Spanish settlers, and so, March 17, 1536,[1]
the King appointed the Licentiate Diego Perez de la Torre to take the
residencia[2] of Guzman. At the same time Torre was commissioned to
replace Guzman as governor of New Galicia, as this northwestern province had been named. The latter had already determined to return to
Spain, leaving Don Christobal de Oñate, a model executive and administrative official, in charge of his province. Guzman almost succeeded
in escaping, but his judge, who had landed at Vera Cruz by the end of
1536, met him at the viceroy's palace in Mexico city, and secured his
arrest before he could depart. After his trial he was detained in Mexico until June 30, 1538, when he was enabled to leave New Spain by an
order which directed him to surrender his person to the officers of the
Casa de Contratacion,[3] at Seville. Guzman lost no time in going to
Spain, where he spent the next four years in urging his claims to a right
to participate in the northern conquests.

Torre, the licentiate, had barely begun to reform the abuses of Guzman's government when he was killed in a conflict with some revolted
Indian tribes. Oñate again took charge of affairs until Mendoza
appointed Luis Galindo chief justice for New Galicia. This was merely
a temporary appointment, however, until a new governor could be
selected. The viceroy's nomination for the position was confirmed by
the King, in a cedula dated April 18, 1539, which commissioned Francisco Vazquez Coronado as governor.[4]

Cortes had been engaged, ever since his return from Spain, in fitting
out expeditions which came to nothing,[5] but by which he hoped to
accomplish his schemes for completing the exploration of the South sea.
His leisure was more than occupied by his efforts to outwit the agents
of the viceroy and the audiencia, who had received orders from the
King to investigate the extent and condition of the estates held by
Cortes. In the spring of 1535, Cortes established a colony on the opposite coast of California, the supposed Island of the Marquis, at Santa

---

[1] The best sources for these proceedings is in Mota Padilla's Historia de la Nueva Galicia (ed.
Icazbalceta, pp. 104–109). A more available account in English is in H. H. Bancroft's Mexico, vol. ii,
p. 457.

[2] An official investigation into the administration of an official who is about to be relieved of his
duties.

[3] The best account, in English, of the Casa de Contratacion is given by Professor Bernard Moses, of
Berkeley, California, in the volume of papers read before the American Historical Association at its
1894 meeting.

[4] See Fragmentos de una Historia de la Nueva Galicia, by Father Tello (Icazbalceta, Documentos de
Mexico, vol. ii, p. 369).

[5] Mendoza, in the "première lettre," gives a brief sketch of the efforts which Cortes had been making, and then adds: "Il ne put donc jamais en faire la conquête; il semblait même que Dieu voulût
miraculeusement l'en éloigner." Ternaux, Cibola volume, p. 287.

Cruz,[1] near the modern La Paz. Storms and shipwreck, hunger and surfeiting, reduced the numbers and the enthusiasm of the men whom he had conducted thither, and when his vessels returned from the mainland with the news that Mendoza had arrived in Mexico, and bringing letters from his wife urging him to return at once, Cortes went back to Mexico. A few months later he recalled the settlers whom he had left at Santa Cruz, in accordance, it may be, with the command or advice of Mendoza.[2] When the stories of Cabeza de Vaca suggested the possibility of making desirable conquests toward the north, Cortes possessed a better outfit for undertaking this work than any of the others who were likely to be rivals for the privilege of exploring and occupying that region.

Pedro de Alvarado was the least known of these rival claimants. He had been a lieutenant of Cortes until he secured an independent command in Guatemala, Yucatan and Honduras, where he subdued the natives, but discovered nothing except that there was nowhere in these regions any store of gold or treasures. Abandoning this field, he tried to win a share in the conquests of Pizarro and Almagro. He approached Peru from the north, and conducted his army across the mountains. This march, one of the most disastrous in colonial history, so completely destroyed the efficiency of his force that the conquerors of Peru easily compelled him to sell them what was left of his expedition. They paid a considerable sum, weighed out in bars of silver which he found, after his return to Panama, to be made of lead with a silver veneering.[3] Alvarado was ready to abandon the work of conquering America, and had forwarded a petition to the King, asking that he might be allowed to return to Spain, when Mendoza, or the audiencia which was controlled by the enemies of Alvarado, furthered his desires by ordering him to go to the mother country and present himself before the throne. This was in 1536. While at court Alvarado must have met Cabeza de Vaca. He changed his plans for making a voyage to the South seas, and secured from the King, whose favor he had easily regained, a commission which allowed him to build a fleet in Central America and explore the South sea—the Pacific—toward the west or the north. He returned to America early in 1539, bringing with him everything needed in the equipment of a large fleet.

Mendoza, meanwhile, 1536–1539, had been making plans and preparations. He had not come to the New World as an adventurer, and he lacked the spirit of eager, reckless, hopeful expectation of wealth and fame, which accomplished so much for the geographical unfolding of the two Americas. Mendoza appears to have arranged his plans as carefully as if he had been about to engage in some intrigue at court. He rec-

---

[1] On the maps it is usually designated as S. †.

[2] The details of this episode are given in the relations and petitions of Cortes. H. H. Bancroft tells the story in his North Mexican States, vol. i, p. 77. The Cortes map of 1536 is reproduced, from a tracing, in Winsor's Narrative and Critical History of America, vol. ii, p. 442.

[3] This is the story which Garcilaso de la Vega tells in his Commentales Reales, pt. II, lib. ii.

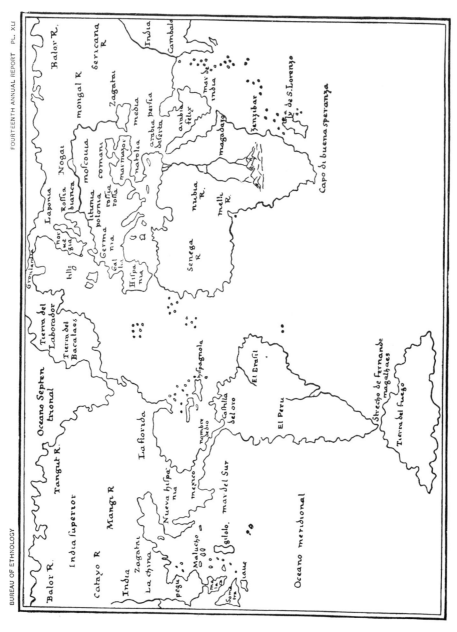

MAP OF THE WORLD BY PTOLEMY, 1548

ognized his rivals and their strength.   Nuño de Guzman was in disgrace and awaiting a trial, but he was at the court, where he could urge his claims persistently in person.   Cortes was active, but he was where Mendoza could watch everything that he tried to do.   He might succeed in anticipating the viceroy's plans, but his sea ventures heretofore had all been failures.   So long as he kept to the water there seemed to be little danger.   Mendoza's chief concern appears to have been to make sure that his rivals should have no chance of uniting their claims against him.   Representing the Crown and its interests, he felt sure of everything else.   The viceroy had no ambition to take the field in person as an explorer, and he selected Alvarado as the most available leader for the expedition which he had in mind, probably about the time that the latter came back to the New World.   He wrote to Alvarado, suggesting an arrangement between them, and after due consideration on both sides, terms and conditions mutually satisfactory were agreed on.   Mendoza succeeded in uniting Alvarado to his interests, and engaged that he should conduct an expedition into the country north of Mexico.   This arrangement was completed, apparently, before the return of Friar Marcos from his reconnoissance, which added so largely to the probabilities of success.

THE RECONNOISSANCE OF FRIAR MARCOS DE NIZA

Mendoza did not confine himself to diplomatic measures for bringing about the exploration and conquest which he had in mind.   In his undated "première lettre" the viceroy wrote that he was prepared to send Dorantes with forty or fifty horses and everything needed for an expedition into the interior; but nothing was done.

About this time, 1537–38, Friar Juan de la Asuncion seems to have visited the inland tribes north of the Spanish settlements.   Mr Bandelier has presented all the evidence obtainable regarding the labors of this friar.[1]   The most probable interpretation of the statements which refer to his wanderings is that Friar Juan went alone and without official assistance, and that he may have traveled as far north as the river Gila.   The details of his journey are hopelessly confused.   It is more than probable that there were a number of friars at work among the outlying Indian tribes, and there is no reason why one or more of them may not have wandered north for a considerable distance.   During the same year the viceroy made an attempt, possibly in person, to penetrate into the country of Topira or Topia, in northwestern Durango,[2] but the mountains and the absence of provisions forced the party to return.   It may be that this fruitless expedition was the same as that in which, according to Castañeda, Coronado took part, while Friar Marcos was on his way to Cibola.   It is not unlikely, also,

---

[1] Contributions to the History of the Southwest, pp. 79–103.

[2] This region is identified by Bandelier in his Contributions, p. 104, note.   The letter from which the details are obtained, written to accompany the report of Friar Marcos when this was transmitted to the King, is in Ramusio, and also in Ternaux, Cibola volume, p. 285.

that Friar Marcos may have made a preliminary trip toward the north, during the same year, although this is hardly more than a guess to explain statements, made by the old chroniclers, which we can not understand.

As yet nothing had been found to verify the reports brought by Cabeza de Vaca, which, by themselves, were hardly sufficient to justify the equipment of an expedition on a large scale. But Mendoza was bent on discovering what lay beyond the northern mountains. He still had the negro Estevan, whom he had purchased of Dorantes, besides a number of Indians who had followed Cabeza de Vaca to Mexico and had been trained there to serve as interpreters. The experience which the negro had gained during the years he lived among the savages made him invaluable as a guide. He was used to dealing with the Indians, knew something of their languages, and was practiced in the all-important sign manual.

Friar Marcos de Niza was selected as the leader of the little party which was to find out what the viceroy wanted to know. Aside from his reconnoitering trip to Cibola, very little is known about this friar. Born in Nice, then a part of Savoy, he was called by his contemporaries a Frenchman. He had been with Pizarro in Peru, and had witnessed the death of Atahualpa. Returning to Central America, very likely with Pedro de Alvarado, he had walked from there barefooted, as was his custom, up to Mexico. He seems to have been somewhere in the northwestern provinces of New Spain, when Cabeza de Vaca appeared there after his wanderings. A member of the Franciscan brotherhood, he had already attained to some standing in the order, for he signs his report or personal narration of his explorations, as vice-commissary of the Franciscans. The father provincial of the order, Friar Antonio de Ciudad-Rodrigo, on August 26, 1539,[1] certified to the high esteem in which Friar Marcos was held, and stated that he was skilled in cosmography and in the arts of the sea, as well as in theology.

This choice of a leader was beyond question an excellent one, and Mendoza had every reason to feel confidence in the success of his undertaking. The viceroy drew up a set of instructions for Friar Marcos, which directed that the Indians whom he met on the way should receive the best of treatment, and provided for the scientific observations which all Spanish explorers were expected to record. Letters were to be left wherever it seemed advisable, in order to communicate with a possible sea expedition, and information of the progress of the party was to be sent back to the viceroy at convenient intervals. These instructions are a model of careful and explicit directions, and show the characteristic interest taken by Mendoza in the details of everything with which he was concerned. They supply to some extent,

---

[1] This certification, with the report of Friar Marcos and other documents relating to him, is printed in the Pacheco y Cardenas Coleccion, vol. iii, pp. 325-351.

also, the loss of the similar instructions which Coronado must have received when he started on his journey in the following February.[1]

Friar Marcos, accompanied by a lay brother, Friar Onorato, according to Mendoza's "première lettre," left Culiacan on March 7, 1539. Coronado, now acting as governor of New Galicia, had escorted them as far as this town and had assured a quiet journey for a part of the way beyond by sending in advance six Indians, natives of this region, who had been "kept at Mexico to become proficient in the Spanish language and attached to the ways of the Christians."[2] The friars proceeded to Petatlan, where Friar Onorato fell sick, so that it was necessary to leave him behind. During the rest of the journey, Friar Marcos was the only white man in the party, which consisted of the negro Estevan, the Indian interpreters, and a large body of natives who followed him from the different villages near which he passed. The friar continued his journey to "Vacapa," which Mr Bandelier identifies with the Eudeve settlement of Matapa in central Sonora, where he arrived two days before Passion Sunday, which in 1539 fell on March 23.[3] At this place he waited until April 6, in order to send to the seacoast and summon some Indians, from whom he hoped to secure further information about the pearl islands of which Cabeza de Vaca had heard.

The negro Estevan had been ordered by the viceroy to obey Friar Marcos in everything, under pain of serious punishment. While the friar was waiting at Vacapa, he sent the negro toward the north, instructing him to proceed 50 or 60 leagues and see if he could find anything which might help them in their search. If he found any signs of a rich and populous country, it was agreed that he was not to advance farther, but should return to meet the friar, or else wait where he heard the good news, sending some Indian messengers back to the friar, with a white cross the size of the palm of his hand. If the news was very promising, the cross was to be twice this size, and if the country about which he heard promised to be larger and better than New Spain, a cross still larger than this was to be sent back. Castañeda preserves a story that Estevan was sent ahead, not only to explore and pacify the country, but also because he did not get on well with his superior, who objected to his eagerness in collecting the turquoises and other things which the natives prized and to the moral effect of his relations with the women who followed him from the tribes which they met on their way. Friar Marcos says nothing about this in his narrative, but he had different and much more important ends to accomplish by his report, compared with those of Castañeda, who may easily have gathered the gossip from some native.

---

[1] The instructions given to Friar Marcos have been translated by Bandelier in his Contributions, p. 109. The best account of Friar Marcos and his explorations is given in that volume.

[2] Herrera, Historia General, dec. VI, lib. VII, cap. VII.

[3] Bandelier, in his Contributions, p. 122, says this was "about the middle of April," but his chronology at this point must be at fault.

Estevan started on Passion Sunday, after dinner. Four days later messengers sent by him brought to the friar "a very large cross, as tall as a man." One of the Indians who had given the negro his information accompanied the messengers. This man said and affirmed, as the friar carefully recorded, "that there are seven very large cities in the first province, all under one lord, with large houses of stone and lime; the smallest one-story high, with a flat roof above, and others two and three stories high, and the house of the lord four stories high. They are all united under his rule. And on the portals of the principal houses there are many designs of turquoise stones, of which he says they have a great abundance. And the people in these cities are very well clothed. . . . Concerning other provinces farther on, he said that each one of them amounted to much more than these seven cities." All this which the Indian told Friar Marcos was true; and, what is more, the Spanish friar seems to have correctly understood what the Indian meant, except that the Indian idea of several villages having a common allied form of government was interpreted as meaning the rule of a single lord, who lived in what was to the Indians the chief, because the most populous, village. These villages of stone and lime—or rather of stone and rolls or balls of adobe laid in mud mortar and sometimes whitened with a wash of gypsum[1]—were very large and wondrous affairs when compared with the huts and shelters of the Seri and some of the Piman Indians of Sonora.[2] The priest can hardly be blamed for translating a house entrance into a doorway instead of picturing it as a bulkhead or as the hatchway of a ship. The Spaniards—those who had seen service in the Indies—had outgrown their earlier custom of reading into the Indian stories the ideas of government and of civilization to which they were accustomed in Europe. But Friar Marcos was at a disadvantage hardly less than that of the companions of Cortes, when they first heard of Moctecuhzoma, because his experience with the wealth of the New World had been in the realm of the Incas. He interpreted what he did not understand, of necessity, by what he had seen in Peru.

The story of this Indian did not convince the friar that what he heard about the grandeur of these seven cities was all true, and he decided not to believe anything until he had seen it for himself, or had at least received additional proof. The friar did not start immediately for the seven cities, as the negro had advised him to do, but waited until he could see the Indians who had been summoned from the seacoast. These told him about pearls, which were found near their homes. Some "painted" Indians, living to the eastward, having their faces, chests, and arms tattooed or decorated with pigments, who were perhaps the Pima or Sobaipuri Indians, also visited him while he was staying at Vacapa and gave him an extended account of the seven cities, very similar to that of the Indian sent by Estevan.

[1] See F. W. Hodge, "Aboriginal Use of Adobes," The Archæologist, Columbus, Ohio, August, 1895.
[2] These are described in the Castañeda narrative.

Friar Marcos started on the second day following Pascua Florida, or Easter, which came on April 6, 1539. He expected to find Estevan waiting at the village where he had first heard about the cities. A second cross, as big as the first, had been received from the negro, and the messengers who brought this gave a fuller and much more specific account of the cities, agreeing in every respect with what had previously been related. When the friar reached the village where the negro had obtained the first information about the cities, he secured many new details. He was told that it was thirty days' journey from this village to the city of Cibola, which was the first of the seven. Not one person alone, but many, described the houses very particularly and showed him the way in which they were built, just as the messengers had done. Besides these seven cities, he learned that there were other kingdoms, called Marata, Acus, and Totonteac. The linguistic students, and especially Mr Frank Hamilton Cushing, have identified the first of these with Matyata or Makyata, a cluster of pueblos about the salt lakes southeast of Zuñi, which were in ruins when Alvarado saw them in 1540, although they appeared to have been despoiled not very long before. Acus is the Acoma pueblo and Totonteac was in all probability the province of Tusayan, northwestward from Zuñi. The friar asked these people why they went so far away from their homes, and was told that they went to get turquoises and cow skins, besides other valuable things, of all of which he saw a considerable store in the village.

Friar Marcos tried to find out how these Indians bartered for the things they brought from the northern country, but all he could understand was that "with the sweat and service of their persons they went to the first city, which is called Cibola, and that they labored there by digging the earth and other services, and that for what they did they received turquoises and the skins of cows, such as those people had." We now know, whatever Friar Marcos may have thought, that they doubtless obtained their turquoises by digging them out of the rocky ground in which they are still found in New Mexico, and this may easily have seemed to them perspiring labor. It is not clear just how they obtained the buffalo skins, although it was doubtless by barter. The friar noticed fine turquoises suspended in the ears and noses of many of the people whom he saw,[1] and he was again informed that the principal doorways of Cibola were ceremonially ornamented with designs made of these stones. Mr Cushing has since learned, through tradition, that this was their custom. The dress of these people of Cibola, including the belts of turquoises about the waist, as it was described to the friar, seemed to him to resemble that of the Bohemians, or gypsies. The cow skins, some of which were given to him, were tanned and finished so well that he thought it was evident that they had been prepared by men who were skilled in this work.

---

[1] In lieu of turquoises the Pima and Maricopa today frequently wear small beaded rings pendent from the ears and septum.

At this point in his narrative Friar Marcos first uses the word *pueblo*, village, in referring to the seven cities, a point which would be of some interest if only we could be sure that the report was written from notes made as he went along. He certainly implies that he kept some such record when he speaks of taking down the statements of the Indian who first told him about the seven cities. It looks as if the additional details which he was obtaining gradually dimmed his vision of cities comparable to those into which he had seen Pizarro gather the golden ransom of Atahualpa.

Friar Marcos had not heard from Estevan since leaving Vacapa, but the natives told him that the negro was advancing toward Cibola, and that he had been gone four or five days. The friar started at once to follow the negro, who had proceeded up Sonora valley, as Mr Bandelier traces the route. Estevan had planted several large crosses along the way, and soon began to send messengers to the friar, urging the latter to hasten, and promising to wait for him at the edge of the wilderness which lay between them and the country of Cibola. The friar followed as fast as he could, although constantly hindered by the natives, who were always ready to verify the stories he had already heard concerning Cibola. They pressed him to accept their offers of turquoises and of cow skins in spite of his persistent refusals. At one village, the lord of the place and his two brothers greeted the friar, having collars of turquoises about their necks, while the rest of the people were all *encaconados*, as they called it, with turquoises, which hung from their ears and noses. Here they supplied their visitor with deer, rabbits, and quail, besides a great abundance of corn and piñon seed. They also continued to offer him turquoises, skins, fine gourds, and other things which they valued. The Sobaipuri Indians, who were a branch of the Papago, among whom the friar was now traveling, according to Bandelier, seemed to be as well acquainted with Cibola as the natives of New Spain were with Mexico, or those of Peru with Cuzco. They had visited the place many times, and whatever they possessed which was made with any skill or neatness had been brought, so they told him, from that country.

Soon after he encountered these people, the friar met a native of Cibola. He was a well-favored man, rather old, and appeared to be much more intelligent than the natives of this valley or those of any of the districts through which the friar had passed in the course of his march. This man reported that the lord of Cibola lived and had his seat of government in one of the seven cities called Ahacus, and that he appointed men in the other cities who ruled for him. Ahacus is readily identified with Hawikuh, one of the present ruins near K'iap-kwainakwin, or Ojo Caliente, about 15 miles southwest of Zuñi. On questioning this man closely, the friar learned that Cibola—by which, as Bandelier and Cushing maintain, the Indian meant the whole range occupied by the Zuñi people—was a large city, in which a great many people dwelt and which had streets and open squares or plazas. In some parts of it there were very large houses, which were ten stories high, and the leading men met together in these on certain days of the year. Possibly this is one of the rare references in the accounts of these early visits to Zuñi, to the ceremonials of the Pueblo Indians, which have been studied and described with so much care by later visitors, notably by Mrs M. C. Stevenson and by Dr J. Walter Fewkes of the Hemenway Southwestern Archeological Expedition.

This native of Cibola verified all the reports which the friar had already heard. Marata, he said, had been greatly reduced by the lord of Cibola during recent wars. Totonteac was a much larger and richer place, while Acus was an independent kingdom and province. The strange thing about all these reports is not that they are true, and that we can identify them by what is now known concerning these Indians, but the hard thing to understand is how the Spanish friar could have comprehended so well what the natives must have tried to tell him. When one considers the difficulties of language, with all its technicalities, and of radically different conceptions of every phase of life and of thought, the result must be an increased confidence in the common sense and the inherent intelligence of mankind.

On his way up this valley of Sonora, Friar Marcos heard that the seacoast turned toward the west. Realizing the importance of this point, he says that he "went in search of it and saw clearly that it turns to the west in 35 degrees." He was at the time between 31 and 31½ degrees north, just opposite the head of the Gulf of California. If Bandelier's identification of the friar's route is accepted—and it has a great deal more in its favor than any other that can be proposed with any due regard to the topography of the country—Friar Marcos was then near the head of San Pedro valley, distant 200 miles in a direct line from the coast, across a rough and barren country. Although the Franciscan superior testified to Marcos' proficiency in the arts of the sea, the friar's calculation was 3½ degrees out of the way, at a latitude where the usual error in the contemporary accounts of expeditions is on the average a degree and a half. The direction of the coast line does change almost due west of where the friar then was, and he may have gone to some point among the mountains from which he could satisfy himself that the report of the Indians was reliable. There is a week or ten days, during this part of the journey, for which his narrative gives no specific reckoning. He traveled rather slowly at times, making frequent stops, so that the side trip is not necessary to fill this gap. The point is a curious one; but, in the absence of any details, it is hardly likely that the friar did more than secure from other Indians stories confirming what he had already been told.

Friar Marcos soon reached the borders of the wilderness—the country in and about the present White Mountain Apache reservation in Arizona. He entered this region on May 9, and twelve days later a young man who had been with Estevan, the son of one of the Indian chiefs accompanying the friar, met him and told the story of the negro's death. Estevan had hastened to reach Cibola before the friar, and just prior to arriving at the first city he had sent a notice of his approach to the chief of the place. As evidence of his position or authority, he sent a gourd, to which were attached a few strings of rattles and two plumes, one of which was white and the other red.

While Cabeza de Vaca and his companions were traveling through Texas, the natives had flocked to see these strange white men and soon began to worship them, pressing about them for even a touch of their garments, from which the Indians trusted to receive some healing power. While taking advantage of the prestige which was thus obtained, Cabeza de Vaca says that he secured some gourds or rattles, which were greatly reverenced among these Indians and which never failed to produce a most respectful behavior whenever they were exhibited. It was also among these southern plains Indians that Cabeza de Vaca heard of the permanent settlements toward the north. Castañeda says that some of these plains Indians came each year to Cibola to pass the winter under the shelter of the adobe villages, but that they were distrusted and feared so much that they were not admitted into the villages unless unarmed, and under no conditions were they allowed to spend the night within the flat-roof houses. The connection between these Indian rattles and the gourd which Estevan prized so highly can not be proven, but it is not unlikely that the negro announced his arrival to the Cibola chiefs by sending them an important part of the paraphernalia of a medicine man of a tribe with which they were at enmity.

There are several versions of the story of Estevan's death, besides the one given in Friar Marcos' narrative, which were derived from the natives of Cibola. Castañeda, who lived among these people for a while the next year, states that the Indians kept the negro a prisoner for three days, "questioning him," before they killed him. He adds that Estevan had demanded from the Indians treasures and women, and this agrees with the legends still current among these people.[1] When Alarcon ascended Colorado river a year later, and tried to obtain news of Coronado, with whom he was endeavoring to cooperate, he heard of Estevan, who was described as a black man with a beard, wearing things that sounded, rattles, bells, and plumes, on his feet and arms— the regular outfit of a southwestern medicine man.[2] Friar Marcos was told that when the messengers bearing the gourd showed it to the chief of the Cibola village, he threw it on to the ground and told the messengers that when their people reached the village they would find out what sort of men lived there, and that instead of entering the place they would all be killed. Estevan was not at all daunted when this answer was reported to him, saying that everything would be right

---

[1] Bandelier, Contributions, pp. 154, 155.

[2] There is an admirable and extended account, with many illustrations, of the Apache medicine men, by Captain John G. Bourke, in the ninth report of the Bureau of Ethnology.

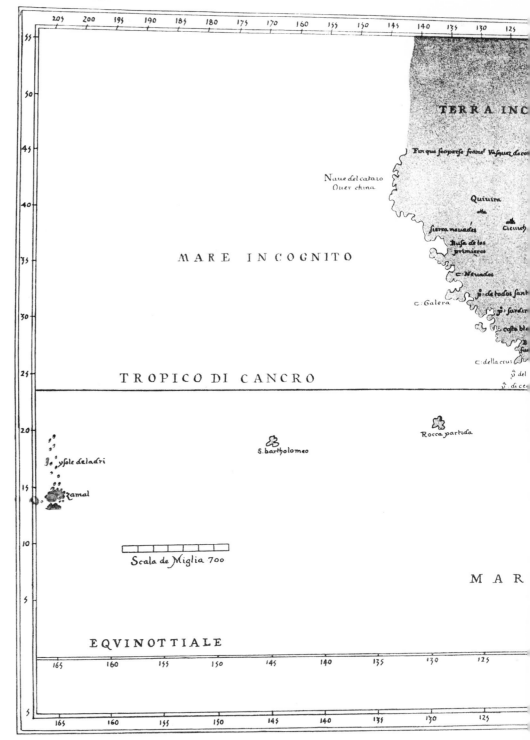

205 200 195 190 185 180 175 170 160 155 150 145 140 135 130 125

55

50

TERRA INC

45

Fin que scoperse frane' Vasquez de co

Naue del cataio
Ouer china

40

Quiuira

sierra neuades *Cieuoh*

35

MARE INCOGNITO

Bufa de los
primieros

c: Neuades

30

p̃: de todos sant

c: Galera *p̃: fardir*

costa ble

25

c: della crus

TROPICO DI CANCRO

p̃: del
p̃: di cee

20

Rocca partida

S. bartholomeo

Jo. ysole de ladri

15

zamal

10

⬜⬜⬜⬜⬜⬜⬜

Scala de Miglia 700

M A R

5

EQVINOTTIALE

165 160 155 150 145 140 135 130 125

5

165 160 155 150 145 140 135 130 125

NVOVA   SPAGNA   PROV.

CHICHIMICAS

GOLFO MEXICANO

SVR

when he reached the village in person. He proceeded thither at once, but instead of being admitted, he was placed under guard in a house near by.[1] All the turquoises and other gifts which he had received from the Indians during his journey were taken from him, and he was confined with the people who accompanied him, over night, without receiving anything to eat or drink. The next morning Estevan tried to run away, but was overtaken and killed. The fugitives who brought this news to Friar Marcos said that most of their companions also had been killed. The Indians who had followed the friar forthwith began to mourn for three hundred of their relations and friends, who had perished, they declared, as a result of their confidence in his forerunner. This number was undoubtedly an exaggeration. Castañeda heard that the natives of Cibola kept a few lads from among those who were with the negro, "and sent back all the rest, numbering about sixty." The story of Estevan's death is reputed to have been preserved among the legends of the Indians of Zuñi. According to this tradition, the village at which the "Black Mexican" was killed was K'iakima, a village now in ruins, situated on a bluff at the southwestern angle of Thunder mountain mesa; but this is totally at variance with the historical evidence, which seems to point quite conclusively to Hawikuh, the first village encountered from the southwest, as the scene of Estevan's death.[2] One of the Indian stories of Estevan's death is that their wise men took the negro out of the pueblo during the night, and "gave him a powerful kick, which sped him through the air back to the south, whence he came!"

The killing of Estevan made it impossible for Friar Marcos, alone and unprepared for fighting, to enter the Cibola region. The first reports of the disaster, as is usually the custom, told of the death of all who accompanied the negro, and in consequence there was much wailing among the Indians who had followed the friar. They threatened to desert him, but he pacified them by opening his bundles and distributing the trinkets brought from Mexico. While they were enjoying these, he withdrew a couple of stone-throws for an hour and a half to pray. Meanwhile, the Indians began again to think of their lost friends, and decided to kill the friar, as the indirect cause of the catastrophe. But when he returned from his devotions, reinvigorated, and learned of their determination, he diverted their thoughts by producing some of the things which had been kept back from the first distribution of the contents of his packs. He expounded to them the folly of killing him, since this would do him no hurt because he was a Christian and so would go at once to his home in the sky, while other Christians would come in search of him and kill all of them, in spite of his own desires to prevent, if possible, any such revenge. "With many other words" he

---

[1] This is precisely the method pursued by the Zuñis today against any Mexicans who may be found in their vicinity during the performance of an outdoor ceremonial.

[2] This question has been fully discussed by F. W. Hodge. See "The First Discovered City of Cibola," American Anthropologist, Washington, April, 1895.

succeeded at last in quieting them and in persuading two of the chief Indians to go with him to a point where he could obtain a view of the "city of Cibola." He proceeded to a small hill, from which he saw that it was situated on a plain on the slope of a round height. "It has a very fine appearance for a village," he writes, "the best that I have seen in these parts. The houses, as the Indians had told me, are all of stone, built in stories, and with flat roofs. Judging by what I could see from the height where I placed myself to observe it, the settlement is larger than the city of Mexico. . . . It appears to me that this land is the best and largest of all those that have been discovered."

"With far more fright than food," the friar says he retraced his way toward New Spain, by hasty marches. During his journey to Cibola, he had heard of a large and level valley among the mountains, distant four or five days from the route which he followed, where he was told that there were many very large settlements in which the people wore clothes made of cotton. He showed his informants some metals which he had, in order to find out what there was in that region, and they picked out the gold, saying that the people in the valley had vessels made of this material and some round things which they hung from their ears and noses. They also had some little shovels of this same metal, with which they scraped themselves to get rid of their sweat. On his way back, although he had not recovered from his fright, the friar determined to see this valley. He did not dare to venture into it, because, as he says, he thought that those who should go to settle and rule the country of the seven cities could enter it more safely than he. He did not wish to risk his own life, lest he should be prevented from making the report of what he had already seen. He went as far as the entrance to the valley and saw seven good-looking settlements at a distance, in a very attractive country, from which arose a great deal of smoke. He understood from the Indians that there was much gold in the valley, and that the natives used it for vessels and ornaments, repeating in his narrative the reports which he had heard on his outward journey.

The friar then hastened down the coast to Culiacan, where he hoped, but failed, to find Coronado, the governor of the province. He went on to Compostela, where Coronado was staying. Here he wrote his report, and sent the announcement of his safe return to the viceroy. A similar notification to the provincial of his order contained a request for instructions as to what he should do next. He was still in Compostela on September 2, and as Mendoza and Coronado also were there, he took occasion to certify under oath before them to the truth of all that he had written in the report of his expedition to Cibola.

THE EFFECT OF FRIAR MARCOS' REPORT

In his official report it is evident that Friar Marcos distinguished with care between what he had himself seen and what the Indians had told him. But Cortes began the practice of attacking the veracity and

good faith of the friar, Castañeda continued it, and scarcely a writer
on these events failed to follow their guidance until Mr Bandelier
undertook to examine the facts of the case, and applied the rules of
ordinary fairness to his historical judgment. This vigorous defender
of the friar has successfully maintained his strenuous contention that
Marcos neither lied nor exaggerated, even when he said that the Cibola
pueblo appeared to him to be larger than the City of Mexico. All the
witnesses agree that these light stone and adobe villages impress one
who first sees them from a distance as being much larger than they
really are. Mexico in 1539, on the other hand, was neither imposing
nor populous. The great communal houses, the " palace of Montezuma," had been destroyed during or soon after the siege of 1521. The
pueblo of Hawikuh, the one which the friar doubtless saw, contained
about 200 houses, or between 700 and 1,000 inhabitants. There is something naïve in Mr Bandelier's comparison of this with Robert Tomson's
report that the City of Mexico, in 1556, contained 1,500 Spanish house-
holds.[1] He ought to have added, what we may be quite sure was true,
that the population of Mexico probably doubled in the fifteen years preceding Tomson's visit, a fact which makes Niza's comparison even more
reasonable.[2]

The credit and esteem in which the friar was held by the viceroy,
Mendoza, is as convincing proof of his integrity as that derived from
a close scrutiny of the text of his narrative. Mendoza's testimony was
given in a letter which he sent to the King in Spain, inclosing the
report written by Friar Marcos, the "première lettre" which Ternaux
translated from Ramusio. This letter spoke in laudatory terms of
the friar, and of course is not wholly unbiased evidence. It is at least
sufficient to counterbalance the hostile declarations of Cortes and Castañeda, both of whom had far less creditable reasons for traducing
the friar than Mendoza had for praising him. " These friars," wrote
Mendoza of Marcos and Onorato, "had lived for some time in the
neighboring countries; they were used to hard labors, experienced in
the ways of the Indies, conscientious, and of good habits." It is possible that Mendoza felt less confidence than is here expressed, for
before he organized the Coronado expedition, late in the fall of this
year 1539, he ordered Melchior Diaz to go and see if what he could discover agreed with the account which Friar Marcos gave.[3]

However careful the friar may have been, he presented to the viceroy a report in which gold and precious stones abounded, and which
stopped just within sight of the goal—the Seven Cities of Nuño de Guzman and of the Indian traders and story tellers. Friar Marcos had

---

[1] Tomson's exceedingly interesting narrative of his experiences in Mexico is printed in Hakluyt,
vol. iii, p. 447, ed. 1600.

[2] Compare the ground plan of Hawikuh, by Victor Mindeleff, in the eighth annual report of the
Bureau of Ethnology, pl. XLVI, with the map of the city of Mexico (1550?), by Alonzo de Santa Cruz,
pl. XLIII of this paper.

[3] Diaz started November 17, 1539. The report of his trip is given in Mendoza's letter of April 17,
1540, in Pacheco y Cardenas, ii, p. 356, and translated herein.

something to tell which interested his readers vastly more than the painful, wonderful story of Cabeza de Vaca. The very fact that he took it for granted, as he says in his report, that they would go to populate and rule over this land of the Seven Cities, with its doorways studded with turquoises, was enough to insure interest. He must, indeed, have been a popular preacher, and when the position of father provincial to the Franciscans became vacant, just now, brother Marcos, already high in the order and with all the fresh prestige of his latest achievements, was evidently the subject for promotion. Castañeda, who is not the safest authority for events preceding the expedition, says that the promotion was arranged by the viceroy. This may have been so. His other statement is probable enough, that, as a result of the promotion, the pulpits of the order were filled with accounts of such marvels and wonders that large numbers were eager to join in the conquest of this new land. Whatever Friar Marcos may have sacrificed to careful truth was atoned for, we may be sure, by the zealous, loyal brethren of blessed Saint Francis.

Don Joan Suarez de Peralta was born, as Señor Zaragoza shows in his admirable edition of the Tratado del Descubrimiento de las Yndias y su Conquista, in Mexico between 1535 and 1540, and probably nearer the first of these five years. In the Tratado, Suarez de Peralta gives a most interesting description of the effect produced in Mexico by the departure and the return of the Coronado expedition. He can hardly have had very vivid personal recollections of the excitement produced by the reports of Friar Marcos, yet his account is so clear and circumstantial that it evidently must be the narrative of an eyewitness, though recorded, it may be, at secondhand. He tells us that "the country was so stirred up by the news which the friar had brought from the Seven Cities that nothing else was thought about. For he said that the city of Cibola was big enough to contain two Sevilles and over, and the other places were not much smaller; and that the houses were very fine edifices, four stories high; and in the country there are many of what they call wild cows, and sheep and goats and rich treasures. He exaggerated things so much, that everybody was for going there and leaving Mexico depopulated. . . . . The news from the Seven Cities inspired so eager a desire in every one that not only did the viceroy and the marquis (Cortes) make ready to start for there, but the whole country wanted to follow them so much that they traded for the licenses which permitted them to go as soldiers, and people sold these as a favor, and whoever obtained one of these thought that it was as good as a title of nobility at the least. For the friar who had come from there exaggerated and said that it was the best place in the world; the people in that country very prosperous, and all the Indians wearing clothes and the possessors of much cattle; the mountains like those of Spain, and the climate the same. For wood, they burnt very large walnut trees, which bear quantities of

walnuts better than those of Spain.   They have many mountain grapes,
which are very good eating, chestnuts, and filberts.   According to the
way he painted it, this should have been the terrestrial paradise.   For
game, there were partridges, geese, cranes, and all the other winged
creatures—it was marvelous what was there."   And then Suarez adds,
writing half a century later, "He told the truth in all this, because
there are mountains in that country, as he said, and herds, especially
of cows. . . . .   There are grapes and game, without doubt, and a
climate like that of Spain." [1]

Second-hand evidence, recorded fifty years after the occurrence, is
far from conclusive.   Fortunately, we are able to supplement it by
legal testimony, taken down and recorded under oath, with all the formalities of the old Spanish law customs.   When the news of Friar
Marcos' journey reached Spain there was much rivalry among those
who claimed the privilege of completing the discovery.   Much evidence was presented and frequent pleas were entered by all the men
who had an active part and leadership in the conquest of the northern
portion of the New World.   In the course of the litigation the representative of the adelantado Hernando de Soto, presented some testimony which had been given in the town of San Cristobal de la Habana
de la Isla Fernandina—Habana and Cuba—dated November 12, 1539.
There were seven witnesses, from a ship which had been obliged to put
into this port in order to procure water and other supplies, and also
because some persons aboard had become very sick.   Each witness
declared that a month or more before—Friar Marcos arrived back
in Mexico before the end of August, 1539—he had heard, and that
this was common talk in Mexico, Vera Cruz, and in Puebla de los Angeles, that a Franciscan friar named Fray Marcos, who had recently
come from the inland regions, said that he had discovered a very rich
and very populous country 400 or 500 leagues north of Mexico.   "He
said that the country is rich in gold, silver and other treasures, and
that it contains very large villages; that the houses are built of stone,
and terraced like those of Mexico, and that they are high and imposing.
The people, so he said, are shrewd, and do not marry more than one
wife at a time, and they wear coarse woolen cloth and ride on some animals," the name of which the witness did not know.   Another testified
that the common report was that this country " was very rich and populous and had great walled cities, and that the lords of the cities were
called kings, and that the people were very shrewd and use the Mexican
language."   But the witness to whose deposition we are most indebted
was Andrés Garcia.   This man declared that he had a son-in-law who
was a barber, who had shaved the friar after he came back from the new
country.   The son-in-law had told the witness that the friar, while being

---

[1] The Spanish text from which I have translated may be found on pages 144 and 148 of Zaragoza's
edition of Suarez de Peralta's Tratado.   This edition is of the greatest usefulness to every student of
early Mexican history.

shaved, had talked about the country which he had discovered beyond the mountains. "After crossing the mountains, the friar said there was a river, and that many settlements were there, in cities and towns, and that the cities were surrounded by walls, with their gates guarded, and were very wealthy, having silversmiths, and that the women wore strings of gold beads and the men girdles of gold and white woolen dresses; and that they had sheep and cows and partridges and slaughterhouses and iron forges."[1]

Friar Marcos undoubtedly never willfully told an untruth about the country of Cibola, even in a barber's chair. But there seems to be little chance for doubting that the reports which he brought to New Spain were the cause of much talk as well as many sermons, which gave rise to a considerable amount of excitement among the settlers, whose old-world notions had been upset by the reputed glory of the Montezumas and the wealth of the Incas. Very many, though perhaps not all, of the colonists were stirred with an eager desire to participate in the rich harvest awaiting the conquerors of these new

[1] The depositions as printed in the Pacheco y Cardenas Docs. de Indias, vol. xv., pp. 392–398, are as follows: Pedro Nuñez, testigo rescebido en la dicha razon, juró segun derecho, é dijo: . . . que estando en la ciudad de México, puede haber tres meses [the evidence being taken November 12, 1539], poco mas ó menos, oyó decir este testigo públicamente, que habia venido un fraile Francisco, que se dice Fray Marcos, que venia la tierra adentro, é que decia el dicho fraile que se habia descobierto una tierra muy rica ó muy poblada; ó que habia cuatrocientas leguas dende México allá; ó que dice que han de ir allá por cerca del rio de Palmas; . . .

Garcia Navarro, . . . oyó decir publicamente, puede haber un mes ó mes y medio [and so all the remaining witnesses] que habia venido un fraile, nuevamente, de una tierra, nuevamente descobierta, que dicen ques quinientas leguas de México, en la tierra de la Florida, que dicen ques hácia la parte del Norte de la dicha tierra; la cual diz, que es tierra rica de oro é plata ó otros resgates, é grandes pueblos; que las casas son de piedra é terrados á la manera de México, ó que tienen peso é medida, é gente de razon, ó que no casan mas de una vez, ó que visten albornoces, é que andan cabalgando en unos animales, que no sabe cómo se llaman, ...

Francisco Serrano, . . . el fraile venia por tierra, por la via de Xalisco; é ques muy rica é muy poblada é grandes ciudades cercadas; é que los señores dellas, se nombran Reyes; ó que las casas son sobradas, é ques gente de mucha razon; que la lengua es mexicana, . . .

Pero Sanchez, tinturero . . . una tierra nueva muy rica ó muy poblada de ciudades é villas; . . . por la vía de Xalisco . . . hácia en medio de la tierra. . . .

Francisco de Leyva . . . en la Vera-Cruz, oyó decir que habia venido un fraile de una tierra nueva muy rica ó muy poblada de ciudades ó villas, é ques á la banda del Sur, . . . Otrosí, dixo: que es verdad que no embargante que no toca en este puerto, dejaba de seguir su viaje; pero que entró en este puerto por necesidad que llevaba de agua é otros bastimentos é de ciertas personas que venian muy enfermos.

Hernando de Sotomayor . . . questando en la Puebla de los Angeles . . . públicamente se decia . . . é que las casas son de piedras sobradadas, é las ciudades cercadas, é gente de razon; . . . é questa dicha tierra es la parte donde vino Dorantes é Cabeza de Vaca, los cuales escaparon de la armada de Narvaez; é que sabe é vido este testigo, que fué mandado al maestre por mandado del Virey ó con su mandamiento, que no tocase en parte ninguna, salvo que fuese derechamente á España, con la dicha nao, ó quel secretario del Virey hizo un requirimiento al dicho maestre, viniendo por la mar, que no tocase en este puerto ni en otra parte destas islas. . . . [This statement appears in each deposition.]

Andrés Garcia, dixo: . . . questando en la ciudad de México, un Francisco de Billegas le dió cartas para dar en esta villa, para dar al Adelantado D. Hernando de Soto, é si no lo hallase, que las llevase á España é las diese al hacedor suyo; é queste testigo tiene un yerno barbero que afeitaba al fraile que vino de la dicha tierra; é quel dicho su yerno, le dixo este testigo, questando afeitando al dicho fraile, le dixo como antes que llegasen á la dicha tierra estaba una sierra, é que pasando la dicha sierra estaba un rio, é que habia muchas poblazones de ciudades ó villas, é que las ciudades son cercadas é guardadas á las puertas, é muy ricas; é que habia plateros; é que las mugeres traian sartas de oro é los hombres cintos de oro, é que habia albarnios é obejas é vacas é perdices é carnicerias é herreria, é peso é medida; é que un Bocanegra, dixo á este testigo que se quedare, que se habia descobierto un nuevo mundo. . . .

lands. Friar Marcos was not a liar, but it is impossible to ignore the charges against him quite as easily as Mr Bandelier has done.

Pedro Castañeda makes some very damaging statements, which are not conclusive proof of the facts. Like the statements of Suarez de Peralta, they represent the popular estimation of the father provincial, and they repeat the stories which passed current regarding him, when the later explorations had destroyed the vision that had been raised by the reports of the friar's exploration. The accusations made by Cortes deserve more careful consideration. Cortes returned to Spain about the time that the preparations for the Coronado expedition were definitely begun. Soon after his arrival at court, June 25, 1540,[1] he addressed a formal memorial to the King, setting forth in detail the ill treatment which he had received from Mendoza. In this he declared that after the viceroy had ordered him to withdraw his men from their station on the coast of the mainland toward the north—where they were engaged in making ready for extended inland explorations—he had a talk with Friar Marcos. "And I gave him," says Cortes, "an account of this said country and of its discovery, because I had determined to send him in my ships to follow up the said northern coast and conquer that country, because he seemed to understand something about matters of navigation. The said friar communicated this to the said viceroy, and he says that, with his permission, he went by land in search of the same coast and country as that which I had discovered, and which it was and is my right to conquer. And since his return, the said friar has published the statement that he came within sight of the said country, which I deny that he has either seen or discovered; but instead, in all that the said friar reports that he has seen, he only repeats the account I had given him regarding the information which I obtained from the Indians of the said country of Santa Cruz, because everything which the said friar says that he discovered is just the same as what these said Indians had told me: and in enlarging upon this and in pretending to report what he neither saw nor learned, the said Friar Marcos does nothing new, because he has done this many other times, and this was his regular habit, as is notorious in the provinces of Peru and Guatemala; and sufficient evidence regarding this will be given to the court whenever it is necessary."[2]

This is a serious charge, but so far as is known it was never substantiated. Cortes was anxious to enforce his point, and he was not always scrupulous in regard to the exact truth. The important point is that such charges were made by a man who was in the position to learn all

---

[1] The document, as printed in Doc. Inéd. Hist. España, vol. iv, pp. 209-217, is not dated. The date given in the text is taken from the heading or title to the petition, which, if not the original, has at least the authority of Señor Navarrete, the editor of this Coleccion when the earlier volumes were printed. This memorial appears, from the contents, to have been one of the documents submitted in the litigation then going on between the rival claimants for the privilege of exploring the country discovered by Friar Marcos, although the document is not printed with the other papers in the case.

[2] Documentos Inéditos Hist. España, vol. iv, p. 211: Memorial que dió el Marqués del Valle en Madrid á 25 de Junio de 1540. . . . "Al tiempo que yo vine de la dicha tierra el dicho Fray Marcos

the facts, and that the accusations were made before anyone knew how little basis there was for the stories which were the cause of the whole trouble. Without trying to clear the character of Cortes, it is possible to suggest the answer to the most evident reply to his accusations—that he never published the stories which he says he received from the Indians. Cortes certainly did persist in his endeavors to explore the country lying about the head of the Gulf of California. If he ever heard from the Indians anything concerning the Cibola region—which is doubtful, partly because Cortes himself complains that if Mendoza had not interfered with the efficiency of his expeditions, he would have secured this information—it would still have been the best policy for Cortes to keep the knowledge to himself, so that possible rivals might remain ignorant of it until he had perfected his own plans. It may be questioned how long such secrecy would have been possible, but we know how successfully the Spanish authorities managed to keep from the rest of the world the correct and complete cartographical information as to what was being accomplished in the New World, throughout the period of exploration and conquest.

The truce—it can hardly be called a friendship—between Mendoza and Cortes, which prevailed during the first years of the viceroy's administration, could not last long. Mendoza, as soon as he was fairly settled in his position in New Spain,[1] asked the King for a license to make explorations. Cortes still looked on every rival in the work of extending this portion of the Spanish world as an interloper, even though he must have recognized that his prestige at the court and in the New World was rapidly lessening. The distrust with which each of the two regarded the other increased the trouble which was inevitable so soon as the viceroy, urged on by the audiencia, undertook to execute the royal orders which instructed him to investigate the extent of the estates held by Cortes, and to enumerate the Indians held to service by the conqueror. Bad feeling was inevitable, and the squabbles over forms of address and of precedence, which Suarez de Peralta records, were only a few of many things which reveal the relations of the two leading men in New Spain.

---

hablö conmigo . . . é yo le di noticia de esta dicha tierra y descubrimiento de ella, porque tenia determinacion de enviarlo en mis navíos en proseguimiento y conquista de la dicha costa y tierra, porque parescia que se le entendia algo de cosas de navegacion: el cual dicho fraile lo comunicó con el dicho visorey, y con su licencia diz que fué por tierra en demanda de la misma costa y tierra que yo habia descubierto, y que era y es de mi conquista; y despues que volvió el dicho fraile ha publicado que diz que llegó á vista de la dicha tierra; lo cual yo niego haber él visto ni descubierto, antes lo que el dicho fraile refiere haber visto, lo ha dicho y dice por sola la relacion que yo le habia hecho de la noticia que tenia de los indios de la dicha tierra de Santa Cruz que yo truje, porque todo lo que el dicho fraile se dice que refiere, es lo mismo que los dichos indios á mí me dijeron; y en haberse en esto adelantado el dicho Fray Marcos fingiendo y refiriendo lo que no sabe ni vió, no hizo cosa nueva, porque otras muchas veces lo ha hecho y lo tiene por costumbre como es notorio en las provincias del Perú y Guatemala, y se dará de ello informacion bastante luego en esta corte, siendo necesario."

[1]The request occurs in the earliest letters from the viceroy, and is repeated in that of December 10, 1537. This privilege was withdrawn from all governors in the colonies by one of the New Laws of 1543. (Icazbalceta, Col. Hist. Mexico, ii, 204.) The ill success of Coronado's efforts did not weaken Mendoza's desire to enlarge his territory, for he begs his agent in Spain, Juan de Aguilar, to secure for him a fresh grant of the privilege in a later letter. (Pacheco y Cardenas, Doc. de Indias, vol. iii, p. 506; B. Smith, Florida, p. 7.)

We can not be certain what the plans of Cortes were, nor can we tell just how much he did to carry his schemes into execution, during the years from 1537 to 1540. Shortly after the men whom Cortes had established at Santa Cruz were recalled, a decree was issued, in the name of the audiencia, to forbid the sending of any expedition for exploration or conquest from New Spain. Cortes declared that he had at this time, September, 1538, nine good ships already built. He was naturally unwilling to give up all hope of deriving any benefit from his previous undertakings, as would be inevitable if Mendoza should succeed in his projects for taking advantage of whatever good things could be found toward the north. The danger must have seemed clear so soon as he learned of the departure of Friar Marcos and the negro on their journey toward the Seven Cities. There is no means of knowing whether Cortes had learned of the actual discovery of Cibola, when he suddenly ordered Francisco de Ulloa to take three vessels and sail up the coast toward the head of the Gulf of California. The friar may have sent Indian messengers to the viceroy so soon as he heard the native reports about the seven cities of Cibola, and it is possible that the news of his approaching return may have reached New Spain before the departure of Ulloa, which took place July 8, 1539, from Acapulco.[1] It seems clear that this action was unexpected, and that it was a successful anticipation of preventive measures. In the statement of his grievances, Cortes declares that Mendoza not only threw every possible obstacle in his way, seizing six or seven vessels which failed to get away with Ulloa, but that even after Ulloa had gone, the viceroy sent a strong force up the coast to prevent the ships from entering any of the ports. When stress of weather forced one of the ships to put into Guatulco, the pilot and sailors were imprisoned and the viceroy persistently refused to return the ship to its owner. About the same time, a messenger who had been sent to Cortes from Santiago in Colima was seized and tortured, in the hope of procuring from him information about the plans of Cortes.[2]

After Friar Marcos came back from the north and filled the people in New Spain with the desire of going to this new country, Cortes realized that he could do nothing, even in the city which he had won for his King and for Europe, to prevent the expedition which Mendoza was already organizing. Early in 1540—we know only that he was on his way when he wrote to Oviedo from Habana[3] on February 5—the conqueror of Motecuhzoma's empire left Mexico for the last time, and went to see what he could gain by a personal application at the court of His Majesty the Emperor, Charles V.

[1] Ulloa's Relation is translated from Ramusio in Hakluyt, vol. iii, p. 397, ed. 1600.
[2] Memorial que dió al Rey el Marques del Valle, en Madrid, 25 de junio, 1540: Printed in Doc. Inéd. España, vol. iv, p. 209. Compare with this account that in H. H. Bancroft's Mexico, vol. ii, p. 425. Mr Bancroft is always a strong advocate of the cause of Cortes.
[3] Oviedo, Historia General, vol. iv, p. 19.

Mendoza had guarded against rival expeditions from his own territory, and so soon as he knew that Friar Marcos had succeeded in his quest, he took precautions to prevent the news of the discovery from reaching other portions of the New World. His chief fear, probably, was lest De Soto, who had recently received a license to explore the country between the Rio de las Palmas, in the present Texas, and Florida,[1] might direct his expedition toward the western limits of his territory, if he should learn of the rich prospects there. Although Mendoza probably did not know it, De Soto had sailed from Habana in May, 1539, and in July, sending back his largest ships, he began the long march through the everglades of Florida, which was to end in the Mississippi. Mendoza, with all the formality of the viceregal authority, ordered that no vessel sailing from New Spain should touch at any port in the New World on its way back to the home peninsula, and this notice was duly served on all departing shipmasters by the secretaries of the viceroy. By the middle of November, however, despite all this care, a ship from Vera Cruz sailed into the harbor of Habana. The master declared, on his oath, that he had been forced to put in there, because sickness had broken out aboard his vessel soon after the departure from New Spain and because he had discovered that his stock of provisions and water was insufficient for the voyage across the Atlantic. Curiously enough, one of the crew, possibly one of those who had been seized with the sickness, had in his possession some letters which he had been asked to deliver to Hernando De Soto, in Habana. Apparently the agent or friend of De Soto living in Mexico, one Francisco de Billegas, did not know that the adelantado had left Cuba, although he had arranged to have the letters carried to Spain and given to the representative of the adelantado there if De Soto was not found at Habana. De Soto had taken care that his interests should be watched and protected, in Spain as well as in the New World, when he started on his search for the land of wealth north of the Gulf of Mexico, the search on which Ayllon and Narvaez had failed so sadly.

It was the regular practice of all the governors and successful explorers in the colonies of the empire to maintain representatives in Spain who should look after their interests at court and before the administrative bureaus. When the news of Friar Marcos' discovery reached Europe, accompanied by reports of the preparations which Mendoza was making for an expedition to take possession of the new territory, protests and counterclaims were immediately presented in behalf of all those who could claim any right to participate in this new field of conquest. The first formal statements were filed with the Council for the Indies, March 3, 1540, and on June 10, 1541, the factor or representative of Cortes, whose petition is first among the papers relating to the case, asked for an extension of six days. This ends the

---

[1] The capitulacion or agreement with De Soto is printed in Pacheco y Cardenas, Doc. de Indias, vol. xv, pp. 354-363.

documents concerning the litigation, so far as they have been printed.[1] Petitions, testimony, narratives of explorations and discoveries, acts taking possession of new lands, notifications and decisions, appeals and countercharges, were filed and referred, each claimant watching his rivals so closely and objecting to their claims so strenuously that the fiscal, Villalobos, in his report on the case, May 25, 1540, gives as one of the most conclusive reasons in favor of the advice which he offers to the Council, that each of the parties has clearly proved that none of the others have any right to claim a share in the newly discovered region by virtue of any grants, licenses, or achievements whatsoever.

Of the various claimants, the representative of the adelantado Hernando De Soto offered perhaps the best argument. The territory granted to De Soto extended on the west to the Rio de las Palmas, and this grant was the same as that previously made to Narvaez. The discovery had grown out of the expedition of Narvaez, to whose rights De Soto had succeeded, through the reports which Cabeza de Vaca carried to New Spain. The newly discovered region was evidently inland, and this fact disposed of the two prominent rivals, Cortes and Alvarado. The adelantado had expended large sums in preparing for this undertaking—a claim advanced with equal vigor by all the parties, and usually supported by specific accounts, which unfortunately are not printed—and it was only right that he should be given every opportunity to reap the full advantage from these outlays. Most important of all was the fact that De Soto was already in the country north of the gulf, in command of a large and well equipped force, and presumably on his way toward the region about which they were disputing. Because De Soto was there, urged his representative with strong and persistent emphasis, all other exploring expeditions ought to be kept away. It was clearly probable that great and notorious scandals would ensue unless this was guarded against, just as had happened in Peru. If this precaution was not taken, and two expeditions representing conflicting interests should be allowed to come together in the country beyond the reach of the royal restraint, many lives would inevitably be lost and great damage be done to the Spaniards, and to the souls of the Indians as well, while the enlargement of the royal patrimony would be hindered.[2]

Cortes reached Spain some time in April, 1540,[3] and was able to direct his case in person for much of the time. He urged the priority of his

[1] These documents fill 108 pages in volume xv of the Pacheco y Cardenas Documentos de Indias. At least one other document presented in the case, the Capitulacion . . . que hizo Ayllon, is printed elsewhere in the same Coleccion. This, also, does not include the two long memorials which Cortes succeeded in presenting to the King in person.

[2] This much feared conjunction came very near to being realized. A comparison of the various plottings of the routes De Soto and Coronado may have followed and of their respective itineraries shows that the two parties could not have been far apart in the present Oklahoma or Indian territory, or perhaps north of that region. This evidence is confirmed by the story of the Indian woman, related by Castañeda. Dr J. G. Shea, in Winsor's Narrative and Critical History, vol. ii, p. 292, states that Coronado heard of his countryman De Soto, and sent a letter to him. This is almost certainly a mistake, which probably originated in a misinterpretation of a statement made by Jaramillo.

[3] See his Carta in Doc. Inéd. España, vol. civ, p. 491.

claims under the royal license, dating from 1529.[1] He told of his many efforts to enlarge the Spanish domain, undertaken at great expense, personal sacrifice and danger, and resulting in the loss of relations and friends. From all of this, as he carefully pointed out, neither His Majesty nor himself had received any proper benefit, though this was not the result of any fault or lack of diligence on his part, as he hastened to explain, but had been caused by the persistent and ill-concealed hostility of the audiencia and the viceroy in New Spain, "concerning all of which His Majesty must have been kept heretofore in ignorance."

Nuño de Guzman presented his case in person, though perhaps this was not so much because it was more effective as because his resources must have been limited and his time little occupied. He was able, indeed, to make out a very good argument, assuming his right to the governorship of New Galicia, a province which had been greatly enlarged by his conquests. These conquests were toward the north, and he had taken possession of all the land in that direction in behalf of His Catholic Majesty. He would have extended the Spanish territory much farther in the same direction, if only his zealous efforts had not been abruptly cut short by his persecutors, through whose malicious efforts he was even yet nominally under arrest. Nor was this all, for all future expeditions into the new region must go across the territory which was rightfully his, and they could only succeed by the assistance and resources which would be drawn from his country. Thus he was the possessor of the key to all that lay beyond.

The commission or license which Pedro de Alvarado took with him from Spain the year before these proceedings opened, granted him permission to explore toward the west and the north—the latter provision probably inserted as a result of the reports which Cabeza de Vaca brought to Spain. Alvarado had prepared an expedition at great expense, and since the new region lay within his grant, his advocate pleaded, it would evidently pertain to him to conquer it. Moreover, he was in very high favor at court, as is shown by the ease with which he regained his position, in spite of the attack by the Mexican audiencia, and also by the ease with which he obtained the papal permission allowing him to marry the sister of his former wife. But Alvarado figures only slightly in the litigation, and he may have appeared as a party in order to maintain an opposition, rather than with any hope or intention of establishing the justice of his claims. Everything seems to add to the probability of the theory that Mendoza effected an alliance with him very early. It is possible that the negotiations may have begun before Alvarado left Spain, although there is no certainty about anything which preceded the written articles of agreement. Some of the contemporary historians appear to have been ignorant even of these.

[1] The Título, etc, dated 6 Julio, 1529, is in Pacheco y Cardenas, Coleccion de Documentos Inéditos de Indias, vol. iv, pp. 572-574.

LONZO DE SANTA CRUZ

The Council for the Indies referred the whole matter of the petitions and accompanying evidence to the fiscal, the licentiate Villalobos, April 21, 1540. He made a report, which virtually decided the case, May 25. The parties were given an opportunity of replying to this, and they continued to present evidence and petitions and countercharges for a year longer. The final decision, if any was made, has not been printed, so far as I know, but the Council could hardly have done anything beyond formally indorsing the report of Villalobos. The duty of the fiscal was plain, and his report advises His Majesty not to grant any of the things asked for by the petitioners. He states that this discovery ought to be made by and in behalf of His Majesty, since the region was not included in any previous grant. Although the Crown had forbidden any further unlicensed explorations, this would not prevent expeditions being undertaken on the part of the Crown, which is always at liberty to explore at will. In effect, of course, the report sanctioned the exploration by Mendoza, who represented the royal interests and power. An objection was at once entered in behalf of De Soto, using the very good argument that Mendoza's expedition would be sent out either at the expense of the Crown or of his private fortune. If the former, it was claimed that as the explorer would have the glory in any event, the Crown ought to save the expense by allowing De Soto, who had already undertaken the same thing at his own cost, to make these discoveries, which he promised should redound to as great an extent to the glory and advantage of the Emperor. If Mendoza was undertaking this at his own expense, it was evident that he would desire to recover his outlay. Here he was merely on the same footing as De Soto, who was prepared to make a better offer to his Royal Master than Mendoza could possibly afford. In either case there was the danger of scandal and disaster, in case the two expeditions should be allowed to come together beyond the range of the royal oversight. No answer to this appeal is recorded, and the parties continued to argue down their opponents' cases, while the viceroy in New Spain started the expedition which, under the command of Francisco Vazquez Coronado, discovered the Pueblo Indians of New Mexico, the Grand canyon of the Colorado, and the bison of the great plains.

The Expedition to New Mexico and the Great Plains

THE ORGANIZATION OF THE EXPEDITION

Two classes of colonists are essential to the security and the permanent prosperity of every newly opened country. In New Spain in the sixteenth century these two classes, sharply divided and almost antagonistic—the established settlers and the free soldiers of fortune—were both of considerable importance. Cortes, so soon as he had conquered the country, recognized the need of providing for its settlement by a stable population. In the petitions and memorials which he wrote in

1539 and 1540 he continually reiterates the declaration of the pains and losses sustained on account of his efforts to bring colonists from Spain to populate the New World. Whether he accomplished all that these memorials claim is doubtful, for there are comparatively few references to this class of immigrants during the years when Cortes was in a position to accomplish his designs. Mendoza declared that the increase of the European population in New Spain came largely after his own arrival there, in 1535, and this was probably true. The "good viceroy" unquestionably did more than anyone else to place the province on a permanent basis.[1]

Mendoza supervised with great care the assignment of land to the newcomers, and provided tools and stock for those who had not the means of equipping their farms. As a royal decree forbade the granting of land to unmarried men, besides directing an increase of royal favor and additional grants proportionate to the increase of children, the viceroy frequently advanced the money which enabled men who were desirous of settling down to get married. When he came from Spain in 1535, he brought with him a number of eligible spinsters, and it is quite probable that, after these had found husbands, he maintained the supply of maids suitable to become the wives of those colonists who wished to experience the royal bounty and favor. Alvarado engaged in a similar undertaking when he came out to Guatemala in 1539, but with less success than we may safely hope rewarded the thoughtfulness of Mendoza.[2] A royal order in 1538 had decreed that all who held encomiendas should marry within three years, if not already possessed of a wife, or else forfeit their estates to married men. Some of the bachelor landholders protested against the enforcement of this order in Guatemala, because eligible white women could not be found nearer than Mexico. To remove this objection, Alvarado brought twenty maidens from Spain. Soon after their arrival, a reception was held, at which they were given a chance to see their prospective husbands. During the evening, one of the girls declared to her companions that she never could marry one of these "old fellows, . . . who were cut up as if they had just escaped from the infernal regions, . . . for some of them are lame, some have only one hand, others have no ears or only one eye, and some of them have lost half their faces. The best of them have one or two scars across their foreheads."

---

[1] Fragmento Visita: Mendoza, Icazbalceta's Mexico, vol. ii, p. 90, § 86. "Porque antes que el dicho visorey viniese . . . habia muy poca gente y los corregimientos bastaban para proveellos y sustentallos, y como despues de la venida del dicho visorey creció la gente y se aumentó, y de cada dia vienen gentes pobres á quien se ha de proveer de comer, con la dicha baja y vacaciones se han proveido y remediado, y sin ella hubieran padecido y padecieran gran necesidad, y no se poblara tanto la tierra, y dello se dió noticia á S. M. y lo aprobó y se tuvo por servido en ello. § 194 (p. 117): Despues que el dicho visorey vino á esta Nueva España, continamente ha acogido en su casa á caballeros y otras personas que vienen necesitados de España y de otras partes, dándoles de comer y vestir, caballos y armas con que sirvan á S. M." . . .

[2] Garcilaso de la Vega, Comentarios Reales, part II, cap. i, lib. ii, p. 58 (ed. 1722), tells the story of Alvarado's experiment. The picture of the life and character of the Spanish conquerors of America, in the eyes of a girl fresh from Europe, is so vivid and suggestive that its omission would be unjustifiable.

The story is that one of the "old fellows" overheard this outburst, reported it to his friends, and promptly went off and married the daughter of a powerful cacique.

Besides assisting his colonists to get wives, Mendoza did a great deal to foster the agricultural interests of the province. He continued the importation of cattle, which Cortes had begun, and also procured horses and sheep from Spain. He writes in one of his letters of the especial satisfaction that he felt because of the rapid increase of his merino sheep, in spite of the depredations of the natives and of wild animals. The chief concern of the officials of the audiencia had been the gold mines, which yielded a considerable revenue in certain districts; but Mendoza, without neglecting these, proved how large and reliable was the additional revenue which could be derived from other sources. The viceroy's success in developing the province can not be shown more clearly than by repeating the description of New Spain in 1555, written by Robert Tomson, an English merchant engaged in the Spanish trade. In the course of a business tour Tomson visited the City of Mexico. His commercial friends in the city entertained him most hospitably, and did their best to make his visit pleasant. He refused, however, to heed their warnings, and his indiscreet freedom of speech finally compelled the officials of the Inquisition to imprison him, thus adding considerably to the length of his residence in the city. After he returned home, he wrote a narrative of his tour, in which he says of New Spain:

"As for victuals in the said Citie, of beefe, mutton, and hennes, capons, quailes, Guiñy-cockes, and such like, all are very good cheape: To say, the whole quarter of an oxe, as much as a slaue can carry away from the Butchers, for fiue Tomynes, that is, fiue Royals of plate, which is iust two shillings and sixe pence, and a fat sheepe at the Butchers for three Royals, which is 18. pence and no more. Bread is as good cheape as in Spaine, and all other kinde of fruites, as apples, peares, pomegranats, and quinces, at a reasonable rate. . . . [The country] doth yeeld great store of very good silke, and Cochinilla. . . . Also there are many goodly fruits, whereof we haue none such, as Plantanos, Guyaues, Sapotes, Tunas, and in the wildernes great store of blacke cheries, and other wholsome fruites. . . . Also the Indico that doeth come from thence to die blew, is a certaine hearbe. . . . Balme, Salsaperilla, cana fistula, suger, oxe hides, and many other good and seruiceable things the Countrey doeth yeeld, which are yeerely brought into Spaine, and there solde and distributed to many nations."[1]

The other class among the colonists of New Spain in the second quarter of the sixteenth century "floated like cork on the water" on those who had established their homes in the New World.[2] The men

[1] Tomson's whole narrative, in Hakluyt, Voyages, vol. iii, p. 447 (ed. 1600), is well worth reading. Considerable additional information in regard to the internal condition of New Spain, at a little later date, may be found in the "Discourses" which follow Tomson's Narrative, in the same volume of Hakluyt.

[2] The proof text for this quotation, as for many of the following statements which are taken from Mota Padilla's Historia de la Nueva Galicia, may be found in footnotes to the passages which they illustrate in the translation of Castañeda's narrative. I hope this arrangement will prove most convenient for those who study the documents included in this memoir. I shall not attempt in the introductory narrative to make any further references showing my indebtedness to Mota Padilla's invaluable work.

who made it possible to live in security on the farms and ranches of the province had rendered many and indispensable services, and there was much that they might still do to enlarge its boundaries and make the security more certain. They were, nevertheless, a serious hindrance to the prosperity of the settlements. For the most part they were young men of all sorts and degrees. Among them were many sons of Spanish noblemen, like Mendoza the viceroy, whose brother had just succeeded his father as Marquis de Mondejar. Very much of the extension of the Spanish world by discovery and conquest was due to the sons of men of rank, who had, perhaps generally, begun to sow their wild oats in Spain and were sent across the Atlantic in order to keep them out of mischief at home, or to atone, it may be, for mischief already done. In action, these young caballeros were most efficient. By personal valor and ability, they held the positions of leadership everywhere, among men who followed whom and when they chose, and always chose the man who led them most successfully. When inactive, these same cavaliers were a most trying annoyance to any community in which they happened to be. Armed with royal letters and comprehensive introductions, they had to be entertained, at heavy charges. Masters of their own movements, they came as they liked, and very often did not go away. Lovers of excitement, they secured it regardless of other men's wives or property.

There had been few attractions to draw these adventurers away from Mexico, the metropolis of the mainland, for some time previous to 1539. Peru still offered excitement for those who had nothing to gain or lose, but the purely personal struggle going on there between Pizarro and Almagro could not arouse the energies of those who were in search of glory as well as of employment. A considerable part of the rabble which followed Nuño de Guzman during the conquest of New Galicia went to Peru after their chief had been superseded by the Licentiate de la Torre, so that one town is said to have disappeared entirely from this cause; but among these there were few men of good birth and spirit. Mendoza had been able, at first, to accommodate and employ those who accompanied him from Spain, like Vazquez Coronado, "being chiefly young gentlemen." But every vessel coming from home brought some companion or friend of those who were already in New Spain, and after Cabeza de Vaca carried the reports of his discoveries to the Spanish court, an increasing number came each season to join the already burdensome body of useless members of the viceregal household. The viceroy recognized the necessity of relieving the community of this burden very soon after he had established himself in Mexico, and he was continually on the watch for some suitable means of freeing himself from these guests. By 1539 the problem of looking after these young gentlemen—whose number is determined quite accurately by the two hundred and fifty or three hundred "gentlemen on horseback" who left New Spain with Coronado in the spring of 1540—had become a serious one to the viceroy. The most desirable employment for all this idle energy would be, of course, the exploration and conquest of new country, or the opening of the border territory for permanent settlement. But no mere work for work's sake, no wild-goose chase, would do. These young gentlemen had many friends near to Charles V, who would have resented any abuse of privilege or of confidence. A suitable expedition could be undertaken only at considerable expense, and unless the cost could all be made good to the accountants in Spain, complaints were sure to be preferred against even the best of viceroys. So Mendoza entertained his guests as best he could, while they loafed about his court or visited his stock farms, and he anxiously watched the reports which came from the officials of the northwestern province of New Galicia and from the priests who were wandering and working among the outlying Indian tribes. When, late in the summer of 1539, Friar Marcos returned from the north, bringing the assurance that Cibola was a desirable field for conquest, the viceroy quickly improved the opportunity for which he had been waiting. Within a month and a half Mendoza had begun to organize the force which was to conquer this new country.

Compostela, on the Pacific coast, was announced as the place at which the force should assemble. The viceroy desired to have the army begin its march so soon as the roads were passable in the spring, and he wished also to relieve the Indians living in the districts between Mexico and the coast from as much as possible of the annoyance and loss which would be inevitable if the army started from Mexico and marched through this territory in a body. How much this forethought for the Indians was needed appears from Mendoza's reply to the accusations against him filed during the visita of 1547, which showed that all his care had not saved the Indians of Michoacan from needless injury at the hands of those who were on their way to join the gathering at Compostela. Incidentally, this arrangement also gave the capital city an earlier relief from its unwelcome guests.

Popular as was the expedition to the Seven Cities, there was a little opposition to the undertaking. When it became evident that a large force was about to leave the country, some of those who were to remain behind complained that all New Spain was being depopulated, and that no one would be left to defend the country in case of an Indian uprising. When Mendoza reached Compostela, by the middle of February, 1540, Coronado asked him to make an official investigation of these complaints. The formal request is dated February 21, and on the following day, Sunday, the viceroy held a grand review of the whole array, with everyone ready equipped for the march. As the men passed before the viceregal party the secretaries made an exact count and description of the force, but this document is not now known. Its loss is partly supplied by the sworn testimony of the officials who were best acquainted with the inhabitants of all parts of New Spain, recorded a few days after the departure of the expedition. They declare that in the whole army there were only two or three men who had ever been settled residents in the country; that these few were men who had failed to make a living as settlers, and that, in short, the whole force was a good riddance.[1]

The men who assembled at Compostela to start for the Seven Cities numbered, Mendoza stated at the time of the visita in 1547, "about two hundred and fifty Spaniards on horseback, . . . and about three hundred Indians, a few more or less." Mota Padilla, who must have used documents of the very best authority, nearly all of which have since disappeared, gives the number of the force as "two hundred and sixty horsemen, . . seventy footmen, . . and more than a thousand friendly Indians and Indian servants." Herrera, who used official documents, says that there were one hundred and fifty horsemen and two hundred footmen. Mendoza's statement of the number of Indians may be explained, if we suppose him to have referred only to the friendly Indians who went on the expedition as native allies. His statement is made in the course of a defense of his administration, when he was naturally desirous of giving as small a number as possible. Castañeda says that there were three hundred horsemen, and this number occurs in other early narratives.

Mendoza spared neither pains nor expense to insure the success of the expedition. Arms, horses, and supplies were furnished in abundance; money was advanced from the royal chest to any who had debts to pay before they could depart, and provision was made for the support of those who were about to be left behind by fathers, brothers, or husbands. The equipment of the force was all that the viceroy could desire. Arms and military supplies had been among the things greatly needed in New Spain when Mendoza reported its condition in his first letters to the home government. In 1537 he repeated his request for these supplies with increased insistence. The subject is not again mentioned in his letters, and we may fairly suppose that he had received the weapons and munitions of war, fresh from the royal arsenals of Spain, with which he equipped the expedition on whose success he had staked so much. It was a splendid array as it passed in review before Mendoza and the officials who helped and watched him govern New Spain, on this Sunday in February, 1540. The young cavaliers curbed the picked horses from the large stock farms of the viceroy, each resplendent in long blankets flowing to the ground. Each rider held his lance erect, while his sword and other weapons hung in their proper places at his side. Some were arrayed in coats of mail, polished to shine like that of their general, whose gilded armor with its brilliant trappings was to bring him many hard blows a few months later. Others wore iron helmets or vizored headpieces of the tough bullhide for which the country

---

[1] The Testimonio contains so much that is of interest to the historical student that I have translated it in full herein.

has ever been famous. The footmen carried crossbows and harquebuses, while some of them were armed with sword and shield. Looking on at these white men with their weapons of European warfare was the crowd of native allies in their paint and holiday attire, armed with the club and the bow of an Indian warrior. When all these started off next morning, in duly ordered companies, with their banners flying, upward of a thousand servants and followers, black men and red men, went with them, leading the spare horses, driving the pack animals, bearing the extra baggage of their masters, or herding the large droves of "big and little cattle," of oxen and cows, sheep, and, maybe, swine,[1] which had been collected by the viceroy to assure fresh food for the army on its march. There were more than a thousand horses in the train of the force, besides the mules, loaded with camp supplies and provisions, and carrying half a dozen pieces of light artillery—the pedreros, or swivel guns of the period.

After the review, the army assembled before the viceroy, who addressed to them an exhortation befitting the occasion. Each man, whether captain or foot soldier, then swore obedience to his commander and officers, and promised to prove himself a loyal and faithful vassal to his Lord the King. During the preceding week the viceroy had divided the force into companies, and now he assigned to each its captain, as Castañeda relates, and announced the other officers of the army.

Francisco Vazquez Coronado—de Coronado it is sometimes written—was captain-general of the whole force. "Who he is, what he has already done, and his personal qualities and abilities, which may be made useful in the various affairs which arise in these parts of the Indies, I have already written to Your Majesty," writes Mendoza to the Emperor, in the letter of December 10, 1537. This previous letter is not known to exist, and there is very little to supply the place of its description of the character and antecedents of Vazquez Coronado. His home was in Salamanca,[2] and he came to America in the retinue of Mendoza in 1535. His relations with his patron, the viceroy, previous to the return of the expedition from Cibola, appear always to have been most cordial and intimate. In 1537 Coronado married Beatrice de Estrada, a cousin by blood, if gossip was true, of the Emperor, Charles V. Her father, Alonso, had been royal treasurer of New Spain. From his mother-in-law Coronado received as a marriage gift a considerable estate, "the half of Tlapa," which was confirmed to him by a royal grant. Cortez complained that the income from this estate was worth more than 3,000 ducados, and that it had been unduly and inconsiderately alienated from the Crown. Coronado obtained also the estate of one Juan de Búrgos, apparently one of those who forfeited

---

[1] Herrera, Historia General, dec. VI, lib. ix, cap. xi, vol. iii, p. 204 (ed. 1730), mentions pigs among the food supply of the army. For the above description, which is not so fanciful as it sounds, see notes from Mota Padilla, etc, accompanying the translation of Castañeda.

[2] Castañeda's statement is supported by Herrera, Historia General, dec. VI, lib. v, cap. ix, vol. iii, p. 121 (ed. 1730), and by Tello, in Icazbalceta's Mexico, vol. ii, p. 370.

their land because they persisted in the unmarried state. This arrangement likewise received the royal approval.[1] When, however, "the new laws and ordinances for the Indies" came out from Spain in 1544,[2] after Coronado's return from the northern expedition, one of the sections expressly ordered an investigation into the extent and value of the estates held by Francisco Vazquez de Coronado, since it had been reported to the King that the number of Indians held to service on these estates was very excessive. Mendoza had to answer the same charge at his visita in 1547.

Mendoza sent Coronado, in 1537, to the mines at Amatepeque, where the negroes had revolted and "elected a king," and where they threatened to cause considerable trouble. The revolt was quelled, after some fighting, with the help of the Indians of the district. A couple of dozen of the rebels were hung and quartered at the mines or in the City of Mexico.[3]

In the following August, Coronado was legally recognized as a citizen of the City of Mexico, where he was one of three witnesses chosen to testify to the formal recognition by Cortes of the royal order which permitted De Soto to explore and conquer Florida.[4] A month later. September 7, 1538, the representative of De Soto, Alvaro de Sanjurjo, summoned Coronado himself to recognize and promise obedience to the same royal order, "as governor, as the said Sanjurjo declared him to be, of New Galicia." Coronado readily promised his loyal and respectful obedience to all of His Majesty's commands, but observed that this matter did not concern him at all, "since he was not governor, nor did he know that His Majesty desired to have him serve in such a position; and if His Majesty should desire his services in that position, he would obey and submit to the royal provision for him whenever he was called on, and would do what was most serviceable to the royal interests." He adds that he knows nothing about the government of Ayllon or that of Narvaez, which were mentioned in the license to De Soto. This part of his statement can hardly have been strictly true. The answer was not satisfactory to Sanjurjo, who replied that he had received information that Coronado was to be appointed governor of New Galicia. The latter stated that he had already given his answer, and thereupon Sanjurjo formally protested that the blame for any expenditures, damages, or scandals which might result from a failure to observe the royal order must be laid at the door of the one to whom they rightfully belonged, and that they would not result from any fault or omission on the part of De Soto. Sanjurjo may have received some hint or suggestion of the intention to appoint Coronado, but it is quite certain that no definite steps had yet been taken to supplant the licentiate, De la

[1] See the Fragmento de Visita, in Icazbalceta's Doc. Hist. Mexico, vol. ii, p. 95.

[2] The laws were signed at Valladolid, June 4 and June 26, 1543, and the copy printed in Icazbalceta's Doc. Hist. Mexico, vol. ii, p. 214, was promulgated in New Spain, March 13, 1544.

[3] See Mendoza's letter to the King, December 10, 1537.

[4] The proceso which was served on Cortes is in Pacheco y Cardenas, Doc. de Indias, vol. xv, p. 371.

Torre, as governor of New Galicia. Coronado's answer shows plainly
that he intentionally refused to commit himself when so many things
were uncertain, and when nothing was definitely known about the
country of which Cabeza de Vaca had heard. Mendoza may have sug
gested his appointment at an earlier date, but the King apparently
waited until he learned of De la Torre's untimely death before approv-
ing the selection. The confirmation was signed April 18, 1539, and at
the same time Coronado was appointed to take the residencia of his
predecessor. The King agreed to allow the new governor a salary of
1,000 ducats from the royal treasure chests and 1,500 more from the
province, with the proviso that the royal revenues were not to be held
responsible for this latter sum in case New Galicia proved too poor to
yield so large an amount. Coronado probably went at once to his
province when he received the notice of his nomination, for he was in
Guadalajara on November 19, 1538, where he approved the selection of
judges and magistrates for the ensuing year by the city of Compostela,
which had held its election before his arrival. At the same time he
appointed the judges for Guadalajara.

Coronado probably spent the winter of 1538–39 in New Galicia,
arranging the administration and other affairs of his government. He
entertained Friar Marcos, when the latter passed through his province
in the spring of 1539, and accompanied the friar as far as Culiacan, the
northernmost of the Spanish settlements. Here he provided the friar
with Indians, provisions, and other things necessary for the journey to
the Seven Cities. Later in the spring, the governor returned to Guadalajara, and devoted considerable attention to the improvement and
extension of this city, so that it was able to claim and obtain from the
King a coat of arms and the title of "city" during the following summer.[1] He was again here on January 9, 1540, when he promulgated
the royal order, dated December 20, 1538, which decreed that inasmuch
as it was reported that the cities in the Indies were not built with sufficient permanency, the houses being of wood and thatched with straw,
so that fires and conflagrations were of frequent occurrence, therefore
no settler should thereafter build a house of any material except stone,
brick, or unbaked brick, and the houses should be built after the fashion of those in Spain, so that they might be permanent, and an adornment to the cities. Between these dates it is very likely that Coronado
may have made some attempt to explore the mountainous regions
north of the province, as Castañeda says, although his evidence is by
no means conclusive.

About midsummer of 1539, Friar Marcos came back from Cibola.
Coronado met him as he passed through New Galicia, and together they
returned to Mexico to tell the viceroy what the friar had seen and
heard. Coronado remained at the capital during the autumn and early

[1] The grant, dated at Madrid, November 8, 1539, is given in Tello's Fragmento (Icazbalceta's Doc. Hist. Mexico, vol. ii, p. 371).

winter, taking an active part in all the preparations for the expedition which he was to command. After the final review in Compostela, he was placed in command of the army, with the title of captain-general.

THE DEPARTURE OF THE EXPEDITION

Monday, February 23, 1540, the army which was to conquer the Seven Cities of Cibola started on its northward march from Compostela.[1] For 80 leagues the march was along the "much-used roads" which followed the coast up to Culiacan.[2]

Everyone was eager to reach the wonderful regions which were to be their destination, but it was impossible to make rapid progress. The cattle could not be hurried, while the baggage animals and the carriers were so heavily laden with equipments and provisions that it was necessary to allow them to take their own time. Several days were lost at the Centizpac river, across which the cattle had to be trans-

---

[1] Before the end of the month Mendoza wrote a letter to the King, in which he gave a detailed account of the preparations he had made to insure the success of the expedition, and of the departure of the army. This letter is not known to exist.

[2] This march from Compostela to Culiacan, according to the letter which Coronado wrote from Granada-Zuñi on August 3, occupied eighty days. The same letter gives April 22 as the date when Coronado left Culiacan, after stopping for several days in that town, and this date is corroborated by another account, the Traslado de las Nuevas. April 22 is only sixty days after February 23, the date of the departure, which is fixed almost beyond question by the legal formalities of the Testimonio of February 21-26. We have only Ramusio's Italian text of Coronado's August 3 letter, so that it is easy to suspect that a slip on the part of the translator causes the trouble. But to complicate matters, eighty days previous to April 22 is about the 1st of February. Mota Padilla, who used material of great value in his Historia de la Nueva Galicia, says that the army marched from Compostela "el 1° de Febrero del año de 1540." Castañeda does not give much help, merely stating that the whole force was assembled at Compostela by "el dia de carnes tollendas," the carnival preceding Shrove tide, which in 1540 fell on February 10, Easter being March 28. Mendoza, who had spent the New Year's season at Pasquaro, the seat of the bishopric of Michoacan, did not hasten his journey across the country, and we know only that the whole force had assembled before he arrived at Compostela. At least a fortnight would have been necessary for completing the organization of the force, and for collecting and arranging all the supplies.

Another combination of dates makes it hard to decide how rapidly the army marched. Mendoza was at Compostela February 26. He presumably started on his return to Mexico very soon after that date. He went down the coast to Colima, where he was detained by an attack of fever for some days. Thence he proceeded to Jacona, where he wrote a letter to the King, April 17, 1540. March 20 Mendoza received the report of Melchior Diaz, who had spent the preceding winter in the country through which Friar Marcos had traveled, trying to verify the friar's report. Diaz, and Saldivar his lieutenant, on their return from the north, met the army at Chiametla as it was about to resume its march, after a few days' delay. Diaz stopped at Chiametla, while Saldivar carried the report to the viceroy, and he must have traveled very rapidly to deliver his packets on March 20, when Mendoza had left Colima, although he probably had not arrived at Jacona.

Everything points to the very slow progress of the force, hampered by the long baggage and provision trains. Castañeda says that they reached Culiacan just before Easter, March 28, less than thirty-five days after February 23. Here Coronado stopped for a fortnight's entertainment and rest, according to Castañeda, who was present. Mota Padilla says that the army stayed here a month, and this agrees with Castañeda's statement that the main body started a fortnight later than their general.

The attempt to arrange an itinerary of the expedition is perplexing, and has not been made easier by modern students. Professor Haynes, in his Early Explorations of New Mexico (Winsor's Narrative and Critical History, vol. ii, p. 481), following Bandelier's statement on page 26 of his Documentary History of Zuñi, says that the start from Compostela was made "in the last days of February, 1540." Mr Bandelier, however, who has given much more time to the study of everything connected with this expedition than has been possible for any other investigator, in his latest work—The Gilded Man, p. 164—adopts the date which is given by Mota Padilla. The best and the safest way out of this tangle in chronology is gained by accepting the three specific dates, February 23—or possibly 24—Easter, and April 22, disregarding every statement about the number of days intervening.

ported one at a time. At Chiametla there was another delay. Here the army camped in the remains of a village which Nuño de Guzman had established. The settlers had been driven away by a pestilence caught from the Indians, and by the fierce onslaught of the natives who came down upon them from the surrounding mountains. The food supply of Coronado's force was beginning to fail, and as the tribes hereabout were still in rebellion, it became necessary to send a force into the mountains to obtain provisions. The army master, Samaniego, who had been warden of one of the royal fortresses,[1] commanded the foraging party. The men found themselves buried in the thick underbrush as soon as they passed beyond the limits of the clearing. One of the soldiers inadvertently, but none the less in disregard of strict orders, became separated from the main party, and the Indians, who were nowhere to be seen, at once attacked him. In reply to his cries, the watchful commander hastened to his assistance. The Indians who had tried to seize him suddenly disappeared. When everything seemed to be safe, Samaniego raised his visor, and as he did so an arrow from among the bushes pierced his eye, passing through the skull. The death of Samaniego was a severe loss to the expedition. Brave and skillful, he was beloved by all who were with him or under him. He was buried in the little chapel of the deserted village. The army postponed its departure long enough to capture several natives of the district, whose bodies were left hanging on the trees in order to counteract the bad augury which followed from the loss of the first life.[2]

A much more serious presage was the arrival at Chiametla, as the army was preparing to leave, of Melchior Diaz and Juan de Saldivar, or Zaldivar, returning from their attempt to verify the stories told by Friar Marcos. Melchior Diaz went to New Galicia with Nuño de Guzman, and when Cabeza de Vaca appeared in that province, in May 1536, Diaz was in command of the outpost of Culiacan. He was still at Culiacan, in the autumn of 1539, when Mendoza directed him to take a mounted force and go into the country toward the north "to see if the account which Friar Marcos brought back agreed with what he could observe." He left Culiacan November 17, with fifteen horsemen, and traveled as far north as the wilderness beyond which Cibola was situated, following much the same route as the friar had taken, and questioning the Indians with great care. Many of the statements made by Friar Marcos were verified, and some new facts were obtained, but nowhere could he find any foundation for the tales of a wealthy and attractive country, except in the descriptions given by the Indians. The cold weather had begun to trouble his men seriously before he reached the limit of his explorations. He pushed on as far as Chichilticalli, however, but here the snows and fierce winds from across the

---

[1] Mota Padilla says, "warden of one of the royal storehouses in Mexico," which may refer to some other position held by Samaniego, or may have arisen from some confusion of names.

[2] This is taken from Mota Padilla's account of the incident, without any attempt to compare or to harmonize it with the story told by Castañeda. Mota Padilla's version seems much the more reasonable.

wilderness forced him to turn back. At Chiametla he encountered
Coronado's force. He joined the army, sending his lieutenant, Saldivar,
with three other horsemen, to carry his report to the viceroy. This was
delivered to Mendoza on March 20, and is embodied in the letter to the
King, dated April 17, 1540.

Coronado did not allow Diaz to announce the results of his reconnoissance to the soldiers, but the rumor quickly spread that the visions inspired by Friar Marcos had not been substantiated. Fortunately, the
friar was himself in the camp. Although he was now the father provincial of the Franciscan order in New Spain, he had determined to accompany the expedition, in order to carry the gospel to the savages
whose salvation had been made possible by his heroic journey of the
preceding spring. The mutterings of suspicion and discontent among
the men grew rapidly louder. Friar Marcos felt obliged to exhort them
in a special sermon to keep up a good courage, and by his eloquence he
succeeded in persuading them that all their labors would soon be well
repaid.

From Chiametla the army resumed its march, procuring provisions
from the Indians along the way. Mendoza stated, in 1547, that he
took every precaution to prevent any injury or injustice being done to
the Indians at the time of Coronado's departure, and that he stationed
officials, especially appointed for this purpose, at convenient points on
the road to Culiacan, who were ordered to procure the necessary provisions for the expedition. There are no means of telling how well this
plan was carried into execution.

A day or two before Easter, March 28, 1540, the army approached
Culiacan. The journey had occupied a little over a month, but when
Coronado, from his lodging in the Cibola village of Granada, three
months later, recalled the slow and tedious marches, the continual
waiting for the lazy cattle and the heavily loaded baggage trains, and
the repeated vexatious delays, we can hardly wonder that it seemed to
him to have been a period of fourscore days' journey.

The town of San Miguel de Culiacan, in the spring of 1540, was one
of the most prosperous in New Spain. Nuño de Guzman had founded
the settlement some years before, and had placed Melchior Diaz in
charge of it. The appointment was a most admirable one. Diaz was
not of gentle birth, but he had established his right to a position of
considerable power and responsibility by virtue of much natural ability.
He was a hard worker and a skillful organizer and leader. He inspired
confidence in his companions and followers, and always maintained the
best of order and of diligence among those who were under his charge.
Rarely does one meet with a man whose record for every position and
every duty assigned to him shows such uniform and thorough efficiency.
The settlement increased rapidly in size and in wealth, and when Coronado's force encamped in the surrounding fields, the citizens of the town
insisted on entertaining in their own homes all of the gentlemen who

were with the expedition. The granaries of the place were filled with the surplus from the bountiful harvests of two preceding years, which sufficed to feed the whole army for three or four weeks, besides providing supplies sufficient for more than two months when the expedition resumed its march. These comfortable quarters and the abundant entertainment detained the general and his soldiers for some weeks.[1] This was the outpost of Spanish civilization, and Coronado made sure that his arrangements were as complete as possible, both for the army and for the administration of New Galicia during his absence.

The soldiers, and especially the gentlemen among them, had started from Compostela with an abundant supply of luxurious furnishings and extra equipment. Many of them were receiving their first rough lessons in the art of campaigning, and the experiences along the way before reaching Culiacan had already changed many of their notions of comfort and ease. When the preparations for leaving Culiacan began, the citizens of the town received from their guests much of the clothing and other surplus baggage, which was left behind in order that the expedition might advance more rapidly, or that the animals might be loaded with provisions. Aside from what was given to the people of the place, much of the heavier camp equipage, with some of the superfluous property of the soldiers, was put on board a ship, the *San Gabriel*, which was waiting in the harbor of Culiacan. An additional supply of corn and other provisions also was furnished for the vessel by the generous citizens.

THE EXPEDITION BY SEA UNDER ALARCON

A sea expedition, to cooperate with the land force, was a part of Mendoza's original plan. After the viceroy left Coronado, and probably while he was at Colima, on his way down the coast from Compostela, he completed the arrangements by appointing Hernando de Alarcon, his chamberlain according to Bernal Diaz, to command a fleet of two vessels. Alarcon was instructed to sail northward, following the coast as closely as possible. He was to keep near the army, and communicate with it at every opportunity, transporting the heavy baggage and holding himself ready at all times to render any assistance which Coronado might desire. Alarcon sailed May 9, 1540, probably from Acapulco.[2]

---

[1] A note, almost as complicated as that which concerns the date of the army's departure, might be written regarding the length of the stay at Culiacan. Those who are curious can find the facts in Coronado's letter from Granada, in Castañeda, and in the footnotes to the translation of the latter.

[2] The complete text of Alarcon's report was translated into Italian by Ramusio (vol. iii, fol. 363, ed. 1556), and the Spanish original is not known to exist. Herrera, however, gives an account which, from the close similarity to Ramusio's text and from the personality of the style, must have been copied from Alarcon's own narrative. The Ramusio text does not give the port of departure. Herrera says that the ships sailed from Acapulco. Castañeda implies that the start was made from La Natividad, but his information could hardly have been better than second hand. He may have known what the viceroy intended to do, when he bade the army farewell, two days north of Compostela. Alarcon reports that he put into the port of Santiago de Buena Esperanza, and as the only Santiago on the coast hereabout is south of La Natividad, which is on the coast of the district of Colima,

14 ETH——25

This port had been the seat of the shipbuilding operations of Cortes on the Pacific coast, and it is very probable that Alarcon's two ships were the same as those which the marquis claimed to have equipped for a projected expedition. Alarcon sailed north to Santiago, where he was obliged to stop, in order to refit his vessels and to replace some artillery and stores which had been thrown overboard from his companion ship during a storm. Thence he sailed to Aguaiauale, as Ramusio has it, the port of San Miguel de Culiacan. The army had already departed, and so Alarcon, after replenishing his store of provisions, added the *San Gabriel* to his fleet and continued his voyage. He followed the shore closely and explored many harbors "which the ships of the marquis had failed to observe," as he notes, but he nowhere succeeded in obtaining any news of the army of Coronado.

THE JOURNEY FROM CULIACAN TO CIBOLA

Melchior Diaz had met with so many difficulties in traveling through the country which the army was about to enter, on its march toward the Seven Cities, and the supply of food to be found there was everywhere so small, that Coronado decided to divide his force for this portion of the journey. He selected seventy-five or eighty horsemen, including his personal friends, and twenty-five or thirty foot soldiers. With these picked men, equipped for rapid marching, he hastened forward, clearing the way for the main body of the army, which was to follow more slowly, starting a fortnight after his own departure. With the footmen in the advance party were the four friars of the expedition, whose zealous eagerness to reach the unconverted natives of the Seven Cities was so great that they were willing to leave the main portion of the army without a spiritual guide. Fortunately for these followers, a broken leg compelled one of the brethren to remain behind. Coronado attempted to take some sheep with him, but these soon proved to be so great a hindrance that they were left at the river Yaquimi, in charge of four horsemen, who conducted them at a more moderate pace.

Leaving Culiacan on April 22, Coronado followed the coast, "bearing off to the left," as Mota Padilla says, by an extremely rough way, to the river Cinaloa. The configuration of the country made it necessary to follow up the valley of this stream until he could find a passage across the mountains to the course of the Yaquimi. He traveled alongside this stream for some distance, and then crossed to Sonora river.[1]

H. H. Bancroft (North Mexican States, vol. i, p. 90) says the fleet probably started from Acapulco. Bancroft does not mention Herrera, who is, I suppose, the conclusive authority. Gen. J. H. Simpson (Smithsonian Report for 1869, p. 315), accepted the start from La Natividad, and then identified this Santiago with the port of Compostela, which was well known under the name of Xalisco. The distance of Acapulco from Colima would explain the considerable lapse of time before Alarcon was ready to start.

[1] Coronado's description of this portion of the route in the letter of August 3 is abbreviated, he says, because it was accompanied by a map. As this is lost, I am following here, as I shall do throughout the Introduction, Bandelier's identification of the route in his Historical Introduction, p. 10, and in his Final Report, part II, pp. 407-409. The itinerary of Jaramillo, confused and perplexing as it is, is the chief guide for the earlier part of the route. There is no attempt in this introductory narrative to repeat the details of the journey, when these may be obtained, much more satisfactorily, from the translation of the contemporary narratives which form the main portion of this memoir.

The Sonora was followed nearly to its source before a pass was discovered. On the northern side of the mountains he found a stream—the Nexpa, he calls it—which may have been either the Santa Cruz or the San Pedro of modern maps. The party followed down this river valley until they reached the edge of the wilderness, where, as Friar Marcos had described it to them, they found Chichilticalli.[1]

Here the party camped for two days, which was as long as the general dared to delay, in order to rest the horses, who had begun to give out sometime before as a result of overloading, rough roads, and poor feed. The stock of provisions brought from Culiacan was already growing dangerously small, although the food supply had been eked out by the large cones or nuts of the pines of this country, which the soldiers found to be very good eating. The Indians who came to see him, told Coronado that the sea was ten days distant, and he expresses surprise, which Mr Bandelier has reëchoed, that Friar Marcos could have gone within sight of the sea from this part of the country.

Coronado entered the wilderness, the White Mountain Apache country of Arizona, on Saint John's eve, and in the quaint language of Hakluyt's translation of the general's letter, "to refresh our former trauailes, the first dayes we founde no grasse, but worser way of mountaines and badde passages."[2] Coronado, following very nearly the line of the present road from Fort Apache to Gila river, proceeded until he came within sight of the first of the Seven Cities. The first few days of the march were very trying. The discouragement of the men increased with the difficulties of the way. The horses were tired, and the slow progress became slower, as horses and Indian carriers fell down and died. The corn was almost gone, and as a result of eating the fruits and herbs which they found along the way, a Spaniard and some of the servants were poisoned so badly that they died. The skull and horns of a great mountain goat, which were lying on the ground, filled the Europeans with wonder, but this was hardly a sign to inspire them with hopes of abundant food and gold. There were 30 leagues of this travailing before the party reached the borders of the inhabited country, where they found "fresh grass and many nutte and mulberrie trees."

The day following that on which they left the wilderness, the advance guard was met, in a peaceable manner, by four Indians. The Spaniards treated them most kindly, gave them beads and clothing, and "willed

[1] This "Red House," in the Nahuatl tongue, has been identified with the Casa Grande ruins in Arizona ever since the revival of interest in Coronado's journey, which followed the explorations in the southwestern portion of the United States during the second quarter of the present century. Bandelier's study of the descriptions given by those who saw the "Red House" in 1539 and 1540, however, shows conclusively that the conditions at Casa Grande do not meet the requirements for Chichilticalli. Bandelier objects to Casa Grande because it is white, although he admits that it may once have been covered with the reddish paint of the Indians. This would suit Mota Padilla's explanation that the place was named from a house there which was daubed over with colored earth—almagre, as the natives called it. This is the Indian term for red ocher. Bandelier thinks that Coronado reached the edge of the wilderness, the White Mountain Apache reservation in Arizona, by way of San Pedro river and Arivaypa creek. This requires the location of Chichilticalli somewhere in the vicinity of the present Fort Grant, Arizona.

[2] Hakluyt, Voyages, vol. iii, p. 375, ed. 1600.

them to return unto their city and bid them stay quiet in their houses fearing nothing." The general assured them that they need have no anxiety, because the newcomers had been sent by His Spanish Majesty, "to defend and ayde them."

THE CAPTURE OF THE SEVEN CITIES

The provisions brought from Culiacan or collected along the way were now exhausted, and as a sudden attack by the Indians, during the last night before their arrival at the cities, had assured the Spaniards of a hostile reception, it was necessary to proceed rapidly. The inhabitants of the first city had assembled in a great crowd, at some distance in front of the place, awaiting the approach of the strangers. While the army advanced, Garcia Lopez de Cardenas, who had been appointed to Samaniego's position as field-master, and Hernando Vermizzo, apparently one of the "good fellows" whose name Castañeda forgot, rode forward and summoned the Indians to surrender, in approved Castilian fashion, as His Majesty commanded always to be done. The natives had drawn some lines on the ground, doubtless similar to those which they still mark with sacred meal in their ceremonial dramatizations, and across these they refused to let the Spaniards pass, answering the summons with a shower of arrows. The soldiers begged for the command to attack, but Coronado restrained them as long as he could. When the influence of the friars was added to the pleas of the men—perhaps without waiting for the command or permission—the whole company uttered the Santiago, the sacred war cry of Saint James, against the infidels, and rushed upon the crowd of Indians, who turned and fled. Coronado quickly recalled his men from the pursuit, and ordered them to prepare for an assault on the city. The force was divided into attacking parties, which immediately advanced against the walls from all sides. The crossbowmen and harquebusiers, who were expected to drive the enemy back from the tops of the walls, were unable to accomplish anything, on account of their physical weakness and of accidents to their weapons. The natives showered arrows against the advancing foes, and as the Spaniards approached the walls, stones of all sizes were thrown upon them with skillful aim and practiced strength. The general, in his glittering armor, was the especial target of the defenders, and twice he was knocked to the ground by heavy rocks. His good headpiece and the devotion of his companions saved him from serious injury, although his bruises confined him to the camp for several days. The courage and military skill of the white men, weak and tired as they were, proved too much for the Indians, who deserted their homes after a fierce, but not protracted, resistance. Most of the Spaniards had received many hard knocks, and Aganiez Suarez—possibly another of the gentlemen forgotten by Castañeda—was severely wounded by arrows, as were also three foot soldiers.

The Indians had been driven from the main portion of the town, and with this success the Spaniards were satisfied. Food—"that which we needed a great deal more than gold or silver," writes one member of the victorious force—was found in the rooms already secured. The Spaniards fortified themselves, stationed guards, and rested. During the night, the Indians, who had retired to the wings of the main building after the conflict, packed up what goods they could, and left the Spaniards in undisputed possession of the whole place.

The mystery of the Seven Cities was revealed at last. The Spanish conquerors had reached their goal. July 7, 1540, white men for the first time entered one of the communal villages of stone and mud, inhabited by the Zuñi Indians of New Mexico.[1] Granada was the name which the Spaniards gave to the first village—the Indian Hawikuh—in honor of the viceroy to whose birthplace they say it bore a fancied resemblance. Here they found, besides plenty of corn, beans and fowls, better than those of New Spain, and salt, "the best and whitest I have seen in all my life," writes one of those who had helped to win the town. But even the abundance of food could not wholly satisfy the men whose toilsome march of more than four months had been lightened by dreams of a golden haven. Friar Marcos was there to see the realization of the visions which the zealous sermons of his brethren and the prolific ardor of rumor and of common talk had raised from his truthful report. One does not wonder that he eagerly accepted the earliest opportunity of returning to New Spain, to escape from the not merely muttered complaints and upbraidings, in expressing which the general was chief.[2]

THE EXPLORATION OF THE COUNTRY

THE SPANIARDS AT ZUÑI

Some of the inhabitants of Hawikuh-Granada returned to the village, bringing gifts, while Coronado was recovering from his wounds. The general faithfully exhorted them to become Christians and to submit themselves to the sovereign over-lordship of His Majesty the Spanish

---

[1] Hawikuh, near Ojo Caliente, was the first village captured by the Spaniards, as Bandelier has shown in his Contributions, p. 166, and Documentary History of Zuñi, p. 29. The definite location of this village is an important point, and the problem of its site was one over which a great deal of argument had been wasted before Mr Bandelier published the results of his critical study of the sources, which he was enabled to interpret by the aid of a careful exploration of the southwestern country, undertaken under the auspices of the Archæological Institute of America. It was under the impetus of the friendly guidance and careful scrutiny of results by Professor Henry W. Haynes and the other members of the Institute that Mr Bandelier has done his best work. It is unfortunate that he did not use the letter which Coronado wrote from Granada-Hawikuh, August 3, 1540, which is the only official account of the march from Culiacan to Zuñi. The fact that Bandelier's results stand the tests supplied by this letter is the best proof of the exactness and accuracy of his work. (This note was written before the appearance of Mr Bandelier's Gilded Man, in which he states that Kiakima, instead of Hawikuh, is the Granada of Coronado. Mr F. W. Hodge, in an exhaustive paper on The First Discovered City of Cibola (American Anthropologist, Washington, April, 1895), has proved conclusively that Mr Bandelier's earlier position was the correct one.)

[2] Marcos returned to Mexico with Juan de Gallego, who left Cibola-Zuñi soon after August 3. Bandelier, in his article on the friars, in the American Catholic Quarterly Review, vol. xv, p. 551, says that "the obvious reason" for Marcos's return "was the feeble health of the friar. Hardship and physical suffering had nearly paralyzed the body of the already aged man. He never recovered his vigor, and died at Mexico, after having in vain sought relief in the delightful climate of Jalapa, in the year 1558"—seventeen years later.

King. The interview failed to reassure the natives, for they packed all their provisions and property on the following day, and with their wives and children abandoned the villages in the valley and withdrew to their stronghold, the secure fastness on top of Taaiyalone or Thunder mountain.

As soon as he was able, Coronado visited the other villages of Cibola-Zuñi, observing the country carefully. He reassured the few Indians whom he found still living in the valley, and after some hesitation on their part succeeded in persuading the chiefs to come down from the mesa and talk with him. He urged them to return to their homes below, but without success. He was more fortunate in obtaining information regarding the surrounding country, which was of much use to him in directing further exploration. Then as now the rule held good that the Indians are much more likely to tell the truth when giving information about their neighbors than about themselves.

THE DISCOVERY OF TUSAYAN AND THE GRAND CANYON

A group of seven villages, similar to those at Cibola, was reported to be situated toward the west, "the chief of the towns whereof they have knowledge." Tucano was the name given to these, according to Ramusio's version of Coronado's letter, and it is not difficult to see in this name that of Tusayan, the Hopi or Moki settlements in northeastern Arizona.

As soon as everything was quiet in the Cibola country, about the middle of July, Don Pedro de Tovar was ordered to take a few horsemen and his company of footmen and visit this district. Don Pedro spent several days in the Tusayan villages, and after he had convinced the people of his peaceable designs, questioned them regarding the country farther west. Returning to the camp at Cibola within the thirty days to which his commission was limited, Tovar reported that the country contained nothing to attract the Spaniards. The houses, however, were better than those at Cibola. But he had heard stories of a mighty river and of giant peoples living toward the west, and so Don Garcia Lopez de Cardenas was instructed to go and verify these reports. Cardenas started, perhaps on August 25. He had authority for eighty days, and within this term he succeeded in reaching the Grand canyon of Colorado river, which baffled his most agile companions in their efforts to descend to the water or to discover some means of crossing to the opposite side. He returned with only the story of this hopeless barrier to exploration westward.

THE RIO GRANDE AND THE GREAT PLAINS

The first expedition toward the east was sent out August 29 in charge of Don Hernando de Alvarado. Passing the rock of Acuco or Acoma—always a source of admiration—Alvarado reached the village and river of Tiguex—the Rio Grande—on September 7. Some time was spent in visiting the villages situated along the stream. The headquarters of the party were at Tiguex, at or near the site of the present town of Bernalillo, and here a list was drawn up and sent to the general giving the names of eighty villages of which he had learned from the natives of this place. At the same time Alvarado reported that these villages were the best that had yet been found, and advised that the winter quarters for the whole force should be established in this district. He then proceeded to Cicuye or Pecos, the most eastern of the walled villages, and from there crossed the mountains to the buffalo plains. Finding a stream which flowed toward the southeast—the Canadian river, perhaps—he followed its course for a hundred leagues or more. Many of the "humpback oxen" were seen, of which some of the men may have remembered Cabeza de Vaca's description.

On his return, Alvarado found the army-master, Garcia Lopez de Cardenas, at Tiguex, arranging winter quarters sufficient to accommodate the whole force in this region.[1] Coronado, who had made a trip to examine the villages farther south, along the Rio Grande, soon joined his lieutenants, leaving only a small force at Cibola to maintain the post. The whole of the advance party was now in Tiguex, and orders had been left at Cibola for the main body to proceed to the eastern settlements so soon as they should arrive from Culiacan and Corazones.

THE MARCH OF THE ARMY FROM CULIACAN TO TIGUEX

The main portion of the army remained at Culiacan, under the command of Don Tristan de Arellano, when the general started for Cibola with his small party of companions. The soldiers completed the work of loading the *San Gabriel* with their surplus equipment and with provisions, and busied themselves about the town for a fortnight after the departure of their general. Some time between the first and middle of May, the army started to follow the route of the advance party. The whole force marched on foot, carrying their lances and other weapons, in order that the horses and other beasts, numbering more than six hundred, might all be loaded with provisions. It had taken Coronado and his party of horsemen, eager to push on toward their destination, more than a month to make the journey to Corazones or Hearts valley. We can only guess how much longer it took the slowly marching army to cover this first half of the distance to Cibola. The orders which the general had left with Arellano were that he should

---

[1] Alvarado's official report is probably the paper known as the Relacion de lo que. . . . Alvarado y Fray Joan de Padilla descubrieron en demanda de la mar del Sur, which is translated herein. The title, evidently the work of some later editor, is a misnomer so far as the Mar del Sur is concerned, for this—the Pacific ocean—was west, and Alvarado's explorations were toward the east. This short report is of considerable value, but it is known only through a copy, lacking the list of villages which should have accompanied it. Muñoz judged that it was a contemporary official copy, which did not commend itself to that great collector and student of Spanish Americana. There is nothing about the document to show the century or the region to which it relates, so that one of Hubert H. Bancroft's scribes was misled into making a short abstract of it for his Central America, vol. ii, p. 185, as giving an account of an otherwise unknown expedition starting from another Granada, on the northern shore of Lake Nicaragua.

take the army to this valley, where a good store of provisions had been found by Melchior Diaz, and there wait for further instructions. Coronado promised to send for his soldiers as soon as he was sure that there was a country of the Seven Cities for them to conquer and settle.

In the valley of Corazones, which had been given its name by Cabeza de Vaca because the natives at this place offered him the hearts of animals for food, Arellano kept the soldiers busy by building a town on Suya river, naming it San Hieronimo de los Corazones—Saint Jerome of the Hearts. A small force was sent down the river to the seacoast, under the command of Don Rodrigo Maldonado, in the hope of communicating with the ships of Alarcon. Maldonado found neither signs nor news of the fleet, but he discovered a tribe of Indian "giants," one of whom accompanied the party back to the camp, where the soldiers were filled with amazement at his size and strength.

Thus the time passed until early in September, when Melchior Diaz and Juan Gallego brought the expected orders from the general. Gallego, who carried the letter which Coronado had written from Granada-Hawikuh on August 3, with the map and the exhibits of the country which it mentions, continued on to Mexico. He was accompanied by Friar Marcos. Diaz had been directed to stay in the new town of San Hieronimo, to maintain this post and to open communication with the seacoast. He selected seventy or eighty men—those least fitted for the hardships and struggles of exploration and conquest—who remained to settle the new town and to make an expedition toward the coast. The remainder of the army prepared to rejoin their general at Cibola, and by the middle of September the start was made.

After a long, rough march, in which little occurred to break the daily monotony, the soldiers reached the pueblo settlements. The bad weather had already begun, but the men were eager to continue their journey in spite of the snow and the fierce, cold winds. After a short rest, the force proceeded to Tiguex, where comfortable quarters were awaiting them, and in these they quickly settled for the winter.

THE WINTER OF 1540-1541 ALONG THE RIO GRANDE

THE INDIAN REVOLT

The first winter spent by white men in the pueblos of New Mexico was a severe one. Fortunately for the strangers, however, they were comfortably domiciled in the best houses of the country, in which the owners had left a plentiful supply of food, and this was supplemented by the livestock brought from New Spain.

During the late autumn the Indians assumed a hostile attitude toward their visitors, and were reduced to peaceful inactivity only after a protracted struggle, which greatly aggravated the conquerors. The Spanish story of this revolt is clear—that the Indians suddenly surprised the Europeans by attacking the horses and mules of the army, killing or driving off a number of them, after which the natives collected their fighting force into two of the strongest villages, from one of which they were able to defy the soldiers until thirst compelled them to abandon the stronghold.   The defenders attempted to escape by stealth, but the sentries of the besieging force discovered them and aroused the camp.   Many of the Indians were killed by the soldiers during the flight which followed, while others perished in the icy waters of the Rio Grande.   During an attack on the second village, a few of the Spaniards who had succeeded in making their way to the highest portion of the buildings, escaped from their perilous position by inducing the native warriors to surrender.   The Indians received an ample promise of protection and safety, but the captain of the attacking party was not informed of this, and in obedience to the general's orders that no prisoners should be taken, he directed that the captives should be burned as a warning to the neighboring tribes.   This affair is a terrible blot on the record of the expedition and of those who composed it.   In condemning it most severely, however, English readers should remember that they are only repeating the condemnations which were uttered by most of the men of rank who witnessed it, which were repeated in New Spain and in old Spain, and which greeted the commander when he led his expedition back to Mexico, to receive the cold welcome of the viceroy.

The Spaniards have told us only one side of the story of what was happening along the Rio Grande in the fall of 1540.   The other side will probably never be heard, for it disappeared with the traditions of the Indian villagers.   Without pretending to supply the loss, it is at least possible to suggest that the preparations by which the army-master procured the excellent accommodations for the force must have appeared very differently to the people in whose homes Cardenas housed the soldiers, and to those who passed the winter in these snug quarters.   Castañeda preserved one or two interesting details which are as significant as is the striking fact that the peaceful natives who entertained Alvarado most freely in September were the leaders of the rebellion three months later.

As soon as Coronado's men had completed the reduction of the refractory natives, and the whole country had been overawed by the terrible punishment, the general undertook to reestablish peaceful relations and confident intercourse between his camp and the surrounding villages.   The Indians seem to have been ready to meet him almost half-way, although it is hardly surprising to find traces of an underlying suspicion, and a readiness for treacherous retaliation.

THE STORIES ABOUT QUIVIRA

While this reconciliation was being effected, Coronado heard from one of the plains Indians,[1] held as a slave in the village of Cicuye

---

[1] Castañeda says that this Indian accompanied Alvarado on the first visit to the buffalo plains, and this may be true without disturbing the statement above.

or Pecos, the stories about Quivira, which were to add so much to the geographic extent of the expedition. When the Spaniards were about to kill this Indian—"The Turk," they called him[1]—he told them that his masters, the people of Cicuye, had induced him to lead the strangers away to the pathless plains, where water was scarce and corn was unknown, to perish there, or, if ever they should succeed in finding the way back to the village settlements, tired and weak, to fall an easy prey to their enemies.

This plan was shrewdly conceived, and it very nearly succeeded. There is little reason why we should doubt the truth of the confession, made when the Indian could scarcely have hoped to save his life, and it affords an easy explanation of the way in which the exaggerated stories of Quivira originated and expanded. The Turk may have accompanied Alvarado on the first visit to the great plains, and he doubtless told the white men about his distant home and the roving life on the prairies. It was later, when the Spaniards began to question him about nations and rulers, gold and treasures, that he received, perhaps from the Spaniards themselves, the hints which led him to tell them what they were rejoiced to hear, and to develop the fanciful pictures which appealed so forcibly to all the desires of his hearers. The Turk, we can not doubt, told the Spaniards many things which were not true. But in trying to trace these early dealings of Europeans with the American aborigines, we must never forget how much may be explained by the possibilities of misinterpretation on the part of the white men, who so often heard of what they wished to find, and who learned, very gradually and in the end imperfectly, to understand only a few of the native languages and dialects. And besides this, the record of their observations, on which the students of today have to depend, was made in a language which knew nothing of the things which it was trying to describe. Much of what the Turk said was very likely true the first time he said it, although the memories of home were heightened, no doubt, by absence and distance. Moreover, Castañeda, who is the chief source for the stories of gold and lordly kings which are said to have been told by the Turk, in all probability did not know anything more than the reports of what the Turk was telling to the superior officers, which were passed about among the common foot soldiers.[2] The present narrative has already shown the wonderful power of gossip, and when it is gossip recorded twenty years afterward, we may properly be cautious in believing it.

Coronado wrote to the King from Tiguex, on April 20, 1541, as he says in his next letter, that of October 20. The April letter, written just before the start for Quivira, must have contained a full and official account of all that had been learned in regard to the country toward

---

[1] He was called "The Turk" because the Spaniards thought that he looked like one. Bandelier, in American Catholic Quarterly Review, vol. xv, p. 555, thinks this was due to the manner in which he wore his hair, characteristic of certain branches of the Pawnee.

[2] This probability is greatly strengthened by Mota Padilla's statement in relation to the Turk and Quivira, quoted in connection with Castañeda's narrative.

the east, as well as more reliable details than we now possess, of what
had happened during the preceding fall and winter. But this April
letter, which was an acknowledgment and answer to one from Charles
V, dated in Madrid, June 11, 1540, has not been found by modern
students. When the reply was dispatched, the messenger—probably
Juan Gallego, who had perhaps brought the Emperor's letter from
Mexico—was accompanied by Pedro de Tovar, who was going back
to Corazones valley for reinforcements. Many mishaps had befallen
the town of San Hieronimo during the year, and when the messengers
arrived there they found it half deserted. Leaving Don Pedro here,
Gallego hastened to Mexico, where he raised a small body of recruits.
He was leading these men, whose number had been increased by some
stragglers and deserters from the original force whom he picked up at
Culiacan, toward Cibola and Quivira, when he met the expedition
returning to New Spain. It was during this, probably his fifth trip
over the road from Mexico to our New Mexico, that he performed the
deeds of valor which Castañeda so enthusiastically recounts at the
very end of his book.

THE JOURNEY ACROSS THE BUFFALO PLAINS

April 23, 1541, Coronado left the Tiguex country and marched toward
the northeast, to the plains where lay the rich land of Quivira. Every
member of the army accompanied the general, for no one was willing to
be left behind when such glorious prospects of fame and fortune lay
before them. A few of the officers suggested the wisdom of verifying
these Indian tales in some measure before setting the whole force in
motion and abandoning their only sure base of supplies. It seems as
if there must have been other reasons influencing Coronado beyond
those revealed in Castañeda's narrative; but, if so, we do not know
what they were. The fear lest he might fail to accomplish any of the
things which had been hoped for, the absence of results on which to
base a justification for all the expense and labor, the thought of what
would await him if he should return empty handed, are perhaps enough
to account for the determination to risk everything and to allow no
possible lack of zeal or of strength to interfere with the realization of
the hopes inspired by the stories of Quivira.

Guided by the Turk, the army proceeded to Cicuye, and in nine days
more they reached the buffalo plains. Here began the long march
which was to be without any guiding landmarks. Just where, or how,
or how far the Spaniards went, I can not pretend to say. After a month
and more of marching—very likely just thirty-five days—their patience
became exhausted. A second native of the plains, who accompanied
the Spaniards from the pueblo country, had declared from the first
that the Turk was lying, but this had not made them trust the latter
any less. When, however, the Indians whom they found living among
the buffalo herds began to contradict the stories of their guide, suspicion was aroused. The Turk, after much persuasive cross-questioning,

was at last induced to confess that he had lied. Quivira, he still insisted, existed, though it was not as he had described it. From the natives of the plains they learned that there were no settlements toward the east, the direction in which they had been traveling, but that toward the north, another good month's journey distant, there were permanent settlements. The corn which the soldiers had brought from Tiguex was almost gone, while the horses were tired and weak from the constant marching and buffalo chasing, with only grass for food. It was clearly impossible for the whole force to attempt this further journey, with the uncertain prospect of finding native tribes like those they had already seen as the only incentive. The general held a council of his officers and friends, and decided to select 30 of the best equipped' horsemen. who should go with him and attempt to verify the new information.

After Coronado had chosen his companions, the rest of the force was sent back to Tiguex, as Castañeda relates. The Indians whom they met on the plains furnished guides, who led the soldiers to the Pueblo settlements by a more direct route than that which the Turk had taken. But the marches were short and slow, so that it was the middle of July before they were again encamped alongside the Rio Grande. So far as is known, nothing of interest happened while they were waiting there for the return of the general.

Coronado and his companion horsemen followed the compass needle for forty-two days after leaving the main force, or, as he writes, "after traveling across these deserts for seventy-seven days in all," they reached the country of Quivira. Here he found some people who lived in permanent settlements and raised a little corn, but whose sustenance came mainly from the buffalo herds, which they hunted at regular seasons, instead of continuously as the plains Indians encountered previously had done.[1]

Twenty-five days were spent among the villages at Quivira, so that Jaramillo, one of the party, doubtless remembered correctly when he said that they were there after the middle of August.[2] There was

[1] The Spaniards had already observed two distinct branches of these pure nomads, whom they knew as Querechos and Teyas. Bandelier, in his Final Report, vol. i. p. 179, identified the Querechos with the Apaches of the plains, but later investigation by Mr James Mooney shows that Querecho is an old Comanche name of the Tonkawa of western central Texas (Hodge, Early Navajo and Apache, Am. Anthropologist, Washington, July, 1895, vol. iii. p. 235). I am unable to find any single tribal group among the Indians whom we know which can be identified with the Teyas, unless, as Mr Hodge has suggested, they may have been the Comanche, who roamed the plains from Yellowstone Park to Durango, Mexico.

[2] I am inclined, also, to believe Jaramillo's statement that the day's marches on the journey to Quivira were short ones. But when he writes that the journey occupied "more than thirty days, or almost thirty days' journey, although not long day's marches,"—seguimos nuestro viaje . . . más de treinta dias ú casi treinta dias de camino, aunque no de jornadas grandes—and again, that they decided to return "because it was already nearly the beginning of winter, . . . and lest the winter might prevent the return,"—nos paresció á todos, que pues que hera ya casi la boca del inbierno, porque si me acuerdo bien, jera media y más de Agosto, y por ser pocos para inbernar allí, . . . y porque el invierno no nos cerrase los caminos de nieves y rios que no nos dexesen pasar (Pacheco y Cardenas, Doc. de Indias, vol. xiv, pp. 312, 314)—we experience some of the difficulties which make it hard to analyse the captain's recollections critically and satisfactorily.

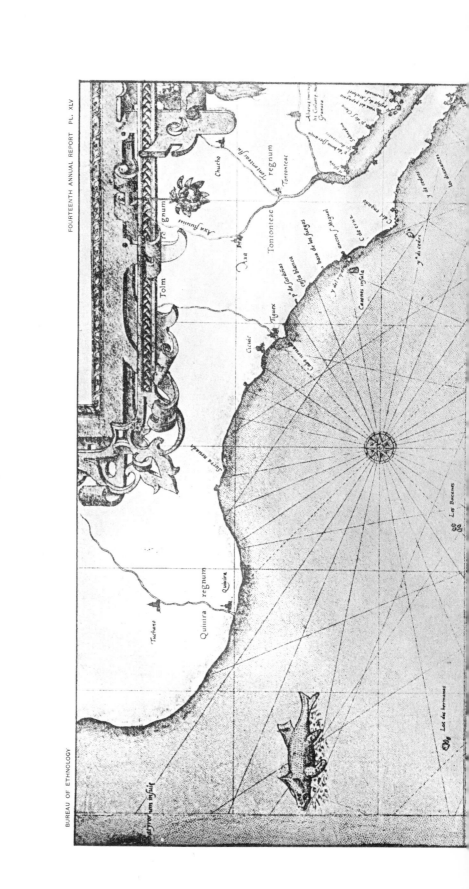

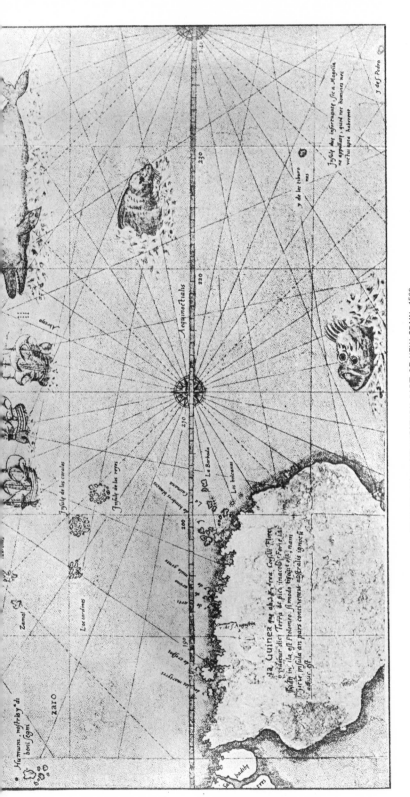

MERCATOR'S NORTHWESTERN PART OF NEW SPAIN, 1569

nothing here except a piece of copper hanging from the neck of a chief, and a piece of gold which one of the Spaniards was suspected of having given to the natives, which gave any promise of mineral wealth, and so Coronado determined to rejoin his main force. Although they had found no treasures, the explorers were fully aware of the agricultural advantages of this country, and of the possibilities for profitable farming, if only some market for the produce could be found.

Students of the Coronado expedition have very generally accepted the location of Quivira proposed by General Simpson, who put the northern point reached by Coronado somewhere in the eastern half of the border country of Kansas and Nebraska. If we take into account the expeditions which visited the outer limits of the Quivira settlements, this is not inconsistent with Bandelier's location of the main seat of these Indians "in northeastern Kansas, beyond the Arkansas river, and more than 100 miles northeast of Great Bend."[1]

It is impossible to ignore the question of the route taken by Coronado across the great plains, although the details chiefly concern local historians. The Spanish travelers spent the summer of 1541 on the prairies west of the Mississippi and south of the Missouri. They left descriptions of these plains, and of the people and animals inhabiting them, which are of as great interest and value as any which have since been written. Fortunately it is not of especial importance for us to know the exact section of the prairies to which various parts of the descriptions refer.

From Cicuye, the Pecos pueblo, Coronado marched northeast until he crossed Canadian river, probably a little to the east of the present river and settlement of Mora.[2] This was about the 1st of May, 1541. From this point General Simpson, whose intimate knowledge of the surface of the country thirty-five years ago makes his map of the route across the plains most valuable, carried the line of march nearly north, to a point halfway between Canadian and Arkansas rivers. Then it turned east, or a trifle north of east, until it reached one of the tributaries of the Arkansas, about 50 miles or so west of Wichita, Kansas. The army returned by a direct route to Cicuye or Pecos river, striking that stream nearly east of Bernalillo-Tiguex, while Coronado proceeded due north to Quivira on the Kansas-Nebraska boundary.

Mr Bandelier has traced a route for the march across the plains which corresponds with the statements of the contemporary narratives somewhat more closely than does that of General Simpson.[3] Crossing

---

[1] Final Report, vol. i, p. 170.

[2] Ibid., vol. i, p. 178.

[3] Bandelier's best discussion of the route is in his article on Fray Juan de Padilla, in the American Catholic Quarterly Review, vol. xv, p. 551. The Gilded Man also contains an outline of the probable route. An element in his calculation, to which he gives much prominence, is the tendency of one who is lost to wander always toward the right. This is strongly emphasized in the Gilded Man; but it can, I think, hardly merit the importance which he gives to it. The emphasis appears, however, much more in Bandelier's words than in his results. I can not see that there is anything to show that the Indian guides ever really lost their reckoning.

Canadian river by a bridge, just south of where Mora river enters it, the Spaniards, according to Bandelier, marched toward the northeast for ten days, until they met the first of the plains Indians, the Querecho or Tonkawa. Thence they turned almost directly toward the rising sun. Bandelier thinks that they very soon found out that the guides had lost their reckoning, which presumably means that it became evident that there was some difference of opinion among the Indians. After marching eastward for thirty-five days or so, the Spaniards halted on the banks of a stream which flowed in the bottom of a broad and deep ravine. Here it was computed that they had already traveled 250 leagues—650 miles—from Tiguex. They had crossed no other large river since leaving the bridge over the Canadian, and as the route had been south of east, as is distinctly stated by one member of the force, they had probably reached the Canadian again. There is a reference to crossing what may have been the North Fork of the Canadian, in which case the army would now be on the north bank of the main river, below the junction of the two forks, in the eastern part of Indian Territory. Here they divided. The Teya guides conducted the main force directly back to the Rio Grande settlements. Coronado went due north, and a month later he reached a larger river. He crossed to the north bank of this stream, and then followed its course for several days, the direction being northeast. This river, manifestly, must be the Arkansas, which makes a sharp turn toward the northeast at the Great Bend, east of Fort Dodge, flowing in that direction for 75 miles. Jaramillo states that they followed the current of the river. As he approached the settled country, Coronado turned toward the north and found Quivira, in northeastern Kansas, not far south of the Nebraska boundary.[1]

The two texts of the Relacion del Suceso differ on a vital point;[2] but in spite of this fact, I am inclined to accept the evidence of this anonymous document as the most reliable testimony concerning the direction of the army's march. According to this, the Spaniards traveled

---

[1] Bandelier accounts for sixty-seven days of short marches and occasional delays between the separation of the force on Canadian river and the arrival at Quivira. It may be that the seventy-seven days of desert marching which Coronado mentions in his letter of October 20, 1541, refers to this part of the journey, instead of to the whole of the journey from the bridge (near Mora on the Canadian) to Quivira. But the number sixty-seven originated in a blunder of Ternaux-Compans, who substituted it for seventy-seven, in translating this letter. The mistake evidently influenced Bandelier to extend the journey over more time than it really took. But this need not affect his results materially, if we extend the amount of ground covered by each day's march and omit numerous halts, which were very unlikely, considering the condition of his party and the desire to solve the mystery of Quivira. If the Spaniards crossed the Arkansas somewhere below Fort Dodge, and followed it until the river turns toward the southeast, Quivira can hardly have been east of the middle part of the state of Kansas. It was much more probably somewhere between the main forks of Kansas river, in the central part of that state. Bandelier seems to have abandoned his documents as he approached the goal, and to have transported Coronado across several branches of Kansas river, in order to fill out his sixty-seven days—which should have been seventy-seven—and perhaps to reach the region fixed on by previous conceptions of the limit of exploration. He may have realized that the difficulty in his explanation of the route was that it required a reduction of about one-fourth of the distance covered by the army in the eastward march, as plotted by General Simpson. This can be accounted for by the wandering path which the army followed.

[2] See the note at the end of the translation.

due east across the plains for 100 leagues—265 miles[1]—and then 50 leagues either south or southeast. The latter is the reading I should prefer to adopt, because it accommodates the other details somewhat better. This took them to the point of separation, which can hardly have been south of Red river, and was much more likely somewhere along the North Fork of the Canadian, not far above its junction with the main stream. From this point the army returned due west to Pecos river, while Coronado rode north "by the needle." From these premises, which are broad enough to be safe, I should be inclined to doubt if Coronado went much beyond the south branch of Kansas river, if he even reached that stream. Coronado probably spent more days on his march than General Simpson allowed for, but I do not think that he traveled nearly so far as General Simpson supposed. Coronado also returned to Cicuye by a direct route, which was about two-thirds as long as that of the outward march. The distances given for various portions of the journey have a real value, because each day's march was paced off by a soldier detailed for the purpose, who carefully recorded the distance covered.

THE WINTER OF 1541-1542

By October 20, 1541, Coronado was back in Tiguex, writing his report to the King, in which he expressed his anxiety lest the failure to discover anything of immediate material profit might react unfavorably on his own prospects. Letters and dispatches from Mexico and Spain were awaiting him at Tiguex. One of these informed Don Garcia Lopez de Cardenas of the death of his brother, by which he became heir to the family estates. Cardenas had broken his arm on the plains, and this injury was still troubling him when he received permission to return to New Spain. He was accompanied by the messengers carrying letters to the viceroy and by ten or twelve other invalids, "not one of whom could have done any fighting." The party had no trouble, however, until they reached Suya, in Corazones valley, the settlement which had taken the place of San Hieronimo. Pedro de Tovar had reduced the already feeble garrison at the latter post by half, when he took away the reinforcements six months before. The town had been much weakened by desertions, as well as by the loss of its commander, the invaluable Melchior Diaz, before this. The Indians quickly discerned the condition of the town, and its defenders were unable to maintain friendly relations with the surrounding tribes. When Cardenas reached the place, he found everything burned to the ground, and the bodies of Spaniards, Indians, and horses lying about. Indeed, he seems barely to have saved the invalids accompanying him from being added to the number of the massacred. The party succeeded in making its way to Cibola in safety, and from there they returned to Tiguex, where they found the general seriously ill. By this time the winter was

---

[1] The Spanish (judicial) league was equivalent to 2.63 statute miles.

fairly begun, but the season, fortunately, was much less severe than the preceding one.

Two parties formed in the Spanish camp at Tiguex during the winter of 1541–42. The men who had seen Quivira can hardly have brought back from there much hope of finding gold or other treasure by further explorations in that country. But there were many who had not been there, who were unwilling to give up the ideas which had been formed during the preceding months. When the general parted from his army on the plains, he may have promised that he would return and lead the whole force to this land, if only it should prove to be such as their inclination pictured it. Many persisted in the belief that a more thorough exploration would discover some of the things about which they thought the Turk had told them. On the other hand, there were many besides the leader who were tired of this life of hardship, which had not even afforded the attractions of adventure and serious conflict. Few of them, doubtless, had wives and estates waiting to welcome them home, like their fortunate general, but most of the gentlemen, surely, were looking forward to the time when they could win wealth and glory, with which to return to old Spain, and add new luster to their family name. Castañeda gives a soldier's gossip of the intriguing and persuading which resulted in the abandonment of the Pueblo country, and Mota Padilla seems to support the main points in his story.

THE FRIARS REMAIN IN THE COUNTRY

When it was determined that the army should return to Mexico, the friars who had accompanied the expedition [1] resolved to remain in the newly discovered regions and continue their labors among the people there. Friar Juan de Padilla was the leader of the three missionaries. Younger and more vigorous than his brethren, he had from the first been the most active in constantly maintaining the oversight and discipline of the church. He was with Tovar when the Tusayan country on the west was discovered, and with Alvarado during the first visit to the Rio Grande and the buffalo plains on the east. When Coronado and his companion horsemen visited the plains of Kansas, Friar Juan de Padilla went with him on foot. His brief experience in the Quivira country led him to decide to go back to that district, when Coronado was preparing to return to New Spain. If the Indians who guided Coronado from Quivira to Cicuye remained in the pueblo country during the winter, Padilla probably returned with them to their homes. He was accompanied by Andres Docampo, a Portuguese, mounted on a mare according to most accounts, besides five Indians, negroes or half bloods, two "donados" or lay brethren, Indians engaged in the church service, who came from Michoacan and were named Lucas and Sebastian, a mestizo or half-blood boy and two other servants from Mexico.

---

[1] Castañeda implies that Friar Antonio Victoria, who broke his leg near Culiacan, accompanied the main force on its march to Cibola. This is the last heard of him, and it is much more probable that he remained in New Galicia.

The friar was successful in his labors until he endeavored to enlarge the sphere of his influence, when the jealousy, or possibly the cupidity, of the Indians led them to kill him, rather than permit the transference to some other tribe of the blessings which he had brought to them.[1]

Friar Juan de la Cruz is not mentioned by Castañeda nor by Jaramillo, but Mendieta and Mota Padilla are very clear in their accounts of him. He was an older man than the others, and had been engaged in missionary work among the natives of the Jalisco country before he joined this expedition. Coronado left him at Tiguex, where he was killed, according to Mota Padilla. The date, in the martyrologies, is November 25, 1542. Many natives of the Mexican provinces stayed in the Pueblo country when Coronado abandoned it. Some of these were still at Cibola when Antonio de Espejo visited it in 1583, while others doubtless made their way back to their old homes in New Spain, and they may have brought the information about the death of Friar Juan.

Friar Luis Descalona, or de Ubeda as Mota Padilla calls him, was a lay brother, who selected Cicuye or Pecos as the seat of his labors in New Mexico. Neither the Spanish chronicles nor the Indian traditions which Mr Bandelier was able to obtain give any hint as to his fate or the results of his devotion to the cause of Christianity.

THE RETURN TO NEW SPAIN

The army started on its return from Tiguex to Cibola and thence to Culiacan and Mexico early in the spring of 1542. The march was without interruption or diversion. As the soldiers reentered New Galicia and found themselves once more among settlements of their own race, beyond the reach of hostile natives, the ranks dwindled rapidly. The men stopped to rest and to recruit their strength at every opportunity, and it was only with the greatest difficulty that Coronado was able to keep together the semblance of a force with which to make his entry into the City of Mexico. Here he presented his personal report to the viceroy. He had little to tell which could interest the disappointed Mendoza, who had drawn so heavily on the royal treasure box two years before to furnish those who formed the expedition with everything that they might need. Besides the loss in his personal estate, there was this use of the royal funds which had to be accounted for to the

---

[1] Vetancurt, in the Menologia, gives the date of the martyrdom of Fray Juan de Padilla as November 30, 1544, and I see no reason to prefer the more general statements of Jaramillo, Castañeda, and Mota Padilla, which seem to imply that it took place in 1542. Docampo and the other companions of the friar brought the news to Mexico. They must have returned some time previous to 1552, for Gomara mentions their arrival in Tampico, on the Mexican gulf, in his Conquista de Mexico published in that year. Herrera and Gomara say that the fugitives had been captured by Indians and detained as slaves for ten months. These historians state also that a dog accompanied the fugitives. Further mention of dogs in connection with the Coronado expedition is in the stories of one accompanying Estevan which Alarcon heard along Colorado river, also in the account of the death of Melchior Diaz, and in the reference by Castañeda to the use of these animals as beasts of burden by certain plains tribes.

Mendieta and Vetancurt say that, of the two donados, Sebastian died soon after his return, and the other lived long as a missionary among the Zacatecas.

14 ETH——26

officials in Spain. It is the best proof of the strength of Mendoza's able and economical administration that no opposition ever succeeded in influencing the home government against him, and that the failure of this expedition, with the attendant circumstances, furnished the most serious charge which those who had displayed hostility toward him were able to produce.

When Coronado reached the City of Mexico, "very sad and very weary, completely worn out and shamefaced," Suarez de Peralta was a boy on the streets. We catch a glimpse of him in the front rows of a crowd watching an execution, this same winter of 1542-43, and we may be sure that he saw all that was going on, and that he picked up and treasured the gossip of the city. His recollections give a vivid picture of the return of the expedition, when Coronado "came to kiss the hand of the viceroy and did not receive so good a reception as he would have liked, for he found him very sad." For many days after the general reached the city the men who had followed him came straggling in, all of them worn out with their toils, clothed in the skins of animals, and showing the marks of their misfortunes and sufferings. "The country had been very joyous when the news of the discovery of the Seven Cities spread abroad, and this was now supplanted by the greatest sadness on the part of all, for many had lost their friends and their fortunes, since those who remained behind had entered into partnerships with those who went, mortgaging their estates and their property in order to procure a share in what was to be gained, and drawing up papers so that those who were to be present should have power to take possession of mines and enter claims in the name of those who were left behind, in accordance with the custom and the ordinances which the viceroy had made for New Spain. Many sent their slaves also, since there were many of these in the country at this time. Thus the loss and the grief were general, but the viceroy felt it most of all, for two reasons: Because this was the outcome of something about which he had felt so sure, which he thought would make him more powerful than the greatest lord in Spain, and because his estates were ruined, for he had labored hard and spent much in sending off the army. Finally, as things go, he succeeded in forgetting about it, and devoted himself to the government of his province, and in this he became the best of governors, being trusted by the King and loved by all his subjects."

THE END OF CORONADO

We do not know what became of Vazquez Coronado. The failure of the expedition was not his fault, and there is nothing to show that he ever sought the position which Mendoza intrusted to him. Neither is there any evidence that Mendoza treated him with any less marks of friendship after his return than before. The welcome home was not cordial, but there are no reports of upbraiding, nor any accusations of negligence or remissness. Coronado soon gave up his position as gov-

ernor of New Galicia, but we need not suppose that he was compelled
to resign. There was every reason why he should have desired to
escape from a position which demanded much skill and unceasing active
administration, but which carried with it no hope of reward or of honor.
It is pleasant to believe that Coronado withdrew to his estates and
lived happily ever after with his wife and children, spending his leisure
in supervising the operations on his farm and ranch, and leading the
uneventful life of a country gentleman. The only break in the monotony of which we happen to know—and this is the only part of this belief
for which there is the slightest evidence that it is correct—came when
he was accused, in 1544 and again in 1547, of holding more Indians to
labor on his estates than were allowed by the royal regulations. We
do not even know the outcome of this accusation. Vazquez Coronado
sinks into oblivion after he made his report to the viceroy in the autumn
of 1542.

SOME RESULTS OF THE EXPEDITION—1540–1547

THE DISCOVERY OF COLORADO RIVER

THE VOYAGE OF ALARCON

Coronado found no gold in the land of the Seven Cities or in Quivira,
but his search added very much to the geographical knowledge of the
Spaniards.[1] In addition to the exploration of the Pueblo country of
New Mexico and Arizona, and of the great plains as far north as
Kansas or Nebraska, the most important subsidiary result of the expedition of 1540–1542 was the discovery of Colorado river. Hernando de
Alarcon, who sailed from Acapulco May 9, 1540, continued his voyage
northward along the coast, after stopping at the port of Culiacan to
add the *San Gabriel* to his fleet, until he reached the shoals and sand-
bars at the head of the Gulf of California. The fleet which Cortes

---

[1] The maps of the New World drawn and published between 1542 and 1600, reproductions of several
of which accompany this memoir, give a better idea of the real value of the geographical discoveries
made by Coronado than any bare statement could give. In 1540, European cartographers knew nothing
about the country north of New Spain. Cortes had given them the name—Nueva España or Hispania
Nova—and this, with the name of the continent, served to designate the inland region stretching
toward the north and west. Such was the device which Mercator adopted when he drew his double
cordiform map in 1538 (plates XLV, XLVI). Six years later, 1544, Sebastian Cabot published his elaborate map of the New World (see plate XL). He had heard of the explorations made by and for Cortes
toward the head of the Gulf of California, very likely from the lips of the conqueror himself. He
confined New Spain to its proper limits, and in the interior he pictured Indians and wild beasts. In 1548
the maps of America in Ptolemy's Geography for the first time show the results of Coronado's discoveries (see plate XLI). During the remainder of the century Granada, Cibola, Quivira, and the other
places whose names occur in the various reports of the expedition, appear on the maps. Their location, relative to each other and to the different parts of the country, constantly changes. Quivira
moves along the fortieth parallel from Espiritu Santo river to the Pacific coast. Tiguex and Totonteac
are on any one of half a dozen rivers flowing into the Gulf of Mexico, the Espiritu Santo, or the South
sea. Acuco and Cicuye are sometimes placed west of Cibola, and so a contemporary map maker may
be the cause of the mistaken title to the report of Alvarado's expedition to the Rio Grande. But
many as were the mistakes, they are insignificant in comparison with the great fact that the people of
Europe had learned that there was an inhabited country north of Mexico, and that the world was, by
so much, larger than before.

had sent out under the command of Ulloa the previous summer, turned
back from these shoals, and Alarcon's sailors begged him not to venture
among them.   But the question of a passage by water through to the
South, or Pacific, sea, which would make an island of the California
peninsula, was still debated, and Alarcon refused to return until he had
definitely determined the possibility of finding such a passage.   His
pilots ran the ships aground, but after a careful examination of the
channel, the fleet was floated across the bar in safety, with the aid of
the rising tide.   Alarcon found that he was at the mouth of a large
river, with so swift and strong a current that it was impossible for the
large vessels to make any headway against it.   He determined to explore
the river, and, taking twenty men in two boats, started upstream on
Thursday, August 26, 1540, when white men for the first time floated on
the waters of the Colorado.   Indians appeared on the river banks during the following day.   The silence with which the strangers answered
the threatening shouts of the natives, and the presence of the Indian
interpreters in the boats, soon overcame the hostile attitude of the savages.   The European trifles which had been brought for gifts and for
trading completed the work of establishing friendly relations, and the
Indians soon became so well disposed that they entirely relieved the
Spaniards of the labor of dragging the boats up the stream.   A crowd
of Indians seized the ropes by which the boats were hauled against the
current, and from this time on some of them were always ready to
render this service to their visitors.   In this fashion the Spaniards continued northward, receiving abundant supplies of corn from the natives,
whose habits and customs they had many excellent opportunities for
observing.   Alarcon instructed these people dutifully in the worship
of the cross, and continually questioned them about the places whose
names Friar Marcos had heard.   He met with no success until he had
traveled a considerable distance up the river, when for the first time he
found a man with whom his interpreter was able to converse.

This man said that he had visited Cibola, which was a month's journey distant.   There was a good trail by which one might easily reach
that country in forty days.   The man said he had gone there merely
to see the place, since it was quite a curiosity, with its houses three
and four stories high, filled with people.   Around the houses there was
a wall half as high again as a man, having windows on each side.   The
inhabitants used the usual Indian weapons—bows and arrows, clubs,
maces, and shields.   They wore mantles and ox hides, which were
painted.   They had a single ruler, who wore a long shirt with a girdle,
and various mantles over this.   The women wore long white cloaks
which completely covered them.   There were always many Indians
waiting about the door of their ruler, ready in case he should wish for
anything.   They also wore many blue stones which they dug out of a
rock—the turquoises of the other narratives.   They had but one wife,
and when they died all their effects were buried with them.   When

their rulers ate, many men waited about the tables. They ate with napkins, and had baths—a natural inference from any attempt to describe the stuffy underground rooms, the estufas or kivas of the Pueblos.

Alarcon continued to question the Indian, and learned that the lord of Cibola had a dog like one which accompanied the Spaniards, and that when dinner was served, the lord of Cibola had four plates like those used by the Spaniards, except that they were green. He obtained these at the same time that he got the dog, with some other things, from a black man who wore a beard, whom the people of Cibola killed. A few days later, Alarcon obtained more details concerning the death of the negro "who wore certain things on his legs and arms which rattled." When asked about gold and silver, the Indians said that they had some metal of the same color as the bells which the Spaniards showed them. This was not made nor found in their country, but came "from a certain mountain where an old woman dwelt." The old woman was called Guatuzaca. One of Alarcon's informants told him about people who lived farther away than Cibola, in houses made of painted mantles or skins during the summer, and who passed the winter in houses made of wood two or three stories high. The Indian was asked about the leather shields, and in reply described a very great beast like an ox, but more than a hand longer, with broad feet, legs as big as a man's thigh, a head 7 hands long, and the forehead 3 spans across. The eyes of the beast were larger than one's fist, and the horns as long as a man's leg, "out of which grew sharp points an handful long, and the forefeet and hind-feet about seven handfuls big." The tail was large and bushy. To show how tall the animal was, the Indian stretched his arms above his head. In a note to his translation of this description, Hakluyt suggests, "This might be the crooke backed oxe of Quivira." Although the height and the horns are clearly those of a buck deer, the rest of the description is a very good account of the bison.

The man who told him all this was called ashore, and Alarcon noticed an excited discussion going on among the Indians, which ended in the return of his informant with the news that other white men like himself were at Cibola. Alarcon pretended to wonder at this, and was told that two men had just come from that country, where they had seen white men having "things which shot fire, and swords." These latest reports seemed to make the Indians doubt Alarcon's honesty, and especially his statements that he was a child of the Sun. He succeeded in quieting their suspicions, and learned more about Cibola, with which these people appeared to have quite frequent intercourse. He was told that the strangers at Cibola called themselves Christians, and that they brought with them many oxen like those at Cibola "and other little blacke beastes with wooll and hornes." Some of them also had animals upon which they rode, which ran very swiftly. Two of the party that had recently returned from Cibola, had fallen in with two of the Christians. The white men asked them where they lived and whether they possessed any fields sown with corn, and gave each of them little caps for themselves and for their companions. Alarcon did his best to induce some of his men to go to Cibola with a message to Coronado, but all refused except one negro slave, who did not at all want to go. The plan had to be given up, and the party returned to the ships. It had taken fifteen days and a half to ascend the river, but they descended with the swift current in two and a half. The men who had remained in the ships were asked to undertake the mission of opening communication with Coronado, but proved as unwilling as the others.

Much against the will of his subordinates, Alarcon determined to make a second trip up the river, hoping to obtain further information which might enable him to fulfill the purposes of his voyage. He took "three boats filled with wares of exchange, with corne and other seedes, hennes and cockes of Castille." Starting September 14, he found the Indians as friendly as before, and ascended the river, as he judged, about 85 leagues, which may have taken him to the point where the canyons begin. A cross was erected to inform Coronado, in case an expedition from Cibola should reach this part of the river,[1] that he had tried to fulfill his duty, but nothing more was accomplished.[2]

While Alarcon was exploring the river, one of the ships was careened and repaired, and everything made ready for the return voyage. A chapel was built on the shore in honor of Nuestra Señora de Buenaguia, and the river was named the Buenaguia, out of regard for the viceroy, who carried this as his device.

The voyage back to Colima in New Spain was uneventful.

THE JOURNEY OF MELCHIOR DIAZ

In September, 1540, seventy or eighty of the weakest and least reliable men in Coronado's army remained at the town of San Hieronimo, in the valley of Corazones or Hearts. Melchior Diaz was placed in command of the settlement, with orders to maintain this post and protect the road between Cibola and New Spain, and also to attempt to find some means of communicating with the fleet under Alarcon. After he had established everything in the town as satisfactorily as possible, Diaz selected twenty-five of these men to accompany him on an exploring expedition to the seacoast. He started before the end of September, going into the rough country west of Corazones valley, and finding only a few naked, weak-spirited Indians, who had come, as he understood, from the land on the farther side of the water, i. e., Lower

---

[1] See Castañeda's account of the finding of   similar message by the party under Diaz.

[2] The account of this trip in Herrera (dec. VI, lib. ix, cap. xv, ed. 1728) is as follows: "Haviendo llegado à ciertas Montañas, adonde el Rio se estrechaba mucho, supo, que vn Encantador andaba preguntando por donde havia de pasar, y haviendo entendido, que por el Rio, puso desde vna Ribera à la otra algunas Cañas, que debian de ser hechiçadas; pero las Barcas pasaron sin daño; y haviendo llegado mui arriba, preguntando por cosas de la Tierra, para entender, si descubriria alguna noticia de Francisco Vazquez de Cornado. . . . Viendo Alarcon, que no hallaba lo que deseaba, i que havia subido por aquel Rio 85 Leguas, determinò de bolver." . . .

California. He hurried across this region and descended the mountains
on the west, where he encountered the Indian giants, some of whom
the army had already seen. Turning toward the north, or northwest,
he proceeded to the seacoast, and spent several days among Indians
who fed him with the corn which they raised and with fish. He traveled
slowly up the coast until he reached the mouth of a river which was
large enough for vessels to enter. The country was cold, and the
Spaniards observed that when the natives hereabouts wished to keep
warm, they took a burning stick and held it to their abdomens and
shoulders. This curious habit led the Spaniards to name the river
Firebrand—Rio del Tizon. Near the mouth of the river was a tree on
which was written, " A letter is at the foot of this." Diaz dug down
and found a jar wrapped so carefully that it was not even moist. The
inclosed papers stated that " Francisco de Alarcon reached this place
in the year '40 with three ships, having been sent in search of Francisco Vazquez Coronado by the viceroy, D. Antonio de Mendoza; and
after crossing the bar at the mouth of the river and waiting many
days without obaining any news, he was obliged to depart, because
the ships were being eaten by worms," the terrible *Teredo navalis*.[1]

Diaz determined to cross the river, hoping that the country might
become more attractive. The passage was accomplished, with considerable danger, by means of certain large wicker baskets, which the
natives coated with a sort of bitumen, so that the water could not leak
through. Five or six Indians caught hold of each of these and swam
across, guiding it and transporting the Spaniards with their baggage,
and being supported in turn by the raft. Diaz marched inland for four
days, but not finding any people in the country, which became steadily
more barren, he decided to return to Corazones valley. The party
made its way back to the country of the giants without accident, and
then one night while Diaz was watching the camp, a small dog began to
bark and chase the flock of sheep which the men had taken with them
for food. Unable to call the dog off, Diaz started after him on horseback and threw his lance while on the gallop. The weapon stuck up in
the ground, and before Diaz could stop or turn his horse, which was
running loose, the socket pierced his groin. The soldiers could do
little to relieve his sufferings, and he died before they reached the settlement, where they arrived January 18, 1541. A few months later,
Alcaraz, who had been placed in charge of the town when Diaz went
away, abandoned Corazones valley for a more attractive situation on
Suya river, some distance nearer Cibola. The post was maintained here

---

[1] Mota Padilla (p. 158, § 1). "Los Indios, para resistir el frio, llevan en las manos un troncon ardiendo
que les calienta el pecho, y del mismo modo la espalda; siendo esto tan comun en todos los indios,
que por eso los nuestros pusieron á este rio el nombre del rio del Tison, cerca de él vieron un árbol en
el cual estaban escritas unas letras, que decian: al pié está una carta: y con efecto; la hallaron en una
olla, bien envuelta, porque no se humedeciese, y su contenido era: que el año de 40 llegó allí Francisco de Alarcon con tres navíos, y entrando por la barra de aquel rio, enviado por el virey D. Antonio de Mendoza, en busca de Francisco Vazquez Coronado; y que habiendo estado allí muchos dias
sin noticia alguna le fué preciso salir porque los navíos se comian de broma."

until late in the summer, when it became so much weakened by dissensions and desertions that the Indians had little difficulty in destroying it. The defenders, with the exception of a few who were able to make their way back to Culiacan, were massacred.

THE INDIAN UPRISING IN NEW SPAIN, 1540–1542

Of the arguments advanced by those who wished to hinder the expedition which Mendoza sent off under Coronado, none was urged more persistently than the claim that this undertaking would require all the men available for the protection of New Spain. It was suggested by all the parties to the litigation in Spain, was repeated by Cortes again and again, reappeared more than once during the visita of 1547, and was the cause of the depositions taken at Compostela on February 26, 1540. These last show the real state of affairs. The men who were withdrawn constituted a great resource in case of danger, but they were worse than useless to the community when things were peaceful. The Indians of New Spain had been quiet since the death of De la Torre, a few years before, but signs of danger, an increasing restlessness, unwilling obedience to the masters and encomenderos, and frequent gatherings, had been noticed by many besides Cortes. There were reasons enough to justify an Indian outbreak, some of them abuses which dated from the time of Nuño de Guzman, but there is every reason to suppose that the withdrawal of Coronado's force, following the irritation which was inevitably caused by the necessity of collecting a large food supply and many servants, probably brought matters to a crisis. Oñate, to whom the administration of New Galicia had again been intrusted during the absence of his superior, began to prepare for the trouble which he foresaw almost as soon as Coronado was gone from the province. In April he learned that two tribes had rebelled and murdered one of their encomenderos. A force was sent to put down the revolt. The rebels requested a conference, and then, early next morning, surprised the camp, which was wholly unprepared for defense. Ten Spaniards, including the unwary commander, and nearly two hundred native allies were killed. Thus began the last and the fiercest struggle of the Indians of New Spain against their European conquerors—the Mixton war.

Oñate prepared to march against the victorious rebels, as soon as the news of the disaster reached him, but when this was followed by additional information from the agents among the Indians, showing how widespread were the alliances of those who had begun the revolt, and that the Indians throughout the province of New Galicia were already in arms, he retired to Guadalajara. The defenses of this town were strengthened as much as possible, and messengers were dispatched to Mexico for reenforcements. The viceroy sent some soldiers and supplies, but this force was not sufficient to prevent the Indians—who were animated by their recent successes, by their numbers, by the knowledge of the weak points as well as of the strong ones in their oppressors, and

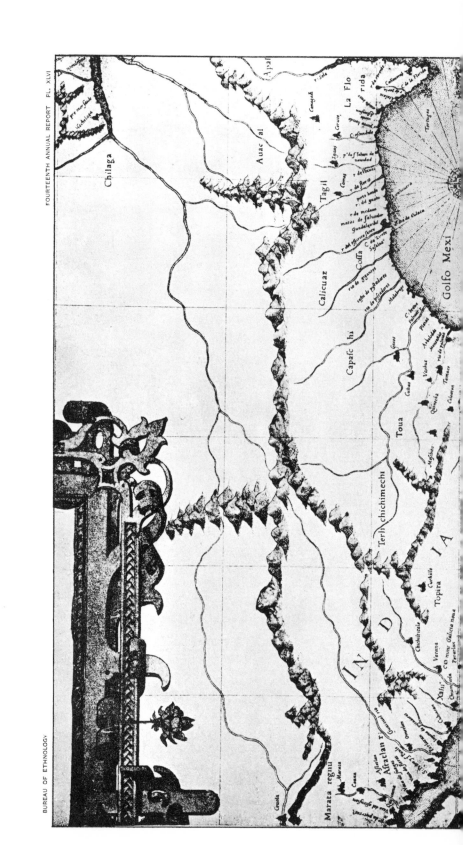

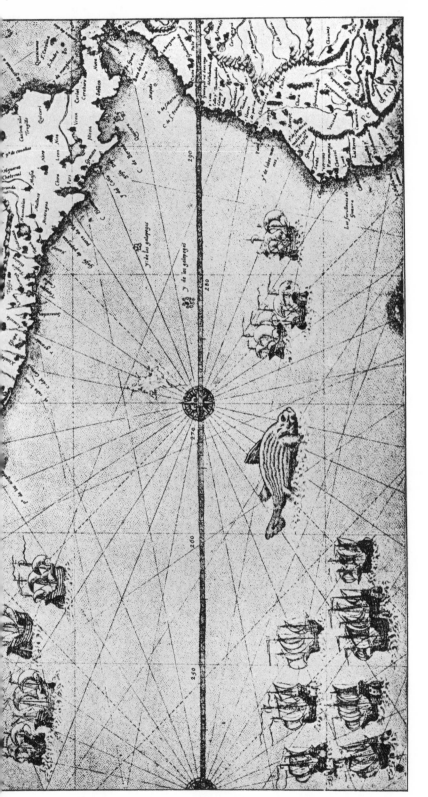

THE INTERIOR OF NEW SPAIN, AFTER MERCATOR, 1569

who were guided by able leaders possessing all the prestige of religious authority—from attacking the frontier settlements and forcing the Spaniards to congregate in the larger towns.

There was much fighting during the early summer of 1540, in which the settlers barely held their own. In August, the adelantado Pedro de Alvarado sailed into the harbor of La Natividad. As the news of his arrival spread, requests were sent to him from many directions, asking for help against the natives. One of the most urgent came from those who were defending the town of Purificacion, and Alvarado was about to start to their assistance, when a message from Mendoza changed his plans. The two men arranged for a personal interview at Tiripitio in Michoacan, where the estate of a relative afforded Alvarado a quasi neutral territory. After some difficulties had been overcome, the terms of an alliance were signed by both parties November 29, 1540. Each was to receive a small share in whatever had already been accomplished by the other, thus providing for any discoveries which might have rewarded Coronado's search before this date. In the future, all conquests and gains were to be divided equally. It was agreed that the expenses of equipping the fleet and the army should offset each other, and that all future expenses should be shared alike. Each partner was allowed to spend a thousand castellanos de minas yearly, and all expenditure in excess of this sum required the consent of the other party. All accounts were to be balanced yearly, and any surplus due from one to the other was to be paid at once, under penalty of a fine, which was assured by the fact that half of it was to go into the royal treasury.

Mendoza secured a half interest in the fleet of between nine and twelve vessels, which were then in the ports of Acapulco and of Santiago de Colima. Cortes accused the viceroy of driving a very sharp bargain in this item, declaring that Alvarado was forced to accept it because Mendoza made it the condition on which he would allow the ships to obtain provisions.[1] Mendoza, as matters turned out, certainly had the best of the bargain, although in the end it amounted to nothing. Whether this would have been true if Alvarado had lived to prosecute his schemes is another possibility. Alvarado took his chances on the results of Coronado's conquests, and it is very likely that, by the end of November, the discouraging news contained in Coronado's letter of August 3 was not generally known, if it had even reached the viceroy.

The contract signed, Alvarado and Mendoza went to Mexico, where they passed the winter in perfecting arrangements for carrying out their plans. The cold weather moderated the fury of the Indian war somewhat, without lessening the danger or the troubles of the settlers in New Galicia, all of whom were now shut up in the few large towns. Alvarado returned to the Pacific coast in the spring of 1541, and as soon as

---

[1] The accusation was made by others at the time. H. H. Bancroft repeats the charge in his Mexico, but it should always be remembered that Mr Bancroft, or his compilers, in everything connected with the conqueror, repeat whatever it may have pleased Cortes to write, without criticism or question.

Oñate learned of this, he sent an urgent request for help, telling of the serious straits in which he had been placed. The security of the province was essential to the successful prosecution of the plans of the new alliance. Alvarado immediately sent reinforcements to the different garrisons, and at the head of his main force hastened to Guadalajara, where he arrived June 12, 1541. Oñate had received reports from the native allies and the Spanish outposts, who were best acquainted with the situation and plans of the hostile Indians, which led him to urge Alvarado to delay the attack until he could be certain of success. An additional force had been promised from Mexico, but Alvarado felt that the glory and the booty would both be greater if secured unaided. Scorning the advice of those who had been beaten by savages, he hastened to chastise the rebels. The campaign was a short one. On June 24 Alvarado reached the fortified height of Nochistlan, where he encountered such a deluge of men and of missiles that he was not able to maintain his ground, nor even to prevent the precipitate retreat of his soldiers. It was a terrible disaster, but one which reflected no discredit on Alvarado after the fighting began. The flight of the Spaniards continued after the Indians had grown tired of the chase. It was then that the adelantado tried to overtake his secretary, who had been one of those most eager to get away from the enemy. Alvarado was afoot, having dismounted in order to handle his men and control the retreat more easily, but he had almost caught up with his secretary, when the latter spurred his jaded horse up a rocky hill. The animal tried to respond, fell, and rolled backward down the hill, crushing the adelantado under him. Alvarado survived long enough to be carried to Guadalajara and to make his will, dying on the 4th of July.

This disaster did not fully convince the viceroy of the seriousness of the situation. Fifty men had already started from Mexico, arriving in Guadalajara in July, where they increased the garrison to eighty-five. Nothing more was done by Mendoza after he heard of the death of Alvarado. The Indians, emboldened by the complete failure of their enemies, renewed their efforts to drive the white men out of the land. They attacked Guadalajara on September 28, and easily destroyed all except the chief buildings in the center of the city, in which the garrison had fortified themselves as soon as they learned that an attack was about to be made. A fierce assault against these defenses was repulsed only after a hard struggle. The miraculous appearance of Saint Iago on his white steed and leading his army of allies, who blinded the idolatrous heathen, alone prevented the destruction of his faithful believers, according to the record of one contemporary chronicler. At last Mendoza realized that the situation was critical. A force of 450 Spaniards was raised, in addition to an auxiliary body of between 10,000 and 50,000 Aztec warriors. The native chieftains were rendered loyal by ample promises of wealth and honors, and the warriors were granted, for the first time, permission to use horses and Spanish weapons. With the help of these Indians, Mendoza eventually succeeded in destroying or reducing the revolted tribes. The campaign was a series of fiercely contested struggles, which culminated at the Mixton peñol, a strongly fortified height where the most bitter enemies of the Spanish conquerors had their headquarters. This place was surrendered during the Christmas holidays, and when Coronado returned in the autumn of 1542, the whole of New Spain was once more quiet.

FURTHER ATTEMPTS AT DISCOVERY

THE VOYAGE OF CABRILLO

Mendoza took possession of the vessels belonging to Alvarado after the death of the latter. In accordance with the plans which the two partners had agreed on, apparently, the viceroy commissioned Juan Rodriguez Cabrillo to take command of two ships in the port of La Natividad and make an exploration of the coast on the western side of the peninsula of Lower California. Cabrillo started June 27, 1542, and sailed north, touching the land frequently. Much bad weather interfered with his plans, but he kept on till the end of December, when he landed on one of the San Lucas islands. Here Cabrillo died, January 3, 1543, leaving his chief pilot, Bartolome Ferrel or Ferrelo, "a native of the Levant," in command. Ferrel left the island of San Miguel, which he named Isla de Juan Rodriguez, on January 29, to continue the voyage. In a little more than a month the fleet had reached the southern part of Oregon or thereabouts, allowing for an error of a degree and a half in the observations, which said that they were 44° north. A severe storm forced the ships to turn back from this point.

The report of the expedition is little more than an outline of distances sailed and places named, although there are occasional statements which give us valuable information regarding the coast Indians.[1] Among the most interesting of these notes are those showing that the news of the expeditions to Colorado river, and perhaps of the occupancy of the Pueblo country by white men, had reached the Pacific coast. About September 1, 1542, a party from the fleet went ashore near the southern boundary of California. Five Indians met the Spanish sailors at a spring, where they were filling the water casks. "They appeared like intelligent Indians," and went on board the ships without hesitation. "They took note of the Spaniards and counted them, and made signs that they had seen other men like these, who had beards and who brought dogs and cross-bows and swords . . . and showed by their signs that the other Spaniards were five days' journey distant. . . . The captain gave them a letter, which he told them to carry to the Spaniards who they said were in the interior." September 28, at San

---

[1] The report or memorandum was written by Juan Paez, or more probably by the pilot Ferrel. It has been translated in the reports of the United States Geological Survey West of the One Hundredth Meridian. (Appendix to part i, vol. vii, Archæology, pp. 293-314.) The translation is accompanied by notes identifying the places named, on which it is safe enough to rely, and by other notes of somewhat doubtful value.

Pedro bay, Ferrel again found Indians who told him by signs that "they had passed people like the Spaniards in the interior." Two days later, on Saturday morning, "three large Indians came to the ship, who told by signs that men like us were traveling in the interior, wearing beards, and armed and clothed like the people on the ships, and carrying cross-bows and swords. They made gestures with the right arm as if they were throwing lances, and went running in a pos- ture as if riding on horseback. They showed that many of the native Indians had been killed, and that this was the reason they were afraid." A week later, October 7, the ships anchored off the islands of Santa Cruz and Anacapa. The Indians of the islands and also of the main- land opposite, near Santa Barbara or the Santa Clara valley, gave the Spaniards additional descriptions of men like themselves in the interior.

The rest of the year 1542 was spent in this locality, off the coast of southern California, and then the voyage northward was resumed. Many points on the land were touched, although San Francisco bay quite escaped observation. Just before a severe storm, in which one of the vessels was lost, forcing him to turn back, Ferrel observed floating drift and recognized that it meant the neighborhood of a large river, but he was driven out to sea before reaching the mouth of the Columbia. The return voyage was uneventful, and the surviving vessel reached the harbor of Natividad in safety by April 14, 1543.

VILLALOBOS SAILS ACROSS THE PACIFIC

Cortes and Alvarado had both conceived plans more than once to equip a great expedition in New Spain and cross the South sea to the isles of the Western ocean. After the death of Alvarado, Mendoza adopted this scheme, and commissioned Ruy Lopez de Villalobos to take command of some of the ships of Alvarado and sail westward. He started on All Saints day, the 1st of November, 1542, with 370 Spanish soldiers and sailors aboard his fleet. January 22, 1547, Friar Jeronimo de Santisteban wrote to Mendoza "from Cochin in the Indies of the King of Portugal." He stated that 117 of the men were still with the fleet, and that these intended to keep together and make their way as best they could home to Spain. Thirty members of the expedition had remained at Maluco, and twelve had been captured by the natives of various islands at which the party had landed. The rest, including Ruy Lopez, had succumbed to hunger and thirst, interminable labors and suffering, and unrelieved discouragement—the record of the pre- vious months. This letter of Friar Jeronimo is the only published account of the fate of this expedition.

The brief and gloomy record of the voyage of Villalobos is a fit end- ing for this story of the Coronado expedition to Cibola and Quivira, of how it came about, of what it accomplished, and of what resulted from it. NOTHING is the epitome of the whole story. The lessons which it teaches are always warnings, but if one will read history rightly, every warning will be found to be an inspiration.

THE NARRATIVE OF CASTAÑEDA

BIBLIOGRAPHIC NOTE

A perusal of the narratives of the expeditions of Coronado and of Friar Marcos of Nice, which were translated by Henri Ternaux-Compans for the ninth volume of his Collection de Voyages, convinced me that the style and the language of these narratives were much more characteristic of the French translator than of the Spanish conquistadores. A comparison of Ternaux's translations with some of the Spanish texts which he had rendered into French, which were available in the printed collections of Spanish documents in the Harvard University library, showed me that Ternaux had not only rendered the language of the original accounts with great freedom, but that in several cases he had entirely failed to understand what the original writer endeavored to relate. On consulting Justin Winsor's Narrative and Critical History of America, in the second edition, I found that the Spanish manuscript of the Castañeda narrative, from which most of our knowledge of Coronado's expedition is derived, was in the Lenox Library in New York City. The trustees of this library readily granted my request, made through Dr Winsor, for permission to copy the manuscript. The Lenox manuscript is not the original one written by Castañeda, but a copy made toward the end of the sixteenth century. It contains a number of apparent mistakes, and the meaning of many passages is obscure, probably due to the fact that the Spanish copyist knew nothing about the North American Indians and their mode of living. These places I have pointed out in the notes to my translation of the narrative, and I have called attention also to the important errors and misconceptions in Ternaux's version. Diligent inquiry among the custodians of the large Spanish libraries at Simancas, Madrid, and at Seville where the Lenox manuscript was copied in 1596, has failed to bring me any information in regard to the original manuscript. The Lenox copy is the one used by Ternaux.

The Spanish text of the Relación Postrera de Sívola is printed now for the first time, through the kindness of the late Señor Joaquin García Icazbalceta, who copied it for me from a collection of papers in his possession, which formerly belonged to the Father Motolinia, the author of a very valuable description of the Indians of New Spain. In the preface to this work, dated 1541, Motolinia says that he was in communication with the brethren who had gone with Coronado. The Relación Postrera appears to be a copy made from a letter written to some of the Franciscans in New Spain by one of the friars who accompanied Coronado.

107

In the bibliography are the references to the exact location of the Spanish texts from which I have translated the other narratives. I am not aware that any of these have been translated entire, although Mr Bandelier has quoted from them extensively in his Documentary History of Zuñi.

There is one other account of the Coronado expedition which might have been included in the present volume. Mota Padilla wrote his Historia de la Nueva Galicia two centuries after the return of Coronado, but he had access to large stores of contemporary documents concerning the early history of New Spain, most of which have since been destroyed. Among these documents were those belonging to Don Pedro de Tovar, one of the captains in Coronado's army. Mota Padilla's account of this expedition is nearly if not quite as valuable as that of Castañeda, and supplements the latter in very many details. The length of the narrative and the limitations inevitable to any work of this nature forced me to abandon the idea of translating it for the present memoir. Much of the text of Mota Padilla will be found, however, in the notes to the translation of Castañeda, while the second half of the historical introduction is based primarily on Mota Padilla's narrative, and a large portion of it is little more than a free rendering of this admirable work.

THE SPANISH TEXT[1]

Relacion de la Jornada de Cibola conpuesta por Pedro de Castañeda de Naçera. Donde se trata de todos aquellos poblados y ritos, y costumbres, la qual fue el Año de 1540.

Historia del Conde Fernando Gonzales impressa.

PROEMIO.

Cosa por sierto me parece muy magnifico señor liçeta y que es exerçi-çio de hombres uirtuosos el desear saber y querer adquirir para su memoria la noticia berdadera de las cosas acasos aconteçidos en partes remotas de que se tiene poca noticia lo qual yo no culpo algunas personas especulatiuas que por uentura con buen çelo por muchas ueces me an sido inportunos no poco rogadome les dixese y aclarase algunas dudas que tenian de cosas particulares q̃ al bulgo auian oydo en cosas y casos acontecidos en la jornada de cibola o tierra nueba que el buen uisorey que dios aya en su gloria don Antonio de Mendoca ordeno y hiço haçer donde embio por general capitan a francisco uasques de coronado y a la berdad ellos tienen raçon de querer saber la uerdad porque como el bulgo muy muchas ueces y cosas que an oydo y por uentura a quien de ellas no tubo noticia ansi las hacen mayores o menores que ellas son y las que son algo las hacen nada y las no tales las hacen tã admirables que pareçen cosas no creederas podria tan bien

---

[1] This text is, as far as possible, a copy of the Relacion in the Lenox Library. No attempt has been made to add marks of punctuation, to accent, or to alter what may have been slips of the copyist's pen.

causarlo que como aquello tierra no permanecio no ubo quien quisiese
gastar tienpo en escrebir sus particularidades porque se perdiese la
noticia de aquello que no fue dios seruido que gosasen el sabe por que
en berdad quien quisiera exercitarse en escrebir asi las cosas acaeçidas
en la jornada como las cosas se bieron en aquellas tierras los ritos y
tratos delos naturales tubiera harta materia por donde pareçiera su
juiçio y creo que no le faltara de quedar relaçion que tratar de berdad
fuera tam admirable que pareciera increyble.

y tambien creo que algunas nobelas que se quentan el aber como a
ueinte años y mas que aquella jornada se hiço lo causa digo esto porque
algunas la haçen tierra inabitable otros confinante a la florida otros a la
india mayor que no parece pequeño desbario pueden tomar alguna ocaçion
y causa sobre que poner su fundamento tambien ay quien da noticia de
algunos animales bien remotos que otros con aber se hallado en aquella
jornada lo niegan y afirman no aber tal ni aberlos bisto otros uariã en
el rumbo de las prouincias y aun en los tractos y trajes atribuyendo lo
que es de los unos a los otros todo lo qual a sido gran parte muy magnifico señor a me mober aunque tarde a querer dar una brebe noticia
general para todos los que se arrean de esta uirtud especulatiua y por
ahorrar el tiempo que con inportunidades soy a quexado donde se halla-
ran cosas por sierto harto graues de crer todas o las mas bistas por
mis ojos y otras por notiçia berdadera inquiridas de los propios naturales creyendo que teniendo entendido como lo tengo que esta mi pequeña obra seria en si ninguna o sin autoridad sino fuese faboreçida y
anparada de tal persona que su autoridad quitase el atrebimiento a los
que sin acatamiento dar libertad a sus murmuradores lenguas y cono-
çiendo yo en quanta obligacion siempre e sido y soy a vr̃a md humil-
mente suplico de baxo de su anparo como de berdadero seruidor y criado
sea recebida esta pequeña obra la qual ba en tres partes repartida para
que mejor se de a entender la primera sera dar noticia del descubrimiento y el armada o campo que hiço con toda la jornada con los capitanes que alla fueron la segunda los pueblos y prouinçias que se hallaron
y en que rumbos y que ritos y costumbres los animales fructas y yerbas
y en que partes de la tierra. la terçera la buelta que el campo hiço y las
ocaciones que ubo para se despoblar aun que no licitas por ser el mejor
paraje que ay para se descubrir el meollo de la tierra que ay en estas
partes de poniente como se uera y despues aca se tiene entendido y en lo
ultimo se tratara de algunas cosas admirables que se bieron y por donde
con mas facilidad se podra tornar a descubrir lo que no bimos que suelo
mejor y que no poco haria al caso para por tierra entrar en la tierra de
que yba en demanda el marques del ualle don fer^{do} cortes de baxo de
la estrella del poniente que no pocas armadas le costo de mar plega a
nr̃o señor me de tal graçia que con mi rudo entendimiento y poca abilidad
pueda tratando berdad agradar con esta me pequeña obra al sabio y
prudente lector siendo por vr̃a md aceptada pues mi intincion no es ganar
gracias de buen componedor ni retorico salbo querer dar berdadera

noticia y hacer a vr̃a md este pequeño seruicio el qual reciba como de berdadero seruidor y soldado que se hallo presente y aunque no por estilo pulido escrebo lo que paso lo que a oydo palpo y bido y tratrato.

siempre beo y es ansi que por la mayor parte quando tenemos entre las manos alguna cosa preciosa y la tratamos sin inpedimento no la tenemos ni la preçiamos en quanto uale si entendemos la falta que nos haria si la perdiesemos y por tanto de continuo la bamos teniendo en menos pero despues que la abemos perdido y carecemos del benefficio de ella abemos gran dolor en el coraçon y siempre andamos ymaginatibos buscando modos y maneras como la tornemos a cobrar y asi me pareçe acaeçio a todos aquellos o a los mas que fueron a la jornada quel año de nr̃o saluador jesu christo de mill y quinientos y quarenta hiço francisco uasques coronado en demanda de las siete ciudades que puesto que no hallaron aquellas riqueças de que les auian dado notiçia hallaron aparejo para las buscar y principio de buena tierra que poblar para de alli pasar adelante y como despues aca por la tierra que conquistaron y despoblaron el tiempo les a dado a entender el rumbo y aparejo donde estaban y el principio de buena tierra que tienan entre manos lloran sus coracones por aber perdido tal oportunidad de tiempo y como sea sierto que ben mas lo honbres quando se suben a la talanquera que quando andan en el coso agora que estan fuera cognoçen y entienden los rumbos y el aparejo donde se hallauan y ya que ben que no lo pueden goçar ni cobrar y el tiempo perdido deleytanse en contar lo que bieron y aun lo que entienden que perdieron especial aquellos que se hallan pobres oy tanto como quando alla fueron y no an dexado de trabajar y gastado el tienpo sin probecho digo esto porque tengo entendido algunos de los que de alla binieron holgarian oy como fuese para pasar adelante boluer a cobrar lo perdido y otros holgarian oy y saber la causa porque se descubrio y pues yo me ofrecido a contarlo tomarlo e del principio que pasa asi.

PRIMERA PARTE.[1]

Capitulo primero donde se trata como se supo la primera poblacion de las siete çiudades y como Nuño de guzman hiço armada para descubrirlla.

en el año y quinientos y treinta siendo presidente de la nueba españa Nuño de guzman ubo en su poder un indio natural del ualle o ualles de oxitipar a quien los españoles nombran tejo este indio dixo que el era hijo de un mercader y su padre era muerto pero que siendo el chiquito su padre entraua la tierra adentro a mercadear con plumas ricas de aues para plumages y que en retorno traya un mucha cantidad de oro y plata que en aquella tierra lo ay mucho y que el fue con el una o dos ueçes y que bido muy grandes pueblos tanto que los quiso comparar con mexico y su comarca y que auia uisto siete pueblos muy grandes donde auia calles de plateria y que para ir a ellos tardauan desde su tierra quarenta dias y todo despoblado y que la tierra por do yban no

[1] The Primera Parte begins a new leaf in the original.

tenia yerba sino muy chiquita de un xeme y que el rumbo que lleuaban
era al largo de la tierra entre las dos mares siguiendo la lauia del norte
debaxo de esta notiçia Nuño de guzman junto casi quatrosientos hombres españoles y ueinte mill amigos de la nueua españa y como se hallo
a el presente en mexico atrabesando la tarasca que es tierra de mechuacan para hallandose el aparejo quel indio deçia boluer atrabesando
la tierra hacia la mar del norte y darian en la tierra que yban a buscar
a la qual ya nombrauan las siete ciudades pues conforme a los quarenta
dias quel texo decia hallaria que abiendo andado doçientas leguas
podrian bien atrabesar la tierra quitado a parte algunas fortunas que
pasaron en esta jornada desque fueron llegados en la prouincia de
culiacan que fue lo ultimo de su gouernaçion que es agora el nueuo
reyno de galiçia quisieron atrabesar la tierra y ubo muy gran dificultad
porque la cordillera de la sierra que cae sobre aquella mar estan agra
que por mucho que trabajo fue inposible hallar camino en aquella
parte y a esta causa se detubo todo su campo en aquella tierra de culiacan hasta tanto que como yban con el hombres poderosos que tenian
repartimientos en tierra de mexico mudaron las boluntades y de cada
dia se querian boluer fuera de esto Nuño de guzman tubo nueua como
auia benido de españa el marques del ualle don fernando cortes con el
nueuo titulo y grandes fabores y prouinçiones y como nuño de guzman
en el tiempo que fue presidente le ubiese sido emulo muy grande y
hecho muchos daños en sus haciendas y en las de sus amigos temiose
que don fer^{do} cortes se quisiese pagar en otras semejantes obras o
peores y determino de poblar aquella uilla de culiacan y dar la buelta
con la demas gente sin que ubiese mas efecto su jornada y de buelta
poblo a xalisco que es la çiudad de conpostela y atonala que llaman
guadalaxara y esto es agora el nuebo reyno de galicia la guia que lleuaban que se decia texo murio en estos comedios y ansi se quedo el
nombre de estas siete ciudades y la demanda de ellas hasta oy dia que
no sean descubierto.

Capitulo segundo como bino a ser gouernador françisco uasques coro-
nado y la segunda relaçion que dio cabeça de uaca.

pasados que fueron ocho años que esta jornada se auia hecho por Nuño
de guzman abiendo sido preso por un juez de residençia que uino de
españa para el efecto con prouiçiones bastantes llamado el lic^{do} diego
de la torre que despues muriendo este juez que ya tenia en si la gouernaçion de aquella tierra el buen don Antonio de mendoça uisorey de la
nueua españa puso por gouernador de aquela gouernaçion a francisco
uasques de coronado un cauallero de salamanca que a la sacon era
casado en la çiudad de mexico cõ una señora hija de Alonso de estrada
thesorero y gouernador que auia sido de mexico uno por quien el bulgo
dice ser hijo del rey catholico don fernando y muchos lo afirman por
osa sierta digo que a la sacon que francisco uasques fue probeydo por
gouernador andaba por uisitador general de la nueua españa por donde

tubo amistad y conuersaçiones de muchas personas nobles que despues le siguieron en la jornada que hiço aconteçio a la saçon que llegaron a mexico tres españoles y un negro que auian por nombre cabeça de uaca y dorantes y castillo maldonado los quales se auian perdido en la armada que metio pamfilo de narbaes en la florida y estos salieron por la uia de culiacan abiendo atrabesado la tierra de mar a mar como lo beran los que lo quisieren saber por un tratado que el mismo cabeça de uaca hiço dirigido a el principe don phelipe que agora es rey de españa y señor nr̄o y estos dieron notiçia a el buen don Antonio de mendoça en como por las tierras que atrabesaron tomaron lengua y notiçia grande de unos poderosos pueblos de altos de quatro y çinco doblados y otras cosas bien diferentes de lo que pareçio por berdad esto comunico el buen uisorey con el nuebo gouernador que fue causa que se apresurase dexando la bisita que tenia entre manos y se partiese para su guernaçion lleuando consigo el negro que auia bendido con los tres frayles de la orden do san franc᷉o el uno auia por nombre fray marcos de niça theologo y saserdote y el otro fray daniel lego y otro fray Antonio de santa maria y como llego a la prouincia de culiacan luego despidio a los frayles ya nonbrados y a el negro que auia por nombre esteuan para que fuesen en demanda de aquella tierra porque el fray marcos de niça se prefirio de llegar a berla por que este frayle se auia hallado en el peru a el tienpo que don pedro de albarado passo por tierra ydos los dichos frayles y el negro esteuan pareçe que el negro no yba a fabor de los frayles porque lleuaba las mugeres que le daban y adquiria turquesas y haçia balumen de todo y aun los indios de aquellos poblados por do yban entendiasen mejor con el negro como ya otra uez lo auian uisto que fue causa que lo ubieron hechar delante que fuese descubriendo y pacificando para que quando ellos llegasen no tubiesen mas que entender de en tomar la relacion de lo que buscauan.

Capitulo terçero como mataron los de cibola a el negro esteuan y fray marcos bolbio huyendo.

apartado que se ubo el esteuan de los dichos frayles presumio ganar en todo reputacion y honra y que se le atribuyese la osadia y atrebimiento de auer el solo descubierto[1] aquellos poblados de altos tan nombrados por aquella tierra y lleuando consigo de aquellas gentes que le seguian procuro de atrabesar los despoblados que ay entre cibola y lo poblado que auia andado y auiase les adelantado tanto a los frayles que quando ellos llegaron a chichieticale ques principio del despoblado ya el estaua a cibola que son ochenta leguas de despoblado que ay desde culiacan a el principio del despoblado docientas y ueinte leguas y en el despoblado ochenta que son trecientas diez mas o menos digo ansi que llegado que fue el negro esteuan a cibola llego cargado de grande numero de turquesas que le auian dado y algunas mugeres hermosas que le auian dado y lleuauan los indios que le acompañauan y le seguian

---

[1] This is a marginal correction of what is clearly a slip of the pen in the text.

de todo lo poblado que auia pasado los quales en yr debajo de su amparo
creyan poder atrabesar toda la tierra sin riesgo ninguno pero como
aquellas gentes de aquella tierra fuesen de mas raçon que no los que seguian a el esteuan aposentaronlo en una sierta hermita que tenian fuera
del pueblo y los mas uiejos y los que gouernauan oyeron sus raçones
y procuraron saber la causa de su benida en aquella tierra y bien infor-
mados por espaçio de tres dias entraron en su consulta y por la notiçia
quel negro les dio como atras uenian dos hombres blancos embiados
por un gran señor que eran entendidos en las cosas del cielo y que
aquellos los uenian a industriar en las cosas diuinas consideraron que
debia ser espia o guia de algunas naçiones que los querian yr a conquistar porque les pareçio desbario decir que la tierra de donde uenia era
la gente blanca siendo el negro y enbiado por ellos y fueron a el y como
despues de otras raçones le pidiese turquesas y mugeres parecioles
cosa dura y determiaronse a le matar y ansi lo hicieron sin que mata-
sen a nadie de los que con el yban y tomaron algunos muchachos y a
los de mas que serian obra de sesenta personas dexaron bolber libres a
sus tierras pues como estos que boluian ya huyendo atemorisados llegasen a se topar y ber con los frayles en el despoblado sesenta leguas de
çibola y les diesen la triste nueba pusieron los en tanto temor que aun
no se fiando de esta gente con aber ydo en compañia del negro abrieron
las petacas que lleuaban y les repartieron quanto trayan que no les
quedo salbo los hornamentos de deçir misa y de alli dieron la buelta sin
ber la tierra mas de lo que los indios les deçian antes caminaban dobla-
das jornadas haldas en sinta.

*Capitulo quarto como el buen don Antonio de mendoça hiço jornada
para el descubrimiento de Cibola.*

despues que francisco uasques coronado ubo embiado a fray marcos
de niça y su conpaña en la demanda ya dicha quedando el en culiacan
entendio en negocios que conbenian a su gouernaçiõ tubo sierta relaçion de una prouinçia que corria en la trabesia de la tierra de culiacan
a el norte que se decia topira y luego salio para la ir a descubrir con
algunos conquistadores y gente de amigos y su yda hiço poco efecto
por que auian de atrabesar las cordilleras y fue les muy dificultoso y la
notiçia no la hallaron tal ni muestra de buena tierra y ansi dio la
buelta y llegado que fue hallo a los frayles que auian acabado de llegar
y fueron tantas las grandeças que les dixeron de lo que el esteuan el
negro auia descubierto y lo que ellos oyeron a los indios y otras noticias
de la mar del sur y de ylas que oyeron deçir y de otras riquesas quel
gouernador sin mas se detener se partio luego para la ciudad de
mexico lleuando a el fray marcos consigo para dar notiçia de ello a el
bisorey en grandesiendo las cosas con no las querer comunicar con
nadie, sino de baxo de puridad y grande secreto a personas particula
res y llegados a mexico y bisto con don Antonio de mendoça luego se
començo a publicar como ya se abian descubierto las siete çiudades

que Nuño de guzman buscaba y haçer armada y portar gente para
las yr a conquistar el buen birrey tubo tal orden con los frayles de la
orden de san françisco que hicieron a fray marcos prouincial que fue
causa que andubiesen los pulpitos de aquella orden llenos de tantas
marabillas y tan grãdes que en pocos dias se juntaron mas de tresientos hombres españoles y obra de ochocientos indios naturales de la nue
(ua) españa y entre los españoles honbres de gran calidad tantos y
tales que dudo en indias aber se juntado tan noble gente y tanta en
tam pequeño numero como fueron treçientos hombres y de todos ellos
capitan general francisco uasques coronado gouernador de la nueba
galiçia por aber sido el autor de todo hico todo esto el buen uirey don
Antonio porque a la saçon era franᶜᵒ uasques la persona mas allegada
a el por pribança porque tenia entendido era hombre sagaz abil y de
buen consejo allende de ser cauallero como lo era tenido tubiera mas
atençion y respecto a el estado en que lo ponia y cargo que llebaua que
no a la renta que dexaba en la nueba españa o a lo menos a la honra
que ganaba y auia de ganar lleuando tales caualleros de baxo de su
bando pero no le salio ansi como a delante se bera en el fin de este
tratado ni el supo conserbar aquel estado ni la gouernacion que tenia.

Capitulo quinto que trata quienes fueron por capitanes a cibola.

ya quel bisorey don Antonio de mendoça bido la muy noble gente
que tenia junta y con los animos y uoluntad q̃ todos se le auian ofreçido
cognoçiendo el ualor de sus personas a cada uno de ellos quisiera haçer
capitan de un exerçito pero como el numero de todos era poco no pudo
lo que quisiera y ansi ordeno las conductas y capitanias que le pareçio
porque yendo por su mano ordenado era tam obedecido y amado que
nadie saliera de su mandado despues que todos entẽdieron quien era
su general hiço alferez general a don pedro de touar cauallero mançebo
hijo de don fernando de tobar guarda y mayordomo mayor de la reyna
doña Juana nr̃a natural señora que sea en gloria y maestre de campo a
lope de samaniego alcayde de las ataraçanas de mexico cauallero para el
cargo bien sufiçiente capitanes fueron don tristan de arellano don pedro
de gueuara hijo de don juan de gueuara y sobrino del conde de oñate
don garçi lopes de cardenas don rodrigo maldonado cuñado del duque
del infantado diego lopes ueinte y quatro de seuilla diego gutierres de
la caualleria todos los demas caualleros yban debajo del guion del general por ser peronas señaladas y algunos de ellos fueron despues capitanes y permanecieron en ello por ordenaçion del birey y otros por el
general francisco uasques nombrare algunos de aquellos de que tengo
memoria que fueron françisco de barrio nuebo un cauallero de granada
juan de saldibar françisco de auando juan gallego y melchior dias capitan y alcalde mayor que auia sido de culiacan, q̃ aunque no era cauallero mereçia de su persona el cargo que tubo los demas caualleros que
fueron sobresalientes fueron don Alonso manrique de lara don lope de
urrea cauallero aragones gomes suares de figueroa luis ramires de uargas

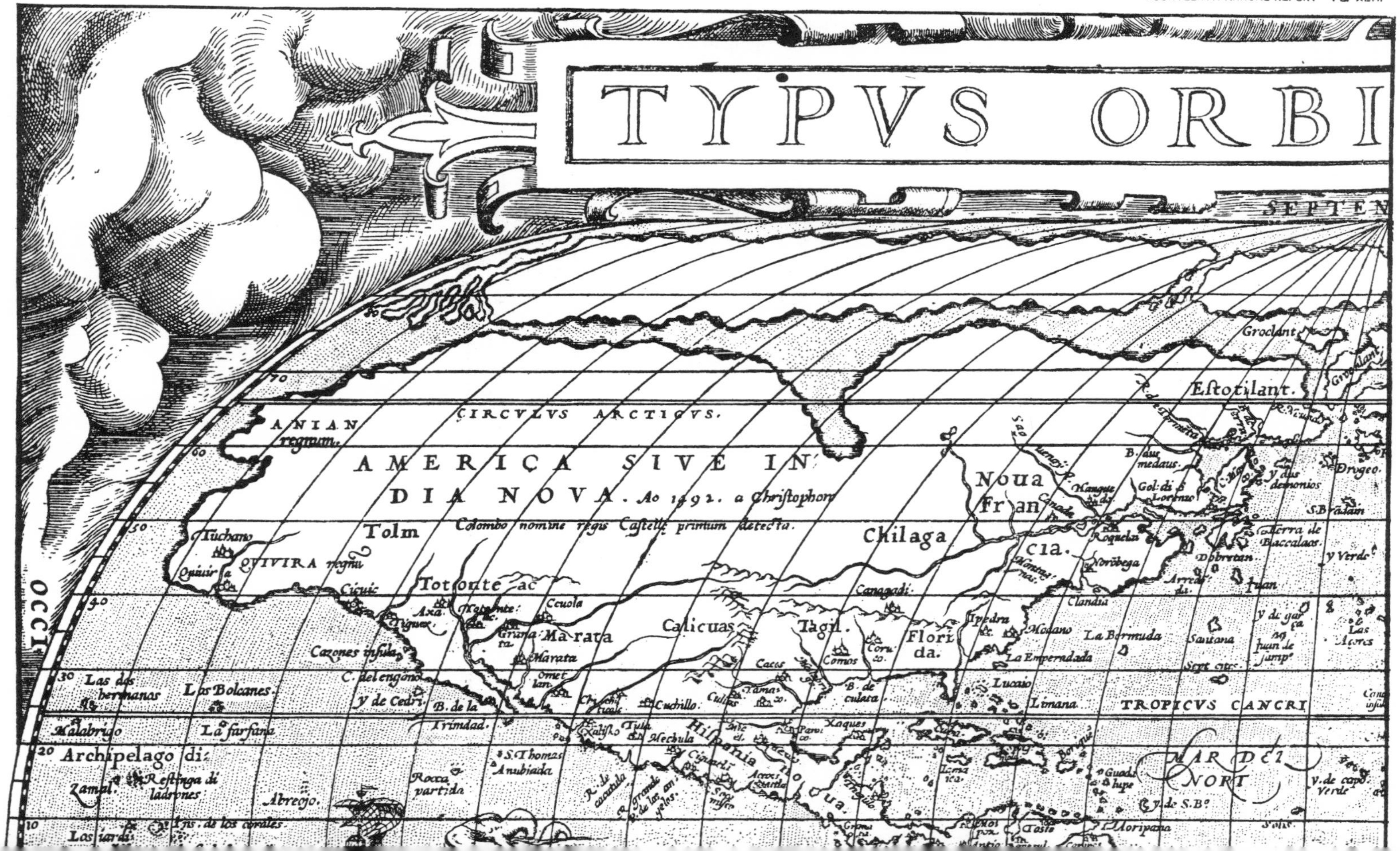
TYPVS ORBI
SEPTEN
CIRCVLVS ARCTICVS.
ANIAN regnum.
AMERICA SIVE INDIA NOVA. Ao 1492. a Christophoro Colombo nomine regis Castellæ primum detecta.
Tolm
QVIVIRA regnu
Totonteac
Marata
Calicuas
Tagil
Florida.
Chilaga
Noua Francia.
Estotilant.
Groclant
La Bermuda
TROPICVS CANCRI
MAR DEL NORT
Hispania
Archipelago di
OCCI

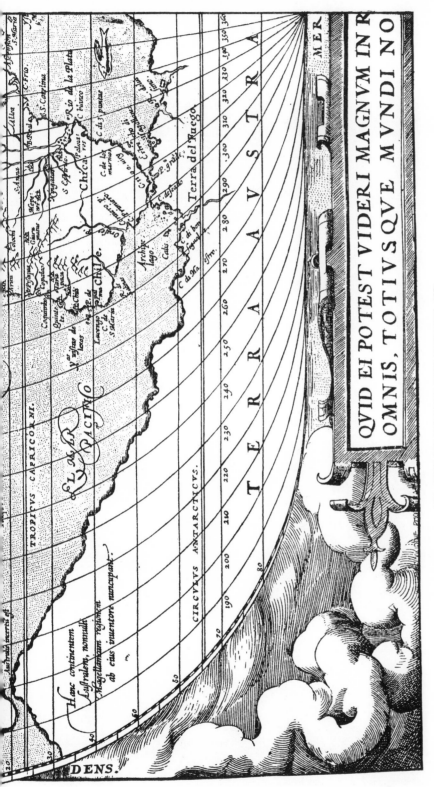

ABR. ORTELIUS' THEATRUM ORBIS TERRARUM, 1570

juan de sotomayor francisco gorbalan el factor riberos y otros caualleros de que agora no me acuerdo y hombres de mucho calidad capitan
de infanteria fue pablo de melgosa burgales y de la artilleria hernando
de albarado cauallero montañes digo que con el tiempo e perdido la
memoria de muchos buenos hijos dalgo que fuera bueno que los nom-
brara por que se biera y cognoçiera la raçon que tengo de decir que
auia para esta jornada la mas lucida gente que sea juntado en indias
para yr en demandas de tierras nuebras sino fueran desdichados en lleuar
capitan que dexaba rentas en la nueba españa y muger moça noble y
generosa que no fueron pocas espuelas para lo que bino a haçer.

Capitulo sexto como se juntaron en conpostela todas las capitanias y
salieron en orden para la jornada.

hecho y ordenado por el birey don Antonio de mendoça lo que abemos
dicho y hechas las capitanias o capitanes dio luego a la gente de guerra
socorros de la caxa de su magestad a las personas mas menesterosas y
por pareçerle que si salia el campo formado desde mexico haria algunos
agrauios por las tierras de los amigos ordeno que se fuesen a juntar a
la ciudad de conpostela cabeça del nuebo reyno de galicia ciento y
diez leguas de mexico para que desde alli ordenadamente comencasen
su jornada lo que paso en este uiaje no ay para que dar de ello relaçion
pues al fin todos se juntaron en conpostela el dia de carnes tollendas
del año de quarenta y uno y como ubo hechado toda la gente de Mexico
dio orden en como pedro de alarcon saliese con dos nauios que estaban
en el puerto de la nabidad en la costa del sur y fuese a el puerto de
xalisco a tomar la ropa de los soldados que no la pudiesen lleuar para
que costa a costa fuese tras del campo porque se tubo entendido que
segun la notiçia auian de ir por la tierra çerca de la costa de el mar y
que por los rios sacariamos los puertos y los nauios siempre tendrian
noticia del campo lo qual despues pareçio ser falso y ansi se perdio toda
la ropa o por mejor deçir la perdio cuya era como adelante se dira asi
que despachado y concluido todo el uisorey se partio para conpostela
acompañado de muchos caualleros y ricos honbres y tubo el año nuebo
de quarenta y uno en pasquaro que es cabeça del obispado de mechuacan y de alli con mucha alegria y placer y grandes reçebimientos atrabeso toda la tierra de la nueba españa hasta Conpostela que son
como tengo dicho çiento y diez leguas adonde hallo toda la gente junta
y bien tratada y hospedada por christobal de oñate que era a la saçon
la persona que tenia enpeso aquella gouernaçion y la auia sostenido y
era capitan de toda aquella tierra puesto que francisco uasques era
gouernador y llegado con mucha alegria de todos hiço alarde de la gēte
que embiaba y hallo toda la que abemos señalado y repartio las capitanias y esto hecho otro dia despues de misa a todos juntos ansi capitanes como a soldados el uisorey les hiço una muy eloquente y breue
oraçion encargandoles la fidelidad q̃ debian a su general dandoles bien
a entender el probecho que de haçer aquella jornada podia redundar a

si a la conuerçion de aquellas gentes como en pro de los que conquista-
sen.aquella tierra y el seruicio de su magestad y la obligaçion en que le
auian puesto para en todo tiempo los faborecer y socorrer y acabada
tomo juramento sobre los euāgelios en un libro misala todos generalmente asi a capitanes como a soldados aunque por orden que siguirian
a su general y harian en aquella jornada y obedecerian todo aquello que
por el les fuese mandado lo qual despues cumplieron fielmente como se
bera y esto hecho otro dia salio el campo con sus banderas tendidas y
el uirey don Antonio le acompaño dos jornados y de alli se despidio
dando la buelta para la nueua españa aconpañado de sus amigos.

*Capitulo septimo como el campo llego a chiametla y mataron a el maestre
de canpo y lo que mas acaeçio hasta llegar a culiacan.*

partido que fue el uirey don Antonio el campo camino por sus jornadas y como era forçado lleuar cada uno sus aberes en cauallos y no
todos los sabian aparejar y los cauallos salian gordos y holgados en las
primeras jornadas ubo grande dificultad y trabajo y muchos dexaron
muchas preseas y las daban de gracia a quien las queria por no las cargar
y a el fin la necesidad que es maestra con el tiempo los hiço maestros
donde se pudierā ber muchos caualleros tornados harrieros y que el que
se despreciaba del officio no era tenido por hombre y con estos trabajos
que entonçes tubieron por grandes llego el canpo en chiametla donde
por fastar bastimentos fue forçado de tenerse alli algunos dias en los
quales el maestre de campo lope de samaniego con sierta compañia fue
a buscar bastimentos y en un pueblo por entrar indiscretamente por un
arcabuco en pos de los enemigos lo flecharon por un ojo y le pasaron el
celebro de que luego murio alli y flecharon otros cinco o seis compañeros
y luego como fue muerto diego lopes ueinte y quatro de seuilla recogio
la gente y lo embio a haçer saber a el general y puso guarda en el pueblo
y en los bastimentos sabido dio gran turbacion en el campo y fue enterrado y hicieron algunas entradas de dōde truxeron bastimentos y algunos
presos de los naturales y se ahorcaron a lo menos los que parecieron ser
de a quella parte a do murio el maestre de campo.

parece que a el tiempo que el general françisco uasques partio de
culiacan con fray marcos a dar la noticia ya dicha a el bisorey don Antonio
de mendoça auia dexado ordenado que saliese el capitan melchior dias
y juan de saldibar con una doçena de buenos hombres de culiacan en
demada de lo que fray marcos auia bisto y oydo los quales salieron y
fueron hasta chichilticale que es principio del despoblado doçientas y
ueinte leguas de Culiacan y no hallaron cosa de tomo bolbieron y a el
tiempo que el campo queria salir de chiametla llegaron y hablaron a el
general y por secreto que se trato la mala nueua luego suena ubo algunos
dichos que aunque se doraban no dexaban de dar lustre de lo que
eran fray marcos de niça cognociendo la turbaçion de algunos deshaçia
aquellos nublados prometiendo ser lo que bieron lo bueno y que el
yba alli y poruia el campo en tierra donde hinchesen las manos y con

esto se aplaco y mostraron buen semblante y de alli camino el campo
hasta llegar a culiacan haçiendo algunas entradas en tierra de
guerra por tomar bastimentos llegaron a dos leguas de la uilla de
culiacan uispera de pasqua de resureçion a donde salieron los uecinos
a reçebir a su gouernador y le rogaron no entrase en la uilla hasta el
segundo dia de pasqua.

*Capitulo otauo como el campo entro en la uilla de culiacan y el reçebi-
miento que se hiço y lo que mas acaeçio hasta la partida.*

como fuese segundo dia de pasqua de resureçion el campo salio de
mañana para entrar en la uilla y en la entrada en un campo esconbrado
los de la uilla ordenados anso de guerra a pie y a cauallo por sus exqua-
drones teniendo asētada su artilleria que eran siete pieças de bronce
salieron en muestra de querer defender la uilla estaban con ellos alguna
parte de nr̃os soldados nr̃o campo por la misma orden comencaron con
ellos una escaramuça y ansi fueron romprendo despues de aber jugado
el artilleria de ambas partes de suerte que les fue tomada la uilla por
fuerça de armas que fue una alegre demostraçion y reçebimiento aun
que no para el artillero que se llebo una mano por aber mandado poner
fuego antes que acabase de sacar el atacador de un tiro tomada la uilla
fueron luego bien aposentados y hospedados por los ueçinos que como
eran todos hombres muy honrados en sus propias posadas metieron a
todos los caualleros y personas le calidad que yban en el campo aunque
auia aposento hecho para todos fuera de la uilla y no les fue algunos
uecinos mal gratificado este hospedaje por que como todos benian adere-
sados de ricos atabios y de alli auian de sacar bastimentos en sus bestias
y de fuerça auian de dejar sus preseas muchos quisieron antes dar las a
sus huespedes que no ponerlas a la bentura de la mar ni que se las llebase
los nabios que auian benido por la costa siguiendo el campo para tomar
el fardaje como ya se dixo ansi que llegados y bien aposentados en la
uilla el general por orden del bisorey don Antonio puso alli por capitan
y tiniente a fernandarias de saabedra tio de hernandarias de saabedra
conde del castellar que fue alguaçil mayor de seuilla y alli reposo el
canpo algunos dias porque los ueçinos auian cogido aquel año muchos
bastimentos y partieron con la gente de nr̃o campo con mucho amor
especial cada uno con sus huespedes de manera que no solamente ubo
abudançia para gastar alli mas aun ubo para sacar que a el tiempo de la
partida salieron mas de seiçientas bestias cargadas y los amigos y
seruiçio que fueron mas de mill personas. pasados quinse dias el general
ordeno de se partir delante con hasta sinquenta de acauallo y pocos
peones y la mayor parte de los amigos y dexar el campo que le siguiese
desde a quinse dias y dexo por su teniente a don tristan de arellano.

en este comedio antes que se partiese el general aconteçio un caso
donoso y yo por tal lo quento y fue que un soldado mançebo que se
decia trugillo fingio aber bisto una biçion estando bañandose en el rio
y façiendo del disfigurado fue traydo ante el general adonde dio a enten-

der que le auia dicho el demonio que matase a el general y lo casaria con doña beatris su muger y le daria grandes thesoros y otras cosas bien donosas por donde fray marcos de niça hiço algunos sermones atribuyendolo a que el demonio con embidia del bien que de aquella jornada auia de resultar lo queria desbaratar por aquella uia y no solamente paro en esto sino que tambien los frayles que yban en la jornada lo escribieron a sus conbentos y fue causa que por los pulpitos de mexico se dixesen hartas fabulas sobre ello.

El general mando quedar a el truxillo en aquella uilla y que no hiciese la jornada que fue lo que el pretendio quando hiço aquel embuste segun despues pareçio por berdad el general salio con la gente ya dicha siguiendo su jornada y despues el campo como se dira.

Capitulo nueue como el canpo salio de culiacan y llego el general a çibola y el campo a señora y lo que mas acaeçio.

el general como esta dicho salio del ualle de culiacan en seguimiento de su uiaje algo a la ligera lleuando consigo los frayles que ninguno quiso quedar con el campo y a tres jornados un frayle llamado fray Antonio uictoria se quebro un pierna y este frayle era de misa y para que se curase lo bolbieron del camino y despues fue con el campo que no fue poca consolaçion para todos el general y su gente atrabesaron la tierra sin contraste que todo lo que hallaron de pax porque los indios cognoçian a fray marcos y algunos de los que auian ydo con el capitan melchior dias quando auia ydo el y juan de saldibar a descubrir como el general ubo atrabesado lo poblado y llegado a chichilticale principio del despoblado y no bio cosa buena no dexo de sentir alguna tristesa porque aunque la notiçia de lo de adelante era grande no auia quien lo ubiese uisto sino los indios que fueron con el negro que ya los auian tomado en algunas mentiras por todos se sintio mucho ber que la fama de chichilticale se resumia en una casa sin cubierta aruynada puesto que pareçia en otro tiempo aber sido casa fuerte en tiempo que fue poblada y bien se cognoçia ser hecha por gentes estrangeras puliticas y guerras benidas de lejos era esta casa de tierra bermeja desde alli prosiguieron el despoblado y llegaron en quinse dias a ocho leguas de çibola a un rio que por yr el agua turbia y bermeja le llamaron el rio bermejo en este rio se hallaron barbos como en españa a qui fue adonde se bieron los primeros indios de aquella tierra que fueron dos que huyeron y fueron a dar mandado y otro dia a dos leguas del pueblo siendo de noche algunos indios en parte segura dieron una grita que aunque la gente estaba aperçebida se alteraron algunos en tanta manera que ubo quien hecho la silla a el rebes y estos fueron gente nueba que los diestros luego caualgaron y corrieron el campo los indios huyeron como quien sabia la tierra que ninguno pudo ser abido.

otro dia bien en orden entraron por la tierra poblada y como bieron el primer pueblo que fue çibola fueron tantas las maldiciones que algunos hecharon a fray marcos quales dios no permita le comprehendan.

el es un pueblo pequeño ariscado y apeñuscado que de lejos ay estan-
cias en la nueua españa que tienen mejor aparençia es pueblo de hasta
doçientos hombres de guerra de tres y de quatro altos y las casas chicas
y poco espaciosas no tienen patios un patio sirue a un barrio auia se
juntado alli la gente de la comarca porque es una prouinçia de siete
pueblos donde ay otros harto mayores y mas fuertes pueblos que no
çibola estas gentes esperarõ en el campo hordenados con sus exqua-
drones a uista del pueblo y como a los requerimientos que le hicieron
con las lenguas no quisieron dar la pax antes se mostraban brauos diese
santiago en ellos y fueron desbaratados luego y despues fueron a tomar
el pueblo que no fue poco dificultoso que como tenian la entrada angosta
y torneada a el entrar deribaron a el general con una gran piedra tendido
y ansi le mataran sino fuera por don garci lopes de cardenas y hernando de albarado que se deribaron sobre el y le sacaron recibiendo
ellos los golpes de piedras que no fueron pocos pero como a la primera
furia de los españoles no ay resistençia en menos de una ora se entro y
gano el pueblo y se descubrieron los bastimentos que era de lo que
mas necesidad auia y de ay adelante toda la prouincia bino de pax.

el campo quo auia quedado a don tristan de arellano partio en seguimiento del general cargados todos de bastimentos las lanças en los
onbros todos a pie por sacar cargados los cauallos y no con pequeño
trabajo de jornadas en jornadas llegaron a una prouinçia que cabeça de
uaca puso por nombre coraçones a causa que alli les ofrecieron muchos
coraçones de animales y luego la començo a poblar una uilla y poner le
nombre sant hieronimo de los coraçones y luego la començo a poblar y
bisto que no se podia sustentar la paso despues a un ualle que llamã
persona digo señora y los españoles le llamaron señora y ansi le llamare
de aqui adelante desde alli se fue a buscar el puerto el rio abajo a la
costa de la mar por saber de los nabios y no los hallaron don rodrigo
maldonado que yba por caudillo en busca de los nabios de buelta truxo
consigo un indio tam grande y tam alto que el mayor honbre y tan alto
quel mayor hombre del campo no le llegaua a el pecho deciase que en a
quella costa auia otros indios mas altos alli reposaron las aguas y despues paso el campo y la uilla señora por que auia en aquella comarca
bastimentos para poder aguardar mandado del general.

mediado el mes de otubre melchior dias y juan gallego capitanes
binieron de çibola el juan gallego para nueba españa y melchior dias
para quedar por capitan en la nueba uilla de los coraçones con la gente
que alli quedase y para que fuese a descubrir los nabios por aquella
costa.

*Capitulo deçimo como el campo salio de la uilla de senora quedando la
uilla poblada y como llego a çibola y lo que le a uino en el camino a el capitan
melchior dias yendo en demanda de los nabios y como descubrio el rio del
tison.*

luego como fue llegado en la uilla de señora melchior dias y juan
gallego se publico la partida del campo para cibola y como auia de que-

dar en aquella uilla melchior dias por capitan con ochenta honbres y como juan gallego yba con mensaje para la nueba españa a el bisorey y llebaba en su compañia a fray marcos que no se tubo por seguro quedar en cibola biendo que auia salido su relaçion falsa en todo porque ni se hallaron los reynos q̃ deçia ni ciudades populosas ni riquesas de oro ni pedreria rica que se publico ni brocados ni otras cosas que se dixeron por los pulpitos pues luego que esto se publico se repartio la gente que auia de quedar y los demas cargaron de bastimentos y por su orden mediado setiembre se partieron la uia de çibola siguiendo su general don tristan de arellano quedo en esta nueba uilla con la gente de menos estofa y asi nunca dexo de aber de alli adelante motines y contrastes porque como fue partido el canpo el capitan melchoir dias tomo uiente y çinco hombres de los mas escogidos dexando en su lugar a un diego de alcaraz hombre no bien acondicionado para tener gente debaxo de su mando y el salio en demanda de la costa de la mar entre norte y poniente con guias y abiendo caminado obra de çiēto y sinquenta leguas dieron en una prouinçia de gētes demasiadamente de altos y membrudos ansi como gigantes aunque gente desnuda y que hacia su abitaçion en choças de paja largas a manera de sa hurdas metidas debaxo de tierra que no salia sobre la tierra mas de la paja entraban por la una parte de largo y salian por la otra dormian en una chosa mas de cien personas chicos y grandes lleuaban de peso sobre las cabeças quando se cargauan mas de tres y de quatro quintales biose querer los nr̃os traer un madero para el fuego y no lo poder traer seis hombres y llegar uno de aquellos y leuantarlo en los braços y ponerselo el solo en la cabeça y lleuallo muy liuianamente.

comen pan de mais cosidoso el rescoldo de la senisa tam grandes como hogasas de castilla grandes. para caminar de unas partes a otras por el gran frio sacan un tison en una mano con que se ban calentādo la otra y el cuerpo y ansi lo ban trocando a trechos y por esto a un gran rio que ba por aquella tierra lo nōbran el rio del tison es poderoso rio y tiene de boca mas de dos leguas por alli tenia media legua de trabesia alli tomo lengua el capitā como los nabios auian estado tres jornadas de alli por bajo hacia la mar y llegados adonde los nabios estubieron que era mas de quinçe leguas el rio arriba de la boca del puerto y hallaron en un arbol escripto aqui llego alarcon a el pie de este arbol ay cartas sacaronse las cartas y por ellas bieron el tiempo que estubieron aguardando nuebas de el campo y como alarcon auia dado la buelta desde alli para la nueba españa con los nabios porque no podia correr adelante porque aquella mar era ancō que tornaba a bolber sobre la isla del marques que diçen California y dieron relaçion como la california no era isla sino punto de tierra firme de la buelta de aquel ancon.

uisto esto por el capitan torno a bolber el rio arriba sin ber la mar por buscar bado para pasar a la otra banda para seguir la otra costa y como andubieron cinco o seis jornadas parecioles podrian pasar con balsas y para esto llamaron mucha gente de los de la tierra los quales

querian ordenar de hacer salto en los nños y andaban buscando ocaçion
oportuna y como bieron que querian pasar acudieron a haçer las balsas
con toda prestesa y diligençia por tomar los ansi en el agua y ahogarlos
o dibidos de suerte que no se pudiesen faboreçer ni ayudar y en este
comedio que las balsas se hacian un soldado que auia ydo a campear
bido en un mõte atrabesar gran numero de gente armada que aguarda-
ban a que pasase la gente dio de ello notiçia y secretamente se ençerro
un indio para saber de el la berdad y como le apretasen dixo toda la
orden que tenian ordenada para quando pasasen q̃ era que como ubiesen
pasado parte de los nños y parte fuesen por el rio y parte quedasen por
pasar que los de las balsas procurasen a hogar los que lleuaban y las
demas gente saliese a dar en ambas partes de la tierra y si como tenian
cuerpos y fuerças tubieran discriçion y esfuerço ellos salierã con su
empresa. bisto su intento el capitan hiço matar secretamente el indio
que confeso el hecho y aquella noche se hecho en el rio con una pesga
porque los indios no sintiesen que eran sentidos y como otra dia sintieron el reçelo de los nños mostraronse de guerra hechãdo roçiadas de
flechas pero como los cauallos los començaron a alcançar y las lanças los
lastimaban sin piadad y los arcabuçeros tambien hacian buenos tiros
ubieron de dexar el campo y tomar el monte hasta que no pareçio honbre de ellos bino por alli y ansi paso la gente a buen recaudo siendo los
amigos balseadores y españoles a las bueltas pasando los cauallos a la
par de las balsas donde los dexaremos caminando.

por contar como fue el campo que caminaba para çibola que como
yba caminando por su orden y el general lo auia dexado todo de pax
por do quiera hallaban la gente de la tierra alegre sin temer y que se
dexaban bien mandar y en una prouinçia que se diçe uacapan auia
gran cantidad de tunas que los naturales haçen conserua de ellas en
cantidad y de esta conserua presentaron mucha y como la gente del
campo comio de ella todos cayeron como amodoridos con dolor de
cabeça y fiebre de suerte que si los naturales quisieran hicieran gran
daño en la gente duro esto ueinti y quatro oras naturales despues que
salieron de alli caminando llegaron a chichilticale despues que salierõ
de alli un dia los de la guardia bieron pasar una manada de carneros y
yo los bi y los segui eran de grande cuerpo en demasia el pelo largo los
cuernos muy gruesos y grandes para correr enhıestran el rostro y hechã
los cuernos sobre el lomo corren mucho por tierra agra que no los pudi-
mos alcançar y los ubimos de dexar.

entrando tres jornadas por el despoblado en la riuera de un rio que
esta en unas grandes honduras de barrancas se hallo un cuerno quel
general despues de aber lo uisto lo dexo alli para que los de su canpo
le biesen que tenia de largo una braça y tam gordo por el naçimiento
como el muslo de un hombre en la faieron pareçia mas ser de cabron
que de otro animal fue cosa de ber pasando adelante y a quel canpo
yba una jornada de çibola començo sobre tarde un gran torbellino de
ayre frigidissimo y luego se signio gran lubia de niebe que fue harta

con friçion para la gente de seruiçio el campo camino hasta llegar a
unos peñascos de socareñas donde se llego bien noche y con harto
riesgo de los amigos que como eran de la nueba españa y la mayor
parte de tierras calientes sintieron mucho la frialdad de aquel dia tanto
que ubo harto que haçer otro dia en los reparar y llebar a cauallo yendo los soldados a pie y con este trabajo llego el campo a çibola donde
los aguardaba su general hecho el aposento y alli se torno a jūtar aunque
algunos capitanes y gente faltaua que auian salido a descubrir otras
prouinçias.

Capitulo onçe como don pedro de touar descubrio a tusayan o tutahaco
y don garci lopes de cardenas bio el rio del tison y lo que mas acaecion.

en el entre tanto que las cosas ya dichas pasaron el general franco
uasques como estaba en cibola de pax procuro saber de los de la tierra
que prouincias le cayan en comarca y que ellos diesen noticia a sus
amigos y uecinos como eran benidos a su tierra cristianos y que no
querian otra cosa salbo ser sus amigos y aber notiçia de buenas tierras
que poblar y que los biniesen aber y comunicar y ansi lo hiçieron luego
saber en aquellas partes que se comunicaban y trataban con ellos y
dieron notiçia de una prouinçia de siete pueblos de su misma calidad
aunque estaban algo discordes que no se trataban con ellos esta prouinçia se diçe tusayan esta de cibola ueinte y çinco leguas son pueblos
de altos y gente belicosa entre ellos.

el general auia embiado a ellos a don pedro de touar con desisiete
hombres de a cauallo y tres o quatro peones fue con ellos un fray juan
de padilla frayle françisco que en su mosedad auia sido hombre belicoso
llegados que fueron entraron por la tierra tam secretamente que no
fueron sentidos de ningun honbre la causa fue que entre prouincia y
prouinçia no ay poblados ni caserias ni las gentes salen de sus pueblos
mas de hasta sus heredades en espeçial en aquel tienpo que tenian
noticia de que çibola era ganada por gentes ferosissimas que andaban
en unos animales que comian gentes y entre los que no auian bisto
cauallos era esta notiçia tam grande que les ponia admiraçion y tanto
que la gente de los nros llego sobre noche y pudieron llegar a encubrirse
se debajo de la barranca del pueblo y estar alli oyendo hablar los
naturales en sus casas pero como fue de mañana fueron descubiertos y
se pusieron en orden los de la tierra salieron a ellos bien ordenados de
arcos y rodelas y porras de madera en ala sin se desconsertar y ubo
lugar que las lenguas hablasen con ellos y se les hiçiese requerimientos
por ser gente bien entendida pero con todo esto hacian rayas requiri-
endo que no pasasen los nuestros aquellas rayas hacia sus pueblos que
fuesen porte pasaronse algunas rayas andando hablando con ellos bino
a tanto que uno se ellos de desmesuro y con una porra dio un golpe
a un cauallo en las camas del freno. el fray juan enojado del tiempo
que se mal gastaba con ellos dixo a el capitan en berdad yo no se a que
benimos aca bisto esto dieron santiago y fue tam supito que derribaron
muchos indios y luego fueron desbaratados y huyeron a el pueblo y a

otros no les dieron ese lugar fue tanta la prestesa con que del pueblo
salieron de pax con presentes que luego se mando recoger la gente y que
no se hiciese mas dano el capitan y los que con el se hallaron buscaron
sitio para asentar su real çerca del pueblo y alli se hallaron digo se
apearon dõde llego la gente de pax diciendo que ellos benian a dar la
obidençia por toda la prouinçia y que los queria tener por amigos que
recibiesen aquel presente que les daban que era alguna ropa de algodon
aunque poca por no lo aber por aquella tierra dieron algunos cueros
adobados y mucha harina y piñol y mais y abes de la tierra despues
dieron algunas turquesas aunque pocas aquel dia se recogio la gente de
la tierra y binieron a dar la obidençia y dieron abiertamente sus pueblos
y que entrasen en ellos a tratar comprar y bender y cambiar.

rigese como çibola por ayuntamiento de los mas ançianos tenien sus
gouernadores y capitanes seria lados aqui se tubo notiçia de un gran
rio y que rio abajo a algunas jornadas auia gẽtes muy grandes de cuerpo
grande.

como don pedro de touar no llebo mas comiçion bolbio de alli y dio
esta notiçia al general que luego despacho alla a don garçi lopes de
cardenas con hasta doçe conpañeros para ber este rio que como llego a
tusayan siendo bien reçebido y hospedado de los naturales le dieron
guias para proseguir sus jornadas y salieron de alli cargados de bastimentos por que auian de yr por tierra despoblada hasta el poblado que
los indios deçian que eran mas de ueinte jornadas pues como ubieron
andado ueinte jornadas llegaron a las barrancas del rio que puestos a
el bado de ellas pareçia al otro bordo que auia mas de tres o quatro
leguas por el ayre esta tierra era alta y llena de pinales bajos y encor-
bados frigidissima debajo del norte que con ser en tiempo caliente no se
podia biuir de frio en esta barranca estubieron tres dias buscando la
bajada para el rio que pareçia de lo alto tendria una braçada de trabesia
el agua y por la notiçia de los indios tendria media legua de ancho fue
la baxada cosa inposible porque acabo de estos tres dias pareçiendo
les una parte la menos dificultosa se pusieron a abajar por mas ligeros
el capitan melgosa y un juan galeras y otro conpañero y tadaron
baxando a bista de ellos de los de arriba hasta que los perdieron de
uista los bultos quel biso no los alcansaba aber y bolbieron a ora de las
quatro de la tarde que no pudieron acabar de bajar por grandes difi-
cultades que hallaron porque lo que arriba parecia façil no lo era antes
muy aspero y agro dixeron que auian baxado la terçia parte y que
desde donde llegaron parecia el rio muy grande y que conforme a lo
que bieron era berdad tener la anchura que los indios deçian de lo alto
determinaban unos peñol sillas desgarados de la baranca a el parecer
de un estado de hombre juran los que baxaron que llegaron a ellos que
eran mayores que la torre mayor de seuilla no caminaron mas arrimados
a la barranca de el rio porque no auia agua y hasta alli cada dia se
desbiaban sobre tarde una legua o dos la tierra adentro en busca de
las aguas y como andubiesen otras quatro jornadas las guias dixeron

que no era posible pasar adelante porque no auia agua en tres ni quatro jornadas porque ellos quando caminauan por alli sacaban mugeres cargadas de agua en calabaços y que en aquellas jornadas enterraban los calabaços del agua para la buelta y que lo que caminaban los nuestros en dos dias lo caminaban ellos en uno.

este rio era el del tison mucho mas hacia los nacimientos del que no por donde lo auian pasado melchior dias y su gente estos indios eran de la misma calidad segun despues pareçio desde alli dieron la buelta que no tubo mas efecto aquella jornado y de camino bieron un descolgadero de aguas que baxaban de una peña y supieron de las guias que unos rasimos que colgauan como sinos de christal era sal y fueron alla y cogieron cantidad de ella que trugeron y repartieron quando llegaron en çibola donde por escripto dieron quenta a su general de lo que bieron por que auia ydo con don garçi lopes un pedro de sotomayor que yba por coronista de el campo aquellos pueblos de aquella prouinçia quedaron de paz que nunca mas se biçitaron ni se supo ni procuro buscar otros poblados por aquella uia.

Capitulo doçe como binieron a çibola gentes de cicuye a ber los christianos y como fue her^{do} de aluarado a ber las uacas.

en el comedio que andaban en estos descubrimientos binieron a çibola siertos indios de un pueblo que esta de alli setenta leguas la tierra adentro al oriente de aquella prouincia a quien nombran cicuye benia entre ellos un capitan a quien los nños pusieron por nombre bigotes por que traya los mostachos largos era mançebo alto y bien dispuesto y robusto de rostro este dixo al general como ellos benian a le seruir por la noticia que les auian dado para que se les ofreçiese por amigos y que si auian de yr por su tierra los tubiesen por tales amigos hicieron sierto presente de cueros adobados y rodelas y capaçetes fue reçebido con mucho amor y dio les el general basos de bidrio y quētas margaritas y caxcabeles que los tubieron en mucho como cosa nunca por ellos uista dieron notiçia de uacas que por una que uno de ellos traya pintada en las carnes se saco ser uaca que por los cueros no se podia entender a causa quel pelo era merino y burelado tanto que no se podia saber de que eran aquellos cueros ordeno el general que fuese con ellos hernando de aluarado con ueinte compañeros y ochenta dias de comiçion y quien bolbiese a dar relaçion de lo que hallauan este capitan aluarado prosiguio su jornada y a çinco jornadas llegaron a un pueblo que estaba sobre un peñol deciase acuco era de obra de doçientos hombres de guerra salteadores temidos por toda la tierra y comarca el pueblo era fortissimo porque estaba sobre la entrada del peñol que por todas partes era de peña tajada en tan grande altura que tubiera un arcabuz bien que haçer en hechar una pelota en lo alto del tenia una sola subida de escalera hecha a mano que començaba sobre un repecho que hacia aquella parte haçia la tierra esta escalera era ancha de obra de doçientos escalones hasta llegar a la peña auia otra luego

angosta arrimada a la peña de obra de cien escalones y en el remate de
ella auian de subir por la peña obra de tres estados por agugeros dõde
hincaban las puntas de los pies y se asian con las manos en lo alto auia
una albarrada de piedra seca y grãde que sin se descubrir podian derribar tanta que no fuese poderoso ningun exerçito a les entrar en lo alto
auia espaçio pa sembrar y coger gran cantidad de maix y cisternas para
recoger nieue y agua esta gente salio de guerra abajo en lo llano y no
aprobechaba con ellos ninguna buena raçon haçiendo rayas y queriendo
defender que no las pasasen los nuestros y como bieron que se les dio
un apreton luego dieron la plaça digo la pax antes que se les hiçiese
daño hicieron sus serimonias de pax que llegar a los cauallos y tomar
del sudor y untarse con el y hacer cruçes con los dedos de las manos y
aun que la pax mas figa es trabarse las manos una con otra y esta
guardan estos inbiolablemente dieron gran cantidad de gallos de papada
muy grandes mucho pan y cueros de benado adobados y piñoles y harina
y mais.

de alli en tres jornadas llegaron a una prouinçia que se dice triguex
salio toda de pax biendo que yban con bigotes hombres temido por
todas aquellas prouinçias de alli embio aluarado a dar auiso a el general para que se biniese a inbernar aquella tierra que no poco se holgo
el general con la nueba que la tierra yba mejorando de alli a cinco jornadas llego a cicuyc un pueblo muy fuerte de quatro altos los del pueblo
salieron a recebir a her^{do} de aluarado y a su capitan con muestras de
alegria y lo metieron en el pueblo con atambores y gaitas que alli ay
muchos a manera de pifanos y le hiçieron grãde presente de ropa y turquesas que las ay en aquella tierra en cantidad alli holgaron algunos
dias y tomaron lengua de un indio esclabo natural de la tierra de
aquella parte que ba hacia la florida ques la parte que don fer^{do} de
soto descubrio en lo ultimo la tierra adentro este dio notiçia que no
debiera de grandes poblados llebolo hernando de aluarado por guia
para las uacas y fueron tantas y tales cosas las que dixo de las riqueças
de oro y plata que auia en su tierra que no curaron de buscar las uacas
mas de quanto bieron algunas pocas luego bolbieron por dar a el general la rica notiçia a el indio llamaron turco porque lo pareçia en el
aspecto y a esta sacon el general auia embiado a don garcia lopes de
lopes de cardenas a tiguex con gente a haçer el aposẽto para lleuar alli
a inbernar el campo que a la sason auia llegado de señora y quando
hernando de albarado llego a tiguex de buelta de cicuyc hallo a don
garcia lopes de cardenas y fue neçesario que no pasase adelante y como
los naturales les inportase que biesen digo diesen a donde se aposenta-
sen los españoles fue les forçado desamparar un pueblo y recogerse
ellos a los otros de sus amigos y no llebaron mas que sus personas y
ropas y alli se descubrio notiçia de muchos pueblos debajo del norte que
creo fuera harto mejor seguir aquella uia que no a el turco que fue causa
de todo el mal suseso que ubo.

Capitulo trece como el general llego con poca gente la uia de tutahaco y dexo el campo a don tristan que lo llebo a tiguex.

todas estas cosas ya dichas auian pasado quando don tristan de are-llano llego de señora en cibola y como llego luego el general por noticia que tenia de una prouincia de ocho pueblos tomo treinta hombres de los mas descansados y fue por la uer y de alli tomar la buelta de tiguex con buenas guias que lleuaba y dexo ordenado que como descansase la gente ueinte dias don tristan de arellano saliese con el campo la uia derecha de tiguex y asi siguio su camino donde le acontecio que desde un dia q̄ salieron de un aposento hasta terçero dia a medio dia que bieron una sierra nebada donde fueron a buscar agua no la bebieron ellos ni sus cauallos ni el seruicio pudo soportala por el gran frio aun que con gran trabajo en ocho jornadas llegaron a tutahaco y alli se supo que aquel rio abaxo auia otros pueblos estos salieron de pax son pue-blos de terrados como los de tiguex y del mismo traje salio el general de alli bisitando toda la probinçia el rio arriba hasta llegar a tiguex donde hallo a hernando de aluarado y a el turco que no pocas fueron las alegrias que hiço con tam buena nueba porque deçia que auia en su tierra un rio en tierra llana que tenia dos leguas de ancho a donde auia peçes tan grandes como cauallos y gran numero de canoas grandissi-mas de mas de a ueinte remeros por banda y que lleuaban uelas y que los señores yban a popa sentados debajo de toldos y en la proa una grande aguila de oro deçia mas quel señor de aquella tierra dormia la siesta debajo de un grande arbol donde estaban colgados gran cantidad de caxcabeles de oro que con el ayre le dabā solas deçia mas quel comun seruicio de todos en general era plata labrada y los jarros platos y escu-dillas eran de oro llamaba a el oro Acochis diose le a el presente credito por la eficaçia con que lo deçia y porque le enseñaron joyas de alaton y oliolo y deçia que no era oro y el oro y la plata cognoçia muy bien y de los otros metales no hacia caso de ellos. embio el general a her-nando de albarado otra bez a cicuyc a pedir unos brasaletes de oro que deçia este turco que le tomaron a el tiempo que lo prendieron albarado fue y los del pueblo recibieron como amigo y como pidio los bracaletes negaron los por todas uias diciendo quel turco los engañaba y que men-tia el capitan aluarado biendo que no auia remedio procuro que biniese a su tienda el capitan bigotes y el gouernador y benidos prendio les en cadena los del pueblo lo salieron de guerra hechando flechas y denostando a hernando de albarado diçiendole de honbre que quebrantaba la fee y amistad her^do de albarado partio con ellos a tiguex al general donde los tubieron presos mas de seis meseis despues quã fue el principio de desacreditar la palabra que de alli adelante se les daba de paz como se uera por lo que despues suçedio.

Capitulo catorce como el campo salio de sibola para tiguex y lo que les acaeçio en el camino con niebe.

ya abemos dicho como quando el general salio de çibola dexo man-dado a don tristan de arellano saliese desde a ueinte dias lo qual se hiço

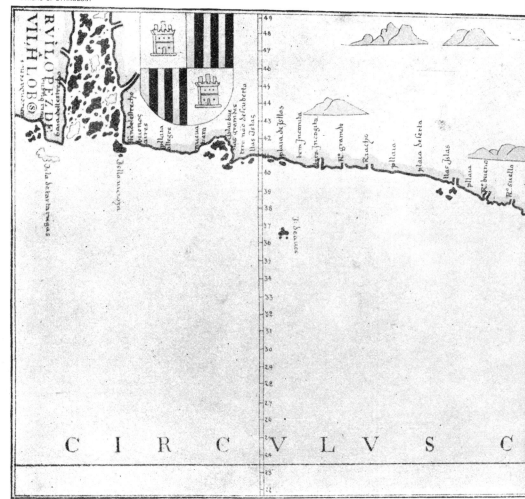

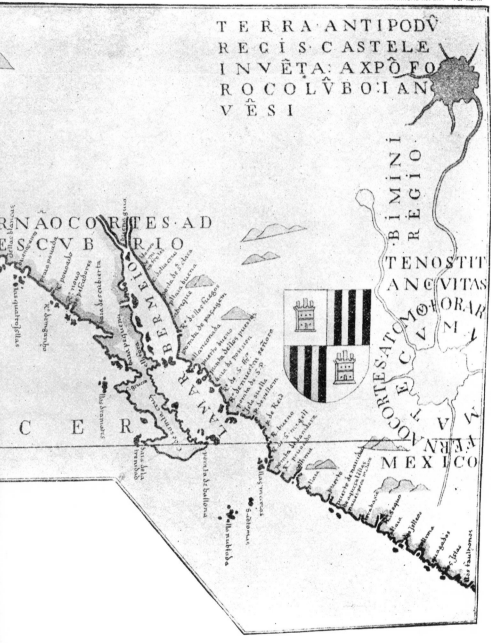

TERRA ANTIPODV
REGIS CASTELE
INVÊTA: AXPÔFO
ROCOLVBO:IAN
VÊSI

BIMINI
REGIO.

TENOSTIT
ANGVITAS
CVMOHORAR
M

RNÃOCORTES·AD
ESCVB·RIO

CER

MEXICO

que como bido que la gente estaba ya descansada y probeydos de bastimentos y ganosos de salir en busca de su general salio con su gente
la buelta de tigues y el primero dia fueron a haçer aposento a un pueblo
de aquella probinçia el mejor mayor y mas hermoso solo este pueblo
tiene casas de siete altos que son casas particulares que siruen en el
pueblo como de fortaleças que son superiores a las otras y salen por
encima como torres y en ellas ay troneras y saeteras para defender
los altos por que como los pueblos no tienen calles y los terrados son
parejos y comunes anse de ganar primero los altos y estas casas mayores es la defença de ellos alli nos començo a nebar y faboreçiose la gente
solas las aues digo alaues del pueblo que salen a fuera unos como balcones con pilares de madera por baxo por que comunmẽte se mandan por
escaleras que suben a aquellos balcones que por baxo no tienen puertas.

como dexo de nebar salío de alli el campo su camino y como ya el
tiempo lo lleuaba que era entrada de diçiembre en diez dias que tardo
el canpo no dexo de nebar sobre tarde y casi todas las noches de suerte
que para haçer los aposentos donde llegaban auian de apalancar un
coldo de niebe y mas no se bio camino empero las guias atino guiaban
cognociendo la tierra ay por toda la tierra sauinas y pinos haciase de
ello grandes hogueras quel humo y calor haçia a la niebe que caya que
se desbiase una braça y dos a la redonda del fuego era nieue seca que
aunque cay medio estado sobre el fardaje no mojaba y con sacudilla
caya y quedaba el hato linpio como caya toda la noche cubria de tal
manera el fardaje y los soldados en sus lechos que si de supito alguien
diera en el campo no biera otra cosa que montones de niebe y los cauallos
aunque fuese medio estado se soportaba y antes daba calor a los que
estaban debajo.

paso el campo por Acuco el gran peñol y como estaban de paz hiçieron
buen hospedaje dando bastimentos y abes aũque ella es poca gente como
tengo dicho a lo alto subieron muchos compañeros por lo ber y los pasos
de la peña con gran dificultad por no lo aber usado porque los naturales
lo suben y bajan tam liberalmente que ban cargados de bastimentos y
las mugeres con agua y parece que no tocan las manos y los nr̄os para
subir auian de dar las armas los unos a los otros por el paso arriba.

desde alli pasaron a tiguex donde fueron bien recebidos y aposentados y la tam buena nueba del turco que no dio poca alegria segun alibia-
ba los trabajos aunque quando el campo llego hallamos aleada aquella
tierra o probincia por ocaçion que para ello ubo que no fue pequeña
como se dira y auian ya los nr̄os quemado un pueblo un dia antes que el
campo llegase y bolbian a el aposento.

*Capitulo quinçe como se alço tiguex y el castigo que en ellos ubo sin que
lo ubiese en el causador.*

dicho sea como el general llego a tiguex donde hallo a don garci lopes
de cardenas y a hernando de albarado y como lo torno a embiar a cicuye
y truxo preso a el capitan bigotes y a el gouernador del pueblo que

era un hombre ançiano de esta prision los tiguex no sintieron bien juntose con esto q̃ el general quiso recoger alguna ropa para repartir a la gente de guerra y para esto hiço llamar a un indio principal de tiguex que ya se tenia con el mucho conosimiento y conbersaçion a quien los nuestros llamauan juan aleman por un juan aleman que estaba en mexico a quien deçian pareçer a queste hablo el general diciendo que le probeyese de tresientas pieças de ropa o mas que auia menester para dar a su gente el dixo que aquello no era a el haçer lo sino a los gouernadores y que sobre ello era menester entrar en consulta y repartirse por los pueblos y que era menester pedir lo particularmente a cada pueblo por si ordenolo ansi el general y que lo fuesen a pedir siertos hombres señalados de los que con el estaban y como eran doçe pueblos que fuesen unos por la una parte del rio y otros por la otra y como fuese de manos aboca no les dieron lugar de se consultar ni tratar sobre ello y como llegaria a el pueblo luego se les pedia y lo abian de dar porque ubiese lugar de pasar adelante y con esto no tenian mas lugar de quitarse los pellones de ençima y darlos hasta que llegase el numero que se les pedia y algunos soldados de los que alli yban que los cogedores les daban algunas mantas o pellones sino eran tales y bian algun indio con otra mejor trocabanse la sin tener mas respecto ni saber la calidad del que despojaban que no poco sintieron esto allende de lo dicho del pueblo del aposento salio un sobre saliente que por su honra no le nombrare y fue a otro pueblo una legua de alli y biendo una muger hermosa llamo a su marido que le tubiese el cauallo de rienda en lo bajo y el subio a lo alto y como el pueblo se mandaba por lo alto creyo el indio que yba a otra parte y detenido alli ubo sierto rumor y el bajo y tomo su cauallo y fuese el indio subio y supo que auia forçado o querido forçar a su muger y juntamente con las personas de calidad del pueblo se uino a quexar diçiendo que un hombre le auia forçado a su muger y conto como auia pasado y como el general hiço pareçer todos los soldados y personas que con el estaban y el indio no lo conoçio o por aberse mudado la ropa o por alguna otra ocaçion que para ello ubo pero dixo que conoçeria el cauallo porq̃ lo tubo de rienda fue lleuado por las cauallerisas y hallo un cauallo enmantado hobero y dixo que su dueño de aquel cauallo era el dueño nego biendo quel no abia conoçido y pudo ser que se herro en el cauallo finalmente el se fue sin aber en mienda de lo que pedia otra dia uino un indio del canpo que guardaba los cauallos herido y huyendo diciendo que le auian muerto un compañero y que los indios de la tierra se llebarian los cauallos ante cogidos hacia sus pueblos fueron a recoger los cauallos y faltaron muchos y siete mulas del general.

otro dia fue don garci lopes de cardenas a ber ¿os pueblos y tomar de ellos lengua y hallo los pueblos serrados con palenques y gran grita dẽtro corriendo los cauallos como en coso de toros y flechandolos y todos de guerra no pudo haçer cosa por que no salieron a el campo que como son pueblos fuertes no les pudieron enojar luego ordeno el general que don garçi lopes de cardenas fuese a çercar un pueblo con toda la

demas gente y este pueblo era donde se hiço el mayor daño y es donde
acaeçio lo de la india fueron muchos capitanes que auian ydo delante
con el general como fue juan de saldiuar y barrio nuebo y diego lopes
y melgosa tomaron a los indios tam de sobresalto que luego les ganaron
los altos con mucho riesgo porque les hirieron muchos de los nuestros
por saeteras que hacian por de dentro de las casas estubieron los nuestros en lo alto a mucho riesgo el dia y la noche y parte de otro dia haçiendo buenos tiros de ballestas y arcabuçes la gente de a cauallo en el
campo con muchos amigos de la nueba españa y daban por los sotanos
que auian aportillado grandes humasos de suerte que pidieron la paz
hallaronse aquella parte pablos de melgosa y diego lopes ueinti quatro
de seuilla y respondieronles cõ las mismas señales que ellos haçian de
paz que es haçer la cruz y ellos luego soltaron las armas y se dieron
a md llebabanlos a la tienda de don garçia el qual segun se dixo no
supo de la paz y creyo que de su boluntad se daban como hombres
benzidos y como tenia mandado del general que no los tomase a uida
porque se hiciese castigo y los demas temiesen mando que luego hin-
casen doçientos palos para los quemar biuos no ubo quien le dixese de
la paz que les auian dado que los soldados tan poco lo sabian y los que
la dieron se lo callaron que no hiçieron caso de ello pues como los enemigos bieron que los yban atando y los començaban a quemar obra
de çien hombres que estaban en la tienda se començaron a haçer fuertes
y defenderse con lo que estaba dentro y con palos que salian a tomar
la gente nuestra de a pie dan en la tiẽda por todas partes estocadas
que los hacian desmanparar la tienda y dio luego la gente de a cauallo
en ellos y como la tierra era llana no les quedo hombre a uida sino
fueron algunos que se auian quedado escondidos en el pueblo que huyeron a quella noche y dieron mandado por toda la tierra como no les
guardaron la paz que les dieron que fue despues harto mal y como esto
fue hecho y luego les nebase desampararon el pueblo y bolbieronse a el
aposento a el tiẽpo que llegaba el campo de cibola.

*Capitulo desiseis como se puso çerco a tiguex y se gano y lo que mas
acontencio mediante el cerco.*

como ya e contado quando acabaron de gañar aquel pueblo començo
a nebar en aquella tierra y nebo de suerte que en aquellos dos meses no
se pudo haçer nada salbo yr por los caminos a les abisar que biniesen
de pax y que serian perdonados dandoles todo seguro a lo qual ellos respondieron que no se fiarian de quien no sabia guardar la fe que daban
que se acordasen que tenian preso a bigotes y que en el pueblo quemado
no les guardaron la paz fue uno de los que fueron a les haçer estos
requerimientos don garcia lopes de cardenas que salio con obra de
treinta compañeros un dia y fue a el pueblo de tiguex y a hablar con
juan aleman y aunque estaban de guerra binieron a hablalle y le dixeron que si queria hablar con ellos q̃ se apease y se llegauan a el a hablar de
paz y que se desbiase la gente de a cauallo y harian apartar su gente

y llegaron a el el juan aleman y otro capitan del pueblo y fue hecho
ansi como lo pedian y a que estaba çerca de ellos dixeron que ellos no
trayan armas que se las quitase don garcia lopes lo hiço por mas los
asegurar cõ gana que tenia de los traer de paz y como llego a ellos el
juan aleman lo bino a abraçar en tanto los dos que con el benian sacaron
dos maçetas que secretamente trayan a las espaldas y dieronle sobre
la çelada dos tales golpes que casi lo aturdieron hallaron dos soldados
de a cauallo çerca que no se auian querido apartar aunque les fue mandado y arremetieron con tanta presteça que lo sacaron de entre sus
manos aunque no puedieron enojar a los enemigos por tener la acogida
çerca y grandes rosiadas de flechas que luego binieron sobre ellos y a
el uno le atrabesaron el cauallo por las narises la gente de acauallo llego
toda de tropel y sacaron a su capitan de la priesa sin poder dañar a los
enemigos antes salieron muchos de los nros mal heridos y asi se retira-
ron quedando algunos haçiendo rostro don garçia lopes de cardenas
con parte de la gente paso a otro pueblo que estaba media legua adelante porque en estos dos lugares se auia recogido toda la mas gente de
aquellos pueblos y como de los requerimientos que les hiçieron no hiçieron caso ni de dar la paz antes con grandes gritos tiraban flechas de
lo alto y se bolbio a la compañia que auia quedado haciendo rostro a
el pueblo de tiguex entonçes salieron los del pueblo en gran cantidad
los nros a media rienda dieron muestra que huyan de suerte que sacaron
los enemigos a lo llano y rebulbieron sobre ellos de manera que se tendieron algunos de los mas señalados los demas se recogieron al pueblo
y a lo alto y ansi se bolbio este capitan a el aposento.

el general luego como esto paso ordeno delos yr açercar y salio un
dia con su gente bien ordenada y con algunas escalas llegado asento su
real junto a el pueblo y luego dieron el combate pero como los enemigos
auia muchos dias que se pertrechaban hecharon tanta piedra sobre los
nros que a muchos tendieron en tierra y hirieron de flechas çerca de
çien hombres de que despues murieron algunos por mala cura de un
mal surugano que yba en el campo el çerco duro sinquenta dias en los
quales algunas ueces se les dieron sobresaltos y lo que mas les aquexo
fue que no tenian agua y hiçieron dentro del pueblo un poso de gran-
dissima hondura y no pudieron sacar agua antes se les derrumbo a el
tiempo que lo hacian y les mato treinta personas murieron de los çerca-
dos doçientos hombres de dentro en los combates y un dia que se les
dio un combate recio mataron de los nros a francisco de obando capitan
y maestre de campo que auia sido todo el tiempo que don garcia lopes
de cardenas andubo en los descubrimientos ya dichos y a un francisco
de pobares buen hidalgo a francisco de obando metieron en el pueblo
que los nros no lo pudieron defender q̃ no poco se sintio por ser como era
persona señalada y por si tam honrado afable y bien quisto que era
marauilla antes que se acabase de ganar un dia llamaron a habla y
sabida su demanda fue deçir que tenian cognoçido que las mugeres ni
a los niños no haciamos mal que querian dar sus mugeres y hijos por

que les gastaban el agua no se pudo acabar con ellos que se diesen de paz
diçiendo que no les guardaria la palabra y asi dieron obra de çien personas de niños y mugeres que no quisieron salir mas y mientras las
dieron estubieron los nr̃os a cauallo en ala delante del pueblo don lope de
urrea a cauallo y sin çelada andaba reçibiendo en los braços los niños y
niñas y como ya no quisieron dar mas el don lope les inportunaba que
se diesen de pax haçiendo les grandes promeças de seguridad ellos le
dixeron que se desbiase que no era su uoluntad de se fiar de gente que
no guardaba la amistad ni palabra que daban y como no se quisiese
desbiar salio uno con un arço a flechar y con una flecha y amenasolo
con ella que se la tiraria sino se yba de alli y por boçes que le dieron
que se pusiese la çelada no quiso diçiendo que mientras alli estubiese
no le harian mal y como el indio bido que no se queria yr tiro y hincole
la flecha par de las manos de el cauallo y en arco luego otra y torno le
a deçir que se fuese sino que le tirarian de beras el don lope se puso su
çelada y paso ante paso se uino a meter entre los de a cauallo sin que
recibiese enojo de ellos y como le bieron que ya estaba en salbo con
gran grita y alarido comencaron arroçiar flecheria el general no quiso
que por a quel dia se les diese bateria por ber si los podian traer por
alguna uia de paz lo qual ellos jamas quisieron.

　　desde a quinçe dias determinaron de salir una noche y ansi lo
hicieron y tomando en medio las mugeres salieron a el quarto de la
modorra uelauan aquel quarto quarenta de a cauallo y dando aclarma
los del quartel de don rodrigo maldonado dieron en ellos los enemigos
derribaron un español muerto y un cauallo y hirieron a otros pero
ubieron los de romper y haçer matança en ellos hasta que retirandose
dieron consigo en el rio que yba corriente y frigidissimo y como la gente
del real acudio presto fueron pocos los que escaparon de muertos o
heridos otro dia pasaron el rio la gente del real y hallaron muchos
heridos que la gran frialdad los auia deribado en el campo y trayan los
para curar y siruirse de ellos y ansi se acabo aquel çerco y se gano el
pueblo aun que algunos que quedaron en el pueblo se rreçibieron en un
barrio y fueron tomados en pocos dias.

　　el otro pueblo grande mediãte de çerco le auian ganado dos capitanes
que fueron don diego de gueuara y juº de saldibar que yendo les una
madrugada a echar una çelada para coger en ella sierta gente de guerra
que acostumbraba a salir cada mañana a haçer muestra por poner algun
temor en nr̃o real las espias que teniã puestas para quando los biesen
benir bieron como saliã gentes y caminaban haçia la tierra salieron de
la çelada y fueron para el pueblo y bieron huir la gente y siguieron la
haciendo en ellos matança como de esto se dio mandado salio gente del
real que fueron sobre el pueblo y lo saquearon prēdiendo toda la gente
que en el hallaron en que ubo obra de çien mugeres y niños acabose este
çerco en fin de marco del año de quarenta y dos en el qual tiempo acae-
çieron otras cosas de que podria dar notiçia que por no cortar el hilo
las he dexado pero deçir sean agora porque conbienese sepan para entender lo de adelante.

Capitulo desisiete como binieron a el campo mensajeros del ualle de señora
y como murio el capitan melchior dias en la jornada de tizon.

ya diximos como melchior dias el capitan auia pasado en balsas el rio
del tiçon para proseguir adelante el descubrimiento de aquella costa
pues a el tiempo que se acabo de ercollegaron mensajeros a el caubo de
la uilla de san hieronimo con cartas de diego de alarcon que auia quedado alli en lugar del melchior dias trayan nuebas como melchior dias
auia muerto en la demanda que lleuaba y la gente se auia buelto sin
ber cosa de lo que deseaban y paso el caso desta manera.

como ubieron pasado el rio caminaron en demanda de la costa que
por alli ya daba la buelta sobre el sur o entre sur y oriente porque
aquel ancon de mar entra derecho al norte y este rio entre en el remate
del ancon trayendo sus corrientes debaxo del norte y corre a el sur yedo
como yban caminando dieron en unos medaños de çenisa ferbiente que
no podia nadie entrar a ellos porque fuera entrarse a hogar en la mar
la tierra que hollaban temblaba como tenpano que pareçia que estaban
debaxo algunos lagos pareçio cosa admirable que asi herbia la çenisa en
algunas partes que pareçia cosa infernal y desbiando se de aqui por el
peligro que pareçia que llebauan y por la falta del agua un dia un lebrel
que lleuaba un soldado antojo se le dar tras de unos carneros que
llebauan para bastimento y como el capitan lo bido arronjole la lança
de enquentro yendo corriendo y hincola en tierra y no pudiendo detener
el cauallo fue sobre la lança y enclabose la por el muslo que le salio el
hierro a la ingle y le rompio la begiga bisto esto los soldados dieron la
buelta con su capitan siendo teniendo cada dia refriegas con los indios
que auian quedado rebelados bibio obra de ueinte dias que por le traer
pasaron gran trabajo y asi bolbieron hasta que murio con buena-orden
sin perder un honbre ya yban saliendo de lo mas trabajoso llegados
a señora hiço alcaraz los mensajeros ya dichos haciendolo saber y como
algunos soldados estaban mal asentados y procuraban algunos motines
y como auia sentenciado a la horca a dos que despues se le auian huydo
de la priçion.

el general bisto esto enbio a quella uilla a don pedro de touar para
que entresacase alguna gente y para que llebase consigo mensajeros
que embiaba a el uisorey don Antonio de mendoça con recaudos de lo
aconteçido y la buena nueba del turco.

don pedro de touar fue y llegado alla hallo que auian los naturales de
aquella probinçia muerto con una flecha de yerba a un soldado de una
muy pequeña herida en una mano sobre esto auian ydo alla algunos
soldados y no fueron bien recebidos don pedro de tobar embio a diego de
alcaraz con gente aprender a los prinçipales y señores de un pueblo que
llaman el ualle de los uellacos que esta en alto llegado alla los prendieron
y presos pareçio le a diego de alcaraz de los soltar a trueque de que
diesen algun hilo y ropa y otras cosas de que los soldados tenian necesidad biendose sueltos alsarose de guerra y subieron a ellos y como
estaban fuertes y tenian yerba mataron algunos españoles y hirieron
otros que despues murieron en el camino bolbiendose retirandose para

su uilla y sino lleuaran consigo amigos de los coraçones lo pasaron peor
bolbieron a la uilla dexando muertos desisiete soldados de la yerba que
con pequeña herida morian rabiando rompiendose las carnes con un
pestelencial hedor inconportable bisto por don pedro de touar el daño
pareçiendoles que no quedaban seguros en aquella uilla la paso quarenta
leguas mas haçia çibola al ualle del suya donde los dexaremos por contar
lo que a bino a el general con el campo despues del cerco de tiguex.

*Capitulo desiocho como el general procuro dexar asentada la tierra para ir
en demanda de quisuira donde deçia el turco auia el prinçipio de la riqueça.*

mediante el çerco de tiguex el general quiso yr a cicuye llebando consigo a el gouernador para lo poner en libertad con promesas que quando
saliese para quiuira daria libertad a bigotes y lo dexaria en su pueblo y
como llego a cicuye fue reçibido de paz y entro en el pueblo con algunos
soldados ellos reçibieron a su gouernador con mucho amor y fiesta bisto
que ubo el pueblo y hablado a los naturales dio la buelta para su canpo
quedando cicuye de paz con esperança de cobrar su capitan bigotes.

acabado que fue el çerco como ya abemos dicho embio un capitan a
chia un buen pueblo y de mucha gente que auia embiado a dar la
obidençia que estaba desbiado del rio al poniente quatro leguas y
hallaronle de paz a qui se dieron aguardar quatro tiros de bronçe ques-
taban mal acondiçionados tambien fueron a quirix probincia de siete
pueblos seis compañeros y en el primer pueblo que seria de çien ueçinos
huyeron que no osaron a esperar a los nros y los fueron atajar arrienda
suelta y los bolbieron a el pueblo a sus casas con toda seguridad y de
alli abisaron a los demas pueblos y los aseguraron y asi poco a poco se
fue asegurando toda la comarca en tanto quel rio se deshelaba y se
dexaba badear para dar lugar a la jornada aunque los doçe pueblos de
tiguex nunca en todo el tiempo que por alli estubo el campo se poblo
ninguno por seguridad ninguna que se les diese.

y como el rio fue deshelado que lo auia estado casi quatro meses que
se pasaba por ençima del yelo a cauallo ordenose la partida para
quibira donde decia el turco que auia algun oro y plata aunque no tanto
como en Arche [Arehe?] y los guaes ya auia algunos del campo sospe-
chosos del turco porque mediante el cerco tenia cargo del un español que
se llamaua seruantes y este español juro con solenidad que auia bisto a
el turco hablar en una olla de agua con el demonio y que teniendolo el
debaxo de llaue que nadie podia hablar con el le auia preguntado el
turco a el que a quien auian muerto de los cristianos los de tiguex y el
le dixo que a no nadie y el turco le respondio mientes que çinco christianos an muerto y a un capitan y que el çeruantes biendo que deçia
berdad se lo conçedio por saber del quien se lo auia dicho y el turco le
dixo quel lo sabia por si y que para aquello no auia neçesidad que
nadie se lo dixese y por esto lo espio y bio hablar con el demonio en la
olla como e dicho.

con todo esto se hiço alarde para salir de tiguex a este tiempo llegaron
gentes de cibola a ber a el general y el general les encargo el buen trata-

miento de los españoles que biniesen de señora con don pedro de touar
y les dio cartas que le diesen a don pedro en que le daba abiso de lo
que debia de haçer y como abia de yr en busca del campo y que hallaria
cartas debajo de las cruçes en las jornadas que el campo abia de haçer
salio el campo de tiguex a çinco de mayo la buelta de cicuye que como
tengo dicho son ueinte y cinco jornadas digo leguas de alli lleuando de
alli a bigotes llegado alla les dio a su capitan que ya andaba suelto con
guardia el pueblo se holgo mucho con el y estubieron de paz y dieron
bastimentos y bigotes y el gouernador dieron a el general un mancebete
que se deçia xabe natural de quiuira para que del se informasen de
la tierra este deçia que abia oro y plata pero no tanto como deçia el
turco toda uia el turco se afirmaua y fue por guia y asi salio el campo
de alli.

*Capitulo desinueue como salieron en demanda de quiuira y lo que aconte-
cio en el camino.*

salio el campo de cicuye dexando el pueblo de paz y a lo que pareçio
contento y obligado a mantener la amistad por les aber restituydo su
gouernador y capitan y caminando para salir a lo llano que esta pasada
toda la cordillera a quatro dias andados de camino dieron en un rio de
gran corriente hondo que baxaba de hacia cicuye y a queste se puso
nombre el rio de cicuye detubieron se aqui por haçer puente para le pasar
acabose en quatro dias con toda diligençia y prestesa hecha paso todo
el campo y ganados por ella y a otras diez jornadas dieron en unas
racherias de gente alarabe que por alli son llamados querechos y auia
dos dias que se auian uisto uacas esta gente biuen en tiendas de cueros
de uacas adobados andan tras las uaças haçiendo carne estos aun que
bieron nrõ campo no hiçieron mudamiento ni se alteraron antes salieron
de sus tiendas a ber esentamente y luego binieron a hablar con la auanguardia y dixeron que se a el campo y el general hablo con ellos y como
ya ellos auian hablado con el turco que yba en la auanguardia cõfor-
maron con el en quanto deçia era gente muy entendida por señas que
pareçiã que lo decian y lo daban tan bien a entender que no auia mas
necesidad de interprete estos dixeron que baxando haçia do sale el sol
auia un rio muy grande y que yria por la riuera del por poblados no-
uenta dias sin quebrar de poblado en poblado deçian quese decia lo
primero del poblado haxa y que el rio era de mas de una legua de ancho
y que auia muchas canoas estos salieron de alli otro dia con harrias de
perros en que llebabã sus aberes desde a dos dias que todauia caminaba
el campo a el rumbo que auian salido de lo poblado que era entre norte
y oriente mas haçia el norte se bieron otros querechos rancheados y
grande numero de uacas que ya pareçia cosa increibble estos dieron
gradissima notiçia de poblados todo a el oriente de donde nos hallamos
a qui se quebro don garçia un braço y se perdio un español que salio a
casa y no aserto a boluer al real por ser la tierra muy llana deçia el
turco que auia a haya una o dos jornadas el general embio adelante a

el capitan diego lopes a la ligera con diez compañeros dandole rumbo
por una guia de mar haçia adonde salia el sol que caminase dos dias a
toda priesa y descubriese a haxa y bolbiese a se topar con el canpo otro
dia salio por el mesmo rumbo y fue tanto el ganado que se topo que los
que yban en la auanguardia cogierō por delante un gran numero de toros
y como huyan y unos a otros serrenpugaban dieron en una barranca y
cayo tanto ganado dentro que la emparejaron y el demas ganado paso
por ençima la gēte de a cauallo que yba en pos de ellos cayeron sobre
el ganado sin saber lo que haçian tres cauallos de los que cayeron ensillados y enfrenados se fueron entre las bacas que no pudieron mas ser
abidos.

Como a el general le parecio que seria ya de buelta diego lopes hiço
que seis compañeros siguisen una ribera arriba de un pequeño rio y
otros tantos la riuera abajo y que se mirase por el rastro de los cauallos
en las entradas o las salidas del rio porque por la tierra no es posible hallarse rastro porque la yerua en pisandola se torna a leuantar
hallose por donde auian ydo y fue bentura que a las bueltas auian ydo
indios del campo en busca de fruta una gran legua de donde se hallo
rastro y toparon con ellos y ansi bajaron el rio abajo a el real y dieron
por nueua a el general que en ueinte leguas que auian andado no auian
uisto otra cosa sino uacas y çielo yba en el campo otro indio pintado
natural de quiuira que se deçia sopete este indio siempre dixo que el
turco mentia y por esto no haçian caso del y aunque en esta saçon
tambien lo deçia como los querechos auian informado con el y el y sopete
no era creydo.

desde aqui embio el general delante a don rodrigo maldonado con su
compañia el qual camino quatro dias y llego a una barranca grande
como las de colima y hallo en lo bajo de ella gran rancheria de gente
por aqui auia atrabesado cabeça de uaca y dorantes aqui presētaron a
don rodrigo un monton de cueros adobados y otras cosas y una tienda
tan grande como una casa en alto lo qual mando que asi la guardasen
hasta quel campo llegase y embio cōpañeros que guiasen el campo haçia
aquella parte porque no se perdiesen aunque auian ydo haçiendo mojones
de guesos y boñigas para que el campo se siguiese y desta manera
se guiaba ya el campo tras la abanguardia.

llego el general con su campo y como bio tan gran multitud de
cueros penso los repartir cō la gente y hiço poner guardas para que
mirasen por ellos pero como la gente llego y bieron los companeros que
el general embiaba algunos hombres particulares con señas para que
les diesen las guardas algunos cueros y los andaban a escoger enojados
de que no se repartia cō orden dan saco mano y en menos de quarto de
ora no dexaron sino el suelo limpio.

los naturales que bieron aquello tambien pusieron las manos en la obra
las mugeres y algunos otros quedaron llorando porque creyeron que no
les auian de tomar nada sino bendeçirse lo como auian hecho cabeça de
uaca y dorantes quando por alli pasaron aqui se hallo una india tam

blanca como muger de castilla saluo que tenia labrada la barua como
morisca de berberia que todas se labran en general de aquella manera
por alli se ahogolan los ojos.

*Capitulo ueinte como cayeron grandes piedras en el campo y como se
descubrio otra barranca donde se dibidio el campo en dos partes.*

estando descansando el campo en esta barranca que abemos dicho
una tarde començo un torbellino con grandissimo ayre y graniço y en
pequeño espaçio bino tam grande multitud de piedra tam grandes como
escudillas y mayores y tam espesas como lubia que en parte cubrieron
dos y tres palmos y mas de tierra y uno dexo el cauallo digo que ningun
cauallo ubo que no se solto sino fueron dos o tres que acudieron a los
tener negros enpabesados y conseladas y rrodelas que todos los demas
llebo por delante hasta pegallos con la barranca y algunos subio donde
con grã trabajo se tornaron abajar y si como los tomo alli dentro fuera
en lo llano de arriba quedara el campo a gran rriesgo sin cauallos que
muchos no se pudieran cobrar rrompio la piedra muchas tiendas y abollo
muchas çeladas y lastimo muchos cauallos y quebro toda la losa del
canpo y calabaços que no puso poca neçesidad porque por alli no ay
losa ni se haçe ni calabaços ni se siembra maiz ni comen pan salbo carne
cruda o mal asada y fructas.

desde alli embio el general a descubrir y dieron en otras rancherias
Alexeres   a quatro jornadas a manera de alixares era tierra muy poblada
adonde auia muchos frisoles y siruelas como las de castilla y
parrales duraban estos pueblos de rancherías tres jornadas desiase cona
desde aqui salieron con el campo algunos teyas porque asi se deçian
aquellas gentes y caminaron con sus harrias de perros y mugeres y hijos
hasta la prostera jornada de las otras donde dieron guias para pasar
adelante a donde fue el canpo a una barranca grande estas guias no las
dexaban hablar con el turco y no hallauan las notiçias que de antes
deçian que quiuira era hacia el norte y que no hallauamos buena derrota
con esto se començo a dar credito a ysopete y ansi llego el campo a la
prostera barrãca que era una legua de borbo a bordo y un pequeño rio
en lo bajo y un llano lleno de arboleda con mucha uba morales y rosales
que es fruta que la ay en françia y sirue de agraz en esta barranca la auiã
madura abia nueses y galinas de la calidad de las de la nueba españa
y siruelas como las de castilla y en cantidad en este camino se bio a un
teya de un tiro pasar un toro por ambas espaldas que un arcubuz tiene
bien que haçer es gēte bien entendida y las mugeres bien tratadas y de
berguença cubren todas sus carnes traen çapatos y borseguiez de cuero
adobado traen mantas las mugeres sobre sus faldellines y mangas cogi-
das por las espaldas todo de cuero y unos como sanbenitillos con rapasejos que llegan a medio muslo sobre los faldellines.

en esta barranca holgo el campo muchos dias por buscar comarca
hicieronse hasta aqui treinta y siete jornadas de camino de a seis y de
a siete leguas porque se daba cargo a quien fuese tasanda y un con

tando por pasos deçian que auian a el poblado do doçientas y sinquenta
leguas bisto ya y cognoçido por el general fran^co uasques como hasta
alli auian andado engañados por el turco y que faltauan los bastimentos
a el campo y que por alli no auia tierra dõde se pudiesen probeer llamo
a los capitanes y alferes a junta para acordar lo que les paresiese se
debiese haçer y de acuerdo de todos fue quel general contreinta de a
cauallo y media doçena de peones y fuese en demanda de quiuira y
que dõ tristan de arellano bolbiese con todo el campo la buelta de tiguex
sabido esto por la gente del canpo y como ya se sabia lo acordado supli-
caron de ello a su general y que no los dexase de lleuar adelante que
todos querian morir con el y no bolber atras esto no aprobecho aunque
el general les conçedio que les embiaria mensajeros dentro de ocho dias
si cõbiniese seguirle o no y con esto se partio con las guias que lleuaba
y con ysopete el turco yba arrecando en cadena.

*Capitulo ueinte y uno como el campo bolbio a tiguex y el general llego a
quiuira.*

partio el general de la barranca con las guias que los teyas le auian
dado hiço su maestre de campo a el ueinte y quatro diego lopes y llebo
de la gẽte que le pareçio mas escogida y de mejores cauallos el canpo quedo con alguna esperança que embiaria por el general y tornaron se lo a
embiar a suplicar a el general con dos hombres de a cauallo a la ligera
y por la posta.　el general llego digo que se le huyeron las guias en las
primeras jornadas y ubo de bolber diego lopes por guias a el campo y
con mandado quel cãpo bolbiese a tiguex a buscar bastimentos y a aguardar a el general dieronle otras guias que les dieron los teyas de boluntad aguardo el campo sus mensajeros y estubo alli quinçe dias haçiendo
carnaje de bacas para lleuar tubose por quenta que se mataron en estos
quinse dias quinientos toros era cosa increyble el numero de los que
auia sin bacas perdiose en este comedio mucha gente de los que salian
a caça y en dos ni tres dias no tornaban a bolber a el campo andando
desatinados a una parte y a otra sin saber bolber por donde auian ydo
y con aber aquella barranca que arriba o abaxo auian de atinar y como
cada noche se tenia quenta con quien faltaua tirauan artilleria y tocauan
trompetas y a tambores y haçian grandes hogaredas y algunos se hallaron tam desbiados y abian desatinado tanto que todo esto no les apro-
bechaua nada aunque a otros les balio el remedio era tornar adonde
mataban el ganado y haçer una uia a una parte y a otra hasta que daban
con la barranca o topaban con quien los encaminaua es cosa de notar
que como la tierra es tam llana en siendo medio dia como an andado
desatinados en pos de la caça a una parte y a otra sean de estar cabe la
caça quedos hasta que decline el sol para ber a que rumbo an de bolber
a donde salieron y aun estos auian de ser hombres entendidos y los que
no lo eran se auian de encomendar a otros.

el general siguio sus guias hasta llegar a quiuira en que gasto quarenta y ocho dias de camino por la grande cayda que auian hecho sobre

la florida y fue reçebido de paz por las guias que lleuaba preguntaron
a el turco que porque auia mētido y los auia guiado tam abieso dixo que
su tierra era haçia aquella parte y que allende de aquello los de cicuye
le auian rogado que los truxese perdidos por los llanos por que faltando
les el bastimento se muriesen los cauallos y ellos flacos quando bolbiesen los podrian matar sin trabajo y bengarse de lo que auian hecho
y que por esto los abia desrumbado creyendo que no supieran caçar ni
mantenerse sin maiz y que lo del oro que no sabia adonde lo auia esto
dixo ya como desesperado y que se hallaba corrido que auain dado credito a el ysopete y los auia guiado mejor que no el y temiendose los que
alli yban que no diese algun abiso por donde les biniese algun daño le
dieron garrote de que el ysopete se holgo porque siēpre solia deçir que
el ysopete era un bellaco y que no sabia lo que se decia y siempre le
estorban ban que no hablase con nadie no se bio entre aquellag ente
oro ni plata ni noticia de ello el señor traya al cuello una patena de
cobre y no la tenia en poca.

los mensajeros quel campo embio en pos del general bolbieron como
dixe y luego como no truxeron otro recaudo que el que el ueinti quatro
auia dicho el campo salio de la barranca la buelta de los teyas a donde
tomaron guias que los bolbiesen por mas derecho camino ellas las dieron
de boluntad porque como es gente que no para por aquellas tierras en
pos del ganado todo lo saben guiaban desta manera luego por la mañana
mirabā a donde salia el sol y tomaban el rumbo que auian de tomar y
tiraban una flecha y antes de llegar a ella tirauan otra por ençima y desta
manera yban todo el dia hasta las aguas adonde se auia de haçer jornada
y por este orden lo que se auia andado a la yda en treinta y siete jornadas se bolbio en ueinte y çinco caçādo en el camino uacas hallaronse
en este camino muchas lagunas de sal que la auia en gran cantidad auia
sobre el agua tablones della mayores que mesas de quatro y de çinco
dedos de grueso debajo del agua a dos y tres palmos sal en grano mas
sabrosa que la de los tablones por que esta amargaba un poco era cris-
talina auia por aquellos llanos unos animales como hardillas en gran
numero y mucha suma de cueuas de ellas uino en esta buelta a tomar el
campo el rio de cicuyc mas de treinta leguas por bajo de ella digo de la
puente que se auia hecho a la yada y subiose por el arriba que en general casi todas sus riueras tenian rosales que son como ubas moscateles
en el comer naçen en unas uaras delgadas de un estado tiene la oja como
peregil auia ubas en agraz y mucho uino y oregano deçian las guias que
se juntaba este rio con el de tiguex mas de ueinte jornadas de alli y
que boluian sus corrientes a el oriente creese que ban a el poderoso rio
del espiritu santo que los de don hernando de soto descubrieron en la
florida en esta jornada a la yda se hundio una india labrada a el capitan juan de saldibar y fue las barrancas abajo huyendo que reconoçio la
tierra por que en tiguex donde se ubo era esclaua esta india ubieron a
las manos siertos españoles de los de la florida que auian entrado descubriendo hacia aquella parte yo les oy deçir quādo bolbieron a la nueba

españa que les auia dicho la india que auia nuebe dias que se auia huydo
de otros y que nombro capitanes por donde se debe creer que no
llegamos lejos de lo que ellos descubrieron aunque dicen que estaban
entonçes mas de dosientas leguas la tierra adentro creese que tiene la
tierra de trabesia por aquella parte mas de seicientas leguas de mar a
mar.

pues como digo el rio arriba fue el campo hasta llegar a el pueblo de
cicuye el qual se hallo de guerra que no quisieron mostrarse de paz
ni dar ningun socorro de bastimento de alli fueron a tiguex que ya
algunos pueblos se auian tornado a poblar que luego se tornaban a
despoblar de temor.

*Capitulo ueinte y dos como el general bolbio de quiuira y se hiçieron otras
entradas debajo del norte.*

luego que don tristan de arellano llego en tiguex mediado el mes de
jullio del año de quarenta y dos hiço recoger bastimentos para el inbierno
benidero y enbio a el capitan francisco de barrio nuebo con alguna gēte
el rio arriba debajo del norte en que bio dos prouinçias que la una se
decia hemes de siete pueblos y la otra yuqueyunque los pueblos de
hemes sâlieron de paz y dieron bastimentos los de yuqueyunque en
tanto que el real se asentaba despoblaron dos muy hermosos pueblos
que tenian el rio en medio y se fueron a la sierra a donde tenian quatro
pueblos muy fuertes en tierra aspera que no se podia yr a ellos a cauallo
en estos dos pueblos se ubo mucho bastimento y loça muy hermoça y
bedriada y de muchas labores y hechuras tambien se hallaron muchas
ollas llenas de metal escogido reluciente con que bedriaban la losa era
señal que por aquella tierra auia minas de plata si se buscaran.

ueinte leguas adelante el rio arriba auia un poderoso y grande rio
digo pueblo que se decia braba a quien los nr̄os pusieron ualladolid
tomaba el rio por medio pasabase por puentes de madera de muy largos
y grandes pinos quadrados y en este pueblo se bieron las mas grandes
y brabas estufas que en toda aquella tierra porque eran de doçe pilares
que cada uno tenia dos braças de ruedo de altura de dos estados este
pueblo auia uisitado hernando de aluarado quando descubrio a çicuye
es tierra muy alta y figridissima el rio yba hondo y de gran corriente
sin ningun uado dio la buelta el capitan barrio nuebo dexando de pax
aquellas prouinçias.

otro capitan fue el rio abajo en busca de los poblados que deçian los
de tutahaco auia algunas jornadas de alli este capitan bajo ochenta leguas
_{Rio que se hundi.} y hallo quatro pueblos grandes que dexo de paz y andubo
hasta que hallo quel rio se sumia debaxo de tierra como guadiana
en extremadura no paso adelāte donde los indios decian q̄ salia muy
poderoso por no llebar mas comiçion de ochēta leguas de camino y
como bolbio este capitan y se llegaba el plaço en que el capitan abia de
bolber de quiuira y no bolbia don tristan señalo quarenta conpañeros y
dexando el campo a franᶜᵒ de barrio nuebo salio con ellos a buscar el

general y como llego a cicuye los del pueblo salieron de guerra que fue
causa que se detubiesen alli quatro dias por les haçer algun daño como
se les hiço que con tiros quese asentaron a el pueblo les mataron alguna
gēte por que no salian a el canpo a causa quel primer dia les mataron
dos hombres señalados.

en este comedio llegaron nuebas [niebas?] como el general benia y por
esto tambien ubo de aguardar alli don tristan para asegurar aquel paso
llegado el general fue bien reçebido de todos con grande alegria el
indio xabe que era el mançebo que auian dado los de cicuye a el
general quando yba en demanda de quiuira estaba con don tristan de
arellano y como supo que el general benia dando muestras que se
holgaba dixo agora que biene el general bereis como ay oro y plata en
quiuira aunque no tanta como deçia el turco y como el general llego y
bio como no auian hallado nada quedo triste y pasmado y afirmãdo
que la auia hiço creer a muchos que era asi porque el general no entro
la tierra adentro que no oso por ser muy poblado y no se hallar
poderoso y dio la buelta por lleuar sus gentes pasadas las aguas
porque ya por alla llobia que era entrada de agosto quando salio tardo
en la buelta quarenta dias con buenas guias con benir a la ligera
como bolbieron deçia el turco quando salio de tiguex el canpo que
para que cargauan los cauallos tanto de bastimẽtos que se cansarian y
no podrian despues traer el oro y la plata donde parese bien andaba
con engaño.

llegado el general con su gēte a cicuyc luego se partio para tiguex
dexando mas asentado el pueblo por que a el luego salieron de paz y le
hablaron llegado a tiguex procuro de inbernar alli para dar la buelta
con todo el campo porque deçia traya noticia de grandes poblaciones
y rios poderossissimos y que la tierra era muy pareciente a la de
españa en las frutas y yerbas y temporales y que no benian satisfechos
de creer que no auia oro antes trayan sospecha que lo auia la tierra
adentro porque puesto que lo negauan entendian que cosa era y tenia
nombre entre ellos que se deçia acochis con lo qual daremos fin a esta
primera parte y trataremos en dar relaçion de las prouincias.

SEGUNDA PARTE EN QUE SE TRATA DE LOS PUEBLOS Y PROUIN-
CIAS DE ALTOS Y DE SUS RITOS Y COSTUMBRES RECOPILADA POR
PEDRO DE CASTAÑEDA UEÇINO DE LA ÇIUDAD DE NAXARA.[1]

laus deo.

no me parece que quedara satisfecho el lector em aber bisto y entendido lo que e contado de la jornada aunque en ello ay bien que notar
en la discordançia de las notiçias porque aber fama tan grande de
grandes thesoros y en el mismo lugar no hallar memoria ni aparençia
de aberlo cosa es muy de notar en lugar de poblados hallar grandes
despoblados y en lugar de ciudades populosas hallar pueblos de doçien-

---

[1] The Segunda Parte begins a new page in the manuscript.

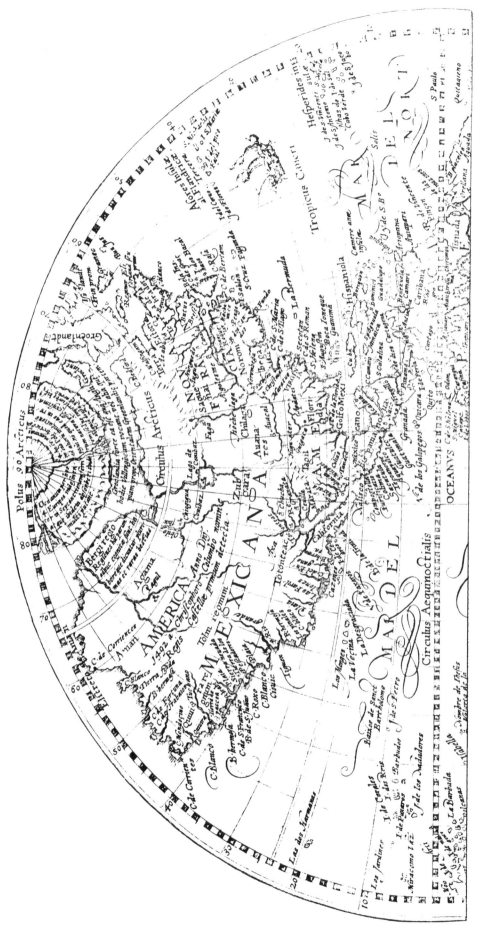

NORTHERN HALF OF DE BRY'S "AMERICA SIVE NOVUS ORBIS," 1596

tos uecinos y el mayor de ocho cientos o mill no se si esto les dara materia para considerar y pēsar en la bariedad de esta uida y para poderlos
agradar les quiero dar relaçion particular de todo lo poblado que se bio
y descubrio en esta jornada y algunas costunbres que tienen y ritos
conforme a lo que de ellos alcançamos a saber y en que rumbo cae cada
prouinçia para que despues se pueda entender a que parte esta la florida y a que parte cae la india mayor y como esta tierra de la nueba
españa es tierra firme con el peru ansi lo es con la india mayor o de la
china sin que por esta parte aya entrecho que la dibida ante es estan
grande la anchura de la tierra que da lugar a que aya tan grandes
despoblados como ay entre las dos mares por que la costa del norte
sobre la florida buelbe sobre los bacallaos y despues torna sobre la
nuruega y la del sur a el poniente haciendo la otra punta debaxo del
sur casi como en arco la buelta de la india dando lugar a que las tierras
que siguen las cordilleras de anbas costas se desbien en tanta manera
unas de otras que dexen en medio de si grandes llanuras y tales que
por ser inabitables sō pobladas de ganados y otros muchos animales de
dibersas maneras aunque no de serpientes por ser como son esentos y
sin montes antes de todo genero de caça y aues como adelante se dira
dexando de contar la buelta quel campo dio para la nueba españa hasta
que se beā la poca ocaçion que para ello ubo començaremos a tratar de
la uilla de culiacan y bersea la diferençia que ay de la una tierra a la
otra para que meresca lo uno estar poblado de españoles y lo otro no
abiendo de ser a el contrario quanto a cristianos porque en los unos ay
raçon de hombres y en los otros barbaridad de animales y mas que de
bestias.

Capitulo primero de la prouincia de Culiacan y de sus ritos y costumbres.

Culiacan es lo ultimo del nuebo reyno de galiçia y fue lo primero que
poblo Nuño de guzman quando conquisto este reyno esta a el poniente de
mexico doçientas y diez leguas en esta prouinçia ay tres lēguas prinçipales sin otras bariables que de ella responden la primera es de tahus
que era la mejor gente y mas entendida y los que en esta saçon estan
mas domesticos y tienen mas lumbre de la fe estos ydolatraban y haçian
presentes a el demonio de sus aberes y requeças que era ropa y turquesas no comian carne humana ni la sacrificauan aconstumbraban a
criar muy grandes culebras y tenian las en beneraçion auia entre ellos
hombres en abito de mugeres que se casaban con otros honbres y les
seruian de mugeres canonicaban con gran fiesta a las mugeres que
querian bibir solteras con un grande areyto o bayle en quese juntaban
todos los señores de la comarca y sacaban la a baylar en cueros y desque todos abian baylado con ella metian la en un rancho que para aquel
efecto estaba bien adornado y las señoras la adereçaban de ropa y bra-
çaletes de finas turquesas y luego entrabran a usar con ella los señores
uno a uno y tras de ellos todos los demas que querian y desde alli adelante no abian de negar a nadie pagandoles sierta paga que estaba cons-

tituyda para ello y aunque despues tomaban maridos no por eso eran reseruadas de c̄uplir con quien se lo pagaba sus mayores fiestas son mercados auia una costumbre que las mugeres que se casaban los maridos las compraban a los padres y parientes por gran preçio y luego la llebaban a un señor que lo tenian como por saserdote para que las desbirgase y biese si estaba donçella y si no lo estaba le abian de bolber todo el preçio y estaba en su escoger si la queria por muger o no o dexalla para que fuese canoniçada haçian grandes borracheras a sus tiempos.

la segunda lengua es de pacaxes que es la gente que abitan en la tierra que esta entre lo llano y las serranias estos son mas barbara gente algunos comen carne humana que son los que confinan con las serranias son grandes someticos toman muchas mugeres aunque sean hermanas adoran en piedras pintados de entalladura son grandes abuçioneros y hechiçeros.

la tercera lengua son acaxes aquestos pose en gran parte de la tierra por la serrania y toda la cordillera y asi andan a caça de hombres como a caça de benados comen todos carne humana y el que tiene mas guesos de hombre y calaberas colgadas a el rededor de su caça es mas temido y en mas tenido biben a barrios y en tierra muy aspera huyen de lo llano para pasar de un barrio a otro a de aber quebrada en medio que aunque se hablē no puedan pasar tam ligeramēte a una grita se juntan quinientos hombres y por pequeña ocaçion se matan y se comen estos an sido malos de sojuzgar por la aspereça de la tierra que es muy grande.

an se hallado en esta tierra muchas minas de plata ricas no ban a lo hondo acabāse en breue desde la costa de esta prouinçia comiença el ancon que mete la mar debajo del norte que entra la tierra adentro doçientas y sinquentas leguas y ienese en la boca del rio del tiçon esta tierra es la una punta a el oriente la punta del poniente es la California ay de punta a punta segun he oydo a hombres que lo an nabegado treinta leguas porque perdiendo de bista a esta tierra ben la otra el ancon diçen es ancho dentro a tener de tierra a tierra çiento y sinquenta leguas y mas desde el rio del tiçon da la buelta la costa a el sur haçiendo arco hasta la california que buelue a el poniente haçiendo aquella punta que otro tiempo se tubo por isla por ser tierra baxa y arenosa poblada de gente bruta y bestial desnuda y que comen su mismo estiercol y se juntaban hombre y muger como animales poniendose la hembra en quatro pies publicamente.

Capitulo segundo de la prouincia de petlatlan y todo lo poblado hasta chichilticale.

petlatlan es una poblaçion de casas cubiertas con una manera de esteras hechas de causo congregadas en pueblos que ban a el luego de un rio desde la sierras hasta la mar son gente de la calidad y ritos de los tahues culhacaneses ay entre ellos muchos someticos tienen grande poblaçion y comarca de otros pueblos a la serrania difieren en la lengua

de los tahues algun tanto puesto que se entienden los unos a los otros
dixose petlatlan por ser las casas de petates dura esta manera de casas
por aquella parte docientas y quarenta leguas y mas que ay hasta el
principio del despoblado de cibola desde petlatlan hace raya aquella
tierra cognoçidamente la causa porque desde alli para adelante no ay
arbol sin espina ni ay frutas sino son tunas y mesquites y pitahayas
ay desde culiacan alla ueinte leguas y desde petlatlan a el ualle de
señora ciento y treinta ay entre medias muchos rios poblados de gente
de la misma suerte como son sinoloa, boyomo, teocomo, y aquimi yotros
mas pequeños estan tambien los coraçones ques nuestro caudal abajo
del ualle de señora.

    senora es un rio y ualle muy poblado de gente muy dispuesta las
mugeres bisten naguas de cuero adobado de benados y sanbeni-
Nagues tillos hasta medio cuerpo los que son señores de los pueblos se
ponen a las mañanas en unos altillos que para aquello tienen hechos y
a manera de pregones o pregoneros estan pregonando por espaçio de
una ora como administrando les en lo que an de haçer tienē unas casi-
llas pequeñas de adoratorios en que hincan muchas flechas que las
ponen por de fuera como un eriso y esto haçen quando asperan tener
guerra a el rededor de esta prouincia hacia las sierras ay grandes pobla-
çiones en probincillas apartadas y congregadas de diez y doçe pueblos
y ocho o siete de ellos que se los nombres sō com u patrico, mochilagua
y arispa, y el uallecillo ay otros que no se bieron.

    desde señora a el ualle de suya ay quarenta leguas en este ualle se
uino a poblar la uilla de san hieronimo que despues se alcaron y mataron parte de la gente que estaba poblada como se bera adelante en lo
terçera parte en este ualle ay muchos puèblos que tienen en su torno
son las gentes de la calidad de los de señora y de un traje y lengua
ritos y costumbres con todo los demas que ay hasta el despoblado de
chichilticale las mugeres se labran en la barba y los ojos como moriscas
de berberia ellos son grandes someticos beben bino de pitahayas que
es fruta de cardones que se abre como granadas hacen se con el bino
tontos haçen conserua de tunas en gran cantidad conseruanse en su
sumo en gran cantidad sin otra miel haçen pan de mesquites como
quesos conseruase todo el año ay en esta tierra melones de ella tam
grandes que tiene una persona que lleuar en uno haçen de ellos tasajos
y curan los a el sol son de comer del sabor de higos pasado guisados son
muy buenos y dulces guardanse todo el año asi pasado.

    y por esta tierra se bieron aguilas candoles tienen las los señores por
grandeça en todos estos pueblos no se bieron gallinas de ninguna suerte
salbo en este ualle de suya que se hallaron gallinas como las de castilla
que no se supo por donde entraron tanta tierra de guerra teniendo como
todos tienen guerra unos con otros entre suya y chichilticale ay muchos
carneros y cabras montesas grandissimas de cuerpos y de cuernos
españoles ubo que afirman aber bisto manada de mas de çiento juntos
corren tanto que en brebe se desparesen.

    14 ETH——29

en chichilticale torna la tierra a hacer raya y pierde la arboleda espinosa y la causa es que como el Ancon llega hasta aquel paraje y da buelta la costa asi da buelta la cordillera de las sierras y alli se biene a trabesar la serrania y se rompe para pasar a lo llano de la tierra

Capitulo tercero de lo ques chichilticale y el despoblado de çibola sus costumbres y ritos y de otras cosas.

chichilticale dixose asi porque hallaron los frayles en esta comarca una casa que fue otros tiempos poblada de gentes que rresquebraban de çibola era de tierra colorado o bermeja la casa era grande y bien pareçia en ella aber sido fortaleça y debio ser despoblada por los de la tierra que es la gente mas barbara de las que se bieron hasta alli biuen en rancherias sin poblados biben de casar y todo lo mas es despoblado y de grandes pinales ay piñones en gran cantidad son los pinos donde se dan parrados de hasta de dos a tres estados de alto ay ençinales de bellota dulce y fanonas que dan una fruta como confites de culantro seco es muy dulce como asucar ay berros en algunas fuètes y rosales y poleo y oregano.

en los rios deste despoblado ay barbos y picones como en españa ay leones pardos que se bieron desde el principio del despoblado siempre se ba subiendo la tierra hasta llegar a çibola que son ochenta leguas la uia del norte y hasta llegar alli desde culiacan se auia caminado lleuando el norte sobre el ojo isquierdo.

çibola son siete pueblos el mayor se dice maçaque comunmente son de tres y quatro altos las casas en maçaque ay casas de quatro altos y de siete estas gentes son bien entendidas andan cubiertas sus berguenças y todas las partes deshonestas con paños a manera de serbilletas de mesa con rapasejos y una borla en cada esquina atan los sobre el quadril bisten pellones de plumas y de pelo de liebres mãtas de algodon las mugeres se bisten de mantas que las atan o añudan sobre el honbro isquierdo y sacan el braço derecho por ençima siriense las a el cuerpo traen capotes de cuero pulidos de buena fayçion cogen el cabello sobre las dos orejas hechos dos ruedas que paresen papos de cosia.

esta tierra es un ualle entre sierras a manera de peñones siembran a hoyos no crese el maiz alto de las maçorcas desdel pie tres y quatro cada caña gruesas y grandes de a ocho çiẽtos granos cosa no bista en estas partes ay en esta prouincia osos en gran cantidad leones gatos çeruales y nutrias ay muy finas tratan turquesas aunque no en la cantidad que deçian recogen y entrogan piñones para su año no tiene un hombre mas de una muger ay en los pueblos estufas que estan en los patios o placas donde se juntan a consulta no ay señores como por la nueba españa rigense por consejo de los mas biejos tienen sus saser-dotes a quien llaman papas que les predican estos son uiejos subense en el terrado mas alto del pueblo y desde alli a manera de pregoneros predican a el pueblo por las mañanas quando sale el sol estando todo el pueblo en silençio asentados por los corredores escuchando dicen les

como an de bibir y creo que les diçen algunos mandamientos que an
de guardar porque entre ellos no ay borrachera ni sodomia ni sacrificios
ni comen carne humana ni hurtan de comun trabajan en el pueblo la
estufas son comunes es sacrilegio que las mugeres entren a dormir en
las estufas por señal de paz dar cruz queman los muertos hechan con
ellos en el fuego los instrumentos que tienen para usar sus officios.

tienen a tusayan entre norte y poniente a ueinte leguas es prouinçia
de siete pueblos de la misma suerte trajes ritos y costumbres que los
de çibola abra en estas dos prouinçias que son catorçe pueblos hasta
tres o quatro mill hombres y ay hasta tiguex quarenta leguas o mas la
buelta del norte ay entre medias el peñon de acuco que contamos en la
primera parte.

*Capitulo quarto como se tratan los de tiguex y de la prouincia de tiguex
y sus comarcas.*

tiguex es prouincia de doçe pueblos riberas de un rio grande y cau-
daloso unos pueblos de una parte y otros de otra es ualle espaçioso de
dos leguas en ancho tiene a el oriente una sierra nebada muy alta y
aspera a el pie de ella por las espaldas ay siete pueblos quatro en llano
y los tres metidos en la halda de la sierra.

tiene a el norte a quirix siete pueblos a siete leguas tiene a el nordeste
la prouincia de hemes siete pueblos a quarenta leguas tiene a el norte o
leste a Acha a quatro leguas a el sueste a tutahaco prouinçia de ocho
pueblos todos estos pueblos en general tienen unos ritos y costumbres
aunque tienen algunas cosas en particulares que no las tienen los otros
gobiernanse por acuerdo de los mas uiejos labran los edificios del pueblo
de comun las mugeres entienden en haçer la mescla y las paredes los
hombres traen la madera y la asientan no ay cal pero haçen una mescla
de çenisa de carbon y tierra ques poco menos que de cal porque con
aber de tener quatro altos la casa no hacen la pared de mas gordor que
de media bara juntan gran cantidad de rama de tomillos y corriso y
ponen le fuego y como esta entre carbon y çenisa hechan mucha tierra
y agua y haçen lo mescla y de ella hacen pellas redondas que ponen en
lugar de piedra despues de seco y traban con la misma mescla de suerte
que despues es como argamasa los mançebos por casar siruen a el pueblo
en general y traen la leña que se a de gastar y la ponen en rima en los
patios de los pueblos de donde la toman las mugeres para lleuar a sus
casas su abitaçion de los mançebos es en las estufas que son en los
patios de el pueblo debajo de tierra quadrados o redondos con pilares
de pino algunas se bieron de doçe pilares y de quatro por nabe de gordor de dos braças los comunes eran de tres o quatro pilares los suelos
de losas grandes y lisas como los baños que se usan ē europa tienen
dentro un fogon a manera de una bitacora de nabio donde ensienden un
puño de tomillo con que sustentan la calor y pueden estar dentro como
en baño lo alto en pareja con la tierra alguna se bio tan espaciosa que
tendra juego de bola quando alguno se a de casar a de ser por orden de

los que gobiernan a de hilar y texer una manta el baron y ponerle la
muger delante y ella cubre con ella y queda por su muger las casas son
de las mugeres las estufas de los hombres si el uaron repudia la muger
a de ir a ello a la estufa es biolable cosa domir las mugeres en la estufa
ni entrar a ningun negoçio mas de meter de comer a el marido o a los
hijos los hombres hilan y texen las mugeres crian los hijos y guisan de
comer la tierra es tan fertil que no desyerban en todo el año mas de para
sembrar porque luego cae la niebe y cubre lo senbrado y debajo de la
niebe cria la maçorca cogen en un año para siete ay grãdissimo numero
de guillas y de ansares y cuerbos y tordos que se mantienen por los sem-
brados y con todo esto quando bueluen a sembrar para otro año estan
los campos cubiertos dè maiz que no lo an podido acabar de encerrar.

auia en estas prouincias grã cantidad de gallinas de la tierra y gallos
de papada sustentabanse muertos sin pelar ni abrir sesenta dias sin
mal olor y los hombres muertos lo mismo y mas tiempo siendo inbierno
los pueblos son limpios de inmundiçias porque salen fuera a estercolar
y desaguan en basijas de barro y las sacan a basiar fuera del pueblo
tienen bien repartidas las casas en grande limpieça donde guisan de
comer y donde muelen la harina que es un apartado o retrete donde
tienen un farnal con tres piedras asentado con argamasa donde entran
tres mugeres cada una en su piedra que la una frangolla y la otra muele
y la otra remuele antes q̃ entren dentro a la puerta se descalçan los
sapatos y cogen el cabello y sacuden la ropa y cubrē la cabeça mientras
que muelē esta un hombre sentado a la puɛ̃ta tañedo con una gayta
al tono traen las piedras y cantã a tres boçes muelen de una bez mucha
cantidad porque todo el pan haçen de harina desleyda con agua caliente
a manera de obleas cogen gran cantidad de yeruas y secan las para
guisar todo el año para comer no ay en la tierra frutas saluo piñones
tienen sus predicadores no se hallo en ellos sodomia ni comer carne
humana ni sacrificarlla no es gente cruel porque en tiguex estubieron
obra de quarenta dias muerto a françisco de ouando y quando se acabo
de ganar el pueblo lo hallaron entero entre sus muertos sin otra liçion
mas de la herida de que murio blanco como niebe sin mal olor de un
indio de los nuestros que auia estado un año catibo entre ellos alcanse
a saber algunas cosas de sus costumbres en especial preguntãdole yo
que porque causa en aquella prouinçia andaban las mugeres moças en
cueros haçiendo tam gran frio dixome que las donçellas auian de andar
ansi hasta que tomasen maridos y que en cognoçiendo uaron se cubrian
trayan los hombres por alli camisetas de cuero de benado adobado y
ençima sus pellones ay por todas estas prouincias loca bedriada de
alcohol y jarros de extremadas labores y de hechuras que era cosa de
ber.

Capitulo quinto de cicuyc y los pueblos de su contorno y de como unas
gentes binieron a conquistar aquella tierra.

ya abemos dicho de tiguex y de todas las prouinçias que estan en la
costa de aquel rio por ser como son todos de una calidad de gente y una

condiçion y costumbres no sera menester en ellos particulariçar ninguna
cosa solo quiero deçir del açiento de cicuye y unos pueblos despoblados
que le caen en comarca en el camino derecho quel campo llebo para alla
y otros que estan tras la sierra nebada de tiguex que tambien caen en
aquella comarca fuera del rio.

cicuye es un pueblo de hasta quinientos hombres de guerra es temido
por toda aquella tierra en su sitio es quadrado asentado sobre peña
en medio un gran patio o plaça con sus estufas las casas son todas
parejas de quatro altos por lo alto se anda todo el pueblo sin que aya
calle que lo estorbe a los dos primeros doblados es todo çercado de
corredores que se anda por ellos todo el pueblo son como balcones que
salen a fuera y debajo de ellos se pueden amparar no tienen las casas
puertas por lo bajo con escaleras leuadisas se siruen y suben a los corredores que son por de dentro del pueblo y por alli se mandan que las
puertas de las casas salen a aquel alto al corredor sirue el corredor por
calle las casas que salen a el campo haçen espaldas con las de dentro
del patio y en tiempo de guerra se mandan por las de dentro es çercado
de una çerca baja de piedra tiene dentro una fuente de agua que se la
pueden quitar la gente deste pueblo se preçiã de que nadie los a podido
sojuzgar y los sojuzgan los pueblos que quieren son de la misma condiçion y costumbres que los otros pueblos tambien andan las doncellas
desnudas hasta que tomã maridos por que diçen que si hacen maldad
que luego se bera y ansi no lo haran ni tienẽ de que tener berguença
pues andan qual naçieron.

ay entre cicuye y la prouinçia de quirix un pueblo chico y fuerte a
quien los españoles pusieron nonbre ximena y otro pueblo casi despoblado que no tiene poblado sino un barrio este pueblo era grande segun
su sitio y fresco parecia aber sido destruydo aqueste se llamo el pueblo
de los cilos porque se hallaron en el grandes silos de maiz.

adelante auia otro pueblo grande todo destruido y asolado en los
patios del muchas pelotas de piedras tan grandes como botijas de arroba
que pareçia aber sido hechadas con ingenios o trabucos con que des-
truyeron aquel pueblo lo que de ello se alcanso a saber fue que abria
desiseis años que unas gentes llamados teyas en gran numero auian
benido en aquella tierra y auian destruydo aquellos pueblos y auian
tenido çercado a cicuye y no lo auian podido tomar por ser fuerte y que
quando salieron de aquella tierra auian hecho amistades con toda la
tierra pareçio debio de ser gente poderosa y que debiã de tener ingenios
para derriba los pueblos no saben decir de que parte binieron mas de
señalar debaxo del norte generalmente llaman estas gentes teyas por
gentes ualiẽtes como diçen los mexicanos chichimecas o teules porque los
teyas que el campo topo puesto que eran ualientes eran cognoçidos de la
gente de los poblados y sus amigos y que se ban a inbernar por alla los
inbiernos debaxo de los alaues de lo poblado porque dẽtro no se atreben
a los reçebir porque no se deben fiar de ellos y puesto que los reçiben
de amistad y tractan con ellos de noche no quedan en los pueblos sino

fuera solas alaues y los pueblos se belanabo çina y grito grito como las fortaleças de españa.

otros siete pueblos ay a la orilla deste camino hacia la sierra nebada que el uno quedo medio destruydo de estas gentes ya dichas que estan debaxo de la obidiençia de cicuye esta cicuye en un pequeño ualle entre sierras y montañas de grandes pinales tiene una pequeña riuera que lleba muy buenas truchas y nutrias crianse por aqui muy grandes osos y buenos halcones.

Capitulo sexto en que se declara quantos fueron los pueblos que se uieron en los poblados de terrados y lo poblado de ello.

pareçiome antes que salga deçir de los llanos de las bacas y lo poblado y rancheado de ellos que sera bien que se sepa que tanto fue lo poblado que se bio de casas de altos en pueblos congregados y en que tanto espaçio de tierra digo que çibola es lo primero.

çibola siete pueblos

tucayan siete pueblos

el peñon de acuco uno

tiguex doçe pueblos

tutahaco ocho pueblos

por abajo del rio estauan estos pueblos.

quirix siete pueblos

a la sierra nebeda siete pueblos

ximena tres pueblos.

cicuye uno pueblo.

hemes siete pueblos

aguas calientes tres pueblos.

yuqueyunque de la sierra seis pueblos.

ualladolid dicho braba un pueblo.

chia un pueblo.

por todos son sesenta y seis pueblos como parece tiguex es el riñon de los pueblos ualladolid lo mas alto el rio arriba a el nordeste los quatro pueblos a el rio abaxo al sueste porque el rio boltea haçia leuante que desde la una punta de lo que se bio el rio abaxo a la otra que se bio el rio arriba en que esta todo lo poblado ay çiento y treinta leguas diez mas o menos que por todos los pueblos con los de las trabesias son sesenta y seis como tengo dicho en todos ellos puede auer como ueinte mill hombres lo qual se puede bien considerar y entender por la poblaçion de los pueblos y entre medias de unos y otros no ay caserias ni otra abitacion sino todo despoblado por donde se be que segun son poca gente y tan diferençiados en trato gouierno y poliçia de todas las naçiones que se an bisto y descubierto en estas partes de poniente son benediços de aquella parte de la india mayor que cae su costa debaxo del poniente de esta tierra que por aqueila parte pueden aber baxado atrabesando aquellas cordilleras baxando por aquel rio abajo poblando en lo mejor que les pareçia y como an ydo multiplicando an ydo poblando hasta que

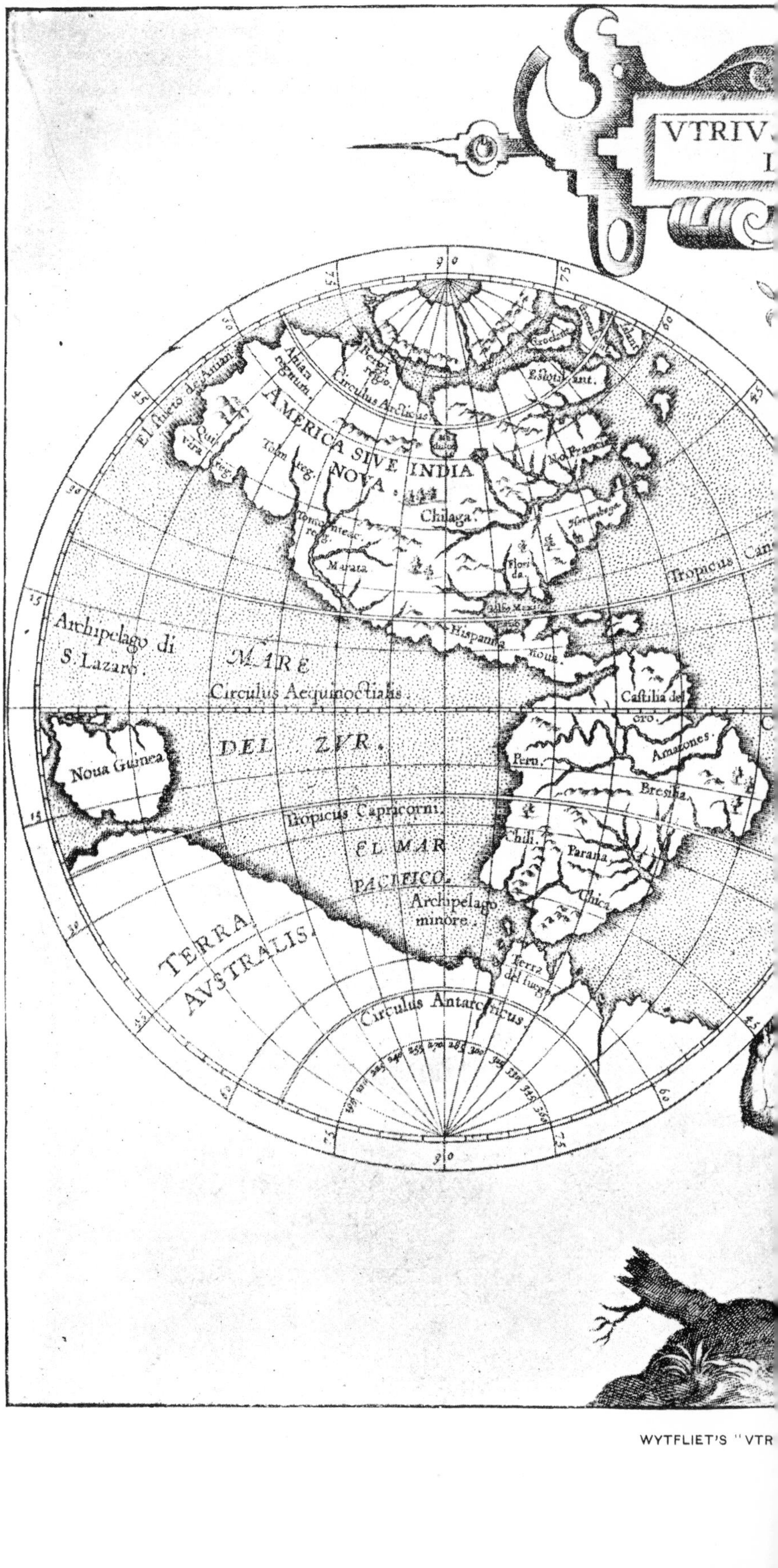

VTRIV
I

AMERICA SIVE INDIA
NOVA

MARE
Circulus Aequinoctialis

DEL ZVR

EL MAR
PACIFICO

Noua Guinea

Tropicus Capricorni

Archipelago di
S. Lazaro

TERRA
AVSTRALIS

Circulus Antarcticus

Peru

Bresilia

Chili

Parana

Chica

Terra
del fuego

Castilia del
oro

Amazones

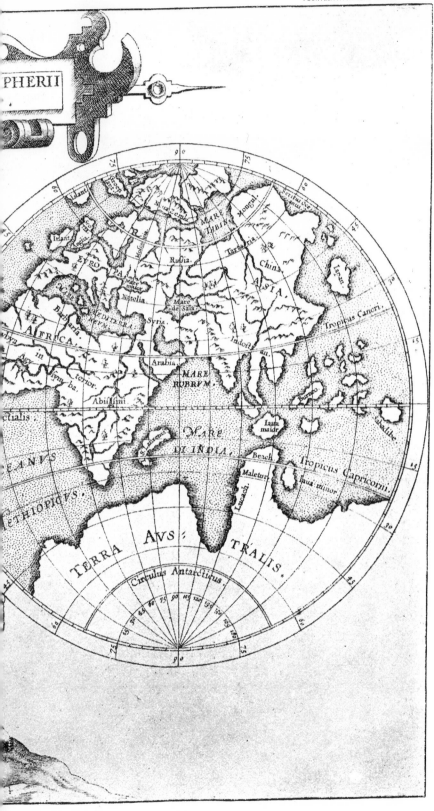

no hallaron rio porque se sume debaxo de tierra haciendo sus corrientes
haçia la florida baxando del nordeste donde se hallaua notiçia todauia
de pueblos quese dexo de seguir al turco que lo deçiā sin aquellas cordilleras do nace aquel rio se atrabesaran yo creo se tomaran ricas noticias y se entrara en las tierras de donde aquellas gentes proçeden que
segun el rūbo es principio de la india mayor aun que partes innotas y
no sabidas ni cognosidas porque segun la demostraçion de la costa es
muy la tierra adentro entre la nuruega y la china en el comedio de la
tierra de mar a mar es grande anchura segun de muestran los rumbos
de ambas costas asi lo q̄ descubrio el capitan uillalobos yendo por esta
mar de poniente en demanda de la china como lo que sea descubierto
por la mar del norte la buelta de los bacallaos que es por la costa de la
florida arriba hacia la nuruega.

ansi que tornado a el proposito de lo començado digo q̄ en espaçio de
setenta leguas en el ancho de aquella tierra poblada y de ciento y
treinta leguas al luego del rio de tiguex no se bieron ni hallaron mas
poblados ni gentes de los ya dichas que ay repartimientos en la nueba
españa no uno sino muchos de mayor numero de gentes en muchos pueblos de ellos se hallaron metales de plata que los tenian para bedriar y
pintar los rotro.

*Capitulo septimo que trata de los llanos que se atrabesaron de bacas y
de las gentes que los habitan.*

dicho abemos de lo poblado de altos que segun parese esta en el
comedio de la cordillera en lo mas llano y espaçioso de ella porque tiene
de atrabesia çiento y sinquenta leguas hasta entrar en la tierra llana
que esta entre las dos cordilleras digo la que esta a la mar del norte y
la que esta a la mar del sur que por esta costa se podria mejor deçir a
la mar de poniente esta cordillera es la que esta a el mar del sur pues
para entender como lo poblado que digo es ba en el comedio de la cordillera digo que desde chichilticale que es el principio de la trabesia a
çibola ay ochenta leguas de çibola que es el primer pueblo a cicuye que
es el prostero en la trabesia ay setenta leguas de cicuye a los llanos ay
treinta leguas hasta el prinçipio de ellos puede ser aberse atrabesado
algo por trabesia o a el sesgo por do parece aber mas tierra que si se
atrabesara por medio y pudiera ser mas dificultoso y aspero y esto no
se puede biē entender por la buelta que la cordillera haçe tras de su costa
del Ancon del rio del tizon.

agora diremos de los llanos que es una tierra llana y espaçiosa que
tiene en anchura mas de quatro cientas leguas por aquella parte entre
las dos cordilleras la una la que atrabeso francisco uasques coronado a la
mar del sur y la otra la que atrabeso la gente de don fernando de soto
a la mar del norte entrando por la florida lo que de estos llanos se bio
todo era despoblado y no se pudo ber la otra cordillera ni çerro ni çierra
que tubiese de altura tres estados con andar doçientas y sinquenta
leguas por ellos atrechos se hallauan algunas lagunas redondas como

platos de un tiro de piedra de ancho y mayores algunas dulçes y algunas de sal en estas lagunas ay alguna yerba cresida fuera de ellas toda
es muy chica de un geme y menos es la tierra de hechura de bola que
donde quiera que un hombre se pone lo çerca el çielo a tiro de ballesta no tiene arboleda sino en los rios que ay en algunas barrancas que
son tam encubiertas que hasta que estan a el bordo de ellas no son
bistas son de tierra muerta tienen entradas que haçen las bacas para
entrar a el agua que esta honda por estos llanos andan gentes como
tengo dicho en la primera parte en pos de las bacas haçiendo caça y
adobādo cueros para lleuar a bender a los poblados los inbiernos porque
ban a inbernar a ellos cada compañia a donde mas çerca se halla unos
a los poblados de cicuye otros haçia quiuira otros haçia la florida a los
poblados que estan haçia aquella parte y puerto estan gentes que los
llamā querechos y teyas dan relaçion de grandes poblados y segun lo
que de estas gentes se bio y de otros que ellos daban notiçia que auia
por otras partes ella es harto mas gente que no la de los poblados mas
dispuesta y mayores hombres de guerra y mas temidos andan como
alarabes con sus tiendas y harrias de perros aparejados con lomillos y
en xalmas y sincha quando se les tuerçe la carga aullan llamando quien
los aderese comen esta gente la carne cruda y beben la sagre no comen
carne humana es gente amoroso y no cruel tienen fiel amistad son muy
entendidos por señas secan la carne a el sol cortandola delgada como
una oja y seca la muelen como harina para guardar y haçer maçamo-
rras para comer que con un puño que hechan en una olla se hinche por
que creçe mucho guisan lo con manteca que siempre procuran traer
quando matan la baca uaçian una gran tripa y hinchen la de sangre y
hechan la a el cuello para beber quando tienen sed quando an abierto
la pança de la baca aprietan para abajo la yerua mascada y el sumo
que queda arriba lo beben que diçen que esto da la sustançia de el
bientre abren las bacas por el lomo y deshaçen los por sus coyunturas
con un pedernal grande como un dedo atado en un palito cō tanta
façilidad como si fuese con una muy buena herramienta dando les los
filos en sus propios dientes es cosa de ber y de notar la presteça con
que lo haçen.

ay por estos llanos muy gran cantidad de lobos que andā tras de las
bacas tienen el pelo blanco los sieruos son remendados de blanco el pelo
ancho y que muriendo ansi con la mano se pelan en caliente y quedan
como puerco pelado las liebres que son en gran numero andan tan
abobadas que yendo a cauallo las matan con las lanças esto es de andar
hechas entre las bacas de la gente de pie huyen.

Capitulo ocho de quiuira y en que rumbo esta y la notiçia que dan.

quiuira es a el poniente de aquellas barrancas por el medio de la tierra
algo arrimada a la cordillera de la mar porque hasta quiuira es tierra
llana y alli se començan a ber algunas sierras la tierra es muy poblada
segun el principio de ella se bio ser esta tierra muy aparente a la de

españa en su manera de yeruas y frutas ay siruelas como las de castilla
ubas nueçes moras uallico y abena poleo oregano lino en gran cantidad
no lo benefficiã porque no saben el uso de ello la gente es casi de la
manera y traje de los teyas tienen los pueblos a la manera como los de
la nueba españa las casas son redondas sin çerca tienen unos altos a
manera de balbacoas por baxo la techũbre adonde duermen y tienen sus
aberes las techumbres son de paja ay en su contorno otras prouincias
muy pobladas en grande numero de gente y aqui en esta prouinçia quedo
un frayle que se deçia fray juº de padilla y un español portugues y
un negro y un mestiso y siertos indios de la prouinçia de capothan de
la nueba españa a el frayle mataron porque se queria yr a la prouinçia
de los guas que eran sus enemigos el español escapo huyendo en una
yegua y despues aporto en la nueba españa saliendo por la uia de panuco
los indios de la nueba españa que yban con el frayle lo enterraron con
consentimiento de los matadores y se binieron en pos del español hasta
que lo alcançaron este español era portugues auia por nombre campo.

el gran rio del espiritu santo que descubrio don ferᵈᵒ de soto en la
tierra de la florida lleua sus corrientes de aquesta tierra pasa por una
prouinçia que se diçe arache segun alli tubo por notiçia berdadera que
no se bieron sus naçimientos porque segun deçian bienen de muy lejos
tierra de la cordillera del sur de la parte que desagua a los llanos y atra-
biesa toda la tierra liana y rompe la cordillera del norte y sale adonde
lo nauegaron los de don fernando de soto esto es mas de treçientas
leguas de donde el ba a salir a la mar y por esto y por las grandes
acogidas que tiene sale tam poderosa a el mar que an perdido la uista
de la tierra y no el agua de ser dulçe.

hasta esta tierra de quiuira fue lo ultimo que se bio y de lo que ya
puedo dar notiçia o relaçion y agora me conbiene dar la buelta a hablar
del campo que dexe en tiguex reposando el inbierno para poder pasar
o bolber a buscar estos poblados de quiuira lo qual despues no suçedio
ansi porque fue dios seruido que estos descubrimientos quedasen para
otras gentes y que nos contentasemos los que alla fuimos con deçir que
fuimos los primeros que lo descubrimos y tubimos notiçia de ello.

como hercules conoçer el sitio adonde jullio çesar auia de fundar a
seuilla o hispales plega a el señor todo poderoso se sirua con todo que
sierto es que si su uoluntad fuera ni franᶜᵒ uasques se bolbiera a la
nueba españa tan sin causa ni raçon ni los de don fernando de soto
dexaran de poblar tan buena tierra como tenian y tambien poblada y
larga mayormente abiendo tenido como tubieron notiçia de nuestro
campo.

TERCERA PARTE COMO Y EN QUE SE TRATA AQUELLO QUE ACON-
TEÇIO A FRANCISCO UASQUES CORONADO ESTANDO INBERNANDO Y
COMO DEXO LA JORNADA Y SE BOLBIO A LA NUEBA ESPAÑA.[1]

laus deo.

*Capitulo primero como bino de Señora don pedro de touar con gente y
se partio para la nueba españa don garci lopes de cardenas.*

en el fin de la primera parte de este libro diximos como francisco
uasques coronado buelto de quiuira auia ordenado de inbernar en
tiguex y benido el inbierno dar la buelta con todo su canpo para
descubrir todos aquellos poblados en estos comedios don pedro de
touar que como diximos auia ydo a sacar gente de la uilla de san hieronimo llego con la gente que traya y a la berdad considerando que pa
ir en demanda de su general a la tierra del indio que llemauan turco le
conbenia lleuar buena gente no saco de alla los cediçiosos ni reboltosos
sino los mas exprimentados y mejores soldados hombres de confiança
que pudo y llegados a tiguex aunque hallaron alli el campo no les
plugo mucho por que benian ya el pico a el biento creyendo hallar a el
general en la tierra rica del indio que deçian turco consolaronse con la
esperança de la buelta que se auia de haçer y biuian en gran plaçer y
alegria con la esperanca de la buelta que se auia de hacer y de que
presto yria el campo a quiuira con don pedro de touar binieron cartas
de la nueba españa ansi del uirrey don Antonio de mendoça como de
particulares entre los quales dieron una a don garçia lopes de cardenas
en que le hiçieron saber la muerte de un su hermano mayorazgo lla-
mandole fuese a heredar a españa por donde ubo liçençia y salio de
tiguex con algunas otras personas que ubieron liçençia para se yr a
reposar a sus casas otros muchos se quisieran yr que lo dexaron por
no mostrar flaqueça procuraba en estos comedios a pasiguar algunos
pueblos de la comarca que estaban no bien asentados y llamar a los de
tiguex a paz y buscar alguna ropa de la tierra porque andaban ya los
soldados desnudos y mal tratados llenos de piojos y no los podian
agotar ni deshechar de si.

el general francisco uasques coronado auia sido entre sus capitanes
y soldados el mas bien quisto y obedeçido capitan que podia auer salido
en indias y como la necesidad careçe de ley y los capitanes que recogian
la ropa la repartiesen mal tomando para si y sus amigos y criados lo
mejor y a los soldados se les repartiese el deshecho comēço a aber algunas murmuraçiones y desabrimentos unos por lo dicho y otros por ber
que algunos sobre salientes eran reseruados del trabajo y de las uelas
y mejor repartidos en lo que se repartia asi de ropa como de bastimentos
par do se cree praticaban y a no aber en la tierra para que bolber a
quiuira que no fue pequeña ocaçion para lo de adelante como se uera.

---

[1] The heading of the third part is written on the same page with the preceding text of the second
part, there being no break between the end of the second part and the heading which follows it. The
following page is left blank.

Capitulo segundo como cayo el general y se hordeno la buelta para la nueba españa.

pasado que fue el inuierno se publico la buelta para quiuira y la gente se comēcaua a perçebir de las cosas necesarias y como ninguna cosa esta en esta uida a la dispusiçion de los hombres sino a la ordenaçion de dios todo poderoso fue su uoluntad que los nr̄os no se efectuasen y fue el caso quel general un dia de fiesta se salio a holgar a cauallo como solia y corriendo parejas con el capitan don rodrigo maldonado el yba en un poderoso cauallo y sus criados auian le puesto una çincha nueba que del tiempo debia de estar podrida en la carrera rebento y bino a caer de lado a la parte que yba don rodrigo y a el pasar a el cansole el cauallo con el pie en la cabeça de que llego a punto de muerte y su cura fue larga y temida.

en este comedio quel estaba en la cama don garci lopes de cardenas que auia salido para salir a la nueba españa bolbio de suya huyendo que hallo despoblada la uilla y muerta la gente y cauallos y ganados y llego a tiguex y sabida la triste nueba como el general estaba en los terminos ya dichos no se lo osaron deçir hasta que estubiese sano y al cabo y a que se lebantaua lo supo y sintio lo tanto que ubo de tornar a recaer y por uentura para benir a haçer lo que hiço segun despues se creyo y fue que como se bio de aquella suerte bino le a la memoria que en salamanca un mathematico su amigo le auia dicho que se auia de ber en tierras estrañas señor y poderoso y abia de dar un cayda de que no se auia de poder leuantar y con esta inmaginaçion de su muerte le dio deseo de boluer a morir a donde tenia muger y hijos y como del mismo fiçico y su surujano que lo curaua y seruia tambien de chismoso suprese las murmuraçiones que andaban entre los soldados trato secreta y oculta-mente con algunos caualleros de su opinion pusieron en pratica la buelta de la nueua españa entre los soldados haçiendo juntas y corrillos y que se hiciesen consultas y lo pidiesen con sus alferes a el general cō carteles firmados de todos sus soldados lo qual ellos trataron muy por entero y no fue menester gastar mucho tienpo segun ya muchos lo tenian en uoluntad el general mostro des que se lo pidieron que no lo queria haçer sino lo confirmauan todos los caualleros y capitanes dando su pareçer firmado y como algunos eran en ello dieronlo luego y aun persuadieron a los otros a haçer lo mismo y ansi dieron pareçer que se deuian de boluer a la nueba españa pues no se auia hallado cosa rica ni auia poblado en lo descubrierto donde se pudiesen haçer reparti-mientos a todo el campo y como les cogio las firmas luego se publico la buelta para la nueua españa y como no puede aber cosa encubierta comēçose a descubrir el trato doble y hallaronse muchos de los caua-lleros faltos y corridos y procuraron por todas uias tornar a cobrar sus firmas del general el qual las guardo tanto que no salia de una camara haçiendo su dolençia muy mayor poniendo guardas en su persona y camara y de noche en los altos a donde dormia con todo esto le hurtaron el cofre y se dixo no hallaron en el sus firmas que las tenia en el colchon

por otro cabo se dixo que las cobraron ellos pidieron quel general les
diese sesenta hombres escogidos y que ellos quedarian y sustentarian
la tierra hasta que el uirrey les embiase socorro o a llamar o que el general dexase el campo y escogiese sesenta hombres con que se fuese pero
los soldados ni de una ni de otra manera no quisieron quedar lo uno por
aber ya puesto la proa a la nueba españa y lo otro por que bieron clara
la discordia que se auia de leuantar sobre quien auia de mandar los
caualleros no se sabe si porque auian jurado fidelidad o por tener creydo
que los soldados no los faboreçerian aunque agrabiados lo ubieron de
su fin y pasar por lo determinado aunque desde alli no obedeçian al
general como solian y el era dellos mal quisto y haçia caudal de los
soldados y honraba los que fue a benir a el efecto de lo quel queria y
que se efetuase la buelta de todo el campo.

Capitulo terçero como se alço Suya y las causas que para ello dieron los
pobladores.

ya diximos en el capitulo pasado como don garcia lopes de cardenas
bolbio huyendo de suya desque hallo alçada la tierra y que de deçir
como y porque se despoblo a la aquella uilla lo qual paso como contare
y fue el caso que como ya en aquella uilla no auia quedado sino la gente
ruyn entereçada honbres reboltosos y sediciosos puesto que quedaron
algunos honrados en los cargos de republica y para gouernar a los demas
podia mas la maliçia de los ruynes y cada dia hacian munipudios y tratos diciendo que estaban bendidos y no para ser aprobechados pues en
aquella tierra se mandaba por otra parte mas aproposito de la nueba
españa que no aquella estaua y ellos quedaban casi por derecho y con
esto mouidos sierta compañia haciendo caudillo a un pedro de auila se
amotinaron y fueron la buelta de culiacan dexando a diego de alcaraz
su capitan con poca gente doliente en aquella uilla de sant hieronimo
que no ubo quiẽ los pudiese seguir para los apremiar a que bolbiesẽ en
el camino en algunos pueblos les mataron alguna gente y al cabo salieron a culiacan adonde hernando arias de saya bendra los detubo
_{saabedra} entretenidos con palabras porque aguardaba a juan gallego
que auia de benir alli con gente de la nueua españa y que los bolberia
algunos temiendolo que auia de ser se huyan de noche para la nueba
españa diego de alcaraz que auia quedado con poca gente y doliente
aunque quisiera no podia alli sustentarse por el peligro de la yerua mortal que por alli usan traer los naturales los quales sintiendo la flaqueça
de los españoles ya no se dexaban tratar como solian abian se ya descubierto antes desto mineros de oro y como estaban en tierra de guerra y
no tenian posibilidad no se labrauan estando en esta confuçion no se
dexaban de belar y recatar mas que solian.

la uilla estaba poblada çerca de un rio pequeño y una noche a desora
bieron fuegos no usados ni acostumbrados que fue causa que doblaron
las uelas pero como en toda la noche no sintieron nada a la madrugada
se descuidarõ y los enemigos entraron tan callados por el pueblo que no

fueron uistos hasta que andaban matando y robando algunas gentes
salieron a lo llano que tubieron lugar y a el salir hiriero de muerte a el
capitan y como algunos españoles se rehiçieron en algunos cauallos
bolbieron sobre los enemigos y socorrieron alguna gente aunque fue poca
y los enemigos se fueron con la presa sin reçebir daño dexando muertos
tres españoles y mucha gente de seruiçio y mas de ueinto cauallos.

los españoles que quedaron salieron aquel dia a pie sin cauallos la
buelta de culiacan por fuera de caminos y sin ningun bastimento hasta
llegar a los coraçones adonde aquellos indios los socorrieron de bastimentos como amigos que siempre fueron y de alli cō grandes trabajos que
pasaron llegaron a culiacan adonde hernandarias de saabedra alcalde
mayor los reçibio y hospedo lo mejor que pudo hasta que juan gallego
llego con el socorro que traya para pasar adelante en busca del campo
que no poco le peso se obiese despoblado aquel paso creyendo quel
campo estaba en la tierra rica que auia dicho el indio que llamaron turco
porque lo parecia en su aspeto.

*Capitulo quarto como se quedo fray juan de padilla y fray luis en la
tierra y el campo se aperçibio la buelta de mexico.*

ya quel general francisco uasques uido que todo estaba pacifico y
que sus negoçios se auian encaminado a su uoluntad mando que para
entrado el mes de abril del año de quinientos y quarenta y tres estu-
biesen todos aperçebidos para salir la buelta de la nueba españa.

biendo esto un fray juan de padilla frayle de misa de la orden de los
menores y otro fray luis lego dixeron a el general que ellos querian
quedarse en aquella tierra el fray juan de padilla en quiuira porque le
parecia haria alli fructo su dotrina y el fray luis en cicuye y para esto
como era quaresma a la saçon predico un domingo aquel sermon del
padre de las compañas y fundo su proposito con autoridad de la sagrada
escritura y como su celo era combertir aquellas gentes y traer los a la
fe y como tubieron liçençia que para esto no era menester embio el general con ellos una compañia que los sacasen hasta cicuye donde se quedo el fray luis y el fray juan paso la buelta de quiuira lleuando el portugues que diximos y el negro y el mestiso y indios de la nueba españa
con las guias que auia traydo el general donde en llegando alla dentro
de muy poco tiempo lo martiriçaron como contamos en la segunda parte
cap̄ otauo y ansi se puede creer murio martir pues su çelo era santo y
bueno.

el fray luis se quedo en cicuye no se a sabido del mas hasta oy aun
que antes quel campo saliese de tiguex lleuandole sierta cantidad de
obejas para que se le quedasen los que las lleuauan toparon acompañado de gente que andaba uiçitando otros pueblos que estaban a quinçe
y a ueinte leguas de cicuye y no dio poca buena esperança que estaba
en graçia del pueblo y haria fruto su dotrina aūque se quexaba que los
uiejos lo desamparaban y creyo al fin lo matarian yo para mi tengo que
como era hombre de buena y santa uida nr̄o señor lo guardaria y daria

gracia que conbirtiese algunas gentes de aquellas y dexase despues de sus dias quien los administrase en la fee y no es de creer otro cosa porque la gente de por alli es piadosa y ninguna cosa cruel antes son amigos o enemigos de la crueldad y guardan la fee y lealtad a los amigos.

el general despachados los frayles temiendo no le dañase el traer gente de aquella tierra a la nueba españa mādo quel seruiçio que los soldados tenian de los naturales lo dexasen yr libres a sus pueblos adonde quisiesen que a mi ber no lo a serto que mas ualiera se dotrinaran entre christianos.

andaba ya el general alegre y contento llegado el plaço y todos probeydos de lo necesario para su jornada el campo salio de tiguex la buelta de cibola aconteçio en este camino una cosa no poco de notar y fue que con salir los cauallos exerçitados a el trabajo gordos y hermosos en diez dias que se tardo en llegar a cibola murieron mas de treinta que no ubo dia que no muriesen dos y tres y mas y despues hasta llegar a culiacan murieron gran numero de ellos cosa no acontecida en toda la jornada.

llegado que fue el campo a çibola se rehiço para salir por el despoblado por ser alli lo ultimo de los poblados de aquella tierra quedando toda aquella tierra pacifica y llana y que se quedaron algunos amigos entre ellos de los nuestros.

Capitulo quinto como el canpo salio del poblado y camino a culiacan y lo que aconteçio en el camino.

dexando ya por popa podemos deçir los poblados que se auian descubierto en la tierra nueba que como tengo dicho eran los siete pueblos de cibola lo primero que se bio y lo prostero que se dexo salio el campo caminando por el despoblado y en dos o tres jornadas nunca dexaron los naturales de seguir el campo tras la retaguardia por coger algun fardaje o gente de seruiçio porque aunque que dabā de paz y auian sido buenos y le a les amigos todauia como bieron que se les dexaba la tierra libre se holgauan de ber en su poder gente de la nuestra a aunque se cre no para los enojar como se supo de algunos que no quiseron yr con ellos que fueron de ellos inportunados y rogados todauia lleuaron alguna gente y otros que se auian quedado uoluntariamēte de los quales el dia de oy abra buenas lenguas el despoblado se camino sin contraste y como salieron en chichilticale en la segunda jornada llego a el campo juan gallego que yba de la nueba españa con socorro de gente y cosas neçesarias para el campo pensando de lo hallar en la tierra del indio que llamauan turco y como juan gallego bido que el canpo se bolbia la prime[ra] palabra que dixo no fue deçir norabuena bengais y no lo sintio tan poco que despues de aber hablado al general y llegados a el campo digo a el aposento no ubiese algunos mobimientos en los caualleros con aquel nuebo socorro que no con poco trabajo auian allegado tras ta alli teniendo cada dia recuentros con los indios de aquellas partes como se a dicho que estaban alcados ubo algunos tratos y platicas de poblar por alli en alguna parte hasta dar relaçion a el bisorey de lo que pasaba la gente de los soldados que uenian de la tierra nueba a ninguna cosa daban consentimiento sino en bolber a la nueba españa por donde no ubo efecto nada de lo que se proponia en sus consultas y aunque ubo algunos alborotos al cabo se apasiaguarō yban con juan gallego algunos de los amotinados que despoblaron la uilla de los coraçones asegurados por el y debajo de su palabra y puesto que el general quisiera haçer algun castigo era poco su poder porque ya era desobe desobedecido y poco acatado y de alli adelante de nuebo començo a temer y haciase doliente andando con guarda en algunas partes ubo algunas gritas y de indios y de heridos y muertes de cauallos hasta llegar a batuco donde salieron a el campo indios amigos del ualle del coraçon por ber a el general como amigos que sienpre fueron y ansi auiā tratado a todos los españoles que por sus tierras auian pasado probeyendoles en sus neçesidades de bastimentos y gente si necesario era y ansi fueron de los nr̄os siempre muy bien tratados y gratificados en esta jornada se aprobo del agua del menbrillo ser buena contra la yerba de estas partes porque en un paso algunas jornadas antes de llegar a el ualle de señora los indios enemigos hirieron a un español llamado mesa y con ser la herida mortal de yerba fresca y tardarse mas de dos oras en curar con el agua no murio puesto que quedolo que la yerba auia inficionado podrido y se cayo la carne hasta dexar los guesos y nierbos desnudos con pestilençial hedor que fue la herida en la muñeca y auia llegado la ponsoña hasta la espalda quando se uino a curar y todo esto desamparo la carne.

caminaba el campo sin tomar reposo porque ya en esta saçon auia falta de bastimentos que como aquellas comarcas estaban alçadas las bituallas no auia adonde las tomar hasta que llego a petlatlan haçiendo algunas entradas en las trabesias por buscar bastimentos patlatlan es de la prouinçia de culiacan y a esta causa estaba de paz aunque despues aca a bido algunas nobedades alli descanso el campo algunos dias por se basteçer y salidos de alli con mayor presteça que de antes procuraron pasar aquellas treinta leguas que ay el ualle de culiacan donde de nuebo los acogieron como gente que benia con su gouernador mal tratado.

Capitulo sexto como el general salio de culiacan para dar quenta a el uisorey del campo que le encargo.

ya parece que en aber llegado a el ualle de culiacan se da fin a los trabajos de esta jornada lo uno por ser el general gouernador y lo otro por estar en tierra de christianos y ansi se començaron luego asentar algunos de la superioridad y dominio que sobre ellos tenian sus capitanes y aun algunos capitanes de la obidencia del general y cada uno haçia ya cabeça de su juego de manera que pasando el general a la uilla que estaua de alli diez leguas mucha de la gente o la mas de ella se le quedo en el ualle reposando y algunos con proposito de no le seguir bien sintio el general que por uia de fuerça ya no era poderoso

aunque la autoridad de ser gouernador le daba otra nueba autoridad
determino llebar lo por otra mejor uia que fue mandar prober a todos
los capitanes de bastimentos y carne de lo que auia en algunos pueblos
que como gouernador estaban en su cabeça y mostrose estar doliente
haçiendo cama porque los que con el ubiesen de negoçiar pudiesen
hablarle o el con ellos mas libremente sin enpacho ni obenpacion y no
dexaba de embiar a llamar algunos particulares amigos para les rogar
y encargar hablasen a los soldados y los animasen a salir de alli en su
compañia la buelta de la nueba españa y les dixesen lleuaba muy a
cargo de los faboreçeran si con el uisorey don Antonio de mendoça
como en su gouernaçion a los que con el quisiesen quedar en ella y
desque ubo negociado salio con su campo en tiempo reçio y principio
de las aguas que era por san juan en el qual tiempo lluebe brabamēte y
los rios de aquel despoblado que se pasan hasta conpostela sō muchos
y muy peligrosos y caudalosos de grandes y brauos lagartos en un rio
de los quales estando asentado el campo pasando un soldado de la una
parte a la otra a bista de todos fue arrebatado de un lagarto y llebado
sin poder ser socorrido el general camino dexando por todas partes
gentes que no le querian seguir y llego a mexico con menos de çien
hombres a dar quenta a el uisorey don Antonio de mendoça no fue del
bien recebido aun que dio sus descargos y desde alli perdio reputaçion
y gouerno poco tiempo la gouernaçion que se le auiā encargado de la
nueba galiçia porque el uisorey la tomo en si hasta que uino a el la audien-
çia como a el presente lo ay y este fue el fin que ubieron aquellos descubrimientos y jornada que se hiço de la tierra nueba.

quedanos agora deçir por que uia se podria entrar y por mas
derecho camino en ella aunque digo que no ay atajo sin trabajo y siempre es lo mejor lo que se sabe porque prebienen bien los hombres lo que
saben que a de benir y necesidades en que ya otra uez se bieron y decir
sea a que parte cae quiuira ques el rumbo que llebo el campo y a qual
parte cae la india mayor que era lo que se pretendia buscar quando el
campo salio para alla que agora por aber uillalobos descubierto esta
costa de la mar del sur que es por esta uia de poniente se cognoçe y be
claramente que se auia de bolber estando como estabamos debajo del
norte a el poniente y no haçia oriente como fuimos y con esto dexaremos
esta materia y daremos fin a este tratado como ay a hecho relaçion de
algunas cosas notables que dexe de contar por las tratar particularmente en los dos capitulos siguientes.

Capitulo septimo de las cosas que le aconteçieron al capitan Juan gallego
por la tierra alçada lleuando el socorro.

bien se sufrira pues en el capitulo pasado pase en silençio las haçañas
quel capitan juan gallego hiço con ueinte compañeros que lleuabase
diga en el presente capitulo para que en los tiempos benideros los que
lo leyeren y de ello dieren notiçia tengan autor sierto con quien apro-
bar y que no escribe fabulas como algunas cosas que en nr̃os tiempos

leemos en los libros de cauallerias que si no fuese por lleuar aquellas
fabulas de encãtamientos ay cosas el dia de oy acontesidas en estas
partes por nr̃os españoles en conquistas y recuentros abidos con los
naturales que sobrepujan en hechos de admiraçion no solo a los libros
ya dichos sino a los que se escriben de los doçe parés de frãçia porque
tanteado y mirado la fatales fuerças que los autores de aquellos tienpos
les atribuyen y las lucidas y resplandesientes armas de que los adornan
y las pequeñas estaturas de que agora son los hombres de nr̃os tiempos
y las pocas y ruynes armas de en estas partes mas es de admirar las
cosas estrañas que con tales armas los nr̃os acometen y hacen el dia de
oy que las que escribẽ de los antiguos pues tambien peleaban ellos con
gentes barbaras y desnudas como los nr̃os con indios donde no dexa de
aber hombres que entre ellos sõ esforçados y ualientes y muy çerteros
flecheros pues le abemos uisto derribar las aues que ban bolando y corriendo tras las liebres flecharlas todo esto he dicho a el fin que algunas
cosas que tenemos por fabulosas pueden ser berdaderas y pues cada
dia bemos en nr̃os tiempos cosas mayores como an sido las de don
fer^do cortes en los benideros tienpos que con tresientos hombres osa
se entrar en el riñon de la nueba españa donde tan grande numero de
gentes como es mexico y con quinientos españoles la acabase de ganar
y señorear en dos años cosa de grande admiraçion.

los hechos de don pedro de aluarado en la conquista de guatimala y
lo de montejo en tabasco las conquistas de terra firme y del peru cosas
eran todas estas para que yo ubiera de callar y pasar en silençio lo que
agora quiero contar pero por que estoy obligado a dar relacion de las
cosas en esta jornada acontecidas e querido se sepan tambien las oue
agora dire con las demas que tengo dicho.

y es ansi quel capitan juan gallego llego a la uilla de culiacan con
bien poca gente y alli recogio la que pudo de la que se auia escapado de
la uilla de los coraçones o por mejor decir de suya que por todos fueron
ueinte y dos hombres y con estos camino por toda aquella tierra poblada
en que andubo doçientas leguas y de tierra de guerra y gente alçada que
auian estado ya en el amistad de los españoles teniendo cada dia o poco
menos recuentros con los enemigos y siempre caminaua dexando atras
el fardaje con las dos partes de las gentes lleuando continuamente la
auangardia con seis o siete españoles sin otros amigos que los lleuaban
entrando en los pueblos por fuerça matando y destruyendo y poniendo
fuego dando en los enemigos tam de supito y con tanta presteça y
denuedo que no les daban lugar a que se juntasen ni entendiesen de
suerte que eran tan temidos que no auia pueblo que esperar los osase
que ansi huyan de ellos como de un poderoso exercito tanto que les
aconteçio yr diez dias todo por poblado que no tenian ora de descanso
y todo lo haciã con siete compañeros que quando llegaua el fardaje con
toda la demas gente no tenian en que entender saluo en robar que ya
ellas auian muerto y preso la gente que auian podido auer a las manos
y la demas auia huydo y como no paraban aunque los pueblos de ade-

14 ETH——30

lante tenian algun abiso eran con ellos tam presto que no les daban
lugar a se recoger en espeçial en aquella parte donde auia sido la uilla
de los coraçones que alli mato y ahorco buena cantidad de gente en
castigo de su rebelion y en todo esto no perdio compañero sin se lo
hirieron saluo uno que por despojar a un indio que casi estaba muerto
le hirio en el parpalo del ojo quando le ronpio el pelejo y por ser con
yerba obiera de morir sino fuera socorrido con el agua del membrillo y
perdio el ojo fueron tales estos hijos digo hechos que aquella gente
tendra en memoria todo quanto la uida les durare en espeçial quatro o
cinco indios amigos que salieron con ellos de los coraçones que quedaron
desto tam admirados que los tenian mas por cosa diuina que humana y
si como nro campo los topo no los topara obieran de llegar a la tierra del
indio que llamauan turco do yban encaminados y lo pasaran sin riesgo
segũ la buena orden y gouierno lleuaba y bien dotrinada y exerçitada
en la guerra de los quales algunos quedaron en esta uilla de culiacan
donde yo a el presente escribo esta relaçion y notiçia a donde ansi ellos
como yo y los demas que en esta prouincia paramos no nos a faltado
trabajos apasiguando y sustentando esta tierra tomando rebeldes y
biniendo en probeça y neçesidad y en esta ora mas por estar la tierra
mas probe y alcançada que nunca lo fue.

*Capitulo otauo en que se quentan algunas cosas admirables que se bieron
en los llanos con la façion de los toros.*

no sin misterio calle y dicimule en la segunda parte deste libro en
el capitulo septimo que habla de los llanos las cosas de que hare men-
çion en este capitulo particular adonde se hallase todo junto pues eran
cosas señaladas y no uistas en otras partes y atrebome a las escrebir
porque escribo en tiempo que son oy biuos muchos hombres que lo bieron
y haran berdadera mi escriptura quien podra crer que caminando por
aquellos llanos mill cauallos y quinientas uacas de las nuestras y mas de
çinco mill carneros y obejas y mas de mill y quinientas personas de los
amigos y seruiçio que acabando de pasar no dexaban mas rastro que si
nunca por alli ubieran pasado nadie tanto que era menester haçer
montones de guesos y boñigas de uacas a trechos para que la retaguardia guiase tras del canpo y no se perdiesen la yerba aunque menuda
en pisandola se enhiestaua tam limpia y derecha como de antes lo
estaba.

otra cosa que se hallo a la orilla de una laguna de sal a la parte del
sur un grande ayuntamiento de guesos de uacas que tenia de largo un
tiro de ballesta o muy poquito menos y de esto casi dos estados en partes
y en ancho tres braças y mas en parte donde no ay gente que lo pudiese
haçer lo que de ello se entendio fue que con la reseca que debe de haçer el
lago o laguna en tiempo de nortes los a juntado de el ganado que muere
dentro en la laguna que de uiejo y flaco entrando no puede salir lo que
se a de notar es que numero de ganado seria menester para tanta osa-
menta.

GRANATA NOVA ET CALIFORNIA.

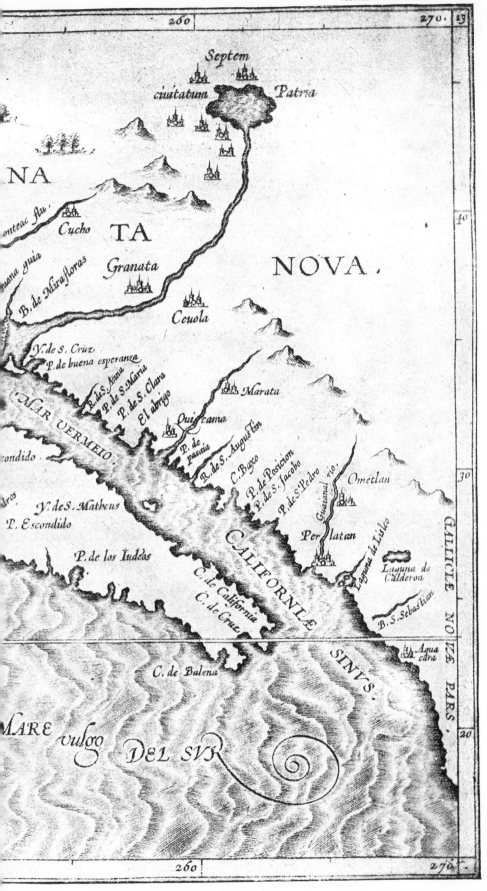

Septem

ciuitatum   Patria

NA

Cucho   TA   NOVA.

B. de Miraflores   Granata

mena guia

Ceuola

Y. de S. Cruz

P. de buena esperanza

E. de S. Anna   Marata

P. de S. Maria

P. de S. Clara

El abrigo

Quiuicama

MAR VERMEIO.   P. de pasaia

R. de S. Augustin

C. Bispo

condido   P. de Posicion

P. de S. Jacobo

dros   Y. de S. Matheus   Guanaual rio.   Ometlan

P. Escondido   P. de S. Pedro

CALIFORNIÆ   Per latan

P. de los Iudeas   Laguna de Lisleo

C. de California   Laguna de

C. de Cruz.   Calderon

B. S. Sebastian

SINVS.

Aqua

clara

C. de Balena

MARE vulgo DEL SVR

GALLICIE NOVÆ PARS.

FORNIA, 1597

pues querer contar la façion de los toros tambien es de admirar que ningun cauallo ubo a los principios que los biese de cara que no huyese de su bista porque ellos tienen el rrostro ancho y corto de ojo a ojo dos palmos de frente los ojos salidos por el lado que yendo huyendo ben a quien los sigue tienen barbas como cabrones muy grandes quando huyen lleuan la cabeça baxa la barba arrastrando por el suelo del medio cuerpo para atras son señidos el pelo muy merino como de ouejas muy finas y de la sinta para adelante el pelo muy largo de faicion de leon raspante y una grã corcoba mayor que de camello los cuernos cortos y gordos que se descubren poco por cima del pelo mudan el pelo de medio cuerpo atras por mayo en un bellon y quedan perfectos leones para mudarse arrimã a algunos arboles pequeños que ay en algunas barranquillas y alli se rrefriegan hasta que dexan el bellon como la culebra el pelejo tienen la cola corta y un pequeño y sopo a el cabo lleuan la quando corren alta a manera de alacrã es cosa de ber que quando son beçerricos son bermejos y de la manera de los nuestros y con el tiempo y la edad se mudan en color y faiçion.

ay otra cosa que todos los toros que se mataron tenian a la oreja isquierda hendida teniendolas sanas quando chiquitos este fue un secreto que no se pudo alcançar la causa de ello de la lana segun la finesa se harian buenos paños aunque no de colores por ser ella de color de buriel.

otra cosa es de notar que andan los toros sin bacas en tanto numero que no ay quien los pueda numerar y tam apartados de las uacas que desde donde començamos a ber toros jasta adonde començamos a ber uacas auia mas de quarenta leguas y la tierra adonde andaban era tan llana y esconbrada que por do quiera que los mirasen se bia el cielo por entre las piernas de suerte que si estaban algo lejos pareçian escombrados pinos que juntaban las copas por lo alto y si un solo toro estaba pareçia quatro pinos y por serca que estubiese no se podia mirando por encima ber tierra de la otra parte causaba todo esto ser la tierra tam redonda que do quiera que un hombre se ponia pareçia que estaba en la cumbre y uia el çielo a el rededor de si a tiro de ballesta y por poca cosa que se le ponia delante le quitaba la uista de la tierra.

otras cosas se bieron que por no ser de tanta calidad no las escribo ni hago de ellas minçion aunque no parece es de callar el tener como tienen en beneraçion en algunas partes de los poblados de altos la señal de la cruz por que en acuco en una fuente que estaba en lo llano tenian una cruz de dos palmos de alto de gordor de un dedo hecha de palo con su peña de una uara de quadro y muchos palitos adornados de plumas a el rededor y muchas flores secas desmenuçadas.

en tutahaco en un sepulcro fuera del pueblo parecia aber se enterrado en el frescamente alguien estaua otra cruz a la cabeçera de dos palitos atados con hilo de algodon y flores desmenusadas secas yo digo que a mi pareçer por alguna uia tienen alguna lunbre de cruz de christo nuestro redentor y podria ser por la uia de la india de do ellos proçeden.

Capitulo nono que trata el rumbo que llebo el campo y como se podria yr a buscar otra uia que mas derecha fuese abiendo de boluer aquella tierra.

mucho quisiera yo agora que para dar a entender lo que quiero deçir ubiera en mi alguna parte de cosmografia o jumetria para que pudiera tantear o compasar la bentaja que puede aber y ay si otra uez saliesen de la nueba españa gentes en demanda de aquella tierra en yr alla por el riñon de la tierra o seguir el camino quel campo llebo pero ayudandome la graçia del señor dire lo que alcanso dandolo a entender lo mejor que a mi sea posible.

ya me pareçe que se tiene entendido quel portugues campo fue el soldado que se escapo quando los de quiuira mataron a fray juan de padilla el quel uino a salir a la nueba españa por panuco abiendo andado por la tierra de los llanos hasta que uino atrabesar la cordillera de la mar del norte dexando siempre la tierra que descubrio don hernando de soto sobre mano isquierda porque este hombre nunca bio el rio del espiritu santo y quando bino acabar de atrabesar la cordillera de la mar del norte cayo sobre panuco de manera que si no se pusiera a demandar por la mar del norte ubiera de salir por la comarca de la marca o tierra de los sacatecas de que ya agora se tiene lumbre.

y para aber de boluer en demanda de quiuira seria aquella uia harto mejor y mas derecha pues ay guias en la nueba españa de las que binieron con el portugues aunque digo que seria mejor y mas derecho por la tierra de los guachichules arrimandose siempre a la cordillera de la mar del sur porque es mas poblada y abria bastimento porque engolfarse en la tierra llana seria perderse por la gran anchura que tiene y ser esteril de comidas aunque sea berdad que dando en las uacas no se pasaria mucha necesidad y esto es solamente para yr en demanda de quiuira y de aquellos pueblos que decia el indio que llemauan turco porque yr por donde fue el campo de fran^co uasques coronado el grandissimo rodeo porque salen de mexico a el poniente siento y diez leguas y despues a el nordeste cien leguas y a el norte docientas y sinquenta y todo esto es hasta los barrancos de las uacas y con aber andado ochoçientas y sinquenta leguas por rumbo derecho no se an desbiado de mexico quatro sientas leguas si es querer yr a la tierra de tiguex para desde alli bolber a el poniente en demanda de la tierra de la india a se de lleuar el camino quel campo llebo porque aunque se quiera tomar otro camino no lo ay que no da lugar el ancon de mar que entra por esta costa adentro hacia el norte sino es que se ubiese de hacer armada de mar que fuese atrabesando este ancon de mar a desembarcar en el paraje de la isla de negros y por alli entrar la tierra adentro atrabesando la cordillera en busca de la tierra do proçeden los de tiguex o de otras gentes que tengan aquella poliçia porque aber de entrar por tierra de la florida por la mar del norte ya se a uisto y conosido que quantas jornadas por alli se an hecho an sido infeliçes y no bien afortunadas allende de ques la tierra de aquella parte llena de cienegas y ahogadiça esteril y la mas mala que calienta el sol sino ban

a desembarcar pasado el rio del espiritu santo como hiço don hernando
de soto y con todo me afirmo que aunque se pase mucho trabajo es lo
mejor por la tierra que aya andado y se sepan los aguajes porque se
lleuauan las cosas necesarias con mas façilidad y mas abundosamente
y en las tierras nueuas los cauallos es lo mas neçesario y lo que mas
haçe temer a los enemigos y los que son señores del campo tambien
es temida el artilleria donde no saben el uso de ella y para poblados
como los que fran^co uasques descubrio fuera buena alguna pieça de
artilleria gruesa para derribar porque el no llebo sino uersillos menores
y no hombre ingenioso para que hiciese un trabuco ni otra maquina
que los atemorisas el qual es muy necesario.

digo pues que con la lunbre que el dia de oy se tiene de los rumbos
que an corrido los nauios por esta costa de la mar del sur an andado
descubriẽdo por esta parte de poniẽte y lo que se sabe de la mar del
norte haçia la nuruega ques la costa de la florida arriba los que agora
entrasen a descubrir por donde fran^co uasques entro y se hallasen en
tierra de çibola o de tiguex bien sabrian a que parte auiã de yr en demanda de la tierra quel marques del ualle don hernando cortes buscaba
y la buelta que da el ancon del tiçon para tomar el rumbo berdadero y
esto bastara para dar fin a nuestra relaçion en todo lo demas probe a
aquel poderoso señor de todas las cosas dios omnipotente quel sabe el
como y quando estas tierras seran descubiertas y para quien esta guar-
dada esta buena uentura.

laus deo.

Acabose de tresladar sabado a ueinte y seis de otubre de mill y quinientos y nouẽta y seis anos en seuilla.

TRANSLATION OF THE NARRATIVE OF CASTAÑEDA

Account of the Expedition to Cibola which took place in the year 1540, in which all those settlements, their ceremonies and customs, are described. Written by Pedro de Castañeda, of Najera.[1]

PREFACE

To me it seems very certain, my very noble lord, that it is a worthy ambition for great men to desire to know and wish to preserve for posterity correct information concerning the things that have happened in distant parts, about which little is known. I do not blame those inquisitive persons who, perchance with good intentions, have many times troubled me not a little with their requests that I clear up for them some doubts which they have had about different things that have been commonly related concerning the events and occurrences that took place during the expedition to Cibola, or the New Land, which the good viceroy—may he be with God in His glory[2]—Don Antonio de Mendoza, ordered and arranged, and on which he sent Francisco Vazquez de Coronado as captain-general. In truth, they have reason for wishing to know the truth, because most people very often make things of which they have heard, and about which they have perchance no knowledge, appear either greater or less than they are. They make nothing of those things that amount to something, and those that do not they make so remarkable that they appear to be something impossible to believe. This may very well have been caused by the fact that, as that country was not permanently occupied, there has not been anyone who was willing to spend his time in writing about its peculiarities, because all knowledge was lost of that which it was not the pleasure of God—He alone knows the reason—that they should enjoy. In truth, he who wishes to employ himself thus in writing out the things that happened on the expedition, and the things that were seen in those lands, and the ceremonies and customs of the natives, will have matter enough to test his judgment, and I believe that the result can not fail to be an account which, describing only the truth, will be so remarkable that it will seem incredible.

---

[1] There were several representatives of the family of Castañeda among the Spaniards in America as early as the middle of the sixteenth century, but the only possible mention of this Pedro, of the Biscayan town of Najera, which I have seen outside of the present document, is the following item from a Relacion de los pesos de oro que están señalados por indios vacos á los conquistadores de Nueva España y á sus hijos, cuyos nombres se expresan (año 1554), in Pacheco y Cardenas, Doc. de Indias, xiv, 206: "A los nueve hijos de Pero Franco, conquistador, é su mujer, que son: María de Acosta, madre de todos, Pero Francisco de Castañeda, Juana de Castañeda, Inés de Castañeda, Francisco de Castañeda, Lorenzo Franco, Marta de Castañeda, Anton de Vargas y Juana de Castañeda, les están señalados de entretenimiento en cada un año duzientos y setenta pesos. CCLXX."

[2] Mendoza died in Lima, July 21, 1552.

186

And besides, I think that the twenty years and more since that expedition took place have been the cause of some stories which are related. For example, some make it an uninhabitable country, others have it bordering on Florida, and still others on Greater India, which does not appear to be a slight difference. They are unable to give any basis upon which to found their statements. There are those who tell about some very peculiar animals, who are contradicted by others who were on the expedition, declaring that there was nothing of the sort seen. Others differ as to the limits of the provinces and even in regard to the ceremonies and customs, attributing what pertains to one people to others. All this has had a large part, my very noble lord, in making me wish to give now, although somewhat late, a short general account for all those who pride themselves on this noble curiosity, and to save myself the time taken up by these solicitations. Things enough will certainly be found here which are hard to believe. All or the most of these were seen with my own eyes, and the rest is from reliable information obtained by inquiry of the natives themselves. Understanding as I do that this little work would be nothing in itself, lacking authority, unless it were favored and protected by a person whose authority would protect it from the boldness of those who, without reverence, give their murmuring tongues liberty, and knowing as I do how great are the obligations under which I have always been, and am, to your grace, I humbly beg to submit this little work to your protection. May it be received as from a faithful retainer and servant. It will be divided into three parts, that it may be better understood. The first will tell of the discovery and the armament or army that was made ready, and of the whole journey, with the captains who were there; the second, of the villages and provinces which were found, and their limits, and ceremonies and customs, the animals, fruits, and vegetation, and in what parts of the country these are; the third, of the return of the army and the reasons for abandoning the country, although these were insufficient, because this is the best place there is for discoveries—the marrow of the land in these western parts, as will be seen. And after this has been made plain, some remarkable things which were seen will be described at the end, and the way by which one might more easily return to discover that better land which we did not see, since it would be no small advantage to enter the country through the land which the Marquis of the Valley, Don Fernando Cortes, went in search of under the Western star, and which cost him no small sea armament. May it please our Lord to so favor me that with my slight knowledge and small abilities I may be able by relating the truth to make my little work pleasing to the learned and wise readers, when it has been accepted by your grace. For my intention is not to gain the fame of a good composer or rhetorician, but I desire to give a faithful account and to do this slight service to your grace, who will, I hope, receive it as from a faithful servant and soldier, who took part in it. Although not in a polished style, I write that which happened—that which I heard, experienced, saw, and did.

I always notice, and it is a fact, that for the most part when we have something valuable in our hands, and deal with it without hindrance, we do not value or prize it as highly as if we understood how much we would miss it after we had lost it, and the longer we continue to have it the less we value it; but after we have lost it and miss the advantages of it, we have a great pain in the heart, and we are all the time imagining and trying to find ways and means by which to get it back again. It seems to me that this has happened to all or most of those who went on the expedition which, in the year of our Savior Jesus Christ 1540, Francisco Vazquez Coronado led in search of the Seven Cities. Granted that they did not find the riches of which they had been told, they found a place in which to search for them and the beginning of a good country to settle in, so as to go on farther from there. Since they came back from the country which they conquered and abandoned, time has given them a chance to understand the direction and locality in which they were, and the borders of the good country they had in their hands, and their hearts weep for having lost so favorable an opportunity. Just as men see more at the bullfight when they are upon the seats than when they are around in the ring,[1] now when they know and understand the direction and situation in which they were, and see, indeed, that they can not enjoy it nor recover it, now when it is too late they enjoy telling about what they saw, and even of what they realize that they lost, especially those who are now as poor as when they went there. They have never ceased their labors and have spent their time to no advantage. I say this because I have known several of those who came back from there who amuse themselves now by talking of how it would be to go back and proceed to recover that which is lost, while others enjoy trying to find the reason why it was discovered at all. And now I will proceed to relate all that happened from the beginning.

FIRST PART.

Chapter 1, which treats of the way we first came to know about the Seven Cities, and of how Nuño de Guzman made an expedition to discover them.

In the year 1530 Nuño de Guzman, who was President of New Spain,[2] had in his possession an Indian, a native of the valley or valleys of Oxitipar, who was called Tejo by the Spaniards. This Indian said he was the son of a trader who was dead, but that when he was a little boy his father had gone into the back country with fine feathers to trade for ornaments, and that when he came back he brought a large amount of gold and silver, of which there is a good deal in that country. He

---

[1] Ternaux renders this: " C'est ainsi que l'homme qui se place derrière la barrière qui, dans les courses des taureaux, sépare le spectateur des combattants, voit bien mieux la position dans laquelle il se trouvait lorsqu'il combattait, qu'alors même qu'il était dans la carrière."

[2] President, or head, of the Audiencia, the administrative and judicial board which governed the province.

went with him once or twice, and saw some very large villages, which
he compared to Mexico and its environs. He had seen seven very
large towns which had streets of silver workers. It took forty days
to go there from his country, through a wilderness in which nothing
grew, except some very small plants about a span high. The way
they went was up through the country between the two seas, following the northern direction. Acting on this information, Nuño de Guzman got together nearly 400 Spaniards and 20,000 friendly Indians of
New Spain, and, as he happened to be in Mexico, he crossed Tarasca,
which is in the province of Michoacan, so as to get into the region
which the Indian said was to be crossed toward the North sea, in this
way getting to the country which they were looking for, which was
already named "The Seven Cities."[1] He thought, from the forty days
of which the Tejo had spoken, that it would be found to be about 200
leagues, and that they would easily be able to cross the country. Omitting several things that occurred on this journey, as soon as they had
reached the province of Culiacan, where his government ended, and
where the New Kingdom of Galicia is now, they tried to cross the
country, but found the difficulties very great, because the mountain
chains which are near that sea are so rough that it was impossible, after
great labor, to find a passageway in that region. His whole army had
to stay in the district of Culiacan for so long on this account that some
rich men who were with him, who had possessions in Mexico, changed
their minds, and every day became more anxious to return. Besides
this, Nuño de Guzman received word that the Marquis of the Valley,
Don Fernando Cortes, had come from Spain with his new title,[2] and
with great favors and estates, and as Nuño de Guzman had been a great
rival of his at the time he was president,[3] and had done much damage
to his property and to that of his friends, he feared that Don Fernando
Cortes would want to pay him back in the same way, or worse. So he
decided to establish the town of Culiacan there and to go back with
the other men, without doing anything more. After his return from
this expedition, he settled at Xalisco, where the city of Compostela is
situated, and at Tonala, which is called Guadalaxara,[4] and now this is
the New Kingdom of Galicia. The guide they had, who was called
Tejo, died about this time, and thus the name of these Seven Cities
and the search for them remains until now, since they have not been
discovered.[5]

[1] The Segunda Relacion Anónima de la Jornada que hizo Nuño de Guzman, 1529, in Icazbelceta's Documentos para la Historia de Mexico, vol. ii, p. 303, also implies that the name of the "Seven Cities" had
already been given to the country which he was trying to discover.

[2] Marqués del Valle de Oaxaca y Capitan General de la Nueva España y de la Costa del Sur.

[3] Guzman had presided over the trial of Cortes, who was in Spain at the time, for the murder of his
first wife seven years previously (October, 1522). See Zaragoza's edition of Suarez de Peralta's Tratado, p. 315.

[4] The name was changed in 1540.

[5] The best discussion of the stories of the Seven Caves and the Seven Cities is in Bandelier's Contributions, p. 9, ff.

Chapter 2, of how Francisco Vazquez Coronado came to be governor, and the second account which Cabeza de Vaca gave.

Eight years after Nuño de Guzman made this expedition, he was put in prison by a juez de residencia,[1] named the licentiate Diego de la Torre, who came from Spain with sufficient powers to do this.[2] After the death of the judge, who had also managed the government of that country himself, the good Don Antonio de Mendoza, viceroy of New Spain, appointed as governor of that province Francisco Vazquez de Coronado, a gentleman from Salamanca, who had married a lady in the city of Mexico, the daughter of Alonso de Estrada, the treasurer and at one time governor of Mexico, and the son, most people said, of His Catholic Majesty Don Ferdinand, and many stated it as certain. As I was saying, at the time Francisco Vazquez was appointed governor, he was traveling through New Spain as an official visitor, and in this way he gained the friendship of many worthy men who afterward went on his expedition with him. It happened that just at this time three Spaniards, named Cabeza de Vaca, Dorantes, and Castillo Maldonado, and a negro, who had been lost on the expedition which Pamfilo de Narvaez led into Florida, reached Mexico.[3] They came out through Culiacan, having crossed the country from sea to sea, as anyone who wishes may find out for himself by an account which this same Cabeza de Vaca wrote and dedicated to Prince Don Philip, who is now King of Spain and our sovereign.[4] They gave the good Don Antonio de Mendoza an account of some large and powerful villages, four and five stories high, of which they had heard a great deal in the countries they had crossed, and other things very different from what turned out to be the truth. The noble viceroy communicated this to the new governor, who gave up the visits he had in hand, on account of this, and hurried his departure for his government, taking with him the negro who had come [with Cabeza de Vaca] with the three friars of the order of Saint Francis, one of whom was named Friar Marcos of Nice, a regular priest, and another Friar Daniel, a lay brother, and the other Friar Antonio de Santa Maria. When he reached the province of Culiacan he sent the friars just mentioned and the negro, who was named Stephen, off in search of that country, because Friar Marcos offered to go and see it, because he had been in Peru at the time Don Pedro de Alvarado went there overland. It seems that, after the friars I have mentioned and the negro had started, the negro did not get on well with the friars, because he took the women that were given him and collected turquoises, and got together a stock of everything. Besides, the Indians in those places through which they went got along with the negro better, because they had seen him before. This was the reason he was sent

---

[1] A judge appointed to investigate the accounts and administration of a royal official.
[2] A full account of the licentiate de la Torre and his administration is given by Mota Padilla (ed. Icazbalceta, pp. 103-106). He was appointed juez March 17, 1536, and died during 1538.
[3] They appeared in New Spain in April, 1536, before Coronado's appointment. Castañeda may be right in the rest of his statement.
[4] This account has been translated by Buckingham Smith. See Bibliography for the full title.

on ahead to open up the way and pacify the Indians, so that when the others came along they had nothing to do except to keep an account of the things for which they were looking.

Chapter 3, of how they killed the negro Stephen at Cibola, and Friar Marcos returned in flight.

After Stephen had left the friars, he thought he could get all the reputation and honor himself, and that if he should discover those settlements with such famous high houses, alone, he would be considered bold and courageous. So he proceeded with the people who had followed him, and succeeded in crossing the wilderness which lies between the country he had passed through and Cibola. He was so far ahead of the friars that, when these reached Chichilticalli, which is on the edge of the wilderness, he was already at Cibola, which is 80 leagues beyond. It is 220 leagues from Culiacan to the edge of the wilderness, and 80 across the desert, which makes 300, or perhaps 10 more or less. As I said, Stephen reached Cibola loaded with the large quantity of turquoises they had given him and several pretty women who had been given him. The Indians who accompanied him carried his things. These had followed him from all the settlements he had passed, believing that under his protection they could traverse the whole world without any danger. But as the people in this country were more intelligent than those who followed Stephen, they lodged him in a little hut they had outside their village, and the older men and the governors heard his story and took steps to find out the reason he had come to that country. For three days they made inquiries about him and held a council. The account which the negro gave them of two white men who were following him, sent by a great lord, who knew about the things in the sky, and how these were coming to instruct them in divine matters, made them think that he must be a spy or a guide from some nations who wished to come and conquer them, because it seemed to them unreasonable to say that the people were white in the country from which he came and that he was sent by them, he being black. Besides these other reasons, they thought it was hard of him to ask them for turquoises and women, and so they decided to kill him. They did this, but they did not kill any of those who went with him, although they kept some young fellows and let the others, about 60 persons, return freely to their own country. As these, who were badly scared, were returning in flight, they happened to come upon the friars in the desert 60 leagues from Cibola, and told them the sad news, which frightened them so much that they would not even trust these folks who had been with the negro, but opened the packs they were carrying and gave away everything they had except the holy vestments for saying mass. They returned from here by double marches, prepared for anything, without seeing any more of the country except what the Indians told them.

Chapter 4, of how the noble Don Antonio de Mendoza made an expedition to discover Cibola.

After Francisco Vazquez Coronado had sent Friar Marcos of Nice and his party on the search already related, he was engaged in Culiacan about some business that related to his government, when he heard an account of a province called Topira,[1] which was to the north of the country of Culiacan. He started to explore this region with several of the conquerors and some friendly Indians, but he did not get very far, because the mountain chains which they had to cross were very difficult. He returned without finding the least signs of a good country, and when he got back, he found the friars who had just arrived, and who told such great things about what the negro Stephen had discovered and what they had heard from the Indians, and other things they had heard about the South sea and islands and other riches, that, without stopping for anything, the governor set off at once for the City of Mexico, taking Friar Marcos with him, to tell the viceroy about it. He made the things seem more important by not talking about them to anyone except his particular friends, under promise of the greatest secrecy, until after he had reached Mexico and seen Don Antonio de Mendoza. Then he began to announce that they had really found the Seven Cities, which Nuño de Guzman had tried to find, and for the conquest of which he had collected a force. The noble viceroy arranged with the friars of the order of Saint Francis so that Friar Marcos was made father provincial, as a result of which the pulpits of that order were filled with such accounts of marvels and wonders that more than 300 Spaniards and about 800 natives of New Spain collected in a few days.[2] There were so many men of such high quality among the Spaniards, that such a noble body was never collected in the Indies, nor so many men of quality in such a small body, there being 300 men. Francisco Vazquez Coronado, governor of New Galicia, was captain-general, because he had been the author of it all. The good viceroy Don Antonio did this because at this time Francisco Vazquez was his closest and most intimate friend, and because he considered him to be wise, skillful, and intelligent, besides being a gentleman. Had he paid more attention and regard to the position in which he was placed and the charge over which he was placed, and less to the estates he left behind in New Spain, or, at least, more to the honor he had and might secure from having such gentlemen under his command, things would not have turned out as they did. When this narrative is ended, it will be seen that he did not know how to keep his position nor the government that he held.

---

[1] Bandelier (Contributions, p. 104) says this was Topia, in Durango, a locality since noted for its rich mines.

[2] Mota Padilla, xxii, 2, p. 111: "Determinó el virey lograr la ocasion de la mucha gente noble que habia en México, que como corcho sobre el agua reposado, se andaba sin tener qué hacer ni en qué ocuparse, todos atenidos á que el virey les hiciese algunas mercedes, y á que los vecinos de México les sustentasen á sus mesas; y asi, le fué fácil aprestar mas de trescientos hombres, los mas de á caballo, porque ya se criaban muchos; dióles á treinta pesos y prometioles repartimientos en la tierra que se poblase, y mas cuando se afirmaba haber un cerro de plata y otras minas."

Chapter 5, concerning the captains who went to Cibola.

When the viceroy, Don Antonio de Mendoza, saw what a noble company had come together, and the spirit and good will with which they had all presented themselves, knowing the worth of these men, he would have liked very well to make every one of them captain of an army; but as the whole number was small he could not do as he would have liked, and so he appointed the captains and officers, because it seemed to him that if they were appointed by him, as he was so well obeyed and beloved, nobody would find fault with his arrangements. After everybody had heard who the general was, he made Don Pedro de Tovar ensign general, a young gentleman who was the son of Don Fernando de Tovar, the guardian and lord high steward of the Queen Doña Juana, our demented mistress—may she be in glory—and Lope de Samaniego, the governor of the arsenal at Mexico,[1] a gentleman fully equal to the charge, army-master. The captains were Don Tristan de Arellano; Don Pedro de Guevara, the son of Don Juan de Guevara and nephew of the Count of Oñate; Don Garcia Lopez de Cardenas; Don Rodrigo Maldonado, brother-in-law of the Duke of the Infantado; Diego Lopez, alderman of Seville, and Diego Gutierres, for the cavalry. All the other gentlemen were placed under the flag of the general, as being distinguished persons, and some of them became captains later, and their appointments were confirmed by order of the viceroy and by the general, Francisco Vazquez. To name some of them whom I happen to remember, there were Francisco de Barrionuevo, a gentleman from Granada; Juan de Saldivar, Francisco de Ovando, Juan Gallego, and Melchior Diaz—a captain who had been mayor of Culiacan, who, although he was not a gentleman, merited the position he held. The other gentlemen, who were worthy substitutes, were Don Alonso Manrique de Lara; Don Lope de Urrea, a gentleman from Aragon; Gomez Suarez de Figueroa, Luis Ramirez de Vargas, Juan de Sotomayor, Francisco Gorbalan, the commissioner Riberos, and other gentlemen, men of high quality, whom I do not now recall.[2] The infantry captain was Pablo de Melgosa of Burgos, and of the artillery, Hernando de Alvarado of the mountain district. As I say, since then I have forgotten the names of many good fellows. It would be well if I could name some of them, so that it might be clearly seen what cause I had for saying that they had on this expedition the most brilliant company ever collected in the Indies to go in search of new lands. But they were unfortunate in having a captain who left in New Spain estates and a pretty wife, a noble and excellent lady, which were not the least causes for what was to happen.

---

[1] See Mendoza's letter to the King, regarding Samaniego's position.

[2] Mota Padilla, xxii, iii, p. 112, mentions among those who had commands on the expedition D. Diego de Guevara and Diego Lopez de Cardenas. The second error may be due to the presence of another Diego Lopez in the party.

Chapter 6, of how all the companies collected in Compostela and set off on the journey in good order.

When the viceroy Don Antonio de Mendoza had fixed and arranged everything as we have related, and the companies and captaincies had been arranged, he advanced a part of their salaries from the chest of His Majesty to those in the army who were in greatest need. And as it seemed to him that it would be rather hard for the friendly Indians in the country if the army should start from Mexico, he ordered them to assemble at the city of Compostela, the chief city in the New Kingdom of Galicia, 110 leagues from Mexico, so that they could begin their journey there with everything in good order. There is nothing to tell about what happened on this trip, since they all finally assembled at Compostela by shrove-tide, in the year (fifteen hundred and) forty-one.[1] After the whole force had left Mexico, he ordered Don Pedro de Alarcon to set sail with two ships that were in the port of La Natividad on the South sea coast, and go to the port of Xalisco to take the baggage which the soldiers were unable to carry,[2] and thence to sail along the coast near the army, because he had understood from the reports that they would have to go through the country near the seacoast, and that we could find the harbors by means of the rivers, and that the ships could always get news of the army, which turned out afterward to be false, and so all this stuff was lost, or, rather, those who owned it lost it, as will be told farther on. After the viceroy had completed all his arrangements, he set off for Compostela, accompanied by many noble and rich men. He kept the New Year of (fifteen hundred and) forty-one at Pasquaro, which is the chief place in the bishopric of Michoacan, and from there he crossed the whole of New Spain, taking much pleasure in enjoying the festivals and great receptions which were given him, till he reached Compostela, which is, as I have said, 110 leagues. There he found the whole company assembled, being well treated and entertained by Christobal de Oñate, who had the whole charge of that government for the time being. He had had the management of it and was in command of all that region when Francisco Vazquez was made governor.[3] All were very glad when he arrived, and he made an examination of the company and found all those whom we have mentioned. He assigned the captains to their companies, and after this was done, on the next day, after they had all heard mass, captains and soldiers together, the viceroy made them a very eloquent short speech, telling them of the fidelity they owed to their general and showing them clearly the benefits which this expedition might afford, from the conversion of those peoples as well as in the profit of those who should conquer the territory, and the advan-

---

[1] The correct date is 1540. Castañeda carries the error throughout the narrative.

[2] See the instructions given by Mendoza to Alarcon, in Buckingham Smith's Florida, p. 1. The last of them reads: "Llevareys ciertas cossas que doña Beatriz de Strada embia para el Capitan General su marido, y mandareys que en ello y en lo que mas llevaredes para algunos de los soldados que con él estan que os ayan recomendado amigos ó parientes suyos haya buen recaudo."

[3] See the writings of Tello and Mota Padilla concerning Oñate. Much of the early prosperity of New Galicia—what there was of it—seems to have been due to Oñate's skillful management.

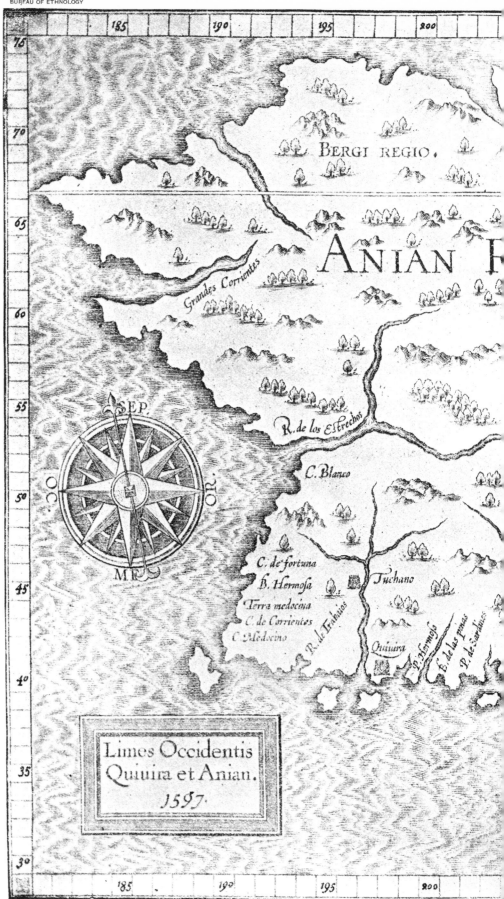

BERGI REGIO.

ANIAN R

Grandes Corrientes

SEP.

OC.

OR.

ME.

R. de los Estrechos

C. Blanco

C. de fortuna

B. Hermosa

Terra medocina

C. de Corrientes

C. Medocino

R. de Trabaios

Tuchano

Quiuira

P. Hermoso

B. de las pinas

P. de Sardinas

Limes Occidentis
Quiuira et Anian.
1597.

210   215   220   225   230   14
75

70

Circulus Arcticus.

65

Pagui

VM.

60

Salboÿ.

Cubirago

55

Tolm Regnum.

50

ꟁIRA REGNꟁVM.

45

S. Francisco

R. grande

Tierra Brana

R. Brnu

B. de pinas

Ciuiac

Tigneis

B. de fuego

R. Hermoso

40

35

Los pinates

C. Blanco

30

210   215   220   225   230

tage to His Majesty and the claim which they would thus have on his favor and aid at all times. After he had finished, they all, both captains and soldiers, gave him their oaths upon the Gospels in a Missal that they would follow their general on this expedition and would obey him in everything he commanded them, which they faithfully performed, as will be seen. The next day after this was done, the army started off with its colors flying. The viceroy, Don Antonio, went with them for two days, and there he took leave of them, returning to New Spain with his friends.[1]

Chapter 7, of how the army reached Chiametla, and the killing of the army-master, and the other things that happened up to the arrival at Culiacan.

After the viceroy Don Antonio left them, the army continued its march. As each one was obliged to transport his own baggage and

---

[1] The following sections from the Fragmento de la Visita hecha á don Antonio de Mendoza, printed in Icazbalceta's Documentos para la Historia de Mexico, ii, 72, add something to the details of the departure of the expedition:

"199. Item, si saben &c. que la gente que salió de la villa de S. Miguel de Culuacan, que es el postrer lugar de Galicia de la Nueva España, para ir en descubrimiento de la tierra nueva de Cíbola con el capitan general Francisco Vazquez de Coronado, fueron hasta doscientos y cincuenta españoles de á caballo, los cuales así para sus personas, como para su carruaje, armas, y bastimentos, y municiones, y otras cosas necesarias para el dicho viaje, llevaron mas de mill caballos y acémilas, y así lo dirán los testigos, porque lo vieron y hallaron presentes, y fueron al dicho viaje: digan lo que saben &c.

"200. Item, . . . que asimismo con la dicha gente española salieron de la dicha villa de S. Miguel de Culuacan hasta trescientos indios, poco mas ó menos, los cuales fueron de su voluntad á servir en la dicha jornada, y el dicho visorey les mandó socorrer, y se les socorrió con dineros y provisiones, y á los que eran casados y dejaban acá sus mujeres les proveyó de lo necesario para su sustentamiento, y esto es público y notorio, . . .

"201. Item, . . . que el dicho visorey proveyó para la gente que fué al dicho descubrimiento, demas de los socorros que les hizo en dineros, y caballos, y armas y otras cosas, les dió mucha cantidad de ganados vacunos y ovejunos, sin otra mucha cantidad de ganados que llevaban los capitanes y soldados, que bastaron para proveerse todo el tiempo que estuvieron al dicho descubrimiento; y asimismo el dicho visorey les dió mucha cantidad de rescates que llevaba á cargo el fator de S. M., para que con ellos comprasen maiz y las otras cosas de bastimentos de la tierra por do pasasen, porque no se hiciese molestia á los indios: . . .

"202. Item, . . . que el dicho visorey mandó y encargó al dicho capitan general tuviese especial cuidado que los indios que desta tierra iban á servir en el dicho descubrimiento, fuesen bien tratados y proveidos de lo que hubiesen menester, y los que se quisiesen volver no fuesen detenidos, antes los enviase ricos y contentos, y el dicho general así lo hizo y cumplió, . . .

"203. Item, si saben que por razon de los dichos caballos y carruaje que llevaron los capitanes y españoles, los indios fueron reservados de llevar cargas de los capitanes y españoles, y si algunos llevaron, seria de su comida, y ropa y bastimentos, como otros españoles lo hacian, que cargaban sus caballos y sus personas de bastimentos, . . .

"204. Item, . . . que de todos los dichos indios que fueron á servir en la dicha jornada, murieron tan solamente hasta veinte ó treinta personas, y si mas murieran, los testigos lo vieran y supieran: . . .

"205. Item, . . . que todos los tamemes que los indios dieron, . . . se les pagó muy á su contento á los indios, por mandado del dicho visorey:" . . .

The evidence of the Informacion, which was taken at Compostela just after the army departed, is so suggestive that I have translated the most valuable portions in full at the end of this memoir.

Mota Padilla, xxii, 3, p. 112: . . . "habiendo llegado la comitiva á Compostela hizo el gobernador reseña de la gente y halló doscientos y sesenta hombres de á caballo con lanzas, espadas y otras armas manuales, y algunos con cotas, celadas y barbotes, unas de hierro y otras de cuero de vaca crudío, y los caballos con faldones de manta de la tierra; sesenta infantes, ballesteros y arcabuceros, y otros con espadas y rodelas: dividió la gente en ocho compañias. . . . Repartida, pues, la gente de esta suerte, con mas de mil caballos sin acémilas, y otros de carga con seis pedreros, pólvora y municion, y mas de mil indios amigos é indias de servicio, vaqueros y pastores de ganado mayor y menor."

all did not know how to fasten the packs, and as the horses started off fat and plump, they had a good deal of difficulty and labor during the first few days, and many left many valuable things, giving them to anyone who wanted them, in order to get rid of carrying them. In the end necessity, which is all powerful, made them skillful, so that one could see many gentlemen become carriers, and anybody who despised this work was not considered a man. With such labors, which they then thought severe, the army reached Chiametla, where it was obliged to delay several days to procure food. During this time the army-master, Lope de Samaniego, went off with some soldiers to find food, and at one village, a crossbowman having entered it indiscreetly in pursuit of the enemies, they shot him through the eye and it passed through his brain, so that he died on the spot.[1] They also shot five or six of his companions before Diego Lopez, the alderman from Seville, since the commander was dead, collected the men and sent word to the general. He put a guard in the village and over the provisions. There was great confusion in the army when this news became known. He was buried here. Several sorties were made, by which food was obtained and several of the natives taken prisoners. They hanged those who seemed to belong to the district where the army-master was killed.

It seems that when the general Francisco Vazquez left Culiacan with Friar Marcos to tell the viceroy Don Antonio de Mendoza the news, as already related, he left orders for Captain Melchior Diaz and Juan de Saldivar to start off with a dozen good men from Culiacan and verify what Friar Marcos had seen and heard. They started and went as far as Chichilticalli, which is where the wilderness begins, 220 leagues from Culiacan, and there they turned back, not finding anything important. They reached Chiametla just as the army was ready to leave, and reported to the general. Although the bad news was kept as secret as possible, some things leaked out which did not seem to add luster to the facts.[2] Friar Marcos, noticing that some were feeling disturbed, cleared away these clouds, promising that what they would see should be good, and that the army was on the way to a country where their hands would be filled, and in this way he quieted them so that they appeared well satisfied. From there the army marched to Culiacan, making some detours into the country to seize provisions. They were two leagues from the town of Culiacan at Easter vespers, when the

---

[1] The account which Mota Padilla gives, cap. xxii, sec. 4, p. 112, is much clearer and more specific than the somewhat confused text of Castañeda. He says: "Á Chametla . . . hallaron la tierra alzada, de suerte que fué preciso entrar á la sierra en busca de maiz, y por cabo el maese de campo, Lopez de Samaniego; internáronse en la espesura de un monte, en donde un soldado que inadvertidamente se apartó, fué aprehendido por los indios, dió voces, á las que, como vigilante, acudió el maese de campo, y libró del peligro al soldado, y pareciéndole estar seguro, alzó la vista á tiempo que de entre unos matorrales se le disparó una flecha, que entrándole por un ojo, le atravesó el cerebro. . . . Samaniego (era) uno de los mas esforzados capitanes y̆ amado de todos; enterróse en una ramada, de donde despues sus huesos fueron trasladados á Compostela."

[2] Compare the Spanish text.—The report of Diaz is incorporated in the letter from Mendoza to the King, translated herein. This letter seems to imply that Diaz stayed at Chichilticalli; but if such was his intention when writing the report to Mendoza, he must have changed his mind and returned with Saldivar as far as Chiametla.

inhabitants came out to welcome their governor and begged him not to enter the town till the day after Easter.

Chapter 8, of how the army entered the town of Culiacan and the reception it received, and other things which happened before the departure.

When the day after Easter came, the army started in the morning to go to the town and, as they approached, the inhabitants of the town came out on to an open plain with foot and horse drawn up in ranks as if for a battle, and having its seven bronze pieces of artillery in position, making a show of defending their town. Some of our soldiers were with them. Our army drew up in the same way and began a skirmish with them, and after the artillery on both sides had been fired they were driven back, just as if the town had been taken by force of arms, which was a pleasant demonstration of welcome, except for the artilleryman who lost a hand by a shot, from having ordered them to fire before he had finished drawing out the ramrod. After the town was taken, the army was well lodged and entertained by the townspeople, who, as they were all very well-to-do people, took all the gentlemen and people of quality who were with the army into their own apartments, although they had lodgings prepared for them all just outside the town. Some of the townspeople were not ill repaid for this hospitality, because all had started with fine clothes and accouterments, and as they had to carry provisions on their animals after this, they were obliged to leave their fine stuff, so that many preferred giving it to their hosts instead of risking it on the sea by putting it in the ship that had followed the army along the coast to take the extra baggage, as I have said. After they arrived and were being entertained in the town, the general, by order of the viceroy Don Antonio, left Fernandarias de Saabedra, uncle of Hernandarias de Saabedra, count of Castellar, formerly mayor of Seville, as his lieutenant and captain in this town. The army rested here several days, because the inhabitants had gathered a good stock of provisions that year and each one shared his stock very gladly with his guests from our army. They not only had plenty to eat here, but they also had plenty to take away with them, so that when the departure came they started off with more than six hundred loaded animals, besides the friendly Indians and the servants—more than a thousand persons. After a fortnight had passed, the general started ahead with about fifty horsemen and a few foot soldiers and most of the Indian allies, leaving the army, which was to follow him a fortnight later, with Don Tristan de Arellano in command as his lieutenant.

At this time, before his departure, a pretty sort of thing happened to the general, which I will tell for what it is worth. A young soldier named Trugillo (Truxillo) pretended that he had seen a vision while he was bathing in the river which seemed to be something extraordinary,[1]

---

[1] Compare the Spanish text for this whole paragraph. Ternaux renders this clause "feignant d'être très-effrayé."

so that he was brought before the general, whom he gave to understand that the devil had told him that if he would kill the general, he could marry his wife, Doña Beatris, and would receive great wealth and other very fine things. Friar Marcos of Nice preached several sermons on this, laying it all to the fact that the devil was jealous of the good which must result from this journey and so wished to break it up in this way. It did not end here, but the friars who were in the expedition wrote to their convents about it, and this was the reason the pulpits of Mexico proclaimed strange rumors about this affair.

The general ordered Truxillo to stay in that town and not to go on the expedition, which was what he was after when he made up that falsehood, judging from what afterward appeared to be the truth. The general started off with the force already described to continue his journey, and the army followed him, as will be related.

Chapter 9, of how the army started from Culiacan and the arrival of the general at Cibola and of the army at Señora and of other things that happened.

The general, as has been said, started to continue his journey from the valley of Culiacan somewhat lightly equipped, taking with him the friars, since none of them wished to stay behind with the army. After they had gone three days, a regular friar who could say mass, named Friar Antonio Victoria, broke his leg, and they brought him back from the camp to have it doctored. He stayed with the army after this, which was no slight consolation for all. The general and his force crossed the country without trouble, as they found everything peaceful, because the Indians knew Friar Marcos and some of the others who had been with Melchior Diaz when he went with Juan de Saldibar to investigate. After the general had crossed the inhabited region and came to Chichilticalli, where the wilderness begins, and saw nothing favorable, he could not help feeling somewhat downhearted, for, although the reports were very fine about what was ahead, there was nobody who had seen it except the Indians who went with the negro, and these had already been caught in some lies. Besides all this, he was much affected by seeing that the fame of Chichilticalli was summed up in one tumble-down house without any roof, although it appeared to have been a strong place at some former time when it was inhabited, and it was very plain that it had been built by a civilized and warlike race of strangers who had come from a distance. This building was made of red earth. From here they went on through the wilderness, and in fifteen days came to a river about 8 leagues from Cibola, which they called Red river,[1] because its waters were muddy and reddish. In this river they found mullets like those of Spain. The first Indians from that country were seen here—two of them, who ran away to give the news. During

---

[1] Bandelier, in his Gilded Man, identifies this with Zuñi river. The Rio Vermejo of Jaramillo is the Little Colorado or Colorado Chiquito.

the night following the next day, about 2 leagues from the village, some
Indians in a safe place yelled so that, although the men were ready for
anything, some were so excited that they put their saddles on hind-side
before; but these were the new fellows. When the veterans had
mounted and ridden round the camp, the Indians fled. None of them
could be caught because they knew the country.

The next day they entered the settled country in good order, and
when they saw the first village, which was Cibola, such were the curses
that some hurled at Friar Marcos that I pray God may protect him
from them.

It is a little, unattractive village, looking as if it had been crumpled all
up together. There are mansions in New Spain which make a better
appearance at a distance.[1] It is a village of about 200 warriors, is
three and four stories high, with the houses small and having only a few
rooms, and without a courtyard. One yard serves for each section.
The people of the whole district had collected here, for there are seven
villages in the province, and some of the others are even larger and
stronger than Cibola. These folks waited for the army, drawn up by
divisions in front of the village. When they refused to have peace on
the terms the interpreters extended to them, but appeared defiant, the
Santiago[2] was given, and they were at once put to flight. The Spaniards then attacked the village, which was taken with not a little difficulty, since they held the narrow and crooked entrance. During the
attack they knocked the general down with a large stone, and would
have killed him but for Don Garcia Lopez de Cardenas and Hernando
de Alvarado, who threw themselves above him and drew him away,
receiving the blows of the stones, which were not few. But the first
fury of the Spaniards could not be resisted, and in less than an hour
they entered the village and captured it. They discovered food there,
which was the thing they were most in need of.[3] After this the whole
province was at peace.[4]

---

[1]Mota Padilla, p. 113: "They reached Tzibola, which was a village divided into two parts, which were
encircled in such a way as to make the village round, and the houses adjoining three and four stories
high, with doors opening on a great court or plaza, leaving one or two doors in the wall, so as to go
in and out. In the middle of the plaza there is a hatchway or trapdoor, by which they go down to a
subterranean hall, the roof of which was of large pine beams, and a little hearth in the floor, and the
walls plastered. The Indian men stayed there days and nights playing (or gaming) and the women
brought them food; and this was the way the Indians of the neighboring villages lived."

[2]The war cry or "loud invocation addressed to Saint James before engaging in battle with the Infidels."—Captain John Stevens' Dictionary.

[3]Compare the translation of the Traslado de las Nuevas herein. There are some striking resem-
blances between that account and Castañeda's narrative.

[4] Gomara, Hist. Indias, cap. ccxiii, ed. 1554: "Llegando a Sibola requirieron a los del pueblo que los
recibiessen de paz; ca no yuan a les hazer mal, sino muy gran bien, y prouecho, y que les diessen
comida, ca lleuauan falta de ella. Ellos respondieron que no querian, pues yuan armados, y en son de
les dar guerra: que tal semblante mostrauan. Assi que cōbatieron el pueblo los nuestros, defendieron
lo gran rato ochocientos hombres, que dentro estauan: descalabraron a Francisco Vazquez, capitan
general del exercito, y a otros muchos Españoles: mas al cabo se salieron huyendo. Entraron los nuestros y nombraron la Granada, por amor del virrey, q̄ es natural dela de España. Es Sibola de hasta
doziētas casas de tierra y madera tosca, altas quatro y cinco sobrados, y las puertas como escotillones
de nao, suben a ellos con escaleras de palo, que quitan de noche y en tiempos de guerra. Tiene delante
cada casa una cueua, donde como en estufa, se recogen los inuiernos, que son largas, y de muchas

The army which had stayed with Don Tristan de Arellano started to follow their general, all loaded with provisions, with lances on their shoulders, and all on foot, so as to have the horses loaded. With no slight labor from day to day, they reached a province which Cabeza de Vaca had named Hearts (Corazones), because the people here offered him many hearts of animals.[1] He founded a town here and named it San Hieronimo de los Corazones (Saint Jerome of the Hearts). After it had been started, it was seen that it could not be kept up here, and so it was afterward transferred to a valley which had been called Señora.[2] The Spaniards call it Señora, and so it will be known by this name.

From here a force went down the river to the seacoast to find the harbor and to find out about the ships. Don Rodrigo Maldonado, who was captain of those who went in search of the ships, did not find them, but he brought back with him an Indian so large and tall that the best man in the army reached only to his chest. It was said that other Indians were even taller on that coast. After the rains ceased the army went on to where the town of Señora was afterward located, because there were provisions in that region, so that they were able to wait there for orders from the general.

About the middle of the month of October,[3] Captains Melchior Diaz and Juan Gallego came from Cibola, Juan Gallego on his way to New Spain and Melchior Diaz to stay in the new town of Hearts, in command of the men who remained there. He was to go along the coast in search of the ships.

Chapter 10, of how the army started from the town of Señora, leaving it inhabited, and how it reached Cibola, and of what happened to Captain Melchior Diaz on his expedition in search of the ships and how he discovered the Tison (Firebrand) river.

After Melchior Diaz and Juan Gallego had arrived in the town of Señora, it was announced that the army was to depart for Cibola; that Melchior Diaz was to remain in charge of that town with 80 men; that Juan Gallego was going to New Spain with messages for the viceroy, and that Friar Marcos was going back with him, because he did not think it was safe for him to stay in Cibola, seeing that his report had

---

nieues. Aunque no esta mas de 37½ grados de la Equinocial: que sino fuesse por las montañas, seria del temple de Sevilla. Las famosas siete ciudades de fray Marcos de Niça, que estan en espacio de seys leguas, ternan obra de 4,000 hombres. Las riquezas de su reyno es no tener que comer, ni que vestir, durādo la nieve siete meses."

[1] Oviedo, Historia, vol. iii, lib. xxxv, cap. vi, p. 610 (ed. 1853), says of Cabeza de Vaca and his companions: "Pues passadas las sierras ques dicho, llegaron estos quatro chripstianos . . . á tres pueblos que estaban juntos é pequeños, en que avia hasta veynte casas en ellos, las quales eran como las passadas é juntas, . . . á este pueblo, ó mejor diçiendo pueblos juntos, nombraron los chripstianos la *Villa de los Coraçones*, porque les dieron allí más de seysçientos coraçones de venados escalados ó secos." Cabeza de Vaca describes this place in his Naufragios, p. 172 of Smith's translation.

[2] It is possible that the persistent use of the form Señora, Madame, for the place Sonora, may be due to the copyists, although it is as likely that the Spanish settlers made the change in their common parlance.

[3] This should be September. See the next chapter; also the Itinerary.

turned out to be entirely false, because the kingdoms that he had told about had not been found, nor the populous cities, nor the wealth of gold, nor the precious stones which he had reported, nor the fine clothes, nor other things that had been proclaimed from the pulpits. When this had been announced, those who were to remain were selected and the rest loaded their provisions and set off in good order about the middle of September on the way to Cibola, following their general.

Don Tristan de Arellano stayed in this new town with the weakest men, and from this time on there was nothing but mutinies and strife, because after the army had gone Captain Melchior Diaz took 25 of the most efficient men, leaving in his place one Diego de Alcaraz, a man unfitted to have people under his command. He took guides and went toward the north and west in search of the seacoast. After going about 150 leagues, they came to a province of exceedingly tall and strong men—like giants. They are naked and live in large straw cabins built underground like smoke houses, with only the straw roof above ground. They enter these at one end and come out at the other. More than a hundred persons, old and young, sleep in one cabin.[1] When they carry anything, they can take a load of more than three or four hundredweight on their heads. Once when our men wished to fetch a log for the fire, and six men were unable to carry it, one of these Indians is reported to have come and raised it in his arms, put it on his head alone, and carried it very easily.[2] They eat bread cooked in the ashes, as big as the large two-pound loaves of Castile. On account of the great cold, they carry a firebrand (tison) in the hand when they go from one place to another, with which they warm the other hand and the body as well, and in this way they keep shifting it every now and then.[3] On this account the large river which is in that country was called Rio del Tison (Firebrand river). It is a very great river and is more than 2 leagues wide at its mouth; here it is half a league across. Here the

---

[1] Bandelier, in his Final Report, vol. i, p. 108, suggests the following from the Relacion of Padre Sedelmair, S. J., 1746, which he quotes from the manuscript: "Sus rancherías, por grandes de gentío que sean, se reducen á una ó dos casas, con techo de terrado y zacate, armadas sobre muchos horcones por pilares con viguelos de unos á otros, y bajas, tan capaces que caben en cada una mas de cien personas, con tres divisiones, la primera una enramada del tamaño de la casa y baja para dormir en el verano, luego la segunda division como sala, y la tercera como alcoba, donde por el abrigo meten los viejos y viejas, muchachitos y muchachitas, escepto los pimas que viven entre ellos, que cada familia tiene su choza aparte." These were evidently the ancestors of the Yuman Indians of Arizona.

[2] Fletcher, in The World Encompassed by Sir Francis Drake, p. 131, (ed. 1854) tells a similar story of some Indians whom Drake visited on the coast of California: "Yet are the men commonly so strong of body, that that which 2 or 3 of our men could hardly beare, one of them would take vpon his backe, and without grudging, carrie it easily away, vp hill and downe hill an English mile together." Mota Padilla, cap. xxxii, p. 158, describes an attempt to catch one of these Indians: "Quiso el capitan [Melchior Diaz] remitir á un indio, porque el virey viese su corpulencia y hallando á un mancebo, trataron de apresarlo; mas hizo tal resistencia, que entre quatro españoles no pudieron amarrarlo, y daba tales gritos, que los obligaron á dejarlo, por no indisponer los ánimos de aquellos indios."

[3] Father Sedelmair, in his Relacion, mentions this custom of the Indians. (See Bandelier, Final Report, vol. i, p. 108): "Su frazada en tiempo de frio es un tizon encendido que aplicándole á la boca del estómago caminan por las mañanas, y calentando ya el sol como á las ocho tiran los tizones, que por muchos que hayan tirado por los caminos, pueden ser guias de los caminantes; de suerte que todos estos rios pueden llamarse rios del Tizon, nombre que algunas mapas ponen á uno solo."

captain heard that there had been ships at a point three days down toward the sea. When he reached the place where the ships had been, which was more than 15 leagues up the river from the mouth of the harbor, they found written on a tree: "Alarcon reached this place; there are letters at the foot of this tree." He dug up the letters and learned from them how long Alarcon had waited for news of the army and that he had gone back with the ships to New Spain, because he was unable to proceed farther, since this sea was a bay, which was formed by the Isle of the Marquis,[1] which is called California, and it was explained that California was not an island, but a point of the mainland forming the other side of that gulf.

After he had seen this, the captain turned back to go up the river, without going down to the sea, to find a ford by which to cross to the other side, so as to follow the other bank. After they had gone five or six days, it seemed to them as if they could cross on rafts. For this purpose they called together a large number of the natives, who were waiting for a favorable opportunity to make an attack on our men, and when they saw that the strangers wanted to cross, they helped make the rafts with all zeal and diligence, so as to catch them in this way on the water and drown them or else so divide them that they could not help one another. While the rafts were being made, a soldier who had been out around the camp saw a large number of armed men go across to a mountain, where they were waiting till the soldiers should cross the river. He reported this, and an Indian was quietly shut up, in order to find out the truth, and when they tortured him he told all the arrangements that had been made. These were, that when our men were crossing and part of them had got over and part were on the river and part were waiting to cross, those who were on the rafts should drown those they were taking across and the rest of their force should make an attack on both sides of the river. If they had had as much discretion and courage as they had strength and power, the attempt would have succeeded.

When he knew their plan, the captain had the Indian who had confessed the affair killed secretly, and that night he was thrown into the river with a weight, so that the Indians would not suspect that they were found out. The next day they noticed that our men suspected them, and so they made an attack, shooting showers of arrows, but when the horses began to catch up with them and the lances wounded them without mercy and the musketeers likewise made good shots, they had to leave the plain and take to the mountain, until not a man of them was to be seen. The force then came back and crossed all right, the Indian allies and the Spaniards going across on the rafts and the horses swimming alongside the rafts, where we will leave them to continue their journey.[2]

---

[1] Cortes.

[2] Mota Padilla, sec. xxxii, p. 158, says: Melchior Dias paso el rio del Tison "en unos cestos grandes que los indios tienen aderezados con un betum que no les pasa el agua, y asidos de él cuatro ó seis indios, lo llevan nadando, . . . á lo que ayudaron tambien las indias."

To relate how the army that was on its way to Cibola got on: Everything went along in good shape, since the general had left everything peaceful, because he wished the people in that region to be contented and without fear and willing to do what they were ordered. In a province called Vacapan there was a large quantity of prickly pears, of which the natives make a great deal of preserves.[1] They gave this preserve away freely, and as the men of the army ate much of it, they all fell sick with a headache and fever, so that the natives might have done much harm to the force if they had wished. This lasted regularly twenty-four hours. After this they continued their march until they reached Chichilticalli. The men in the advance guard saw a flock of sheep one day after leaving this place. I myself saw and followed them. They had extremely large bodies and long wool; their horns were very thick and large, and when they run they throw back their heads and put their horns on the ridge of their back. They are used to the rough country, so that we could not catch them and had to leave them.[2]

Three days after we entered the wilderness we found a horn on the bank of a river that flows in the bottom of a very steep, deep gully, which the general had noticed and left there for his army to see, for it was six feet long and as thick at the base as a man's thigh. It seemed to be more like the horn of a goat than of any other animal. It was something worth seeing. The army proceeded and was about a day's march from Cibola when a very cold tornado came up in the afternoon, followed by a great fall of snow, which was a bad combination for the carriers. The army went on till it reached some caves in a rocky ridge, late in the evening. The Indian allies, who were from New Spain, and for the most part from warm countries, were in great danger. They felt the coldness of that day so much that it was hard work the next day taking care of them, for they suffered much pain and had to be carried on the horses, the soldiers walking. After this labor the army reached Cibola, where their general was waiting for them, with their quarters all ready, and here they were reunited, except some captains and men who had gone off to discover other provinces.

Chapter 11, of how Don Pedro de Tovar discovered Tusayan or Tutahaco[3] and Don Garcia Lopez de Cardenas saw the Firebrand river and the other things that had happened.

While the things already described were taking place, Cibola being at peace, the General Francisco Vazquez found out from the people of the

---

[1] The Zunis make a similar sort of preserves from the fruit of the tuna and the yucca. See Cushing in The Millstone, Indianapolis, July, 1884, pp. 108–109.

[2] Compare the Spanish text for this whole description. Mota Padilla, sec. xxii, 6, p. 113, says: "Chichilticali (que quiere decir casa colorada, por una que estaba en él embarrada con tierra colorada, que llaman almagre); aquí se hallaron pinos con grandes piñas de piñones muy buenos; y mas adelante, en la cima de unas peñas, se hallaron cabezas de carneros de grandes cuernos, y algunos dijeron haber visto tres ó cuatro carneros de aquellos, y que eran muy ligeros (de estos animales se han visto en el Catay, que es la Tartaria.)"

[3] Compare chapter 13. These two groups of pueblos were not the same.

province about the provinces that lay around it, and got them to tell their friends and neighbors that Christians had come into the country, whose only desire was to be their friends, and to find out about good lands to live in, and for them to come to see the strangers and talk with them. They did this, since they know how to communicate with one another in these regions, and they informed him about a province with seven villages of the same sort as theirs, although somewhat different. They had nothing to do with these people. This province is called Tusayan. It is twenty-five leagues from Cibola. The villages are high and the people are warlike.

The general had sent Don Pedro de Tovar to these villages with seventeen horsemen and three or four foot soldiers. Juan de Padilla, a Franciscan friar, who had been a fighting man in his youth, went with them. When they reached the region, they entered the country so quietly that nobody observed them, because there were no settlements or farms between one village and another and the people do not leave the villages except to go to their farms, especially at this time, when they had heard that Cibola had been captured by very fierce people, who traveled on animals which ate people. This information was generally believed by those who had never seen horses, although it was so strange as to cause much wonder. Our men arrived after nightfall and were able to conceal themselves under the edge of the village, where they heard the natives talking in their houses. But in the morning they were discovered and drew up in regular order, while the natives came out to meet them, with bows, and shields, and wooden clubs, drawn up in lines without any confusion. The interpreter was given a chance to speak to them and give them due warning, for they were very intelligent people, but nevertheless they drew lines and insisted that our men should not go across these lines toward their village.[1] While they were talking, some men acted as if they would cross the lines, and one of the natives lost control of himself and struck a horse a blow on the cheek of the bridle with his club. Friar Juan, fretted by the time that was being wasted in talking with them, said to the captain: "To tell the truth, I do not know why we came here." When the men heard this, they gave the Santiago so suddenly that they ran down many Indians and the others fled to the town in confusion. Some indeed did not have a chance to do this, so quickly did the people in the village come out with presents, asking for peace.[2] The captain ordered his force to collect, and, as the natives did not do any more harm, he and those who were with him found a place to establish their headquarters near the village. They had dismounted here when the natives came peacefully, saying that they had come to give in the submission of the whole province and that they wanted him to be friends with them and to accept the presents which they gave him.

[1] Compare the lines which the Hopi or M ki Indians still mark with sacred meal during their festivals, as described by Dr Fewkes in his "Few Summer Ceremonials," in vol. ii of the Journal of American Ethnology and Archæology.

[2] Compare the Spanish text.

This was some cotton cloth, although not much, because they do not make it in that district. They also gave him some dressed skins and corn meal, and pine nuts and corn and birds of the country. Afterward they presented some turquoises, but not many. The people of the whole district came together that day and submitted themselves, and they allowed him to enter their villages freely to visit, buy, sell, and barter with them.

It is governed like Cibola, by an assembly of the oldest men. They have their governors and generals. This was where they obtained the information about a large river, and that several days down the river there were some people with very large bodies.

As Don Pedro de Tovar was not commissioned to go farther, he returned from there and gave this information to the general, who dispatched Don Garcia Lopez de Cardenas with about twelve companions to go to see this river. He was well received when he reached Tusayan and was entertained by the natives, who gave him guides for his journey. They started from here loaded with provisions, for they had to go through a desert country before reaching the inhabited region, which the Indians said was more than twenty days' journey. After they had gone twenty days they came to the banks of the river, which seemed to be more than 3 or 4 leagues above the stream which flowed between them.[1] This country was elevated and full of low twisted pines, very cold, and lying open toward the north, so that, this being the warm season, no one could live there on account of the cold. They spent three days on this bank looking for a passage down to the river, which looked from above as if the water was 6 feet across, although the Indians said it was half a league wide. It was impossible to descend, for after these three days Captain Melgosa and one Juan Galeras and another companion, who were the three lightest and most agile men, made an attempt to go down at the least difficult place, and went down until those who were above were unable to keep sight of them. They returned about 4 oclock in the afternoon, not having succeeded in reaching the bottom on account of the great difficulties which they found, because what seemed to be easy from above was not so, but instead very hard and difficult. They said that they had been down about a third of the way and that the river seemed very large from the place which they reached, and that from what they saw they thought the Indians had given the width correctly. Those who stayed above had estimated that some huge rocks on the sides of the cliffs seemed to be about as tall as a man, but those who went down swore that when they reached these rocks they were bigger than the great tower of Seville. They did not go farther up the river, because they could not get water. Before this they had had to go a league or two inland every day late in the evening in order to find water, and the guides said that if they should go four days farther it would not be possible

---

[1] Compare the Spanish text. Ternaux translates it: "Les bords sont tellement élevés qu'ils croyaient être à trois ou quatre lieues en l'air."

to go on, because there was no water within three or four days, for when they travel across this region themselves they take with them women loaded with water in gourds, and bury the gourds of water along the way, to use when they return, and besides this, they travel in one day over what it takes us two days to accomplish.

This was the Tison (Firebrand) river, much nearer its source than where Melchior Diaz and his company crossed it. These were the same kind of Indians, judging from what was afterward learned. They came back from this point and the expedition did not have any other result. On the way they saw some water falling over a rock and learned from the guides that some bunches of crystals which were hanging there were salt. They went and gathered a quantity of this and brought it back to Cibola, dividing it among those who were there. They gave the general a written account of what they had seen, because one Pedro de Sotomayor had gone with Don Garcia Lopez as chronicler for the army. The villages of that province remained peaceful, since they were never visited again, nor was any attempt made to find other peoples in that direction.

Chapter 12, of how people came from Cicuye to Cibola to see the Christians, and how Hernando de Alvarado went to see the cows.

While they were making these discoveries, some Indians came to Cibola from a village which was 70 leagues east of this province, called Cicuye. Among them was a captain who was called Bigotes (Whiskers) by our men, because he wore a long mustache. He was a tall, well-built young fellow, with a fine figure. He told the general that they had come in response to the notice which had been given, to offer themselves as friends, and that if we wanted to go through their country they would consider us as their friends. They brought a present of tanned hides and shields and head-pieces, which were very gladly received, and the general gave them some glass dishes and a number of pearls and little bells which they prized highly, because these were things they had never seen. They described some cows which, from a picture that one of them had painted on his skin, seemed to be cows, although from the hides this did not seem possible, because the hair was woolly and snarled so that we could not tell what sort of skins they had. The general ordered Hernando de Alvarado to take 20 companions and go with them, and gave him a commission for eighty days, after which he should return to give an account of what he had found.[1]

Captain Alvarado started on this journey and in five days reached a village which was on a rock called Acuco[2] having a population of about 200 men. These people were robbers, feared by the whole country

---

[1] The report of Alvarado, translated herein, is probably the official account of what he accomplished.

[2] In regard to the famous rock fortress of Acoma see Bandelier's Introduction, p. 14, and his Final Report, vol. i, p. 133. The Spaniards called it by a name resembling that which they heard applied to it in Zuñi-Cibola. The true Zuñi name of Acoma, on the authority of Mr F. W. Hodge, is Hákukia; that of the Acoma people, Hákukwe.

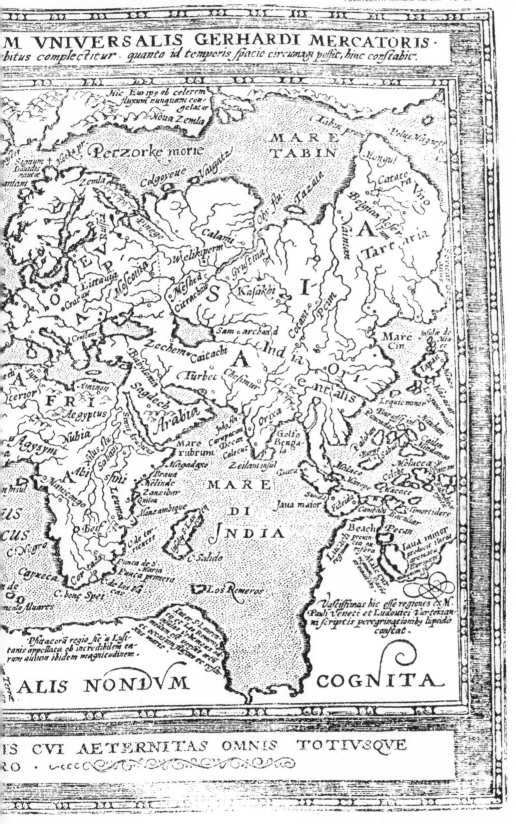

round about. The village was very strong, because it was up on a rock out of reach, having steep sides in every direction, and so high that it was a very good musket that could throw a ball as high. There was only one entrance by a stairway built by hand, which began at the top of a slope which is around the foot of the rock. There was a broad stairway for about 200 steps, then a stretch of about 100 narrower steps, and at the top they had to go up about three times as high as a man by means of holes in the rock, in which they put the points of their feet, holding on at the same time by their hands. There was a wall of large and small stones at the top, which they could roll down without showing themselves, so that no army could possibly be strong enough to capture the village. On the top they had room to sow and store a large amount of corn, and cisterns to collect snow and water. These people came down to the plain ready to fight, and would not listen to any arguments. They drew lines on the ground and determined to prevent our men from crossing these, but when they saw that they would have to fight they offered to make peace before any harm had been done. They went through their forms of making peace, which is to touch the horses and take their sweat and rub themselves with it, and to make crosses with the fingers of the hands. But to make the most secure peace they put their hands across each other, and they keep this peace inviolably. They made a present of a large number of [turkey-] cocks with very big wattles, much bread, tanned deerskins, pine [piñon] nuts, flour [corn meal], and corn.

From here they went to a province called Triguex,[1] three days distant. The people all came out peacefully, seeing that Whiskers was with them. These men are feared throughout all those provinces. Alvarado sent messengers back from here to advise the general to come and winter in this country. The general was not a little relieved to hear that the country was growing better. Five days from here he came to Cicuye,[2] a very strong village four stories high. The people came out from the village with signs of joy to welcome Hernando de Alvarado and their captain, and brought them into the town with drums and pipes something like flutes, of which they have a great many. They made many presents of cloth and turquoises, of which there are quantities in that region. The Spaniards enjoyed themselves here for several days and talked with an Indian slave, a native of the country toward Florida, which is the region Don Fernando de Soto discovered. This fellow said that there were large settlements in the farther part of that country. Hernando de Alvarado took him to guide them to the cows; but he told them so many and such great things about the wealth of gold and silver in his country that they did not care about looking for cows, but returned after they had seen some few, to report the rich news to the general.

---

[1] An error for Tiguex, at or near the present Bernalillo. Simpson located this near the mouth of the river Puerco, southeast of Acoma, but I follow Bandelier, according to whom Alvarado pursued a northeasterly direction from Acoma. See his Introduction, p. 30, and Final Report, vol. i, p. 129.

[2] Pecos. Besides his Final Report, vol. i, p. 127, see Bandelier's Report on the Pecos Ruins.

They called the Indian "Turk," because he looked like one.[1] Meanwhile the general had sent Don Garcia Lopez de Cardenas to Tiguex with men to get lodgings ready for the army, which had arrived from Señora about this time, before taking them there for the winter; and when Hernando de Alvarado reached Tiguex, on his way back from Cicuye, he found Don Garcia Lopez de Cardenas there, and so there was no need for him to go farther. As it was necessary that the natives should give the Spaniards lodging places, the people in one village had to abandon it and go to others belonging to their friends, and they took with them nothing but themselves and the clothes they had on. Information was obtained here about many towns up toward the north, and I believe that it would have been much better to follow this direction than that of the Turk, who was the cause of all the misfortunes which followed.

Chapter 13, of how the general went toward Tutahaco with a few men and left the army with Don Tristan, who took it to Tiguex.

Everything already related had happened when Don Tristan de Arellano reached Cibola from Señora. Soon after he arrived, the general, who had received notice of a province containing eight villages, took 30 of the men who were most fully rested and went to see it, going from there directly to Tiguex with the skilled guides who conducted him. He left orders for Don Tristan de Arellano to proceed to Tiguex by the direct road, after the men had rested twenty days. On this journey, between one day when they left the camping place and midday of the third day, when they saw some snow-covered mountains, toward which they went in search of water, neither the Spaniards nor the horses nor the servants drank anything. They were able to stand it because of the severe cold, although with great difficulty. In eight days they reached Tutahaco,[2] where they learned that

---

[1]The account which Mota Padilla (cap. xxxii, 5, p. 161) gives of the Turk and his stories is very significant: Alvarado "halló un indio en aquellos llanos quien le dijo, mas por señas que por voces, ser de una provincia que distaba treinta soles, la cual se llamaba Copala, y al indio se le puso por nombre el Turco, por ser muy moreno, apersonado y de buena disposicion; y les dijo tantas cosas de aquella provincia, que los puso en admiracion, y en especial que habia tanta cantidad de oro, que no solo podian cargar los caballos, sino carros; que habia una laguna en la que navegaban canoas, y que las del cacique tenian argollas de oro; y para que se explicase, le mostraban plata, y decia que no, sino como un anillo que vió de oro: decia qué á su cacique lo sacaban en andas á las guerras, y que cuando queria, les quitaban los bozales á unos lebreles que despedazaban á los enemigos; que tenian una casa muy grande, adonde todos acudian á servirle; que en las puertas tenian mantas de algodon."

Gomara, Indias, cap. ccxiiii, adds some details: "Viendo la poca gente, y muestra de riqueza, dieron los soldados muy pocas gracias a los frayles, que conellos yuan, y que loauan aquella tierra de Sibola: y por no boluer a Mexico sin hazer algo, ni las manos vazias, acordaron de passar adelante, que les dezian ser mejor tierra. Assi que fueron a Acuco, lugar sobre vn fortissimo peñol, y desde alli fue don Garci lopez de Cardenas con su compañia de cauallos a la mar, y Francisco Vazquez con los demas a Tiguex, que esta ribera de vn gran rio. Alli tuuieron nueua de Axa, y Quiuira: donde dezian, que estaua vn Rey, dicho por nombre Tatarrax, barbudo, canos, y rico, que ceñia vn bracamarte, que rezaua en horas, que adoraua vna cruz de oro, y vna ymagen de muger, Señora Del cielo. Mucho alegro, y sostuuo esta nueua al exercito, aunque algunos la tuuieron por falsa, y echadiza de frayles. Determinaron yr alla con intencion de inuernar en tierra tan rica como se sonaua."

[2]Coronado probably reached the Rio Grande near the present Isleta. Jaramillo applies this name to Acoma, and perhaps he is more correct, if we ought to read it Tutahaio, since the Tiguas (the inhabitants of Isleta, Sandia, Taos, and Picuris pueblos) call Acoma Tuthea-uáy, according to Bandelier, Gilded Man, p. 211.

there were other towns down the river. These people were peaceful. The villages are terraced, like those at Tiguex, and of the same style. The general went up the river from here, visiting the whole province, until he reached Tiguex, where he found Hernando de Alvarado and the Turk. He felt no slight joy at such good news, because the Turk said that in his country there was a river in the level country which was 2 leagues wide, in which there were fishes as big as horses, and large numbers of very big canoes, with more than 20 rowers on a side, and that they carried sails, and that their lords sat on the poop under awnings, and on the prow they had a great golden eagle. He said also that the lord of that country took his afternoon nap under a great tree on which were hung a great number of little gold bells, which put him to sleep as they swung in the air. He said also that everyone had their ordinary dishes made of wrought plate, and the jugs and bowls were of gold. He called gold acochis. For the present he was believed, on account of the ease with which he told it and because they showed him metal ornaments and he recognized them and said they were not gold, and he knew gold and silver very well and did not care anything about other metals.

The general sent Hernando de Alvarado back to Cicuye to demand some gold bracelets which this Turk said they had taken from him at the time they captured him. Alvarado went, and was received as a friend at the village, and when he demanded the bracelets they said they knew nothing at all about them, saying the Turk was deceiving him and was lying. Captain Alvarado, seeing that there were no other means, got the captain Whiskers and the governor to come to his tent, and when they had come he put them in chains. The villagers prepared to fight, and let fly their arrows, denouncing Hernando de Alvarado, and saying that he was a man who had no respect for peace and friendship. Hernando de Alvarado started back to Tiguex, where the general kept them prisoners more than six months. This began the want of confidence in the word of the Spaniards whenever there was talk of peace from this time on, as will be seen by what happened afterward.

Chapter 14, of how the army went from Cibola to Tiguex and what happened to them on the way, on account of the snow.

We have already said that when the general started from Cibola, he left orders for Don Tristan de Arellano to start twenty days later. He did so as soon as he saw that the men were well rested and provided with food and eager to start off to find their general. He set off with his force toward Tiguex, and the first day they made their camp in the best, largest, and finest village of that (Cibola) province.[1] This is the only village that has houses with seven stories. In this village certain houses are used as fortresses; they are higher than the others and set

[1] This was Matsaki, at the northwestern base of Thunder mountain, about 18 miles from Hawikuh, where the advance force had encamped.

up above them like towers, and there are embrasures and loopholes in them for defending the roofs of the different stories, because, like the other villages, they do not have streets, and the flat roofs are all of a height and are used in common. The roofs have to be reached first, and these upper houses are the means of defending them. It began to snow on us there, and the force took refuge under the wings of the village, which extend out like balconies, with wooden pillars beneath, because they generally use ladders to go up to those balconies, since they do not have any doors below.

The army continued its march from here after it stopped snowing, and as the season had already advanced into December, during the ten days that the army was delayed, it did not fail to snow during the evenings and nearly every night, so that they had to clear away a large amount of snow when they came to where they wanted to make a camp. The road could not be seen, but the guides managed to find it, as they knew the country. There are junipers and pines all over the country, which they used in making large brushwood fires, the smoke and heat of which melted the snow from 2 to 4 yards all around the fire. It was a dry snow, so that although it fell on the baggage and covered it for half a man's height it did not hurt it. It fell all night long, covering the baggage and the soldiers and their beds, piling up in the air, so that if anyone had suddenly come upon the army nothing would have been seen but mountains of snow. The horses stood half buried in it. It kept those who were underneath warm instead of cold. The army passed by the great rock of Acuco, and the natives, who were peaceful, entertained our men well, giving them provisions and birds, although there are not many people here, as I have said. Many of the gentlemen went up to the top to see it, and they had great difficulty in going up the steps in the rock, because they were not used to them, for the natives go up and down so easily that they carry loads and the women carry water, and they do not seem even to touch their hands, although our men had to pass their weapons up from one to another.

From here they went on to Tiguex, where they were well received and taken care of, and the great good news of the Turk gave no little joy and helped lighten their hard labors, although when the army arrived we found the whole country or province in revolt, for reasons which were not slight in themselves, as will be shown, and our men had also burnt a village the day before the army arrived, and returned to the camp.[1]

Chapter 15, of why Tiguex revolted, and how they were punished, without being to blame for it.

It has been related how the general reached Tiguex, where he found Don Garcia Lopez de Cardenas and Hernando de Alvarado, and how he

---

[1] The Spanish manuscript is very confusing throughout this chapter. As usual, Ternaux passes over most of the passages which have given trouble, omitting what he could not guess.

sent the latter back to Cicuye, where he took the captain Whiskers and the governor of the village, who was an old man, prisoners. The people of Tiguex did not feel well about this seizure. In addition to this, the general wished to obtain some clothing to divide among his soldiers, and for this purpose he summoned one of the chief Indians of Tiguex, with whom he had already had much intercourse and with whom he was on good terms, who was called Juan Aleman by our men, after a Juan Aleman[1] who lived in Mexico, whom he was said to resemble. The general told him that he must furnish about three hundred or more pieces of cloth, which he needed to give his people. He said that he was not able to do this, but that it pertained to the governors; and that besides this, they would have to consult together and divide it among the villages, and that it was necessary to make the demand of each town separately. The general did this, and ordered certain of the gentlemen who were with him to go and make the demand; and as there were twelve villages, some of them went on one side of the river and some on the other. As they were in very great need, they did not give the natives a chance to consult about it, but when they came to a village they demanded what they had to give, so that they could proceed at once. Thus these people could do nothing except take off their own cloaks and give them to make up the number demanded of them. And some of the soldiers who were in these parties, when the collectors gave them some blankets or cloaks which were not such as they wanted, if they saw any Indian with a better one on, they exchanged with him without more ado, not stopping to find out the rank of the man they were stripping, which caused not a little hard feeling.

Besides what I have just said, one whom I will not name, out of regard for him, left the village where the camp was and went to another village about a league distant, and seeing a pretty woman there he called her husband down to hold his horse by the bridle while he went up; and as the village was entered by the upper story, the Indian supposed he was going to some other part of it. While he was there the Indian heard some slight noise, and then the Spaniard came down, took his horse, and went away. The Indian went up and learned that he had violated, or tried to violate, his wife, and so he came with the important men of the town to complain that a man had violated his wife, and he told how it happened. When the general made all the soldiers and the persons who were with him come together, the Indian did not recognize the man, either because he had changed his clothes or for whatever other reason there may have been, but he said that he could tell the horse, because he had held his bridle, and so he was taken to the stables, and found the horse, and said that the master of the horse must be the man. He denied doing it, seeing that he had not been recognized, and it may be that the Indian was mistaken in the horse;

---

[1] Dutch Jack, perhaps.

anyway, he went off without getting any satisfaction.[1] The next day one of the Indians, who was guarding the horses of the army, came running in, saying that a companion of his had been killed, and that the Indians of the country were driving off the horses toward their villages. The Spaniards tried to collect the horses again, but many were lost, besides seven of the general's mules.[2]

The next day Don Garcia Lopez de Cardenas went to see the villages and talk with the natives. He found the villages closed by palisades and a great noise inside, the horses being chased as in a bull fight and shot with arrows. They were all ready for fighting. Nothing could be done, because they would not come down onto the plain and the villages are so strong that the Spaniards could not dislodge them. The general then ordered Don Garcia Lopez de Cardenas to go and surround one village with all the rest of the force. This village was the one where the greatest injury had been done and where the affair with the Indian woman occurred. Several captains who had gone on in advance with the general, Juan de Saldivar and Barrionuevo and Diego Lopez and Melgosa,[3] took the Indians so much by surprise that they gained the upper story, with great danger, for they wounded many of our men from within the houses. Our men were on top of the houses in great danger for a day and a night and part of the next day, and they made some good shots with their crossbows and muskets. The horsemen on the plain with many of the Indian allies from New Spain smoked them out from the cellars[4] into which they had broken, so that they begged for peace.[5] Pablo de Melgosa and Diego Lopez, the alderman from Seville, were left on the roof and answered the Indians with the same signs they were making for peace, which was to make a cross. They then put down their arms and received pardon. They were taken to the tent of Don Garcia, who, according to what he said, did not know about the peace and thought that they had given themselves up of their own accord because they had been conquered. As he had been ordered by the general not to take them alive, but to make an example of them so that the other natives would fear the Spaniards, he ordered 200 stakes to be prepared at once to burn them alive.

[1] The instructions which Mendoza gave to Alarcon show how carefully the viceroy tried to guard against any such trouble with the natives. Buckingham Smith's Florida, p. 4: "Iten: si poblaredes en alguna parte, no sea entre los yndios, sino apartado dellos, y mandareys que ningun español ni otra persona de las vuestras vaya al lugar ni á las cassas de los yndios sino fuere con expressa licencia vuestra, y al que lo contrario hiziere castigalle eys muy asperamente, y la licencia aveys de dalla las vezes que fuere necessario para alguna cossa que convenga y á personas de quien vos esteys confiado que no hará cossa mal hecha, y estad muy advertido en guardar esta orden, porque es cossa que conviene mas de lo que vos podeys pensar."

[2] Espejo, Relacion del Viaje, 1584 (Pacheco y Cardenas, Doc. de Indias, vol. xv, p. 175), says that at Puala (Tiguex) pueblo, "hallamos relacion muy verdadera; que estubo en esta provincia Francisco Vazquez Coronado y le mataron en ella nueve soldados y cuarenta caballos, y que por este respeto habia asolado la gente de un pueblo desta provincia, y destos nos dieron razon los naturales destos pueblos por señas que entendimos."

[3] Ternaux says Diego Lopez Melgosa, and when Melgosa's name appears again he has it Pablo Lopez Melgosa.

[4] Evidently the underground, or partially underground, ceremonial chambers or kivas.

[5] Compare the Spanish text.

Nobody told him about the peace that had been granted them, for the soldiers knew as little as he, and those who should have told him about it remained silent, not thinking that it was any of their business. Then when the enemies saw that the Spaniards were binding them and beginning to roast them, about a hundred men who were in the tent began to struggle and defend themselves with what there was there and with the stakes they could seize. Our men who were on foot attacked the tent on all sides, so that there was great confusion around it, and then the horsemen chased those who escaped. As the country was level, not a man of them remained alive, unless it was some who remained hidden in the village and escaped that night to spread throughout the country the news that the strangers did not respect the peace they had made, which afterward proved a great misfortune. After this was over, it began to snow, and they abandoned the village and returned to the camp just as the army came from Cibola.[1]

Chapter 16, of how they besieged Tiguex and took it and of what happened during the siege.

As I have already related, it began to snow in that country just after they captured the village, and it snowed so much that for the next two months it was impossible to do anything except to go along the roads to advise them to make peace and tell them that they would be pardoned and might consider themselves safe, to which they replied that they did not trust those who did not know how to keep good faith after they had once given it, and that the Spaniards should remember that they were keeping Whiskers prisoner and that they did not keep their word when they burned those who surrendered in the village. Don Garcia Lopez de Cardenas was one of those who went to give this notice. He started out with about 30 companions and went to the village of Tiguex to talk with Juan Aleman. Although they were hostile, they talked with him and said that if he wished to talk with them he must dismount and they would come out and talk with him about a peace, and

---

[1]Gomara, cap. ccxiiii, gives the following account of these events: "Fueronse los Indios vna noche y amanecieron muertos treynta cauallos, que puso temor al exercito. Caminando, quemaron vn lugar, y en otro que acometieron, les mataron ciertos Españoles, y hirieron cinquenta cauallos, y metieron dentro los vezinos a Francisco de Ouãdo, herido, o muerto, para comer, y sacrificar, a lo que pensaron, o quiça para mejor ver, que hombres eran los Españoles, ca no se hallo por alli rastro de sacrificio humano. Pusieron cerco los nuestros al lugar, pero no lo pudieron tomar en mas de quarenta, y cinco dias. Beuian nieue los cercados por falta de agua, y viendose perdidos, hizieron vna hoguera, echaron en ella sus mãtas, plumajes, Turquesas, y cosas preciadas, porque no las gozassen aquellos estrangeros. Salieron en esquadron, con los niños, y mugeres en medio, para abrir camino por fuerça, y saluarse: mas pocos escaparon de las espadas, y cauallos, y de vn rio q̃ cerca estaua. Murieron en la pelea siete Españoles y quedaron heridos ochẽta, y muchos cauallos, porq̃ veays quanto vale la determinacion en la necessidad. Muchos Indios se boluieron al pueblo, con la gente menuda, y se defendieron hasta que se les puso fuego. Elose tanto aquel rio estãdo en siete y treynta grados de la Equinocial, que sufria passar encima hombres a cauallo, y cauallos con carga. Dura la nieue medio año. Ay en aq̃lla ribera melones, y algodon blanco, y colorado, de que hazen muy mas anchas mantas, que en otras partes de Indias."

Mota Padilla, xxxii, 6, p. 161: "Esta accion se tuvo en España por mala, y con razon, porque fué una crueldad considerable; y habiendo el maese de campo, García Lopez pasado á España á heredar un mayorazgo, estuvo preso en una fortaleza por este cargo."

that if he would send away the horsemen and make his men keep away, Juan Aleman and another captain would come out of the village and meet him. Everything was done as they required, and then when they approached they said that they had no arms and that he must take his off. Don Garcia Lopez did this in order to give them confidence, on account of his great desire to get them to make peace. When he met them, Juan Aleman approached and embraced him vigorously, while the other two who had come with him drew two mallets[1] which they had hidden behind their backs and gave him two such blows over his helmet that they almost knocked him senseless. Two of the soldiers on horseback had been unwilling to go very far off, even when he ordered them, and so they were near by and rode up so quickly that they rescued him from their hands, although they were unable to catch the enemies because the meeting was so near the village that of the great shower of arrows which were shot at them one arrow hit a horse and went through his nose. The horsemen all rode up together and hurriedly carried off their captain, without being able to harm the enemy, while many of our men were dangerously wounded.[2] They then withdrew, leaving a number of men to continue the attack. Don Garcia Lopez de Cardenas went on with a part of the force to another village about half a league distant, because almost all the people in this region had collected into these two villages. As they paid no attention to the demands made on them except by shooting arrows from the upper stories with loud yells, and would not hear of peace, he returned to his companions whom he had left to keep up the attack on Tiguex. A large number of those in the village came out and our men rode off slowly, pretending to flee, so that they drew the enemy on to the plain, and then turned on them and caught several of their leaders. The rest collected on the roofs of the village and the captain returned to his camp.

After this affair the general ordered the army to go and surround the village. He set out with his men in good order, one day, with several scaling ladders. When he reached the village, he encamped his force near by, and then began the siege; but as the enemy had had several days to provide themselves with stores, they threw down such quantities of rocks upon our men that many of them were laid out, and they wounded nearly a hundred with arrows, several of whom afterward died on account of the bad treatment by an unskillful surgeon who was with the army. The siege lasted fifty days, during which time several

---

[1] Wooden warclubs shaped like potato-mashers.

[2] Mota Padilla, xxxii, 7, p. 161, describes this encounter: "D. García pasó al pueblo mayor á requerir al principal cacique, que se llamaba D. Juan Loman, aunque no estaba bautizado, y se dejó ver por los muros sin querer bajar de paz, y á instancias de D. García, ofreció salirle á hablar, como dejase el caballo y espada, porque tenia mucho miedo; y en esta conformidad, desmontó D. García del caballo, entrególe con la espada á sus soldados, á quienes hizo retirar, y acercándose á los muros, luego que Juan Loman se afrontó, se abrazó de él, y al punto, entre seis indios que habia dejado apercibidos, lo llevaron en peso y lo entraran en el pueblo si la puerta no es pequeña, por lo que en ella hizo hincapié, y pudo resistir hasta que llegaron soldados de á caballo, que le defendieron. Quisieron los indios hacer alguna crueldad con dicho D. García, por lo que intentaron llevarlo vivo, que si los indios salen con macanas ó porras que usaban, le quitan la vida."

assaults were made. The lack of water was what troubled the Indians most. They dug a very deep well inside the village, but were not able to get water, and while they were making it, it fell in and killed 30 persons. Two hundred of the besieged died in the fights. One day when there was a hard fight, they killed Francisco de Obando, a captain who had been army-master all the time that Don Garcia Lopez de Cardenas was away making the discoveries already described, and also Francisco Pobares, a fine gentleman. Our men were unable to prevent them from carrying Francisco de Obando inside the village, which was regretted not a little, because he was a distinguished person, besides being honored on his own account, affable and much beloved, which was noticeable.[1] One day, before the capture was completed, they asked to speak to us, and said that, since they knew we would not harm the women and children, they wished to surrender their women and sons, because they were using up their water. It was impossible to persuade them to make peace, as they said that the Spaniards would not keep an agreement made with them. So they gave up about a hundred persons, women and boys, who did not want to leave them. Don Lope de Urrea[2] rode up in front of the town without his helmet and received the boys and girls in his arms, and when all of these had been surrendered, Don Lope begged them to make peace, giving them the strongest promises for their safety. They told him to go away, as they did not wish to trust themselves to people who had no regard for friendship or their own word which they had pledged. As he seemed unwilling to go away, one of them put an arrow in his bow ready to shoot, and threatened to shoot him with it unless he went off, and they warned him to put on his helmet, but he was unwilling to do so, saying that they would not hurt him as long as he stayed there. When the Indian saw that he did not want to go away, he shot and planted his arrow between the fore feet of the horse, and then put another arrow in his bow and repeated that if he did not go away he would really shoot him. Don Lope put on his helmet and slowly rode back to where the horsemen were, without receiving any harm from them. When they saw that he was really in safety, they began to shoot arrows in showers, with loud yells and cries. The general did not want to make an assault that day, in order to see if they could be brought in some way to make peace, which they would not consider.

Fifteen days later they decided to leave the village one night, and did so, taking the women in their midst. They started about the fourth watch, in the very early morning, on the side where the cavalry was.[3] The alarm was given by those in the camp of Don Rodrigo

---

[1] But see the Spanish. Ternaux translates it: "Les Indiens parvinrent à s'emparer de (d'Obando) et l'emmenèrent vivant dans leur village, . . . car c'était un homme distingué qui, par sa vertu et son affabilité, s'était fait aimer de tout le monde."

[2] Ternaux substituted the name of Don Garci-Lopez for that of Don Lope throughout this passage.

[3] Compare the Spanish text. Ternaux: "Ils prirent le parti d'abandonner le village pendant la nuit: ils se mirent donc en route: les femmes marchaient au milieu d'eux. Quand ils furent arrivés à un endroit où campait don Rodrigo Maldonado, les sentinelles donnèrent l'alarme."

Maldonado. The enemy attacked them and killed one Spaniard and a horse and wounded others, but they were driven back with great slaughter until they came to the river, where the water flowed swiftly and very cold. They threw themselves into this, and as the men had come quickly from the whole camp to assist the cavalry, there were few who escaped being killed or wounded. Some men from the camp went across the river next day and found many of them who had been overcome by the great cold. They brought these back, cured them, and made servants of them. This ended that siege, and the town was captured, although there were a few who remained in one part of the town and were captured a few days later.[1]

Two captains, Don Diego de Guevara and Juan de Saldivar, had captured the other large village after a siege. Having started out very early one morning to make an ambuscade in which to catch some warriors who used to come out every morning to try to frighten our camp, the spies, who had been placed where they could see when they were coming, saw the people come out and proceed toward the coun-

[1] There is much additional information of the siege and capture of Tiguex in the account given by Mota Padilla, xxxii, 8, p. 161: "Habiéndose puesto el cerco, estuvieron los indios rebeldes á los requerimientos, por lo que se intentó abrir brecha, y rota la argamasa superficial, se advirtió que el centro del muro era de palizada, troncos y mimbres bien hincados en la tierra, por lo que resistian los golpes que daban con unas malas barras, en cuyo tiempo hacian de las azoteas mucho daño en los nuestros con las piedras y con la flechas por las troneras; y quoriendo un soldado tapar con lodo una tronera de donde se hacia mucho daño, por un ojo le entraron una flecha, de que cayó muerto: llamábase Francisco Pobares; y á otro que se llamaba Juan Paniagua, muy buen cristiano y persona noble, le dieron otro flechazo en el párpado de un ojo, y publicaba que á la devocion del rosario, que siempre rezaba, debió la vida; otro soldado, llamado Francisco de Ovando, se entró de bruzas por una portañuela, y apenas hubo asomado la cabeza, cuando le asieron y le tiraron para adentro, quitándole la vida: púsose una escala por donde á todo trance subieron algunos; pero con arte, los indios tenian muchas piezas á cielo descubierto, para que se no comunicasen; y como á cortas distancias habia torrecillas con muchas saeteras y troneras, hacian mucho daño, de suerte que hirieron mas de sesenta, de los que murieron tres: un fulano Carbajal, hermano de Hernando Trejo, quien fué despues teniente de gobernador por Francisco de Ibarra, en Chametla: tambien murió un vizcaino, llamado Alonso de Castañeda, y un fulano Benitez; y esto fué por culpa de ellos, pues ya que habia pocas armas de fuego con que ofender, pudieron haber pegado fuego á los muros, pues eran de troncones y palizadas con solo el embarrado de tierra.

"9. Viendo el gobernador el poco efecto de su invasion, mandó se tocase á recoger, con ánimo de rendirlos por falta de agua, ya que no por hambre, porque sabia tenian buenas trojes de maiz. Trataron de curar los heridos, aunque se enconaron, y se cicatrizaban; y segun se supo, era la causa el que en unas vasijas de mimbre encerraban los indios vívoras, y con las flechas las tocaban para que mordiesen las puntas y quedasen venenosas; y habiéndose mantenido algun tiempo, cuando se esperaba padeciesen falta de agua, comenzó á nevar, con cuya nieve se socorrieron y mantuvieron dos meses, en los que intentaron los nuestros muchos desatinos: el uno fué formar unos ingenios con unos maderos, que llamaban vaivenes, y son los antiguos arietes con que se batian las fortalezas en tiempo que no se conocia la pólvora; mas no acertaron: despues, por falta de artillería, intentaron hacer unos cañones de madera bien liados de cordeles á modo de cohetes; mas tampoco sirvió; y no arbitraron el arrimar leña á los muros y prenderles fuego: á mi ver entiendo que la crueldad con que quitaron la vida á los ciento y treinta gandules, los hizo indignos del triunfo; y así, en una noche los sitiados salieron y se pusieron en fuga, dejando á los nuestros burlados y sin cosa de provecho que lograsen por despojos de la plaza sitiada y se salieron los indios con su valeroso hecho.

"10. Por la parte que salieron estaban de centinelas dos soldados poco apercibidos, de los cuales el uno no pareció, y el otro fué hallado con el corazon atravesado con una flecha; y traido el cuerpo, le pusieron junto á la lumbrada comun del campo; y cuando volvieron los soldados, que intentaron el alcance de los indios, al desmontar uno de ellos del caballo, le pisó la boca al miserable, y se atribuyó su fatal muerte á haber sido renegador y blasfemo. Luego que amaneció, se trató de reconocer el pueblo, y entrando, se halló abastecido pero sin agua, y se reconoció un pozo profundo en la plaza que aquellos indios abrieron en busca de agua, y por no encontrarla, se resolvieron á la fuga, que consiguieron." . . .

try. The soldiers left the ambuscade and went to the village and saw the people fleeing. They pursued and killed large numbers of them. At the same time those in the camp were ordered to go over the town, and they plundered it, making prisoners of all the people who were found in it, amounting to about a hundred women and children. This siege ended the last of March, in the year '42.[1] Other things had happened in the meantime, which would have been noticed, but that it would have cut the thread. I have omitted them, but will relate them now, so that it will be possible to understand what follows.

Chapter 17, of how messengers reached the army from the valley of Señora and how Captain Melchior Diaz died on the expedition to the Firebrand river.

We have already related how Captain Melchior Diaz crossed the Firebrand river on rafts, in order to continue his discoveries farther in that direction. About the time the siege ended, messengers reached the army from the city of San Hieronimo with letters from Diego de Alarcon,[2] who had remained there in the place of Melchior Diaz. These contained the news that Melchior Diaz had died while he was conducting his search, and that the force had returned without finding any of the things they were after. It all happened in this fashion:

After they had crossed the river they continued their search for the coast, which here turned back toward the south, or between south and east, because that arm of the sea enters the land due north and this river, which brings its waters down from the north, flowing toward the south, enters the head of the gulf. Continuing in the direction they had been going, they came to some sand banks of hot ashes which it was impossible to cross without being drowned as in the sea. The ground they were standing on trembled like a sheet of paper, so that it seemed as if there were lakes underneath them. It seemed wonderful and like something infernal, for the ashes to bubble up here in several places. After they had gone away from this place, on account of the danger they seemed to be in and of the lack of water, one day a greyhound belonging to one of the soldiers chased some sheep which they were taking along for food. When the captain noticed this, he threw his lance at the dog while his horse was running, so that it stuck up in the ground, and not being able to stop his horse he went over the lance so that it nailed him through the thighs and the iron came out behind, rupturing his bladder. After this the soldiers turned back with their captain, having to fight every day with the Indians, who had remained hostile. He lived about twenty days, during which they proceeded with great difficulty on account of the necessity of carrying him.[3] They

---

[1] Ternaux translated this, "à la fin de 1542." Professor Haynes corrected the error in a note in Winsor's Narrative and Critical History, vol. ii, p. 491, saying that "it is evident that the siege must have been concluded early in 1541."

[2] Should be Alcaraz.

[3] Mota Padilla's account of the death of Diaz is translated in the Introduction.

returned in good order without losing a man, until he died, and after that they were relieved of the greatest difficulty. When they reached Señora, Alcaraz dispatched the messengers already referred to, so that the general might know of this and also that some of the soldiers were ill disposed and had caused several mutinies, and that he had sentenced two of them to the gallows, but they had afterward escaped from the prison.

When the general learned this, he sent Don Pedro de Tovar to that city to sift out some of the men. He was accompanied by messengers whom the general sent to Don Antonio de Mendoza the viceroy, with an account of what had occurred and with the good news given by the Turk. When Don Pedro de Tovar arrived there, he found that the natives of that province had killed a soldier with a poisoned arrow, which had made only a very little wound in one hand. Several soldiers went to the place where this happened to see about it, and they were not very well received. Don Pedro de Tovar sent Diego de Alcaraz with a force to seize the chiefs and lords of a village in what they call the Valley of Knaves (de los Vellacos), which is in the hills. After getting there and taking these men prisoners, Diego de Alcaraz decided to let them go in exchange for some thread and cloth and other things which the soldiers needed. Finding themselves free, they renewed the war and attacked them, and as they were strong and had poison, they killed several Spaniards and wounded others so that they died on the way back. They retired toward the town, and if they had not had Indian allies from the country of the Hearts, it would have gone worse with them. They got back to the town, leaving 17 soldiers dead from the poison. They would die in agony from only a small wound, the bodies breaking out with an insupportable pestilential stink. When Don Pedro de Tovar saw the harm done, and as it seemed to them that they could not safely stay in that city, he moved 40 leagues toward Cibola into the valley of Suya, where we will leave them, in order to relate what happened to the general and his army after the siege of Tiguex.

Chapter 18, of how the general managed to leave the country in peace so as to go in search of Quivira, where the Turk said there was the most wealth.

During the siege of Tiguex the general decided to go to Cicuye and take the governor with him, in order to give him his liberty and to promise them that he would give Whiskers his liberty and leave him in the village, as soon as he should start for Quivira. He was received peacefully when he reached Cicuye, and entered the village with several soldiers. They received their governor with much joy and gratitude. After looking over the village and speaking with the natives[1] he returned

---

[1] Compare the Spanish text. Ternaux: "Le général le rétablit dans sa dignité, examina le pays, et retourna au camp."

primera

pareçio bien tam grande multi
tud de piedra tan grande y uno
es cudillas y mayores y tanmesse
fay como lubra que en parte
cubrieron los yndios sus mess y
mas de tierra y uno dexo el ca
uallo dixo que mii que caua
llo vio que nose foll fmofra
rondos otros que acudieronales
tener negros en sus besados y
confeladas y un de las que tu
dos los demas llebo por delan
te hasta se gallopron la barun
ca y algunos lubio donde congri
tabaxo se tornaron aba fax
si como los tomo alli denhosfue
rae enllollano dea un piedra
se elleam fr a gran riesgo sin
cauallos que muchos nose fu
hiera recobrar com fio la piedra

mm

parte

og

muchas hendas y aosto muchas
dela doo y laptimo mur chof ca ua
llof y quebro toda lalofa delun
to y ea laba eof que no pufo yo
ca neeefidad porque por alli
no ayssa ni fe hace ni calabrof
nife fiembra maiz ni comenfar
falbo conre cruda o malafada
y fmtag

lef de alli embio algeneral
a defcubrir y diezon ento taf
ronherias aguaho jornadas
a manera dechixeatrep e cahe   Aluxeres
ua muy srbla do adonde auia
muchof fisof lef y fi me laf como
laf decasttla yfareulafduza
banefhof pueblof te ronheriaf
tref jornadaf defiafccoma
alf dea epifa hezoreo nef

to his army, leaving Cicuye at peace, in the hope of getting back their captain Whiskers.

After the siege was ended, as we have already related, he sent a captain to Chia, a fine village with many people, which had sent to offer its submission. It was 4 leagues distant to the west of the river. They found it peaceful and gave it four bronze cannon, which were in poor condition, to take care of. Six gentlemen also went to Quirix, a province with seven villages. At the first village, which had about a hundred inhabitants, the natives fled, not daring to wait for our men; but they headed them off by a short cut, riding at full speed, and then they returned to their houses in the village in perfect safety, and then told the other villagers about it and reassured them. In this way the entire region was reassured, little by little, by the time the ice in the river was broken up and it became possible to ford the river and so to continue the journey. The twelve villages of Tiguex, however, were not repopulated at all during the time the army was there, in spite of every promise of security that could possibly be given to them.

And when the river, which for almost four months had been frozen over so that they crossed the ice on horseback, had thawed out, orders were given for the start for Quivira, where the Turk said there was some gold and silver, although not so much as in Arche and the Guaes. There were already some in the army who suspected the Turk, because a Spaniard named Servantes,[1] who had charge of him during the siege, solemnly swore that he had seen the Turk talking with the devil in a pitcher of water, and also that while he had him under lock so that no one could speak to him, the Turk had asked him what Christians had been killed by the people at Tiguex. He told him "nobody," and then the Turk answered: "You lie; five Christians are dead, including a captain." And as Cervantes knew that he told the truth, he confessed it so as to find out who had told him about it, and the Turk said he knew it all by himself and that he did not need to have anyone tell him in order to know it. And it was on account of this that he watched him and saw him speaking to the devil in the pitcher, as I have said.

While all this was going on, preparations were being made to start from Tiguex. At this time people came from Cibola to see the general, and he charged them to take good care of the Spaniards who were coming from Señora with Don Pedro de Tovar. He gave them letters to give to Don Pedro, informing him what he ought to do and how he should go to find the army, and that he would find letters under the crosses which the army would put up along the way. The army left Tiguex on the 5th of May[2] and returned to Cicuye, which, as I have said, is twenty-five marches, which means leagues, from there, taking Whiskers with them. Arrived there, he gave them their captain, who already went about freely with a guard. The village was very glad to see him, and the people were peaceful and offered food. The governor and

---

[1] Or Cervantes, as Ternaux spells it.
[2] Coronado says, in his letter of October 20, that he started April 23.

Whiskers gave the general a young fellow called Xabe, a native of Quivira, who could give them information about the country. This fellow said that there was gold and silver, but not so much of it as the Turk had said. The Turk, however, continued to declare that it was as he had said. He went as a guide, and thus the army started off from here.

Chapter 19, of how they started in search of Quivira and of what happened on the way.

The army started from Cicuye, leaving the village at peace and, as it seemed, contented, and under obligations to maintain the friendship because their governor and captain had been restored to them. Proceeding toward the plains, which are all on the other side of the mountains, after four days' journey they came to a river with a large, deep current, which flowed down toward Cicuye, and they named this the Cicuye river.[1] They had to stop here to make a bridge so as to cross it. It was finished in four days, by much diligence and rapid work, and as soon as it was done the whole army and the animals crossed. After ten days more they came to some settlements of people who lived like Arabs and who are called Querechos in that region. They had seen the cows for two days. These folks live in tents made of the tanned skins of the cows. They travel around near the cows, killing them for food. They did nothing unusual when they saw our army, except to come out of their tents to look at us, after which they came to talk with the advance guard, and asked who we were. The general talked with them, but as they had already talked with the Turk, who was with the advance guard, they agreed with what he had said. That they were very intelligent is evident from the fact that although they conversed by means of signs they made themselves understood so well that there was no need of an interpreter.[2] They said that there was a very large river over toward where the sun came from, and that one could go along this river through an inhabited region for ninety days without a break from settlement to settlement. They said that the first of these settlements was called Haxa, and that the river was more than a league wide and that there were many canoes on it. These folks started off from here next day with a lot of dogs which dragged their possessions. For two days, during which the army marched in the same direction as that in which they had come from the settlements— that is, between north and east, but more toward the north[3]—they saw

---

[1] The Rio Pecos. The bridge, however, was doubtless built across the upper waters of the Canadian.

[2] There is an elaborate account of the sign language of the Indians, by Garrick Mallery, in the first annual report of the Bureau of Ethnology, 1879-80.

[3] Mota Padilla, xxxiii, 3, p. 165, says: "Hasta allí caminaron los nuestros, guiados por el Turco para el Oriente, con mucha inclinacion al Norte, y desde entónces los guió vía recta al Oriente; y habiendo andado tres jornadas, hubo de hacer alto el gobernador para conferir sobre si seria acertado dejarse llevar de aquel indio, habiendo mudado de rumbo, en cuyo intermedio un soldado, ó por travesura, ó por hacer carne, se apartó, y aunque lo esperaron, no se supo mas de él; y á dos jornadas que anduvieron, guiados todavía del indio, pasaron una barranca profunda, que fué la primera quiebra que vieron de la tierra desde Tigües." Compare the route of the expedition in the Introduction, and also in the translation of Jaramillo.

LA HISTORIA GENERAL

y enojan : finalmente es animal feo y fiero de ro-
ftro, y cuerpo. Huyē de los los cauallos por fu mala catadura, o por nunca los auer vifto. No tienen
fus dueños otra riqueza , ni hazienda , dellos comen, beuen, viften, calçan , y hazen muchas cofas
de los cueros, cafas, calçado, veftido y fogas : delos
hueffos, punçones : delos neruios, y pelos, hiloide
los cuernos, buches, y bexigas , vafos : delas boñí-
gas, lumbre : y delas terneras , odres , en que traen
y tieuen agua : hazen en fin tantas cofas dellos
quantas han menefter , o quantas las baftan para
fu biuienda. Ay tambien otros animales, tan gran
des como cauallos, que por tener cuernos , y lana
fina, los llaman carneros, y dizen , que cada cuerno pefa dos arrouas. Ay tambien grandes perros,
que

THE BUFFALO OF GOMARA, 1554

other roaming Querechos and such great numbers of cows that it already seemed something incredible. These people gave a great deal of information about settlements, all toward the east from where we were. Here Don Garcia broke his arm and a Spaniard got lost who went off hunting so far that he was unable to return to the camp, because the country is very level. The Turk said it was one or two days to Haya (Haxa). The general sent Captain Diego Lopez with ten companions lightly equipped and a guide to go at full speed toward the sunrise for two days and discover Haxa, and then return to meet the army, which set out in the same direction next day. They came across so many animals that those who were on the advance guard killed a large number of bulls. As these fled they trampled one another in their haste until they came to a ravine. So many of the animals fell into this that they filled it up, and the rest went across on top of them. The men who were chasing them on horseback fell in among the animals without noticing where they were going. Three of the horses that fell in among the cows, all saddled and bridled, were lost sight of completely.

As it seemed to the general that Diego Lopez ought to be on his way back, he sent six of his companions to follow up the banks of the little river, and as many more down the banks, to look for traces of the horses at the trails to and from the river. It was impossible to find tracks in this country, because the grass straightened up again as soon as it was trodden down. They were found by some Indians from the army who had gone to look for fruit. These got track of them a good league off, and soon came up with them. They followed the river down to the camp, and told the general that in the 20 leagues they had been over they had seen nothing but cows and the sky. There was another native of Quivira with the army, a painted Indian named Ysopete. This Indian had always declared that the Turk was lying, and on account of this the army paid no attention to him, and even now, although he said that the Querechos had consulted with him, Ysopete was not believed.[1]

The general sent Don Rodrigo Maldonado, with his company, forward from here. He traveled four days and reached a large ravine like those of Colima,[2] in the bottom of which he found a large settlement of people. Cabeza de Vaca and Dorantes had passed through this place, so that they presented Don Rodrigo with a pile of tanned skins and other things, and a tent as big as a house, which he directed them to keep until the army came up. He sent some of his companions to guide the army to that place, so that they should not get lost, although he had been making piles of stones and cow dung for the army to follow. This was the way in which the army was guided by the advance guard.

---

[1] Compare the Spanish. Ternaux: "Mais cette fois on n'avait pas voulu le croire; les Querechos ayant rapporté la même chose que le Turc."

[2] Ternaux read this Coloma. The reference is clearly to the district of Colima in western Mexico, where one of the earliest Spanish settlements was made.

When the general came up with the army and saw the great quantity of skins, he thought he would divide them among the men, and placed guards so that they could look at them. But when the men arrived and saw that the general was sending some of his companions with orders for the guards to give them some of the skins, and that these were going to select the best, they were angry because they were not going to be divided evenly, and made a rush, and in less than a quarter of an hour nothing was left but the empty ground.

The natives who happened to see this also took a hand in it. The women and some others were left crying, because they thought that the strangers were not going to take anything, but would bless them as Cabeza de Vaca and Dorantes had done when they passed through here. They found an Indian girl here who was as white as a Castilian lady, except that she had her chin painted like a Moorish woman. In general they all paint themselves in this way here, and they decorate their eyes.

Chapter 20, of how great stones fell in the camp, and how they discovered another ravine, where the army was divided into two parts.

While the army was resting in this ravine, as we have related, a tempest came up one afternoon with a very high wind and hail, and in a very short space of time a great quantity of hailstones, as big as bowls, or bigger, fell as thick as raindrops, so that in places they covered the ground two or three spans or more deep. And one hit the horse— or I should say, there was not a horse that did not break away, except two or three which the negroes protected by holding large sea nets over them, with the helmets and shields which all the rest wore;[1] and some of them dashed up on to the sides of the ravine so that they got them down with great difficulty. If this had struck them while they were upon the plain, the army would have been in great danger of being left without its horses, as there were many which they were not able to cover.[2] The hail broke many tents, and battered many helmets, and wounded many of the horses, and broke all the crockery of the army, and the gourds, which was no small loss, because they do not have any crockery in this region. They do not make gourds, nor sow corn, nor eat bread, but instead raw meat—or only half cooked— and fruit.

---

[1] The Spanish text is very confused. Ternaux says: " Les chevaux rompirent leurs liens et s'échap- pèrent tous à l'exception de deux ou trois qui furent retenus par des nègres qui avaient pris des cas- ques et des boucliers pour se mettre à l'abri. Le vent en enleva d'autres et les colla contre les parois du ravin."

[2] Mota Padilla, xxxiii, 3, p. 165: "A la primera barranca. . . . á las tres de la tarde hicieron alto, y repentinamente un recio viento les llevó una nube tan cargada, que causó horror el granizo, que des- pedia tan gruesos como nueces, huevos de gallina y de ánsares, de suerte que era necesario arrodelarse para la resistencia; los caballos dieron estampida y se pusieron en fuga, y no se pudieran hallar si la barranca no los detiene; las tiendas que se habian armado quedaron rotas, y quebradas todas las ollas, cazuelas, comales y demas vasijas; y afligidos con tan varios sucesos, determinaron en aquel dia que fué el de Ascension del Señor de 541, que el ejército se volviese á Tigües á reparar, como que era tierra abastecida de todo."

From here the general sent out to explore the country,[1] and they found another settlement four days from there[2] . . . The country was well inhabited, and they had plenty of kidney beans and prunes like those of Castile, and tall vineyards. These village settlements extended for three days. This was called Cona. Some Teyas,[3] as these people are called, went with the army from here and traveled as far as the end of the other settlements with their packs of dogs and women and children, and then they gave them guides to proceed to a large ravine where the army was. They did not let these guides speak with the Turk, and did not receive the same statements from these as they had from the others. These said that Quivira was toward the north, and that we would not find any good road thither. After this they began to believe Ysopete. The ravine which the army had now reached was a league wide from one side to the other, with a little bit of a river at the bottom, and there were many groves of mulberry trees near it, and rosebushes with the same sort of fruit that they have in France. They made verjuice from the unripe grapes at this ravine, although there were ripe ones.[4] There were walnuts and the same kind of fowls as in New Spain, and large quantities of prunes like those of Castile. During this journey a Teya was seen to shoot a bull right through both shoulders with an arrow, which would be a good shot for a musket. These people are very intelligent; the women are well made and modest. They cover their whole body. They wear shoes and buskins made of tanned skin. The women wear cloaks over their small under petticoats, with sleeves gathered up at the shoulders, all of skin, and some wore something like little sanbenitos[5] with a fringe, which reached half-way down the thigh over the petticoat.

The army rested several days in this ravine and explored the country. Up to this point they had made thirty-seven days' marches, traveling

---

[1]Herrera, Historia General, dec. vi, lib. ix, cap. xi, xii, vol. iii, p. 206, ed. 1728: "La relacion que este Indio hacia, de la manera con que se governaban en vna Provincia mas adelante, llamada Harae, i juzgandose, que era imposible que alli dexase de haver algunos Christianos perdidos del Armada de Panfilo de Narvaez, Francisco Vazquez acordò de escrivir vna Carta, i la embiò con el Indio fiel de aquellos dos, porque el que havia de quedar, siempre le llevaron de Retaguarda, porque el bueno no le viese. . . . Embiada la Carta, dando cuenta de la jornada que hacia el Exercito, i adonde havia llegado, pidiendo aviso, i relacion de aquella Tierra, i llamando aquellos Christianos, si por caso los huviese, ò que avisasen de lo que havian menester para salir de cautiverio."

[2]A manera de alixares. The margin reads Alexeres, which I can not find in the atlases. The word means threshing floor, whence Ternaux: "autres cabanes semblables à des bruyères (alixares)."

[3]Bandelier suggests that the name may have originated in the Indian exclamation, Texia! Texia!—friends! friends!—with which they first greeted the Spaniards.

[4]Ternaux: "il y avait des vignes, des mûriers et des rosiers (rosales), dont le fruit que l'on trouve en France, sert en guise de verjus; il y en avait de mûr."

[5]Captain John Stevens's New Dictionary says the sanbenito was "the badge put upon converted Jews brought out by the Inquisition, being in the nature of a scapula or a broad piece of cloth hanging before and behind, with a large Saint Andrews cross on it, red and yellow. The name corrupted from Saco Benito, answerable to the sackcloth worn by penitents in the primitive church." Robert Tomson, in his Voyage into Nova Hispania, 1555, in Hakluyt, iii, 536, describes his imprisonment by the Holy Office in the city of Mexico: "We were brought into the Church, euery one with a S. Benito vpon his backe, which is a halfe a yard of yellow cloth, with a hole to put in a mans head in the middest, and cast ouer a mans head: both flaps hang one before, and another behinde, and in the middest of euery flap, a S. Andrewes crosse, made of red cloth, sowed on vpon the same, and that is called S. Benito."

6 or 7 leagues a day.   It had been the duty of one man to measure and count his steps.   They found that it was 250 leagues to the settlements.[1] When the general Francisco Vazquez realized this, and saw that they had been deceived by the Turk heretofore, and as the provisions were giving out and there was no country around here where they could procure more, he called the captains and ensigns together to decide on what they thought ought to be done.   They all agreed that the general should go in search of Quivira with thirty horsemen and half a dozen foot-soldiers, and that Don Tristan de Arellano should go back to Tiguex with all the army.   When the men in the army learned of this decision, they begged their general not to leave them to conduct the further search, but declared that they all wanted to die with him and did not want to go back.   This did not do any good, although the general agreed to send messengers to them within eight days saying whether it was best for them to follow him or not, and with this he set off with the guides he had and with Ysopete.   The Turk was taken along in chains.

Chapter 21, of how the army returned to Tiguex and the general reached Quivira.

The general started from the ravine with the guides that the Teyas had given him.   He appointed the alderman Diego Lopez his army-master, and took with him the men who seemed to him to be most efficient, and the best horses.   The army still had some hope that the general would send for them, and sent two horsemen, lightly equipped and riding post, to repeat their petition.

The general arrived—I mean, the guides ran away during the first few days and Diego Lopez had to return to the army for guides, bringing orders for the army to return to Tiguex to find food and wait there for the general.   The Teyas, as before, willingly furnished him with new guides.   The army waited for its messengers and spent a fortnight here, preparing jerked beef to take with them.   It was estimated that during this fortnight they killed 500 bulls.   The number of these that were there without any cows was something incredible.   Many fellows were lost at this time who went out hunting and did not get back to the army for two or three days, wandering about the country as if they were crazy, in one direction or another, not knowing how to get back where they started from, although this ravine extended in either direction so that they could find it.[2]   Every night they took account of who was missing, fired guns and blew trumpets and beat drums and built great fires, but yet some of them went off so far and wandered about so much that all this did not give them any help, although it helped others.   The only way was to go back where they had killed an animal and start from there in one direction and another until

[1] The Tiguex country is often referred to as the region where the settlements were.   Ternaux says "depuis Tiguex jusqu'au dernier village."
[2] Compare the Spanish text.

LES SINGVLARITEZ

tre ceſte Floride & la riuiere de Palme ſe trouuent

Torcau
ſauuage.

*diuerſes eſpeces de beſtes monſtrueuſes: entre leſquel-
les lon peut voir vne eſpece de grands taureaux, por-*

*tans cornes longues ſeulement d'vn pié, & ſur le dos
vne tumueur ou eminence, c̃ome vn chameau: le poil
long par tout le corps, duquel la couleur s'approche fort
de celle d'vne mule fauue, & encores l'eſt plus celuy
qui eſt deſſoubs le ment̃o. Lon en amena vne fois deux
tous vifs en Eſpagne, de l'vn deſquels j'ay veu la peau
& non autre choſe, & n'y peurent viure long temps.
Ceſt animal ainſi que lon dit, eſt perpetuel ennemy du
cheual, & ne le peut endurer pres de luy. De la Flori-*

Cap de
Baxe.

*de tirant au promontoire de Baxe, ſe trouue quelque
petite riuiere, ou les eſclaues vont peſcher huitres, qui
portent perles. Or depuis que ſommes venus iuſque là,*

Huitres
portans
perles.

*que de toucher la collection des huitres, ne veux ou-
blier par quel moyen les parles en ſont tirées, tant aux
Indes*

THE BUFFALO OF THEVET, 1558

they struck the ravine or fell in with somebody who could put them on the right road. It is worth noting that the country there is so level that at midday, after one has wandered about in one direction and another in pursuit of game, the only thing to do is to stay near the game quietly until sunset, so as to see where it goes down, and even then they have to be men who are practiced to do it. Those who are not, had to trust themselves to others.

The general followed his guides until he reached Quivira, which took forty-eight days' marching, on account of the great detour they had made toward Florida.[1] He was received peacefully on account of the guides whom he had. They asked the Turk why he had lied and had guided them so far out of their way. He said that his country was in that direction and that, besides this, the people at Cicuye had asked him to lead them off on to the plains and lose them, so that the horses would die when their provisions gave out, and they would be so weak if they ever returned that they could be killed without any trouble, and thus they could take revenge for what had been done to them. This was the reason why he had led them astray, supposing that they did not know how to hunt or to live without corn, while as for the gold, he did not know where there was any of it. He said this like one who had given up hope and who found that he was being persecuted, since they had begun to believe Ysopete, who had guided them better than he had, and fearing lest those who were there might give some advice by which some harm would come to him. They garroted him, which pleased Ysopete very much, because he had always said that Ysopete was a rascal and that he did not know what he was talking about and had always hindered his talking with anybody. Neither gold nor silver nor any trace of either was found among these people. Their lord wore a copper plate on his neck and prized it highly.

The messengers whom the army had sent to the general returned, as I said, and then, as they brought no news except what the alderman had delivered, the army left the ravine and returned to the Teyas, where they took guides who led them back by a more direct road. They readily furnished these, because these people are always roaming over this country in pursuit of the animals and so know it thoroughly. They keep their road in this way: In the morning they notice where the sun rises and observe the direction they are going to take, and then shoot an arrow in this direction. Before reaching this they shoot another over it, and in this way they go all day toward the water where they are to end the day. In this way they covered in 25 days

---

[1] Herrera, Historia General, dec. vi, lib. ix, cap. xii, vol. iii, p. 206 (ed. 1728): "Los treinta Caballos fueron en busca de la Tierra poblada, i hallaron buenos Pueblos, fundados junto à Buenos Arroios, que van à dàr al Rio Grande, que pasaron. Anduvieron cinco, ò seis dias por estos Pueblos, llegaron à lo vltimo de Quivira, que decian los Indios ser mucho, i hallaron vn Rio de mas Agua, i poblacion que los otros; i preguntando que si adelante havia otra cosa, dixeron, que de Quivira no havia sino Harae, i que era de la misma manera en Poblaciones, i tamaño. . . . Embiòse à llamar al Señor, el qual era vn Hombre grande, y de grandes miembros, de buena proporcion, llevò docientos Hombres desnudos, i mal cubiertas sus carnes, llevaban Arcos, i Flechas, i Plumas en las cabeças." Compare Jaramillo's statement and Coronado's letter, as discussed in the introduction.

what had taken them 37 days going, besides stopping to hunt cows on the way. They found many salt lakes on this road, and there was a great quantity of salt. There were thick pieces of it on top of the water bigger than tables, as thick as four or five fingers. Two or three spans down under water there was salt which tasted better than that in the floating pieces, because this was rather bitter. It was crystalline. All over these plains there were large numbers of animals like squirrels and a great number of their holes. On its return the army reached the Cicuye river more than 30 leagues below there—I mean below the bridge they had made when they crossed it, and they followed it up to that place. In general, its banks are covered with a sort of rose bushes, the fruit of which tastes like muscatel grapes.[1] They grow on little twigs about as high up as a man. It has the parsley leaf. There were unripe grapes and currants (?)[2] and wild marjoram. The guides said this river joined that of Tiguex more than 20 days from here, and that its course turned toward the east. It is believed that it flows into the mighty river of the Holy Spirit (Espiritu Santo), which the men with Don Hernando de Soto discovered in Florida. A painted Indian woman ran away from Juan de Saldibar and hid in the ravines about this time, because she recognized the country of Tiguex where she had been a slave. She fell into the hands of some Spaniards who had entered the country from Florida to explore it in this direction. After I got back to New Spain I heard them say that the Indian told them that she had run away from other men like them nine days, and that she gave the names of some captains; from which we ought to believe that we were not far from the region they discovered, although they said they were more than 200 leagues inland. I believe the land at that point is more than 600 leagues across from sea to sea.

As I said, the army followed the river up as far as Cicuye, which it found ready for war and unwilling to make any advances toward peace or to give any food to the army. From there they went on to Tiguex where several villages had been reinhabited, but the people were afraid and left them again.

Chapter 22, of how the general returned from Quivira and of other expeditions toward the North.

After Don Tristan de Arellano reached Tiguex, about the middle of July, in the year '42,[3] he had provisions collected for the coming winter. Captain Francisco de Barrionuevo was sent up the river toward the north with several men. He saw two provinces, one of which was called Hemes and had seven villages, and the other Yuqueyunque.[4] The inhabitants of Hemes came out peaceably and furnished provisions. At Yuqueyunque the whole nation left two very fine villages which

---

[1] Ternaux: "les rives, qui sont couvertes d'une plante dont le fruit ressemble au raisin muscat."
[2] Compare the Spanish text; Ternaux omits this sentence.
[3] Castañeda's date is, as usual, a year later than the actual one.
[4] Yuge-uing-ge, as Bandelier spells it, is the aboriginal name of a former Tewa village, the site of which is occupied by the hamlet of Chamita, opposite San Juan. The others are near by.

segunda

por ellomo y des hazer las tre
sus coyunturas con un pe
dernal grande como un
dedo atado en un palitro
tanta facilidad como si fue
se un una muy buena he
rra mienta dandoles los fi
los e n su pro prios dientes es
cosa de ber y de no tar la prest
eza con que lo hacen
on su reses llanos muy gran
cantidad de lobos que andan
tras de los bacas tienen es se
lo llaman los ser nos son re
mendados de blanco el pelo
ancho y que muriendo an
sie en la mano se pela en
caliente y queda como jaes
co pelado las lie bres que son

en

parte

en gran m̄ mese andauan
abo bn̄ das que yendo aca
uallo las ma ta con las lan
cas es to es de andar he rras
entre las bocas dela gente de
pie hu yens

Ca pi tulo otho de qui mi
ra y en que rum ba esta
y la no ti cia queda rse

qui mi ra es ael fu miente
dea que llas ba rra ncas por
el medio dela tie rra algun
rre mada a la cor dillera de
la mar por que hasta qui
mi ra es tie rra llana y alli
se co miencan a ver algu
nas sie rras la tie rra es muy
pobla da segun el tu rco

they had on either side of the river entirely vacant, and went into the mountains, where they had four very strong villages in a rough country, where it was impossible for horses to go. In the two villages there was a great deal of food and some very beautiful glazed earthenware with many figures and different shapes. Here they also found many bowls full of a carefully selected shining metal with which they glazed the earthenware. This shows that mines of silver would be found in that country if they should hunt for them.

There was a large and powerful river, I mean village, which was called Braba, 20 leagues farther up the river, which our men called Valladolid.[1] The river flowed through the middle of it. The natives crossed it by wooden bridges, made of very long, large, squared pines. At this village they saw the largest and finest hot rooms or estufas that there were in the entire country, for they had a dozen pillars, each one of which was twice as large around as one could reach and twice as tall as a man. Hernando de Alvarado visited this village when he discovered Cicuye. The country is very high and very cold. The river is deep and very swift, without any ford. Captain Barrionuevo returned from here, leaving the province at peace.

Another captain went down the river in search of the settlements which the people at Tutahaco had said were several days distant from there. This captain went down 80 leagues and found four large villages which he left at peace. He proceeded until he found that the river sank into the earth, like the Guadiana in Estremadura.[2] He did not go on to where the Indians said that it came out much larger, because his commission did not extend for more than 80 leagues march. After this captain got back, as the time had arrived which the captain had set for his return from Quivira, and as he had not come back, Don Tristan selected 40 companions and, leaving the army to Francisco de Barrionuevo, he started with them in search of the general. When he reached Cicuye the people came out of the village to fight, which detained him there four days, while he punished them, which he did by firing some volleys into the village. These killed several men, so that they did not come out against the army, since two of their principal men had been killed on the first day. Just then word was brought that the general was coming, and so Don Tristan had to stay there on this account also, to keep the road open.[3] Everybody welcomed the general on his arrival, with great joy. The Indian Xabe, who was the young fellow who had been given to the general at Cicuye when he started off in search of Quivira, was with Don Tristan de Arellano and when he learned that the gen-

---

[1] Taos, or Te-uat-ha. See Bandelier's Final Report, vol. i, p. 123, for the identification of these places.

[2] This rendering, doubtless correct, is due to Ternaux. The Guadiana, however, reappears above ground some time before it begins to mark the boundary of the Spanish province of Estremadura. The Castañeda family had its seat in quite the other end of the peninsula.

[3] Mota Padilla, xxxiii, 4., p. 165: "Al cabo de dos meses, poco mas ó ménos, volvió con su gente el general á Tigües, y dieron razon que habiendo caminado mas de cien leguas. · · · Quivira se halló ser un pueblo de hasta cien casas."

eral was coming he acted as if he was greatly pleased, and said, "Now when the general comes, you will see that there is gold and silver in Quivira, although not so much as the Turk said." When the general arrived, and Xabe saw that they had not found anything, he was sad and silent, and kept declaring that there was some. He made many believe that it was so, because the general had not dared to enter into the country on account of its being thickly settled and his force not very strong, and that he had returned to lead his army there after the rains, because it had begun to rain there already, as it was early in August when he left. It took him forty days to return, traveling lightly equipped. The Turk had said when they left Tiguex that they ought not to load the horses with too much provisions, which would tire them so that they could not afterward carry the gold and silver, from which it is very evident that he was deceiving them.

The general reached Cicuye with his force and at once set off for Tiguex, leaving the village more quiet, for they had met him peaceably and had talked with him. When he reached Tiguex, he made his plans to pass the winter there, so as to return with the whole army, because it was said that he brought information regarding large settlements and very large rivers, and that the country was very much like that of Spain in the fruits and vegetation and seasons. They were not ready to believe that there was no gold there, but instead had suspicions that there was some farther back in the country, because, although this was denied, they knew what the thing was and had a name for it among themselves—acochis. With this we end this first part, and now we will give an account of the provinces.

SECOND PART, WHICH TREATS OF THE HIGH VILLAGES AND PROVINCES AND OF THEIR HABITS AND CUSTOMS, AS COLLECTED BY PEDRO DE CASTAÑEDA, NATIVE OF THE CITY OF NAJARA.

Laus Deo.

It does not seem to me that the reader will be satisfied with having seen and understood what I have already related about the expedition, although that has made it easy to see the difference between the report which told about vast treasures, and the places where nothing like this was either found or known. It is to be noted that in place of settlements great deserts were found, and instead of populous cities villages of 200 inhabitants and only 800 or 1,000 people in the largest. I do not know whether this will furnish grounds for pondering and considering the uncertainty of this life. To please these, I wish to give a detailed account of all the inhabited region seen and discovered by this expedition, and some of their ceremonies and habits, in accordance with what we came to know about them, and the limits within which each province falls, so that hereafter it may be possible to understand in what direction Florida lies and in what direction Greater India; and

THE BUFFALO OF DE BRY, 1595

this land of New Spain is part of the mainland with Peru, and with Greater India or China as well, there not being any strait between to separate them. On the other hand, the country is so wide that there is room for these vast deserts which lie between the two seas, for the coast of the North sea beyond Florida stretches toward the Bacallaos[1] and then turns toward Norway, while that of the South sea turns toward the west, making another bend down toward the south almost like a bow and stretches away toward India, leaving room for the lands that border on the mountains on both sides to stretch out in such a way as to have between them these great plains which are full of cattle and many other animals of different sorts, since they are not inhabited, as I will relate farther on. There is every sort of game and fowl there, but no snakes, for they are free[2] from these. I will leave the account of the return of the army to New Spain until I have shown what slight occasion there was for this. We will begin our account with the city of Culiacan, and point out the differences between the one country and the other, on account of which one ought to be settled by Spaniards and the other not. It should be the reverse, however, with Christians, since there are intelligent men in one, and in the other wild animals and worse than beasts.

Chapter 1, of the province of Culiacan and of its habits and customs.

Culiacan is the last place in the New Kingdom of Galicia, and was the first settlement made by Nuño de Guzman when he conquered this kingdom. It is 210 leagues west of Mexico. In this province there are three chief languages, besides other related dialects. The first is that of the Tahus, who are the best and most intelligent race. They are now the most settled and have received the most light from the faith. They worship idols and make presents to the devil of their goods and riches, consisting of cloth and turquoises. They do not eat human flesh nor sacrifice it. They are accustomed to keep very large snakes, which they venerate. Among them there are men dressed like women who marry other men and serve as their wives. At a great festival they consecrate the women who wish to live unmarried, with much singing and dancing,[3] at which all the chiefs of the locality gather and dance naked, and after all have danced with her they put her in a hut that has been decorated for this event and the chiefs adorn her with clothes and bracelets of fine turquoises, and then the chiefs go in one by one to lie with her, and all the others who wish, follow them. From this time on these women can not refuse anyone who pays them a certain amount agreed on for this. Even if they take husbands, this does not exempt them from obliging anyone who pays them. The greatest festivals are on market days. The custom is for the husbands to buy the women

---

[1] The Newfoundland region.

[2] Ternaux's rendering. Compare the Spanish text.

[3] Compare the Spanish. Several words in the manuscript are not very clear. Ternaux omits them, as usual.

14 ETH——33

whom they marry, of their fathers and relatives at a high price, and then to take them to a chief, who is considered to be a priest, to deflower them and see if she is a virgin; and if she is not, they have to return the whole price, and he can keep her for his wife or not, or let her be consecrated, as he chooses. At these times they all get drunk.

The second language is that of the Pacaxes, the people who live in the country between the plains and the mountains. These people are more barbarous. Some of them who live near the mountains eat human flesh.[1] They are great sodomites, and have many wives, even when these are sisters. They worship painted and sculptured stones, and are much given to witchcraft and sorcery.

The third language is that of the Acaxes, who are in possession of a large part of the hilly country and all of the mountains They go hunting for men just as they hunt animals. They all eat human flesh, and he who has the most human bones and skulls hung up around his house is most feared and respected. They live in settlements and in very rough country, avoiding the plains. In passing from one settlement to another, there is always a ravine in the way which they can not cross, although they can talk together across it.[2] At the slightest call 500 men collect, and on any pretext kill and eat one another. Thus it has been very hard to subdue these people, on account of the roughness of the country, which is very great.

Many rich silver mines have been found in this country. They do not run deep, but soon give out. The gulf of the sea begins on the coast of this province, entering the land 250 leagues toward the north and ending at the mouth of the Firebrand (Tizon) river. This country forms its eastern limit, and California the western. From what I have been told by men who had navigated it, it is 30 leagues across from point to point, because they lose sight of this country when they see the other. They say the gulf is over 150 leagues broad (or deep), from shore to shore. The coast makes a turn toward the south at the Firebrand river, bending down to California, which turns toward the west, forming that peninsula which was formerly held to be an island, because it was a low sandy country. It is inhabited by brutish, bestial, naked people who eat their own offal. The men and women couple like animals, the female openly getting down on all fours.

Chapter 2, of the province of Petlatlan and all the inhabited country as far as Chichilticalli.

Petlatlan is a settlement of houses covered with a sort of mats made of *plants*.[3] These are collected into villages, extending along a river from the mountains to the sea. The people are of the same race and

---

[1] Omitted by Ternaux, who (p. 151) calls these the Pacasas.

[2] Compare the Spanish text. Ternaux (p. 152) renders: "Ils ont soin de bâtir leurs villages de manière à ce qu'ils soient séparés les uns des autres par des ravins impossibles à franchir," which is perhaps the meaning of the Spanish.

[3] Ternaux, p. 156: "couvertes en nattes de glaïeul." The Spanish manuscript is very obscure.

habits as the Culuacanian Tahues. There is much sodomy among them. In the mountain district there is a large population and more settlements. These people have a somewhat different language from the Tahues, although they understand each other. It is called Petlatlan because the houses are made of petates or palm-leaf mats.[1] Houses of this sort are found for more than 240 leagues in this region, to the beginning of the Cibola wilderness. The nature of the country changes here very greatly, because from this point on there are no trees except the pine,[2] nor are there any fruits except a few tunas,[3] mesquites,[4] and pitahayas.[5]

Petlatlan is 20 leagues from Culiacan, and it is 130 leagues from here to the valley of Señora. There are many rivers between the two, with settlements of the same sort of people—for example, Sinoloa, Boyomo, Teocomo, Yaquimi, and other smaller ones. There is also the Corazones or Hearts, which is in our possession, down the valley of Señora.[6]

Señora is a river and valley thickly settled by able-bodied people. The women wear petticoats of tanned deerskin, and little san benitos reaching half way down the body.[7] The chiefs of the villages go up on some little heights they have made for this purpose, like public criers, and there make proclamations for the space of an hour, regulating those things they have to attend to. They have some little huts for shrines, all over the outside of which they stick many arrows, like a hedgehog. They do this when they are eager for war. All about this province toward the mountains there is a large population in separate little provinces containing ten or twelve villages. Seven or eight of them, of which I know the names, are Comupatrico, Mochilagua, Arispa, and the Little Valley.[8] There are others which we did not see.

It is 40 leagues from Señora to the valley of Suya. The town of Saint Jerome (San Hieronimo) was established in this valley, where there was

---

[1] An account of these people is given in the Trivmphos, lib. 1, cap. ii, p. 6, Andres Perez de Ribas, S. J. "Estas [casas] hazian, vnas de varas de monte hincadas en tierra, entretexidas, y atadas con vejucos, que son vnas ramas como de çarçaparrilla, muy fuertes, y que duran mucho tiĕpo. Las paredes que haziã con essa barazon las afortauan con vna torta de barro, para que no las penetrasse el Sol, ni los vientos, cubriendo la casa con madera, y encima tierra, ó barro, con que hazian açotea, y con esso se contentauan. Otros hazian sus casas de petates q̃ es genero de esteras texidas de caña taxada." Bandelier found the Opata Indians living in houses made with "a slight foundation of cobblestones which supported a framework of posts standing in a thin wall of rough stones and mud, while a slanting roof of yucca or palm leaves covered the whole."—Final Report, pt. i, p. 58.

[2] The meaning of this sentence in the Spanish is not wholly clear. Ternaux, p. 156: "Cette manière de bâtir . . . change dans cet endroit probablement, parce qu'il n'y a plus d'arbres sans épines."

[3] The *Opuntia tuna* or prickly pear.

[4] *Prosopis juliflora.*

[5] *Cereus thurberii.*

[6] Sonora.

[7] Oviedo, Historia, vol. iii, p. 610 (ed. 1853): "Toda esta gente, dende las primeras casas del mahiz, andan los hombres muy deshonestos, sin se cobrir cosa alguna de sus personas; é las mugeres muy honestas, con unas sayas de cueros de venados hasta los piés, ó con falda que detrás les arrastra alguna cosa, ó abiertas por delante hasta el suelo y enlaçadas con unas correas. É traen debaxo, por donde están abiertas, una mantilla de algodon é otra ençima, é unas gorgueras de algodon, que les cubren todos los pechos."

[8] Ternaux, pp. 157–158: "une multitude de tribus à part, réunis en petites nations de sept ou huit, dix ou douze villages, ce sont: Upatriço, Mochila, Guagarispa, El Vallecillo, et d'autres qui son près des montagues."

a rebellion later, and part of the people who had settled there were killed, as will be seen in the third part.   There are many villages in the neighborhood of this valley.   The people are the same as those in Señora and have the same dress and language, habits, and customs, like all the rest as far as the desert of Chichilticalli.   The women paint their chins and eyes like the Moorish women of Barbary.   They are great sodomites. They drink wine made of the pitahaya, which is the fruit of a great thistle which opens like the pomegranate.   The wine makes them stupid.   They make a great quantity of preserves from the tuna; they preserve it in a large amount of its sap without other honey.   They make bread of the mesquite, like cheese, which keeps good for a whole year.[1]   There are native melons in this country so large that a person can carry only one of them.   They cùt these into slices and dry them in the sun.   They are good to eat, and taste like figs, and are better than dried meat; they are very good and sweet, keeping for a whole year when prepared in this way.[2]

In this country there were also tame eagles, which the chiefs esteemed to be something fine.[3]   No fowls of any sort were seen in any of these villages except in this valley of Suya, where fowls like those of Castile were found.   Nobody could find out how they came to be so far inland, the people being all at war with one another.   Between Suya and Chichilticalli there are many sheep and mountain goats with very large bodies and horns.   Some Spaniards declare that they have seen flocks of more than a hundred together, which ran so fast that they disappeared very quickly.

At Chichilticalli the country changes its character again and the spiky vegetation ceases.   The reason is that the gulf reaches as far up as this place, and the mountain chain changes its direction at the same time that the coast does.   Here they had to cross and pass through the mountains in order tò get into the level country.

Chapter 3, of Chichilticalli and the desert, of Cibola, its customs and habits, and of other things.

Chichilticalli is so called because the friars found a house at this place which was formerly inhabited by people who separated from Cibola.   It was made of colored or reddish earth.[4]   The house was large and appeared to have been a fortress.   It must have been destroyed by the people of the district, who are the most barbarous people that have yet been seen. They live in separate cabins and not in settlements.   They live by hunt-

---

[1] Bandelier, Final Report, pt. i, p. 111, quotes from the Relaciones of Zárate-Salmeron, of some Arizona Indians: "Tambien tienen para su sustento Mescali que es conserva de raiz de maguey."   The strong liquor is made from the root of the Mexican or American agave.

[2] These were doubtless cantaloupes.   The southwestern Indians still slice and dry them in a manner similar to that here described.

[3] The Pueblo Indians, particularly the Zuñi and Hopi, keep eagles for their feathers, which are highly prized because of their reputed sacred character.

[4] Chichiltic-calli, a red object or house, according to Molina's Vocabulario Mexicano, 1555.   Bandelier, Historical Introduction, p. 11, gives references to the ancient and modern descriptions.   The location is discussed on page 387 of the present memoir.

ON THE TERRACES AT ZUÑI

ing. The rest of the country is all wilderness, covered with pine forests. There are great quantities of the pine nuts. The pines are two or three times as high as a man before they send out branches. There is a sort of oak with sweet acorns, of which they make cakes like sugar plums with dried coriander seeds. It is very sweet, like sugar. Watercress grows in many springs, and there are rosebushes, and pennyroyal, and wild marjoram.

There are barbels and picones,[1] like those of Spain, in the rivers of this wilderness. Gray lions and leopards were' seen.[2] The country rises continually from the beginning of the wilderness until Cibola is reached, which is 85 leagues, going north. From Culiacan to the edge of the wilderness the route had kept the north on the left hand.

Cibola[3] is seven villages. The largest is called Maçaque.[4] The houses are ordinarily three or four stories high, but in Maçaque there are houses with four and seven stories. These people are very intelligent. They cover their privy parts and all the immodest parts with cloths made like a sort of table napkin, with fringed edges and a tassel at each corner, which they tie over the hips. They wear long robes of feathers and of the skins of hares, and cotton blankets.[5] The women wear blankets, which they tie or knot over the left shoulder, leaving the right arm out. These serve to cover the body. They wear a neat well-shaped outer garment of skin. They gather their hair over the two ears, making a frame which looks like an old-fashioned headdress.[6]

---

[1] Ternaux (p. 162) succeeded no better than I have in the attempt to identify this fish.

[2] Ternaux, p. 162: "A l'entrée du pays inhabité on rencontre une espèce de lion de couleur fauve." Compare the Spanish text. These were evidently the mountain lion and the wild cat.

[3] Albert S. Gatschet, in his Zwölf Sprachen, p. 106, says that this word is now to be found only in the dialect of the pueblo of Isleta, under the form sibúlodá, buffalo.

[4] Matsaki, the ruins of which are at the northwestern base of Thunder mountain. See Bandelier's Final Report, pt. i, p. 133, and Hodge, First Discovered City of Cibola.

[5] The mantles of rabbit hair are still worn at Moki, but those of turkey plumes are out of use altogether. See Bandelier's Final Report, pt. i, pp. 37 and 158. They used also the fiber of the yucca and agave for making clothes.

[6] J. G. Owens, Hopi Natal Ceremonies, in Journal of American Archæology and Ethnology, vol. ii, p. 165 n., says: "The dress of the Hopi [Moki, or Tusayan] women consists of a black blanket about 3½ feet square, folded around the body from the left side. It passes under the left arm and over the right shoulder, being sewed together on the right side, except a hole about 3 inches long near the upper end through which the arm is thrust. This is belted in at the waist by a sash about 3 inches wide. Sometimes, though not frequently, a shirt is worn under this garment, and a piece of muslin, tied together by two adjacent corners, is usually near by, to be thrown over the shoulders. Most of the women have moccasins, which they put on at certain times."

Gomara, ccxiii, describes the natives of Sibola: "Hazen con todo esso vnas mantillas de pieles de conejos, y liebres, y de venados, que algodon muy poco alcançan: calçan çapatos de cuero, y de inuierno vnas como botas hasta las rodillas. Las mugeres van vestidas de Metl hasta en pies, andan ceñidas, trençan los cabellos, y rodeanselos ala cabeça por sobre las orejas. La tierra es arenosa, y de poco fruto, creo q̃ por pereza dellos, pues donde siembran, lleua mayz, frisoles, calabaças, y frutas, y aun se crian en ella gallipauos, que no se hazen en todos cabos."

In his Relacion de Viaje, p. 173, Espejo says of Zuñi: "en esta provincia se visten algunos de los naturales, de mantas de algodon y cueros de las vacas, y de gamuzas aderezadas; y las mantas de algodon las traen puestas al uso mexicano, eceto que debajo de partes vergonzosas traen unos paños de algodon pintados, y algunos dellos traen camisas, y las mugeres traen naguas de algodon y muchas dellas bordadas con hilo de colores, y encima una manta como la traen los indios mexicanos, y atada con un paño de manos como tohalla labrada, y se lo atan por la cintura con sus borlas, y las naguas son que sirven de faldas de camisa á raiz de las carnes, y esto cada una lo trae con la mas ventaja que puede; y todos, asi hombres como mujeres. andan calzados con zapatos y botas, las suelas de cuero

This country is a valley between rocky mountains. They cultivate corn, which does not grow very high. The ears start at the very foot, and each large fat stalk bears about 800 grains, something not seen before in these parts.[1] There are large numbers of bears in this province, and lions, wild-cats, deer, and otter. There are very fine turquoises, although not so many as was reported. They collect the pine nuts each year, and store them up in advance. A man does not have more than one wife. There are estufas or hot rooms in the villages, which are the courtyards or places where they gather for consultation. They do not have chiefs as in New Spain, but are ruled by a council of the oldest men.[2] They have priests who preach to them, whom they call papas.[3] These are the elders. They go up on the highest roof of the village and preach to the village from there, like public criers, in the morning while the sun is rising, the whole village being silent and sitting in the galleries to listen.[4] They tell them how they are to live, and I believe that they give certain commandments for them to keep, for there is no drunkenness among them nor sodomy nor sacrifices, neither do they eat human flesh nor steal, but they are usually at work. The estufas belong to the whole village. It is a sacrilege for the women to go into the estufas to sleep.[5] They make the cross as a sign of peace. They burn their dead, and throw the implements used in their work into the fire with the bodies.[6]

---

de vacas, y lo de encima de cuero de venado aderezado; las mugeres traen el cabello muy peinado y bien puesto y con sus moldes que traen en la cabeza uno de una parte y otro de otra, á donde ponen el cabello con curiosidad sin traer nengun tocado en la cabeza."

Mota Padilla, xxxii, 4, p. 160: "Los indios son de buenas estaturas, las indias bien dispuestas: traen unas mantas blancas, que las cubren desde los hombros hasta los piés y por estar cerradas, tienen por donde sacar los brazos; asimismo, usan traer sobre las dichas otras mantas que se ponen sobre el hombro izquierdo, y el un cabo tercian por debajo del brazo derecho como capa: estiman en mucho los cabellos; y así, los traen muy peinados, y en una jícara de agua, se miran como en un espejo; pártense el cabello en dos trenzas, liadas con cintas de algodon de colores, y en cada lado de la cabeza forman dos ruedas ó círculos, que dentro de ellos rematan, y dejan la punta del cabello levantado como plumajes y en unas tablitas de hasta tres dedos, fijan con pegamentos unas piedras verdes que llaman chalchihuites, de que se dice hay minas, como tambien se dice las hubo cerca de Sombrerete, en un real de minas que se nombra Chalchihuites, por esta razon; . . . con dichas piedras forman sortijas que con unos palillos fijan sobre el cabello como ramillete: son las indias limpias, y se precian de no parecer mal."

[1] Ternaux, p. 164: "les épis partent presque tous du pied, et chaque épi a sept ou huit cents grains, ce que l'on n'avait pas encore vu aux Indes." The meaning of the Spanish is by no means clear, and there are several words in the manuscript which have been omitted in the translation.

[2] Ternaux, p. 164: "ni de conseils de vieillards."

[3] Papa in the Zuñi language signifies "elder brother," and may allude either to age or to rank.

[4] Dr J. Walter Fewkes, in his Few Summer Ceremonials at the Tusayan Pueblos, p. 7, describes the Dä'wä-wýmp-ki-yas, a small number of priests of the sun. Among other duties, they pray to the rising sun, whose course they are said to watch, and they prepare offerings to it.

Mota Padilla, cap. xxxii, 5, p. 160, says that at Cibola, "no se vió templo alguno, ni se les conoció ídolo, por lo que se tuvo entendido adoraban al sol y á la luna, lo que se confirmó, porque una noche que hubo un eclipse, alzaron todos mucha gritería."

[5] Ternaux, p. 165: "Les étuves sont rares dans ce pays. Ils regardent comme un sacrilége que les femmes entrent deux à la fois dans un endroit."

In his Few Summer Ceremonials at Tusayan, p. 6, Dr Fewkes says that "with the exception of their own dances, women do not take part in the secret kibva [estufa] ceremonials; but it can not be said that they are debarred entrance as assistants in making the paraphernalia of the dances, or when they are called upon to represent dramatizations of traditions in which women figure."

[6] Mr Frank Hamilton Cushing, in the Compte-rendu of the Congrès International des Americanistes, Berlin, 1888, pp. 171-172, speaking of the excavations of "Los Muertos" in southern Arizona,

Tercera

mirar que ningun cauallo vio
alos españoles que les biese de
ca ra que no huyese desu bis
ta por que ellos henan chros
ho an choyerctos delos vaqs
dos por mas dessente los españa
les dos por ella do que yendo
huyendo ven aquien los si
que henen tan tas como cabe
nes muy grandes quando hu
yen te nan la cabeca baxa
la barba arras tando por el
suelo del medio cuerpo para
atras son tenidos es pelo muy
merino como lee nejas muy
finas y dela sunta para adelan
te el pelo muy largo desa rison
deleon rras ol abe y una gra
corcoba mayor que decame
llo los cuernos corttos y gordos

que

parte

quese des cubren poco por cima
des pelo madan el pelo de
medio cuerpo aras por mayor
un bellon y que don pujestos
leones para mudarse a nini
a algunos arbo les pequeños
que ay en algunas barranqui
llas y allise me jie gan hasta
que dexarel bellon como lo
cule bra el pelejo he nen la cola
corta y en pequeñyssyos pa
dea bolle uanla quando co
rren alta a manera de alacru
es cosa de ber que quando son
se cerricos son bermejos y de
la manera delos ratos hos y
conel hiembo y la edad se mu
dan en otra color faicion
ay oha asa que todos listuios
quese ma la un temior nalao

It is 20 leagues to Tusayan, going northwest. This is a province with seven villages, of the same sort, dress, habits, and ceremonies as at Cibola. There may be as many as 3,000 or 4,000 men in the fourteen villages of these two provinces. It is 40 leagues or more to Tiguex, the road trending toward the north. The rock of Acuco, which we described in the first part, is between these.

Chapter 4, of how they live at Tiguex, and of the province of Tiguex and its neighborhood.

Tiguex is a province with twelve villages on the banks of a large, mighty river; some villages on one side and some on the other. It is a spacious valley two leagues wide, and a very high, rough, snow-covered mountain chain lies east of it. There are seven villages in the ridges at the foot of this—four on the plain and three situated on the skirts of the mountain.

There are seven villages 7 leagues to the north, at Quirix, and the seven villages of the province of Hemes are 40 leagues northwest. It is 40 leagues north or east to Acha,[1] and 4 leagues southeast to Tuta-

---

says: "All the skeletons, especially of adults [in the intramural burials], were, with but few exceptions, disposed with the heads to the east and slightly elevated as though resting on pillows, so as to face the west; and the hands were usually placed at the sides or crossed over the breast. With nearly all were paraphernalia, household utensils, articles of adornment, etc. This paraphernalia quite invariably partook of a sacerdotal character." In the pyral mounds outside the communal dwellings, "each burial consisted of a vessel, large or small, according to the age of the person whose thoroughly cremated remains it was designed to receive, together, ordinarily, with traces of the more valued and smaller articles of personal property sacrificed at the time of cremation. Over each such vessel was placed either an inverted bowl or a cover (roughly rounded by chipping) of potsherds, which latter, in most cases, showed traces of having been firmly cemented, by means of mud plaster, to the vessels they covered. Again, around each such burial were found always from two or three to ten or a dozen broken vessels, often, indeed, a complete set; namely, eating and drinking bowls, water-jar and bottle, pitcher, spheroidal food receptacle, ladles large and small, and cooking-pot. Sometimes, however, one or another of these vessels actually designed for sacrifice with the dead, was itself used as the receptacle of his or her remains. In every such case the vessel had been either punctured at the bottom or on one side, or else violently cracked—from Zuñi customs, in the process of 'killing' it." The remains of other articles were around, burned in the same fire.

Since the above note was extracted, excavations have been conducted by Dr. J. Walter Fewkes at the prehistoric Hopi pueblo of Sikyatki, an exhaustive account of which will be published in a forthcoming report of the Bureau of Ethnology. Sikyatki is located at the base of the First Mesa of Tusayan, about 3 miles from Hano. The house structures were situated on an elongated elevation, the western extremity of the village forming a sort of acropolis. On the northern, western, and southern slopes of the height, outside the village proper, cemeteries were found, and in these most of the excavations were conducted. Many graves were uncovered at a depth varying from 1 foot to 10 feet, but the skeletons were in such condition as to be practically beyond recovery. Accompanying these remains were hundreds of food and water vessels in great variety of form and decoration, and in quality of texture far better than any earthenware previously recovered from a pueblo people. With the remains of the priests there were found, in addition to the usual utensils, terra cotta and stone pipes, beads, prayer-sticks, quartz crystals, arrowpoints, stone and shell fetiches, sacred paint, and other paraphernalia similar to that used by the Hopi of today. The house walls were constructed of small, flat stones brought from the neighboring mesa, laid in adobe mortar and plastered with the same material. The rooms were invariably small, averaging perhaps 8 feet square, and the walls were quite thin. No human remains were found in the houses, nor were any evidences of cremation observed.

Mota Padilla, cap. xxxii, 5, p. 160, describes a funeral which was witnessed by the soldiers of Coronado's army: "en una ocasion vieron los españoles, que habiendo muerto un indio, armaron una grande balsa ó luminaria de leña, sobre que pusieron el cuerpo cubierto con una manta, y luego todos los del pueblo, hombres y mujeres, fueron poniendo sobre la cama de leña, pinole, calabazas, frijoles, atole, maiz tostado, y de lo demas que usaban comer, y dieron fuego por todas partes, de suerte que en breve todo se convirtió en cenizas con el cuerpo."

[1] The pueblo of Picuris.

haco, a province with eight villages. In general, these villages all have the same habits and customs, although some have some things in particular which the others have not.[1] They are governed by the opinions of the elders. They all work together to build the villages, the women being engaged in making the mixture and the walls, while the men bring the wood and put it in place.[2] They have no lime, but they make a mixture of ashes, coals, and dirt which is almost as good as mortar, for when the house is to have four stories, they do not make the walls more than half a yard thick. They gather a great pile of twigs of thyme and sedge grass and set it afire, and when it is half coals and ashes they throw a quantity of dirt and water on it and mix it all together. They make round balls of this, which they use instead of stones after they are dry, fixing them with the same mixture, which comes to be like a stiff clay. Before they are married the young men serve the whole village in general, and fetch the wood that is needed for use, putting it in a pile in the courtyard of the villages, from which the women take it to carry to their houses.

The young men live in the estufas, which are in the yards of the village.[3] They are underground, square or round, with pine pillars.

---

[1] Bandelier gives a general account of the internal condition of the Pueblo Indians, with references to the older Spanish writers, in his Final Report, pt. i, p. 135.

[2] Bandelier, Final Report, pt. i, p. 141, quotes from Benavides, Memorial, p. 43, the following account of how the churches and convents in the pueblo region were built: "los hã hecho tan solamẽte las mugeres, y los muchachos, y muchachas de la dotrina; porque entre estos naciones se vsa hazer las mugeres las paredes, y los hombres hilan y texen sus mantas, y van á la guerra, y a la caza, y si obligamos a algũ hombre á hazer pared, se corre dello, y las mugeres se rien."

Mota Padilla, cap. xxxii, p. 159: "estos pueblos [de Tigües y Tzibola] estaban murados . . . si bien se diferenciaban en que los pueblos de Tzibola son fabricados de pizarras unidas con argamasa de tierra; y los de Tigües son de una tierra güijosa, aunque muy fuerte; sus fábricas tienen las puertas para adentro del pueblo, y la entrada de estos muros son puertas pequeñas y se sube por unas escalerillas angostas, y se entra de ellas á una sala de terraplen, y por otra escalera se baja al plan de la poblacion."

Several days before Friar Marcos reached Chichilticalli, the natives, who were telling him about Cibola, described the way in which these lofty houses were built: "para dármelo á entender, tomaban tierra y ceniza, y echábanle agua, y señalábanme como ponian la piedra y como subian el edificio arriba, poniendo aquello y piedra hasta ponello en lo alto; preguntábales á los hombres de aquella tierra si tenian alas para subir aquellos sobrados; reíanse y señalábanme el escalera, tambien como la podria yo señalar, y tomaban un palo y poníanlo sobre la cabeza y decian que aquel altura hay de sobrado á sobrado." Relacion de Fray Marcos in Pacheco y Cardenas, Doc. de Indias, vol. iii, p. 339.

Lewis H. Morgan, in his Ruins of a Stone Pueblo, Peabody Museum Reports, vol. xii, p. 541, says: "Adobe is a kind of pulverized clay with a bond of considerable strength by mechanical cohesion. In southern Colorado, in Arizona, and New Mexico there are immense tracts covered with what is called adobe soil. It varies somewhat in the degree of its excellence. The kind of which they make their pottery has the largest per cent of alumina, and its presence is indicated by the salt weed which grows in this particular soil. This kind also makes the best adobe mortar. The Indians use it freely in laying their walls, as freely as our masons use lime mortar; and although it never acquires the hardness of cement, it disintegrates slowly . . . This adobe mortar is adapted only to the dry climate of southern Colorado, Arizona, and New Mexico, where the precipitation is less than 5 inches per annum . . . To the presence of this adobe soil, found in such abundance in the regions named, and to the sandstone of the bluffs, where masses are often found in fragments, we must attribute the great progress made by these Indians in house building."

[3] Bandelier discusses the estufas in his Final Report, pt. i, p. 144 ff., giving quotations from the Spanish writers, with his usual wealth of footnotes. Dr Fewkes, in his Zuñi Summer Ceremonials, says: "These rooms are semisubterranean (in Zuñi), situated on the first or ground floor. never, so far as I have seen, on the second or higher stories. They are rectangular or square rooms, built of stone, with openings just large enough to admit the head serving as windows, and still preserve the old form of entrance by ladders through a sky hole in the roof. Within, the estufas have bare walls and are unfurnished, but have a raised ledge about the walls, serving as seats."

MIDDLE COURT AT ZUÑI

ZUÑI COURT, SHOWING "BALCONY"

Some were seen with twelve pillars and with four in the center as large as two men could stretch around. They usually had three or four pillars. The floor was made of large, smooth stones, like the baths which they have in Europe. They have a hearth made like the binnacle or compass box of a ship,[1] in which they burn a handful of thyme at a time to keep up the heat, and they can stay in there just as in a bath. The top was on a level with the ground. Some that were seen were large enough for a game of ball. When any man wishes to marry, it has to be arranged by those who govern. The man has to spin and weave a blanket and place it before the woman, who covers herself with it and becomes his wife.[2] The houses belong to the women, the estufas to the men. If a man repudiates his woman, he has to go to the estufa.[3] It is forbidden for women to sleep in the estufas, or to enter these for any purpose except to give their husbands or sons something to eat. The men spin and weave. The women bring up the children and prepare the food. The country is so fertile that they do not have to break up the ground the year round, but only have to sow the seed, which is presently covered by the fall of snow, and the ears come up under the snow. In one year they gather enough for seven. A very large number of cranes and wild geese and crows and starlings live on what is sown, and for all this, when they come to sow for another year, the fields are covered with corn which they have not been able to finish gathering.

There are a great many native fowl in these provinces, and cocks with great hanging chins.[4] When dead, these keep for sixty days, and longer in winter, without losing their feathers or opening, and without any bad smell, and the same is true of dead men.

The villages are free from nuisances, because they go outside to excrete, and they pass their water into clay vessels, which they empty

---

[1] The Spanish is almost illegible. Ternaux (pp. 169–170) merely says: "Au milieu est un foyer allumé."

[2] Mota Padilla, cap. xxxii, p. 160: "En los casamientos [á Tigües] hay costumbre, que cuando un mozo da en servir á una doncella, la espera en la parte donde va á acarrear agua, y coge el cántaro, con cuya demostracion manifiesta á los deudos de ella, la voluntad de casarse: no tienen estos indios mas que una muger."

Villagra, Historia de la Nueva Mexico, canto xv, fol. 135:

> Y tienen vna cosa aquestas gentes,
> Que en saliendo las mozas de donzellas,
> Son á todos comunes, sin escusa,
> Con tal que se lo paguen, y sin paga,
> Es vna vil bageza, tal delito,
> Mas luego que se casan viuen castas,
> Contenta cada qual con su marido,
> Cuia costumbre, con la grande fuerça,
> Que por naturaleza ya tenian,
> Teniendo por certissimo nosotros,
> Seguiamos tambien aquel camino,
> Iuntaron muchas mantas bien pintadas,
> Para alcançar las damas Castellanas,
> Que mucho apetecieron y quisieron.

It is hoped that a translation of this poem, valuable to the historian and to the ethnologist, if not to the student of literature, may be published in the not distant future.

[3] This appears to be the sense of a sentence which Ternaux omits.

[4] The American turkey cocks.

at a distance from the village.[1] They keep the separate houses where they prepare the food for eating and where they grind the meal, very clean. This is a separate room or closet, where they have a trough with three stones fixed in stiff clay. Three women go in here, each one having a stone, with which one of them breaks the corn, the next grinds it, and the third grinds it again.[2] They take off their shoes, do up their hair, shake their clothes, and cover their heads before they enter the door. A man sits at the door playing on a fife while they grind, moving the stones to the music and singing together. They grind a large quantity at one time, because they make all their bread of meal soaked in warm water, like wafers. They gather a great quantity of brushwood and dry it to use for cooking all through the year. There are no fruits good to eat in the country, except the pine nuts. They have their preachers. Sodomy is not found among them. They do not eat human flesh nor make sacrifices of it. The people are not cruel, for they had Francisco de Ovando in Tiguex about forty days, after he was dead, and when the village was captured, he was found among their dead, whole and without any other wound except the one which killed him, white as snow, without any bad smell. I found out several things about them from one of our Indians, who had been a captive among them for a whole year. I asked him especially for the reason why the young women in that province went entirely nakèd, however cold it might be, and he told me that the virgins had to go around this way until they took a husband, and that they covered themselves after they had known man. The men here wear little shirts of tanned deerskin and their long robes over this. In all these provinces they have earthenware glazed with antimony and jars of extraordinary labor and workmanship, which were worth seeing.[3]

---

[1] A custom still common at Zuñi and other pueblos. Before the introduction of manufactured dyes the Hopi used urine as a mordant.

[2] Mr Owens, in the Journal of American Ethnology and Archæology, vol. ii, p. 163 n., describes these mealing troughs: "In every house will be found a trough about 6 feet long, 2 feet wide, and 8 inches deep, divided into three or more compartments. In the older houses the sides and partitions are made of stone slabs, but in some of the newer ones they are made of boards. Within each compartment is a stone (trap rock preferred) about 18 inches long and a foot wide, set in a bed of adobe and inclined at an angle of about 35°. This is not quite in the center of the compartment, but is set about 3 inches nearer the right side than the left, and its higher edge is against the edge of the trough. This constitutes the nether stone of the mill. The upper stone is about 14 inches long, 3 inches wide, and varies in thickness according to the fineness of the meal desired. The larger stone is called a máta and the smaller one a matáki. The woman places the corn in the trough, then kneels behind it and grasps the matáki in both hands. This she slides, by a motion from the back, back and forth over the máta. At intervals she releases her hold with her left hand and with it places the material to be ground upon the upper end of the máta. She usually sings in time to her grinding motion."

There is a more extended account of these troughs in Mindeleff's Pueblo Architecture, in the Eighth Report of the Bureau of Ethnology, p. 208. This excellent monograph, with its wealth of illustrations, is an invaluable introduction to any study of the southwestern village Indians.

Mota Padilla, cap. xxxii, 3, p. 159: "tienen las indias sus cocinas con mucho aseo, y en el moler el maiz se diferencian de las demas poblaciones [á Tigües], porque en una piedra mas áspera martajan el maiz, y pasa á la segunda y tercera, de donde le sacan en polvo como harina; no usan tortillas que son el pan de las indias y lo fabrican con primor, porque en unas ollas ponen á darle al maiz un cocinimiento con una poca de cal, de donde lo sacan ya con el nombre de mixtamal."

[3] See W. H. Holmes, Pottery of the Ancient Pueblos, Fourth Annual Report of the Bureau of Ethnology; also his Illustrated Catalogue of a portion of the collections made during the field season of 1881, in the Third Annual Report. See p. 519 n., regarding pottery found at Sikyatki.

AFTER SKETCH BY W. L. METCALF, 1883

ZUÑI INTERIOR

Chapter 5, of Cicuye and the villages in its neighborhood, and of how some people came to conquer this country.

We have already said that the people of Tiguex and of all the provinces on the banks of that river were all alike, having the same ways of living and the same customs. It will not be necessary to say anything particular about them. I wish merely to give an account of Cicuye and some depopulated villages which the army saw on the direct road which it followed thither, and of others that were across the snowy mountains near Tiguex, which also lay in that region above the river.

Cicuye[1] is a village of nearly five hundred warriors, who are feared throughout that country. It is square, situated on a rock, with a large court or yard in the middle, containing the estufas. The houses are all alike, four stories high. One can go over the top of the whole village without there being a street to hinder. There are corridors going all around it at the first two stories, by which one can go around the whole village. These are like outside balconies, and they are able to protect themselves under these.[2] The houses do not have doors below, but they use ladders, which can be lifted up like a drawbridge, and so go up to the corridors which are on the inside of the village. As the doors of the houses open on the corridor of that story, the corridor serves as a street. The houses that open on the plain are right back of those that open on the court, and in time of war they go through those behind them. The village is inclosed by a low wall of stone. There is a spring of water inside, which they are able to divert.[3] The people of this village boast that no one has been able to conquer them and that they conquer whatever villages they wish. The people and their customs are like those of the other villages. Their virgins also go nude until they take husbands, because they say that if they do anything wrong then it will be seen, and so they do not do it. They do not need to be ashamed because they go around as they were born.

There is a village, small and strong, between Cicuye and the province of Quirix, which the Spaniards named Ximena,[4] and another village almost deserted, only one part of which is inhabited.[5] This was a large village, and judging from its condition and newness it appeared to have been destroyed. They called this the village of the granaries or silos, because large underground cellars were found here stored with corn. There was another large village farther on, entirely destroyed and

[1] Bandelier, in his Visit to Pecos, p. 114, n., states that the former name of the pueblo was Âquiu, and suggests the possibility of Castañeda having originally written Acuyé. The Relacion del Suceso, translated herein, has Acuique. As may be seen by examining the Spanish text, the Lenox manuscript copy of Castañeda spells the name of this village sometimes Cicuyc and sometimes Cicuye.

[2] Compare Bandelier's translation of this description, from Ternaux's text, in his Gilded Man, p. 206. See the accompanying illustrations, especially of Zuñi, which give an excellent idea of these terraces or "corridors" with their attached balconies.

[3] The spring was "still trickling out beneath a massive ledge of rocks on the west sill" when Bandelier sketched it in 1880.

[4] The former Tano pueblo of Galisteo, a mile and a half northeast of the present town of the same name, in Santa Fé county.

[5] According to Mota Padilla, this was called Coquite.

pulled down, in the yards of which there were many stone balls, as big as 12-quart bowls, which seemed to have been thrown by engines or catapults, which had destroyed the village. All that I was able to find out about them was that, sixteen years before, some people called Teyas,[1] had come to this country in great numbers and had destroyed these villages. They had besieged Cicuye but had not been able to capture it, because it was strong, and when they left the region, they had made peace with the whole country. It seems as if they must have been a powerful people, and that they must have had engines to knock down the villages. The only thing they could tell about the direction these people came from was by pointing toward the north. They usually call these people Teyas or brave men, just as the Mexicans say chichimecas or braves,[2] for the Teyas whom the army saw were brave. These knew the people in the settlements, and were friendly with them, and they (the Teyas of the plains) went there to spend the winter under the wings of the settlements. The inhabitants do not dare to let them come inside, because they can not trust them. Although they are received as friends, and trade with them, they do not stay in the villages over night, but outside under the wings. The villages are guarded by sentinels with trumpets, who call to one another just as in the fortresses of Spain.

There are seven other villages along this route, toward the snowy mountains, one of which has been half destroyed by the people already referred to. These were under the rule of Cicuye. Cicuye is in a little valley between mountain chains and mountains covered with large pine forests. There is a little stream which contains very good trout and otters, and there are very large bears and good falcons hereabouts.

Chapter 6, which gives the number of villages which were seen in the country of the terraced houses, and their population.

Before I proceed to speak of the plains, with the cows and settlements and tribes there, it seems to me that it will be well for the reader to know how large the settlements were, where the houses with stories, gathered into villages, were seen, and how great an extent of country they occupied.[3] As I say, Cibola is the first:

Cibola, seven villages.

Tusayan, seven villages.

The rock of Acuco, one.

---

[1] These Indians were seen by Coronado during his journey across the plains. As Mr Hodge has suggested, they may have been the Comanches, who on many occasions are known to have made inroads on the pueblo of Pecos.

[2] Ternaux's rendering of the uncertain word teules in the Spanish text. Molina, in the Vocabulario Mexicano (1555), fol. 36, has "brauo hombre . . . tlauele." Gomara speaks of the chichimecas in the quotation in the footnote on page 529. The term was applied to all wild tribes.

[3] Bandelier, Final Report, pt. i, p. 34: "With the exception of Acoma, there is not a single pueblo standing where it was at the time of Coronado, or even sixty years later, when Juan de Oñate accomplished the peaceable reduction of the New Mexican village Indians." Compare with the discussion in this part of his Final Report, Mr Bandelier's attempt to identify the various clusters of villages, in his Historical Introduction, pp. 22-24.

Tiguex, twelve villages.

Tutahaco,[1] eight villages.

These villages were below the river.

Quirix,[2] seven villages.

In the snowy mountains, seven villages.

Ximena,[3] three villages.

Cicuye, one village.

Hemes,[4] seven villages.

Aguas Calientes,[4] or Boiling Springs, three villages.

Yuqueyunque,[5] in the mountains, six villages.

Valladolid, called Braba,[6] one village.

Chia,[7] one village.

In all, there are sixty-six villages.[8] Tiguex appears to be in the center of the villages. Valladolid is the farthest up the river toward the northeast. The four villages down the river are toward the southeast, because the river turns toward the east.[9] It is 130 leagues—10 more or less—from the farthest point that was seen down the river to the farthest point up the river, and all the settlements are within this region. Including those at a distance, there are sixty-six villages in all, as I have said, and in all of them there may be some 20,000 men, which may be taken to be a fair estimate of the population of the villages. There are no houses or other buildings between one village and another, but where we went it is entirely uninhabited.[10] These people, since they are few, and their manners, government, and habits are so different from all the nations that have been seen and discovered in these western regions, must come from that part of Greater India, the coast of which lies to the west of this country, for they could have come down from that country, crossing the mountain chains and following down the river, settling in what seemed to them the best place.[11] As they multiplied, they have kept on making settlements until they lost the river when it buried itself underground, its course being in the direction of Florida. It comes down from the northeast, where they[12] could certainly have found signs of villages. He preferred, however, to follow the reports of

---

[1] For the location of this group of pueblos see page 492, note.

[2] The Queres district, now represented by Santo Domingo, San Felipe, Santa Ana, Sia (Castañeda's Chia), and Cochiti. Acoma and Laguna, to the westward, belong to the same linguistic group. Laguna, however, is a modern pueblo.

[3] One of these was the Tano pueblo of Galisteo, as noted on page 523.

[4] The Jemes pueblo clusters in San Diego and Guadalupe canyons. See pl. LXX.

[5] The Tewa pueblo of Yugeningge, where the village of Chamita, above Santa Fé, now stands.

[6] Taos.

[7] The Keres or Queres pueblo of Sia.

[8] As Ternaux observes, Castañeda mentions seventy-one. Sia may not have been the only village which he counted twice.

[9] The trend of the river in the section of the old pueblo settlements is really westward.

[10] Compare the Spanish text.

[11] The Tusayan Indians belong to the same linguistic stock as the Ute, Comanche, Shoshoni, Bannock, and others. The original habitat of the main body of these tribes was in the far north, although certain clans of the Tusayan people are of southern origin. See Powell, Indian Linguistic Families, 7th Annual Report of the Bureau of Ethnology, p. 108.

[12] The Spaniards under Coronado. The translation does not pretend to correct the rhetoric or the grammar of the text.

the Turk, but it would have been better to cross the mountains where this river rises.   I believe they would have found traces of riches and would have reached the lands from which these people started, which from its location is on the edge of Greater India, although the region is neither known nor understood, because from the trend of the coast it appears that the land between Norway and China is very far up.[1]   The country from sea to sea is very wide, judging from the location of both coasts, as well as from what Captain Villalobos discovered when he went in search of China by the sea to the west,[2] and from what has been discovered on the North sea concerning the trend of the coast of Florida toward the Bacallaos, up toward Norway.[3]

To return then to the proposition with which I began, I say that the settlements and people already named were all that were seen in a region 70 leagues wide and 130 long, in the settled country along the river Tiguex.[4]   In New Spain there are not one but many establishments, containing a larger number of people.   Silver metals were found in many of their villages, which they use for glazing and painting their earthenware.[5]

Chapter 7, which treats of the plains that were crossed, of the cows, and of the people who inhabit them.

We have spoken of the settlements of high houses which are situated in what seems to be the most level and open part of the mountains, since it is 150 leagues across before entering the level country between the two mountain chains which I said were near the North sea and the South sea, which might better be called the Western sea along this coast. This mountain series is the one which is near the South sea.[6]   In order to show that the settlements are in the middle of the mountains, I will state that it is 80 leagues from Chichilticalli, where we began to cross this country, to Cibola; from Cibola, which is the first village, to Cicuye, which is the last on the way across, is 70 leagues; it is 30 leagues from Cicuye to where the plains begin.   It may be we went across in an indirect or roundabout way, which would make it seem as if there was more country than if it had been crossed in a direct line, and it may be more difficult and rougher.   This can not be known certainly, because the mountains change their direction above the bay at the mouth of the Firebrand (Tizon) river.

---

[1] Ternaux, p. 184: "D'après la route qu'ils ont suivie, ils ont dû venir de l'extrémité de l'Inde orientale, et d'une partie très-inconnue qui, d'après la configuration des côtes, serait située très-avant dans l'intérieur des terres, entre la Chine et la Norwège."

[2] See the Carta escrita por Santisteban á Mendoza, which tells nearly everything that is known of the voyage of Villalobos.   We can only surmise what Castañeda may have known about it.

[3] The Spanish text fully justifies Castañeda's statement that he was not skilled in the arts of rhetoric and geography.

[4] Compare the Spanish text.   I here follow Ternaux's rendering.

[5] In a note Ternaux, p. 185, says: "Le [dernier] mot est illisible, mais comme l'auteur parle de certain émail que les Espagnols trouvèrent, . . . j'ai cru pouvoir hasarder cette interprétation."   The word is legible enough, but the letters do not make any word for which I can find a meaning.

[6] More than once Castañeda seems to be addressing those about him where he is writing in Culiacan.

ZUÑIS IN TYPICAL MODERN COSTUME

Now we will speak of the plains. The country is spacious and level, and is more than 400 leagues wide in the part between the two mountain ranges—one, that which Francisco Vazquez Coronado crossed, and the other that which the force under Don Fernando de Soto crossed, near the North sea, entering the country from Florida. No settlements were seen anywhere on these plains.

In traversing 250 leagues, the other mountain range was not seen, nor a hill nor a hillock which was three times as high as a man. Several lakes were found at intervals; they were round as plates, a stone's throw or more across, some fresh and some salt. The grass grows tall near these lakes; away from them it is very short, a span or less. The country is like a bowl, so that when a man sits down, the horizon surrounds him all around at the distance of a musket shot.[1] There are no groves of trees except at the rivers, which flow at the bottom of some ravines where the trees grow so thick that they were not noticed until one was right on the edge of them. They are of dead earth.[2] There are paths down into these, made by the cows when they go to the water, which is essential throughout these plains. As I have related in the first part, people follow the cows, hunting them and tanning the skins to take to the settlements in the winter to sell, since they go there to pass the winter, each company going to those which are nearest, some to the settlements at Cicuye,[3] others toward Quivira, and others to the settlements which are situated in the direction of Florida. These people are called Querechos and Teyas. They described some large settlements, and judging from what was seen of these people and from the accounts they gave of other places, there are a good many more of these people than there are of those at the settlements.[4] They have better figures, are better warriors, and are more feared. They travel like the Arabs, with their tents and troops of dogs loaded with poles[5] and having Moorish pack saddles with girths.[6] When the load gets disarranged, the dogs howl, calling some one to fix them right. These people eat raw flesh and drink blood. They do not eat human flesh. They are a kind people and not cruel. They are faithful friends. They are able to make themselves very well understood by means of signs. They dry the flesh in the sun, cutting it thin like a leaf, and when dry they grind it like meal to keep it and make a sort of sea soup of it to eat. A handful thrown into a pot swells up so as to increase very

---

[1] Ternaux omits all this, evidently failing completely in the attempt to understand this description of the rolling western prairies.

[2] Compare the Spanish. This also is omitted by Ternaux.

[3] Espejo, Relacion, p. 180: "los serranos acuden á servir á los de las poblaciones, y los de las poblaciones les llaman á estos, querechos; tratan y contratan con los de las poblaciones, llevandoles sal y caza, venados, conejos y liebres y gamuzas aderezadas y otros géneros de cosas, á trueque de mantas de algodon y otras cosas con que les satisfacen la paga el gobierno."

[4] Compare the Spanish.

[5] The well known travois of the plains tribes.

[6] Benavides: Memorial (1630), p. 74: "Y las tiendas las lleuan cargadas en requas de perros aparejados cõ sus en xalmillas, y son los perros medianos, y suelẽ lleuar quiniẽtos perros en vna requa vno delante de otro, y la gente lleua cargada su mercaduria, que trueca por ropa de algodon, y por otras cosas de q̃ carecen."

much. They season it with fat, which they always try to secure when they kill a cow.[1] They empty a large gut and fill it with blood, and carry this around the neck to drink when they are thirsty. When they open the belly of a cow, they squeeze out the chewed grass and drink the juice that remains behind, because they say that this contains the essence of the stomach. They cut the hide open at the back and pull it off at the joints, using a flint as large as a finger, tied in a little stick, with as much ease as if working with a good iron tool. They give it an edge with their own teeth. The quickness with which they do this is something worth seeing and noting.[2]

There are very great numbers of wolves on these plains, which go around with the cows. They have white skins. The deer are pied with white. Their skin is loose, so that when they are killed it can be pulled off with the hand while warm, coming off like pigskin.[3] The rabbits, which are very numerous, are so foolish that those on horseback killed them with their lances. This is when they are mounted among the cows. They fly from a person on foot.

Chapter 8, of Quivira, of where it is and some information about it.

Quivira is to the west of those ravines, in the midst of the country, somewhat nearer the mountains toward the sea, for the country is level as far as Quivira, and there they began to see some mountain chains. The country is well settled. Judging from what was seen on the borders of it, this country is very similar to that of Spain in the varieties of vegetation and fruits. There are plums like those of Castile, grapes, nuts, mulberries, oats, pennyroyal, wild marjoram, and large quantities of flax, but this does not do them any good, because they do not know how to use it.[4] The people are of almost the same sort and appearance as the Teyas. They have villages like those in New Spain. The houses are round, without a wall, and they have one story like a loft, under the roof, where they sleep and keep their belongings. The roofs

[1] Pemmican

[2] Mota Padilla, cap. xxxii, 2, p. 165: " Habiendo andado cuatro jornadas por estos llanos, con grandes neblinas, advirtieron los soldados rastro como de picas de lanzas arrastradas por el suelo, y llevados por la curiosidad, le siguieron hasta dar con cincuenta gandules, que con sus familias, seguian unas manadas de dichas vacas, y en unos perrillos no corpulentos, cargaban unas varas y pieles, con las que formaban sus tiendas ó toritos, en donde se entraban para resistir el sol ó el agua. Los indios son de buena estatura, y no se supo si eran haraganes ó tenian pueblos; presumióse los tendrian, porque ninguna de las indias llevaba niño pequeño; andaban vestidas con unos faldellines de cuero de venado de la cintura para abajo, y del mismo cuero unos capisayos ó vizcainas, con que se cubren; traen unas medias calzas de cuero adobado y sandalias de cuero crudo: ellos andan desnudos, y cuando mas les aflige el frio, se cubren con cueros adobados; no usan, ni los hombres ni las mujeres, cabello largo, sino trasquilados, y de media cabeza para la frente rapados á navaja; usan por armas las flechas, y con los sesos de las mismas vacas benefician y adoban los cueros: llámanse cíbolos, y tienen mas ímpetu para embestir que los toros, aunque no tanta fortaleza; y en las fiestas reales que se celebraron en la ciudad de México por la jura de nuestro rey D. Luis I, hizo el conde de San Mateo de Valparaiso se llevase una cíbola para que se torease, y por solo verla se despobló México, por hallar lugar en la plaza, que le fué muy útil al tablajero aquel dia."

[3] Compare the Spanish. Omitted by Ternaux.

[4] Mr Savage, in the Transactions of the Nebraska Historical Society, vol. i, p. 198, shows how closely the descriptions of Castañeda, Jaramillo, and the others on the expedition, harmonize with the flora and fauna of his State.

HOPI MAIDENS, SHOWING PRIMITIVE PUEBLO HAIRDRESSING

are of straw. There are other thickly settled provinces around it containing large numbers of men. A friar named Juan de Padilla remained
in this province, together with a Spanish-Portuguese and a negro and
a half-blood and some Indians from the province of Capothan,[1] in New
Spain. They killed the friar because he wanted to go to the province
of the Guas,[2] who were their enemies. The Spaniard escaped by taking
flight on a mare, and afterward reached New Spain, coming out by way
of Panuco. The Indians from New Spain who accompanied the friar
were allowed by the murderers to bury him, and then they followed
the Spaniard and overtook him. This Spaniard was a Portuguese,
named Campo.[3]

The great river of the Holy Spirit (Espiritu Santo),[4] which Don Fernando de Soto discovered in the country of Florida, flows through this
country. It passes through a province called Arache, according to the
reliable accounts which were obtained here. The sources were not
visited, because, according to what they said, it comes from a very
distant country in the mountains of the South sea, from the part that
sheds its waters onto the plains. It flows across all the level country
and breaks through the mountains of the North sea, and comes out
where the people with Don Fernando de Soto navigated it. This is
more than 300 leagues from where it enters the sea. On account of
this, and also because it has large tributaries, it is so mighty when it
enters the sea that they lost sight of the land before the water ceased
to be fresh.[5]

This country of Quivira was the last that was seen, of which I am able
to give any description or information. Now it is proper for me to return
and speak of the army, which I left in Tiguex, resting for the winter, so
that it would be able to proceed or return in search of these settlements of Quivira, which was not accomplished after all, because it was

---

[1] Ternaux, p. 194, read this Çapetlan.

[2] Ternaux, ibid., miscopied it Guyas.

[3] Herrera, Historia General, dec. vi, lib. ix, cap. xii, vol. iii, p. 207 (ed. 1730): "Toda esta Tierra [Qui-
vira] tiene mejor aparencia, que ninguna de las mejores de Europa, porque no es mui doblada, sino
de Lomas, Llanos, i Rios de hermosa vista, i buena para Ganados, pues la experiencia lo mostraba.
Hallaronse Ciruelas de Castilla, entre coloradas, i verdes, de mui gentil sabor; entre las Vacas se hallò
Lino, que produce la Tierra, mui perfecto, que como el Ganado no lo come, se queda por alli con sus
cabeçuelas, i flor azul; i en algunos Arroios, se hallaron Vbas de buen gusto, Moras, Nueces, i otras
Frutas; las Casas, que estos Indios tenian eran de Paja, muchas de ellas redondas, que la Paja llegaba
hasta el suelo, i encima vna como Capilla, ò Garita, de donde se asomaban."

Gomara, cap. ccxiiii: "Esta Quiuira en quarenta grados, es tierra templada, de buenas aguas, de
muchas yeruas, ciruelas, moras, nuezes, melones, y vuas, que maduran bien: no ay algodon, y visten
cueros de vacas, y venados. Vieron por la costa naos, que trayan arcatrazes de oro, y de plata en las
proas, cõ mercaderias, y pensaron ser del Catayo, y China, porq̃ señalauan auer navegado treynta dias.
Fray Iuan de Padilla se quedo en Tiguex, con otro frayle Francisco, y torno a Quiuira, con hasta doze
Indios de Mechuacan, y con Andres do Campo Portugues, hortelano de Francisco de Solis. Lleuo
caualgaduras. y azemilas con prouision. Leuo ouejas, y gallinas de Castilla, y ornamentos para dezir
missa. Los de Quiuira mataron a los frayles, y escapose el Portugues, con algunos Mechuacanes. El
qual, aun que se libro entonces de la muerte, no se libro de catiuerio, porque luego le prendieron: mas
de alli a diez meses, que fue esclauo, huyo con dos perros. Santiguaua por el camino con vna cruz,
aque le ofrecian mucho, y do quiera que llegaua, le dauan limosna, aluergue, y de comer. Vino a tierra
de Chichimecas, y aporto a Panuco."

[4] The Mississippi and Missouri rivers.

[5] This is probably a reminiscence of Cabeza de Vaca's narrative.

God's pleasure that these discoveries should remain for other peoples and that we who had been there should content ourselves with saying that we were the first who discovered it and obtained any information concerning it, just as Hercules knew the site where Julius Cæsar was to found Seville or Hispales. May the all-powerful Lord grant that His will be done in everything. It is certain that if this had not been His will Francisco Vazquez would not have returned to New Spain without cause or reason, as he did, and that it would not have been left for those with Don Fernando de Soto to settle such a good country, as they have done, and besides settling it to increase its extent, after obtaining, as they did, information from our army.[1]

THIRD PART, WHICH DESCRIBES WHAT HAPPENED TO FRANCISCO VAZQUEZ CORONADO DURING THE WINTER, AND HOW HE GAVE UP THE EXPEDITION AND RETURNED TO NEW SPAIN.

Laus Deo.

Chapter 1, of how Don Pedro de Tovar came from Señora with some men, and Don Garcia Lopez de Cardenas started back to New Spain.

At the end of the first part of this book, we told how Francisco Vazquez Coronado, when he got back from Quivira, gave orders to winter at Tiguex, in order to return, when the winter was over, with his whole army to discover all the settlements in those regions. Don Pedro de Tovar, who had gone, as we related, to conduct a force from the city of Saint Jerome (San Hieronimo), arrived in the meantime with the men whom he had brought. He had not selected the rebels and seditious men there, but the most experienced ones and the best soldiers—men whom he could trust—wisely considering that he ought to have good men in order to go in search of his general in the country of the Indian called Turk. Although they found the army at Tiguex when they arrived there, this did not please them much, because they had come with great expectations, believing that they would find their general in the rich country of the Indian called Turk. They consoled themselves with the hope of going back there, and lived in anticipation of the pleasure of undertaking this return expedition, which the army would soon make to Quivira. Don Pedro de Tovar brought letters from New Spain, both from the viceroy, Don Antonio de Mendoza, and from individuals. Among these was one for Don Garcia Lopez de Cardenas, which informed him of the death of his brother, the heir, and summoned him to Spain to receive the inheritance. On this account he was given permission, and left Tiguex with several other persons who

---

[1] Mota Padilla, cap. xxxiii, 4, p. 166, gives his reasons for the failure of the expedition: "It was most likely the chastisement of God that riches were not found on this expedition, because, when this ought to have been the secondary object of the expedition, and the conversion of all those heathen their first aim, they bartered with fate and struggled after the secondary; and thus the misfortune is not so much that all those labors were without fruit, but the worst is that such a number of souls have remained in their blindness."

HOPI GRINDING AND PAPER-BREAD MAKING

(From photograph of a model in the National Museum)

received permission to go and settle their affairs. There were many others who would have liked to go, but did not, in order not to appear faint-hearted. During this time the general endeavored to pacify several villages in the neighborhood which were not well disposed, and to make peace with the people at Tiguex. He tried also to procure some of the cloth of the country, because the soldiers were almost naked and poorly clothed, full of lice, which they were unable to get rid of or avoid.

The general, Francisco Vazquez Coronado, had been beloved and obeyed by his captains and soldiers as heartily as any of those who have ever started out in the Indies. Necessity knows no law, and the captains who collected the cloth divided it badly, taking the best for themselves and their friends and soldiers, and leaving the rest for the soldiers, and so there began to be some angry murmuring on account of this. Others also complained because they noticed that some favored ones were spared in the work and in the watches and received better portions of what was divided, both of cloth and food. On this account it is thought that they began to say that there was nothing in the country of Quivira which was worth returning for, which was no slight cause of what afterward happened, as will be seen.

Chapter 2, of the general's fall, and of how the return to New Spain was ordered.

After the winter was over, the return to Quivira was announced, and the men began to prepare the things needed. Since nothing in this life is at the disposition of men, but all is under the ordination of Almighty God, it was His will that we should not accomplish this, and so it happened that one feast day the general went out on horseback to amuse himself, as usual,[1] riding with the captain Don Rodrigo Maldonado. He was on a powerful horse, and his servants had put on a new girth, which must have been rotten at the time, for it broke during the race and he fell over on the side where Don Rodrigo was, and as his horse passed over him it hit his head with its hoof, which laid him at the point of death, and his recovery was slow and doubtful.[2]

During this time, while he was in his bed,[3] Don Garcia Lopez de Cardenas, who had started to go to New Spain, came back in flight from Suya, because he had found that town deserted and the people and horses and cattle all dead. When he reached Tiguex and learned the sad news

---

[1] Or perhaps as Ternaux, p. 202, rendered it, "courir la bague."

[2] Mota Padilla, cap. xxxiii, 6, p. 166: "así el [gobernador] como los demas capitanes del ejército, debian estar tan ciegos de la pasion de la codicia de riquezas, que no trataban de radicarse poblando en aquel paraje que veian tan abastecido, ni de reducir á los indios é instruirlos en algo de la fé, que es la que debian propagar: solo trataron de engordar sus caballos para lo que se ofreciese pasado el invierno; y andando adiestrando el gobernador uno que tenia muy brioso, se le fué la silla, y dando la boca en el suelo, quedó sin sentido, y aunque despues se recobró, el juicio le quedó diminuto, con lo cual trataron todos de desistir de la empresa." Gomara, cap. ccxiiii: "Cayo en Tiguex del cauallo Francisco Vazquez, y con el golpe salio de sentido, y deuaneaua: lo qual vnos tuuierõ por dolor, y otros por fingido, ca estauan mal con el, porque no poblaua."

[3] Or, During the time that he was confined to his bed, ...

that the general was near his end, as already related, they did not dare to tell him until he had recovered, and when he finally got up and learned of it, it affected him so much that he had to go back to bed again. He may have done this in order to bring about what he afterward accomplished, as was believed later. It was while he was in this condition that he recollected what a scientific friend of his in Salamanca had told him, that he would become a powerful lord in distant lands, and that he would have a fall from which he would never be able to recover. This expectation of death made him desire to return and die where he had a wife and children. As the physician and surgeon who was doctoring him, and also acted as a talebearer,[1] suppressed the murmurings that were going about among the soldiers, he treated secretly and underhandedly with several gentlemen who agreed with him. They set the soldiers to talking about going back to New Spain, in little knots and gatherings, and induced them to hold consultations about it, and had them send papers to the general, signed by all the soldiers, through their ensigns, asking for this. They all entered into it readily, and not much time needed to be spent, since many desired it already. When they asked him, the general acted as if he did not want to do it, but all the gentlemen and captains supported them, giving him their signed opinions, and as some were in this, they could give it at once, and they even persuaded others to do the same.[2] Thus they made it seem as if they ought to return to New Spain, because they had not found any riches, nor had they discovered any settled country out of which estates could be formed for all the army. When he had obtained their signatures, the return to New Spain was at once announced, and since nothing can ever be concealed, the double dealing began to be understood, and many of the gentlemen found that they had been deceived and had made a mistake. They tried in every way to get their signatures back again from the general, who guarded them so carefully that he did not go out of one room, making his sickness seem very much worse, and putting guards about his person and room, and at night about the floor on which he slept. In spite of all this, they stole his chest, and it is said that they did not find their signatures in it, because he kept them in his mattress; on the other hand, it is said that they did recover them. They asked the general to give them 60 picked men, with whom they would remain and hold the country until the viceroy could send them support, or recall them, or else that the general would leave them the army and pick out 60 men to go back with him. But the soldiers did not want to remain either way, some because they had turned their prow toward New Spain, and others because they saw clearly the trouble that would arise over who should have the command. The gentlemen, I do not know whether because they had sworn fidelity or because they

---

[1] Compare the Spanish. Ternaux, p. 203: " Le chirurgien qui le pansait et qui lui servait en même temps d'espion, l'avait averti du mécontentement des soldats."
[2] Compare the Spanish.

feared that the soldiers would not support them, did what had been decided on,[1] although with an ill-will, and from this time on they did not obey the general as readily as formerly, and they did not show any affection for him. He made much of the soldiers and humored them, with the result that he did what he desired and secured the return of the whole army.

Chapter 3, of the rebellion at Suya and the reasons the settlers gave for it.

We have already stated in the last chapter that Don Garcia Lopez de Cardenas came back from Suya in flight, having found that country risen in rebellion. He told how and why that town was deserted, which occurred as I will relate. The entirely worthless fellows were all who had been left in that town, the mutinous and seditious men, besides a few who were honored with the charge of public affairs and who were left to govern the others. Thus the bad dispositions of the worthless secured the power, and they held daily meetings and councils and declared that they had been betrayed and were not going to be rescued, since the others had been directed to go through another part of the country, where there was a more convenient route to New Spain, which was not so, because they were still almost on the direct road. This talk led some of them to revolt, and they chose one Pedro de Avila as their captain. They went back to Culiacan, leaving the captain, Diego de Alcaraz, sick in the town of San Hieronimo, with only a small force. He did not have anyone whom he could send after them to compel them to return. They killed a number of people at several villages along the way. Finally they reached Culiacan, where Hernando Arias de Saabedra, who was waiting for Juan Gallego to come back from New Spain with a force, detained them by means of promises, so that Gallego could take them back. Some who feared what might happen to them ran away one night to New Spain. Diego de Alcaraz, who had remained at Suya with a small force, sick, was not able to hold his position, although he would have liked to, on account of the poisonous herb which the natives use. When these noticed how weak the Spaniards were, they did not continue to trade with them as they formerly had done. Veins of gold had already been discovered before this, but they were unable to work these, because the country was at war. The disturbance was so great that they did not cease to keep watch and to be more than usually careful.

The town was situated on a little river. One night all of a sudden[2] they saw fires which they were not accustomed to, and on this account they doubled the watches, but not having noticed anything during the whole night, they grew careless along toward morning, and the enemy entered the village so silently that they were not seen until they began to kill and plunder. A number of men reached the plain as well as

---

[1] Compare the Spanish text.

[2] Ternaux, p. 209: "à une heure très-avancée."

they could, but while they were getting out the captain was mortally wounded. Several Spaniards came back on some horses after they had recovered themselves and attacked the enemy, rescuing some, though only a few. The enemy went off with the booty, leaving three Spaniards killed, besides many of the servants and more than twenty horses.

The Spaniards who survived started off the same day on foot, not having any horses. They went toward Culiacan, keeping away from the roads, and did not find any food until they reached Corazones, where the Indians, like the good friends they have always been, provided them with food. From here they continued to Culiacan, undergoing great hardships. Hernandarias de Saabedra,[1] the mayor, received them and entertained them as well as he could until Juan Gallego arrived with the reinforcements which he was conducting, on his way to find the army. He was not a little troubled at finding that post deserted, when he expected that the army would be in the rich country which had been described by the Indian called Turk, because he looked like one.

Chapter 4, of how Friar Juan de Padilla and Friar Luis remained in the country and the army prepared to return to Mexico.

When the general, Francisco Vazquez, saw that everything was now quiet, and that his schemes had gone as he wished, he ordered that everything should be ready to start on the return to New Spain by the beginning of the month of April, in the year 1543.[2]

Seeing this, Friar Juan de Padilla, a regular brother of the lesser order,[3] and another, Friar Luis, a lay brother, told the general that they wanted to remain in that country—Friar Juan de Padilla in Quivira, because his teachings seemed to promise fruit there, and Friar Luis at Cicuye. On this account, as it was Lent at the time, the father made this the subject of his sermon to the companies one Sunday, establishing his proposition on the authority of the Holy Scriptures. He declared his zeal for the conversion of these peoples and his desire to draw them to the faith, and stated that he had received permission to do it, although this was not necessary. The general sent a company to escort them as far as Cicuye, where Friar Luis stopped, while Friar Juan went on back to Quivira with the guides who had conducted the general, taking with him the Portuguese, as we related, and the half-blood, and the Indians from New Spain. He was martyred a short time after he arrived there, as we related in the second part, chapter 8. Thus we may be sure that he died a martyr, because his zeal was holy and earnest.

Friar Luis remained at Cicuye. Nothing more has been heard about him since, but before the army left Tiguex some men who went to take

---

[1] Compare the spelling of this name on page 460 of the Spanish text.
[2] The correct date is, of course, 1542.
[3] A Franciscan. He was a "frayle de misa."

HOPI BASKET MAKER

(From photograph of a model in the National Museum)

him a number of sheep that were left for him to keep, met him as he was on his way to visit some other villages, which were 15 or 20 leagues from Cicuye, accompanied by some followers. He felt very hopeful that he was liked at the village and that his teaching would bear fruit, although he complained that the old men were falling away from him. I, for my part, believe that they finally killed him. He was a man of good and holy life, and may Our Lord protect him and grant that he may convert many of those peoples, and end his days in guiding them in the faith. We do not need to believe otherwise, for the people in those parts are pious and not at all cruel. They are friends, or rather, enemies of cruelty, and they remained faithful and loyal friends.[1]

---

[1] General W. W. H. Davis, in his Spanish Conquest of New Mexico, p. 231, gives the following extract, translated from an old Spanish MS. at Santa Fé: "When Coronado returned to Mexico, he left behind him, among the Indians of Cibola, the father fray Francisco Juan de Padilla, the father fray Juan de la Cruz, and a Portuguese named Andres del Campo. Soon after the Spaniards departed, Padilla and the Portuguese set off in search of the country of the Grand Quivira, where the former understood there were innumerable souls to be saved. After traveling several days, they reached a large settlement in the Quivira country. The Indians came out to receive them in battle array, when the friar, knowing their intentions, told the Portuguese and his attendants to take to flight, while he would await their coming, in order that they might vent their fury on him as they ran. The former took to flight, and, placing themselves on a height within view, saw what happened to the friar. Padilla awaited their coming upon his knees, and when they arrived where he was they immediately put him to death. The same happened to Juan de la Cruz, who was left behind at Cibola, which people killed him. The Portuguese and his attendants made their escape, and ultimately arrived safely in Mexico, where he told what had occurred." In reply to a request for further information regarding this manuscript, General Davis stated that when he revisited Santa Fé, a few years ago, he learned that one of his successors in the post of governor of the territory, having despaired of disposing of the immense mass of old documents and records deposited in his office, by the slow process of using them to kindle fires, had sold the entire lot—an invaluable collection of material bearing on the history of the southwest and its early European and native inhabitants—as junk.

Mota Padilla, cap. xxxiii, 7, p. 167, gives an extended account of the friars: "Pero porque el padre Fr. Juan de Padilla cuando acompañó á D. Francisco Vazquez Coronado hasta el pueblo de Quivira, puso en él una cruz, protestando no desampararla aunque le costase la vida, por tener entendido hacer fruto en aquellos indios y en los comarcanos, determinó volverse, y no bastaron las instancias del gobernador y demas capitanes para que desistiese por entónces del pensamiento. El padre Fr. Luis de Ubeda rogó tambien le dejasen volver con el padre Fr. Juan de Padilla hasta el pueblo de Coquite, en donde le parecia podrian servir de domesticar algo á aquellos indios por parecerle se hallaban con alguna disposicion; y que pues él era viejo, emplearia la corta vida que le quedase en procurar la salvacion de las almas de aquellos miserables. A su imitacion tambien el padre Fr. Juan de la Cruz, religioso lego (como lo era Fr. Luis de Ubeda) pretendió quedarse en aquellas provincias de Tigües, y porque se discurrió que con el tiempo se conseguiria la poblacion de aquellas tierras, condescendió el gobernador á los deseos de aquellos apostólicos varones, y les dejaron proveidos de lo que por entónces pareció necesario; y tambien quiso quedarse un soldado, de nacion portugues, llamado Andres del Campo, con ánimo de servir al padre Padilla, y tambien dos indizuelos donados nombrados Lúcas y Sebastian, naturales de Michoacan; y otros dos indizuelos que en el ejército hacian oficios de sacristanes, y otro muchacho mestizo: dejáronle á dicho padre Padilla ornamentos y provision para que celebrase el santo sacrificio de la misa, y algunos bienecillos que pudiese dar á los indios para atraerlos á su voluntad.

"8. . . . Quedaron estos benditos religiosos como corderos entre lobos; y viéndose solos, trató el padre Fr. Juan de Padilla con los de Tigües, el fin que le movia á quedarse entre ellos, que no era otro que el de tratar de la salvacion de sus almas; que ya los soldados se habian ido, que no les serian molestos, que él pasaba á otras poblaciones y les dejaba al padre Fr. Juan de la Cruz para que les fuese instruyendo en lo que debian saber para ser cristianos é hijos de la Santa Iglesia, como necesario para salvar sus almas, que les tratasen bien, y que él procuraria volver á consolarles: despídese con gran ternura, dejando, como prelado, lleno de bendiciones, á Fr. Juan de la Cruz, y los indios de Tigües señalaron una escuadra de sus soldados que guiasen a dichos padres Fr. Juan de Padilla y Fr. Luis de Ubeda hasta el pueblo de Coquite, en donde les recibieron con demostraciones de alegría, y haciendo la misma recomendacion por el padre Fr. Luis de Ubeda, le dejó, y guiado de otros naturales del mismo pueblo, salió

After the friars had gone, the general, fearing that they might be injured if people were carried away from that country to New Spain, ordered the soldiers to let any of the natives who were held as servants go free to their villages whenever they might wish. In my opinion, though I am not sure, it would have been better if they had been kept and taught among Christians.

The general was very happy and contented when the time arrived and everything needed for the journey was ready, and the army started from Tiguex on its way back to Cibola. One thing of no small note happened during this part of the trip. The horses were in good condition for their work when they started, fat and sleek, but more than thirty died during the ten days which it took to reach Cibola, and there was not a day in which two or three or more did not die. A large number of them also died afterward before reaching Culiacan, a thing that did not happen during all the rest of the journey.

After the army reached Cibola, it rested before starting across the wilderness, because this was the last of the settlements in that country. The whole country was left well disposed and at peace, and several of our Indian allies remained there.[1]

para Quivira con Andres del Campo, donados indizuelos y el muchacho mestizo: llegó á Quivira y se postró al pié de la cruz, que halló en donde la habia colocado; y con limpieza, toda la circunfe- rencia, como lo habia encargado, de que se alegró, y luego comenzó á hacer los oficios de padre maes- tro y apóstol de aquellas gentes; y hallándolas dóciles y con buen ánimo, se inflamó su corazon, y le pareció corto número de almas para Dios las de aquel pueblo, y trató de ensanchar los senos de nuestra madre la Santa Iglesia, para que acogiese á cuantos se le decia haber en mayores distancias.

"9. Salió de Quivira, acompañado de su corta comitiva, contra la voluntad de los indios de aquel pueblo, que le amaban como á su padre, mas á una jornada le salieron indios de guerra, y conociendo mal ánimo de aquellos bárbaros, le rogó al portugues, que pues iba á caballo huyese, y que en su conserva llevase aquellos donados y muchachos, que como tales podrian correr y escaparse: hiciéronlo así por no hallarse capaces de otro modo para la defensa, y el bendito padre, hincado de rodillas ofreció la vida, que por reducir almas á Dios tenia sacrificada. logrando los ardientes deseos de su corazon, la felicidad de ser muerto flechado por aquellos indios bárbaros, quienes le arrojaron en un hoyo, cubriendo el cuerpo con innumerables piedras. Y vuelto el portugues con los indizuelos á Quivira, dieron la noticia, la que sintieron mucho aquellos naturales, por el amor que tenian á dicho padre, y mas lo sintieran si hubieran tenido pleno conocimiento de la falta que les hacia; no sabe el dia de su muerte, aunque sí se tiene por cierto haber sido en el año de 542: y en algunos papeles que dejó escritos D. Pedro de Tovar en la villa de Culiacan, se dice que los indios habian salido á matar á este bendito padre, por robar los ornamentos, y que habia memoria de que en su muerte se vieron grandes prodigios, como fué inundarse la tierra, verse globos de fuego, cometas y oscurecerse el sol.

"10. . . . Del padre Fr. Juan de la Cruz, la noticia que se tiene es, que despues de haber trabajado en la instruccion de los indios en Tigües y en Coquite, murió flechado de indios, porque no todos abrazaron su doctrina y consejos, con los que trataba detestasen sus bárbaras costumbres, aunque por lo general era muy estimado de los caciques y demas naturales, que habian visto la veneracion con que el general, capitanes y soldados le trataban. El padre Fr. Luis de Ubeda se mantenia en una choza por celda ó cueva, en donde le ministraban los indios, con un poco de atole, tortillas y frijoles, el limitado sustento, y no se supo de su muerte; sí quedó entre cuantos le conocieron la memoria de su pefecta vida."

When the reports of these martyrdoms reached New Spain, a number of Franciscans were fired with the zeal of entering the country and carrying on the work thus begun. Several received official permission, and went to the pueblo country. One of them was killed at Tiguex, wh ere most of them settled. A few went on to Cicuye or Pecos, where they found a cross which Padilla had set up. Proceeding to Quivira, the natives there counseled them not to proceed farther. The Indians gave them an account of the death of Fray Padilla, and said that if he had taken their advice he would not have been killed.

[1] Antonio de Espejo, in the Relacion of his visit to New Mexico in 1582 (Pacheco y Cardenas, Docu- mentos de Indias, vol. xv, p. 180), states that at Zuñi-Cibola, "hallamos tres indios cristianos que se digeron llamar Andrés de Cuyacan y Gaspar de México y Anton de Guadalajara, que digeron haber entrado con Francisco Vazquez, y reformándolos en la lengua mexicana que ya casi la tenian olvi- dada; destos supimos que habia llegado allí el dicho Francisco Vazquez Coronado."

Chapter 5, of how the army left the settlements and marched to Culiacan, and of what happened on the way.

Leaving astern, as we might say, the settlements that had been discovered in the new land, of which, as I have said, the seven villages of Cibola were the first to be seen and the last that were left, the army started off, marching across the wilderness. The natives kept following the rear of the army for two or three days, to pick up any baggage or servants, for although they were still at peace and had always been loyal friends, when they saw that we were going to leave the country entirely, they were glad to get some of our people in their power, although I do not think that they wanted to injure them, from what I was told by some who were not willing to go back with them when they teased and asked them to. Altogether, they carried off several people besides those who had remained of their own accord, among whom good interpreters could be found today. The wilderness was crossed without opposition, and on the second day before reaching Chichilticalli Juan Gallego met the army, as he was coming from New Spain with reenforcements of men and necessary supplies for the army, expecting that he would find the army in the country of the Indian called Turk. When Juan Gallego saw that the army was returning, the first thing he said was not, "I am glad you are coming back," and he did not like it any better after he had talked with the general. After he had reached the army, or rather the quarters, there was quite a little movement among the gentlemen toward going back with the new force which had made no slight exertions in coming thus far, having encounters every day with the Indians of these regions who had risen in revolt, as will be related. There was talk of making a settlement somewhere in that region until the viceroy could receive an account of what had occurred. Those soldiers who had come from the new lands would not agree to anything except the return to New Spain, so that nothing came of the proposals made at the consultations, and although there was some opposition, they were finally quieted. Several of the mutineers who had deserted the town of Corazones came with Juan Gallego, who had given them his word as surety for their safety, and even if the general had wanted to punish them, his power was slight, for he had been disobeyed already and was not much respected. He began to be afraid again after this, and made himself sick, and kept a guard. In several places yells were heard and Indians seen, and some of the horses were wounded and killed, before Batuco[1] was reached, where the friendly Indians from Corazones came to meet the army and see the general. They were always friendly and had treated all the Spaniards who passed through their country well, furnishing them with what food they needed, and men, if they needed these. Our men had always treated them well and repaid them for these things. During this journey the juice of the quince was proved to be a good protection against the poison of the

---

[1] There were two settlements in Sonora bearing this name, one occupied by the Eudeve and the other by the Tegui division of the Opata. The former village is the one referred to by Castañeda.

natives, because at one place, several days before reaching Señora,[1] the hostile Indians wounded a Spaniard called Mesa, and he did not die, although the wound of the fresh poison is fatal, and there was a delay of over two hours before curing him with the juice. The poison, however, had left its mark upon him. The skin rotted and fell off until it left the bones and sinews bare, with a horrible smell. The wound was in the wrist, and the poison had reached as far as the shoulder when he was cured. The skin on all this fell off.[2]

The army proceeded without taking any rest, because the provisions had begun to fail by this time. These districts were in rebellion, and so there were not any victuals where the soldiers could get them until they reached Petlatlan, although they made several forays into the cross country in search of provisions. Petlatlan is in the province of Culiacan, and on this account was at peace, although they had several surprises after this.[3] The army rested here several days to get provisions. After leaving here they were able to travel more quickly than before, for the 30 leagues of the valley of Culiacan, where they were welcomed back again as people who came with their governor, who had suffered ill treatment.

Chapter 6, of how the general started from Culiacan to give the viceroy an account of the army with which he had been intrusted.

It seemed, indeed, as if the arrival in the valley of Culiacan had ended the labors of this journey, partly because the general was governor there and partly because it was inhabited by Christians. On this account some began to disregard their superiors and the authority which their captains had over them, and some captains even forgot the obedience due to their general. Each one played his own game, so that while the general was marching toward the town, which was still 10 leagues away, many of the men, or most of them, left him in order to rest in the valley, and some even proposed not to follow him. The general understood that he was not strong enough to compel them, although his position as governor gave him fresh authority. He determined to accomplish it by a better method, which was to order all the captains to provide food and meat from the stores of several villages that were under his control as governor. He pretended to be sick, keeping his bed, so that those who had any business with him could speak to him or he with

---

[1] Mota Padilla, cap. xxxiii, 5, p. 166, says that at Sonora . . . "murió un fulano Temiño, hermano de Baltasar Bañuelos, uno de los quatro mineros de Zacatecas; Luis Hernandez, Domingo Fernandez y otros."

[2] Rudo Ensayo, p. 64: "Mago, en lengua Opata [of Sonora], es un arbol pequeño, mui lozano de verde, y hermoso á la vista; pero contiene una leche mortal que á corta incision de su corteza brota, con la que los Naturales suelen untar sus flechas; y por esto la llaman hierba de la flecha, pero ya pocos lo usan. Sirbe tambien dicha leche para abrir tumores rebeldes, aunque no lo aconsejara, por su calidad venenoso." This indicates a euphorbiacea. Bandelier (Final Report, pt. i, p. 77) believes that no credit is to be given to the notion that the poison used by the Indians may have been snake poison. The Seri are the only Indians of northern Mexico who in recent times have been reported to use poisoned arrows.

[3] Ternaux, p. 223: "On parvint ainsi à Petatlan, qui dépend de la province de Culiacan. A cette époque, ce village était soumis. Mais quoique depuis il y ait eu plusieurs soulèvements, on y resta quelques jours pour se refaire." Compare the Spanish.

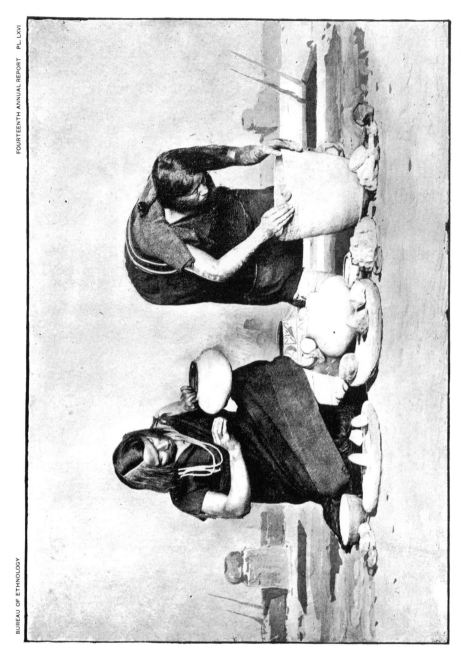

PUEBLO POTTERY MAKING

(From photograph of a model in the National Museum)

them more freely, without hindrance or observation, and he kept sending for his particular friends in order to ask them to be sure to speak to the soldiers and encourage them to accompany him back to New Spain, and to tell them that he would request the viceroy, Don Antonio de Mendoza, to show them especial favor, and that he would do so himself for those who might wish to remain in his government. After this had been done, he started with his army at a very bad time, when the rains were beginning, for it was about Saint John's day, at which season it rains continuously. In the uninhabited country which they passed through as far as Compostela there are numerous very dangerous rivers, full of large and fierce alligators. While the army was halting at one of these rivers, a soldier who was crossing from one side to the other was seized, in sight of everybody, and carried off by an alligator without it being possible to help him. The general proceeded, leaving the men who did not want to follow him all along the way, and reached Mexico with less than 100 men. He made his report to the viceroy, Don Antonio de Mendoza, who did not receive him very graciously, although he gave him his discharge. His reputation was gone from this time on. He kept the government of New Galicia, which had been entrusted to him, for only a short time, when the viceroy took it himself, until the arrival of the court, or audiencia, which still governs it. And this was the end of those discoveries and of the expedition which was made to these new lands.[1]

It now remains for us to describe the way in which to enter the country by a more direct route, although there is never a short cut without hard work. It is always best to find out what those know who have prepared the way, who know what will be needed.[2] This can be found elsewhere, and I will now tell where Quivira lies, what direction the army took, and the direction in which Greater India lies, which was what they pretended to be in search of, when the army started thither. Today, since Villalobos has discovered that this part of the coast of the South sea trends toward the west, it is clearly seen and acknowledged that, since we were in the north, we ought to have turned to the west instead of toward the east, as we did. With this, we will leave this subject and will proceed to finish this treatise, since there are several noteworthy things of which I must give an account, which I have left to be treated more extensively in the two following chapters.

---

[1]Gomara, cap. ccxiiii: "Quando llego a Mexico traya el cabello muy largo, y la barua trençada, y contaua estrañezas de las tierras, rios, y montañas, q̃ a trauesso. Mucho peso a don Antonio de Mendoça, que se boluiessen, porque auia gastado mas de sesenta mil pesos de oro en la empresa, y aun deuia muchos dellos, y no trayan cosa ninguna de alla, ni muestra de plata, ni de oro, ni de otra riqueza. Muchos quisieron quedarse alla, mas Francisco Vazquez de Coronado, que rico, y rezien casado era con hermosa muger, no quiso, diziendo, que no se podrian sustentar, ni defender, en tan pobre tierra, y tan lexos del socorro. Caminaron mas de nouecientas leguas de largo esta jornada."

[2]Ternaux, p. 228: "il n'y ait pas de succès à espérer sans peine; mais il vaut mieux que ceux qui voudront tenter l'entreprise, soient informés d'avance des peines et des fatigues qu'ont éprouvées leurs prédécesseurs."

Chapter 7, of the adventures of Captain Juan Gallego while he was bringing reenforcements through the revolted country.

One might well have complained when in the last chapter I passed in silence over the exploits of Captain Juan Gallego with his 20 companions. I will relate them in the present chapter, so that in times to come those who read about it or tell of it may have a reliable authority on whom to rely. I am not writing fables, like some of the things which we read about nowadays in the books of chivalry. If it were not that those stories contained enchantments, there are some things which our Spaniards have done in our own day in these parts, in their conquests and encounters with the Indians, which, for deeds worthy of admiration, surpass not only the books already mentioned, but also those which have been written about the twelve peers of France, because, if the deadly strength which the authors of those times attributed to their heroes and the brilliant and resplendent arms with which they adorned them, are fully considered, and compared with the small stature of the men of our time and the few and poor weapons which they have in these parts,[1] the remarkable things which our people have undertaken and accomplished with such weapons are more to be wondered at today than those of which the ancients write, and just because, too, they fought with barbarous naked people, as ours have with Indians, among whom there are always men who are brave and valiant and very sure bowmen, for we have seen them pierce the wings while flying, and hit hares while running after them. I have said all this in order to show that some things which we consider fables may be true, because we see greater things every day in our own times, just as in future times people will greatly wonder at the deeds of Don Fernando Cortez, who dared to go into the midst of New Spain with 300 men against the vast number of people in Mexico, and who with 500 Spaniards succeeded in subduing it, and made himself lord over it in two years.

The deeds of Don Pedro de Alvarado in the conquest of Guatemala, and those of Montejo in Tabasco, the conquests of the mainland and of Peru, were all such as to make me remain silent concerning what I now wish to relate; but since I have promised to give an account of what happened on this journey, I want the things I am now going to relate to be known as well as those others of which I have spoken.

The captain Juan Gallego, then, reached the town of Culiacan with a very small force. There he collected as many as he could of those who had escaped from the town of Hearts, or, more correctly, from Suya, which made in all 22 men, and with these he marched through all of the settled country, across which he traveled 200 leagues with the country in a state of war and the people in rebellion, although they had formerly been friendly toward the Spaniards, having encounters with

---

[1] The letters of Mendoza during the early part of his administration in Mexico repeatedly call attention to the lack of arms and ammunition among the Spaniards in the New World.

the enemy almost every day. He always marched with the advance guard, leaving two-thirds of his force behind with the baggage. With six or seven Spaniards, and without any of the Indian allies whom he had with him, he forced his way into their villages, killing and destroying and setting them on fire, coming upon the enemy so suddenly and with such quickness and boldness that they did not have a chance to collect or even to do anything at all, until they became so afraid of him that there was not a town which dared wait for him, but they fled before him as from a powerful army; so much so, that for ten days, while he was passing through the settlements, they did not have an hour's rest. He did all this with his seven companions, so that when the rest of the force came up with the baggage there was nothing for them to do except to pillage, since the others had already killed and captured all the people they could lay their hands on and the rest had fled. They did not pause anywhere, so that although the villages ahead of him received some warning, they were upon them so quickly that they did not have a chance to collect. Especially in the region where the town of Hearts had been, he killed and hung a large number of people to punish them for their rebellion. He did not lose a companion during all this, nor was anyone wounded, except one soldier, who was wounded in the eyelid by an Indian who was almost dead, whom he was stripping. The weapon broke the skin and, as it was poisoned, he would have had to die if he had not been saved by the quince juice; he lost his eye as it was. These deeds of theirs were such that I know those people will remember them as long as they live, and especially four or five friendly Indians who went with them from Corazones, who thought that they were so wonderful that they held them to be something divine rather than human. If he had not fallen in with our army as he did, they would have reached the country of the Indian called Turk, which they expected to march to, and they would have arrived there without danger on account of their good order and the skill with which he was leading them, and their knowledge and ample practice in war. Several of these men are still in this town of Culiacan, where I am now writing this account and narrative, where they, as well as I and the others who have remained in this province, have never lacked for labor in keeping this country quiet, in capturing rebels, and increasing in poverty and need, and more than ever at the present hour, because the country is poorer and more in debt than ever before.

Chapter 8, which describes some remarkable things that were seen on the plains, with a description of the bulls.

My silence was not without mystery and dissimulation when, in chapter 7 of the second part of this book, I spoke of the plains and of the things of which I will give a detailed account in this chapter, where all these things may be found together; for these things were remarkable and something not seen in other parts. I dare to write of them because I am writing at a time when many men are still living who saw them and who will vouch for my account. Who could believe that 1,000 horses and 500 of our cows and more than 5,000 rams and ewes and more than 1,500 friendly Indians and servants, in traveling over those plains, would leave no more trace where they had passed than if nothing had been there—nothing—so that it was necessary to make piles of bones and cow dung now and then, so that the rear guard could follow the army. The grass never failed to become erect after it had been trodden down, and, although it was short, it was as fresh and straight as before.

Another thing was a heap of cow bones, a crossbow shot long, or a very little less, almost twice a man's height in places, and some 18 feet or more wide, which was found on the edge of a salt lake in the southern part,[1] and this in a region where there are no people who could have made it. The only explanation of this which could be suggested was that the waves which the north winds must make in the lake had piled up the bones of the cattle which had died in the lake, when the old and weak ones who went into the water were unable to get out. The noticeable thing is the number of cattle that would be necessary to make such a pile of bones.

Now that I wish to describe the appearance of the bulls, it is to be noticed first that there was not one of the horses that did not take flight when he saw them first, for they have a narrow, short face, the brow two palms across from eye to eye, the eyes sticking out at the side, so that, when they are running, they can see who is following them. They have very long beards, like goats, and when they are running they throw their heads back with the beard dragging on the ground. There is a sort of girdle round the middle of the body.[2] The hair is very woolly, like a sheep's, very fine, and in front of the girdle the hair is very long and rough like a lion's. They have a great hump, larger than a camel's. The horns are short and thick, so that they are not seen much above the hair. In May they change the hair in the middle of the body for a down, which makes perfect lions of them. They rub against the small trees in the little ravines to shed their hair, and they continue this until only the down is left, as a snake changes his skin. They have a short tail, with a bunch of hair at the end. When they run, they carry it erect like a scorpion. It is worth noticing that the little calves are red and just like ours, but they change their color and appearance with time and age.

Another strange thing was that all the bulls that were killed had their left ears slit, although these were whole when young. The reason for this was a puzzle that could not be guessed. The wool ought to

---

[1] Ternaux, p. 236: "l'on trouva sur le bord oriental d'un des lacs salés qui sont vers le sud, un endroit qui avait environ une demi-portée de mousquet de longueur, et qui était entièrement couvert d'os de bisons jusqu'à la hauteur de deux toises sur trois de large, ce qui est surprenant dans un pays désert, et où personne n'aurait pu rassembler ces os."

[2] Compare the Spanish. Ternaux, p. 237: "Ils ont sur la partie antérieure du corps un poil frisé semblable à la laine de moutons, il est très-fin sur la croupe, et lisse comme la crinière du lion."

PUEBLO SPINNING AND WEAVING
(From photograph of a model in the National Museum)

make good cloth on account of its fineness, although the color is not good, because it is the color of buriel.[1]

Another thing worth noticing is that the bulls traveled without cows in such large numbers that nobody could have counted them, and so far away from the cows that it was more than 40 leagues from where we began to see the bulls to the place where we began to see the cows. The country they traveled over was so level and smooth that if one looked at them the sky could be seen between their legs, so that if some of them were at a distance they looked like smooth-trunked pines whose tops joined, and if there was only one bull it looked as if there were four pines. When one was near them, it was impossible to see the ground on the other side of them. The reason for all this was that the country seemed as round as if a man should imagine himself in a three-pint measure, and could see the sky at the edge of it, about a crossbow shot from him, and even if a man only lay down on his back he lost sight of the ground.[2]

---

[1] The kersey, or coarse woolen cloth out of which the habits of the Franciscan friars were made. Hence the name, grey friars.

[2] The earliest description of the American buffalo by a European is in Cabeza de Vaca's Naufragios, fol. xxvii verso (ed 1555): "Alcançã aqui vacas y yo las he visto tres vezes, y comido dellas: y paresceme que seran del tamaño de las de España: tienẽ los cuernos pequeños como moriscas, y el pelo muy largo merino como vna bernia, vnas son pardillas y otras negras; a mi parescer tienen mejor y mas gruessa carne que de las de aca. De las que no son grandes hazen los indios mãtas para cubrirse, y de las mayores hazen çapatos y rodelas: estas vienen de hazia el norte . . . mas de quatrociẽtas leguas· y en todo este camino por los valles por donde ellas vienẽ baxan las gentes que por alli habitan y se mantienen dellas, y meten en la tierra grande contidad de cueros."

Fray Marcos heard about these animals when he was in southern Arizona, on his way toward Cibola-Zuñi: "Aquí . . . me truxeron un cuero, tanto y medio mayor que de una gran vaca, y me dixeron ques de un animal, que tiene solo un cuerno en la frente y queste cuerno es corbo hácia los pechos, y que de allí sale una punta derecha, en la cual dicen que tiene tanta fuerza, que ninguna cosa, por recia que sea, dexa de romper, si topa con ella; y dicen que hay muchos animales destos en aquella tierra; la color del cuero es á manera de cabron y el pelo tan largo como el dedo."—Pacheco y Cardenas, Documentos de Indias, vol. iii, p. 341.

Gomara, cap. ccxv, gives the following description to accompany his picture of these cows (plate LV, herein): "Son aquellos bueyes del tamaño, y color, que nuestros toros, pero no de tan grandes cuernos. Tienen vna gran giba sobre la cruz, y mas pelo de medio adelante, que de medio atras, y es lana. Tienen como clines sobre el espinazo, y mucho pelo, y muy largo de las rodillas abaxo. Cuelganes por la frente grandes guedejas, y parece que tienen baruas, segun los muchos pelos del garguero, y varrillas. Tienen la cola muy larga los machos, y con vn flueco grande al cabo: assi que algo tienen de leon, y algo de camello. Hieren con los cuernos, corren, alcançan, y matan vn cauallo, quando ellos se embrauecen, y enojan: finalmente es animal feo y fiero de rostro, y cuerpo. Huyẽ de los cauallos por su mala catadura, o por nunca los auer visto. No tienen sus dueños otra riqueza, ni hazienda, dellos comen, beuen, visten, calçan, y hazen muchas cosas de los cueros, casas, calçado, vestido y sogas: delos huessos, punçones: de los neruios, y pelos, hilo: de los cuernos, buches, y bexigas, vasos: de las boñigas, lumbre: y de las terneras, odres, en que traen y tienen agua: hazen en fin tantas cosas dellos quantas han menester, o quantas las bastan para su biuienda. Ay tambien otros animales, tan grandes como cauallos, que por tener cuernos, y lana fina, los llaman carneros, y dizen, que cada cuerno pesa dos arrouas. Ay tambien grandes perros, que lidian con vn toro, y que lleuan dos arrouas de carga sobre salmas, quando vã a caça, o quando se mudan con el ganado, y hato."

Mota Padilla, cap. xxxiii, p. 164, says: "son estas vacas menores que las nuestras; su lana menuda y mas fina que la merina; por encima un poco morena, y entre sí un pardillo agraciado, á la parte de atras es la lana mas menuda; y de allí para la cabeza, crian unos guedejones grandes no tan finos; tienen cuernos pequeños, y en todo lo demas son de la hechura de las nuestras, aunque mas cenceñas: los toros son mayores, y sus pieles se curten dejándoles la lana, y sirven, por su suavidad, de mullidas camas; no se vió becerrilla alguna, y puede atribuirse, ó á los muchos lobos que hay entre ellas, ó á tener otros parajes mas seguros en que queden las vacas con sus crias, y deben de mudarse por temporadas, ó porque falten las aguas de aquellas lagunas, ó porque conforme el sol se retira, les dañe la mutacion del temperamento, y por eso se advierten en aquellos llanos, trillados caminos ó veredas por donde entran y salen, y al mismo movimiento de las vacas, se mueven cuadrillas de indios. . . . y se dijo ser desabrida la carne de la hembra, y es providencia del Altísimo, para que los indios maten los machos y reserven las hembras para el multiplico."

I have not written about other things which were seen nor made any mention of them, because they were not of so much importance, although it does not seem right for me to remain silent concerning the fact that they venerate the sign of the cross in the region where the settlements have high houses. For at a spring which was in the plain near Acuco they had a cross two palms high and as thick as a finger, made of wood with a square twig for its crosspiece, and many little sticks decorated with feathers around it, and numerous withered flow-ers, which were the offerings.[1] In a graveyard outside the village at Tutahaco there appeared to have been a recent burial. Near the head there was another cross made of two little sticks tied with cotton thread, and dry withered flowers. It certainly seems to me that in some way they must have received some light from the cross of Our Redeemer, Christ, and it may have come by way of India, from whence they proceeded.

Chapter 9, which treats of the direction which the army took, and of how another more direct way might be found, if anyone was to return to that country.

I very much wish that I possessed some knowledge of cosmography or geography, so as to render what I wish to say intelligible, and so that I could reckon up or measure the advantage those people who might go in search of that country would have if they went directly through the center of the country, instead of following the road the army took. However, with the help of the favor of the Lord, I will state it as well as I can, making it as plain as possible.

It is, I think, already understood that the Portuguese, Campo, was the soldier who escaped when Friar Juan de Padilla was killed at Qui-vira, and that he finally reached New Spain from Panuco,[2] having trav-eled across the plains country until he came to cross the North Sea mountain chain, keeping the country that Don Hernando de Soto dis-covered all the time on his left hand, since he did not see the river of the Holy Spirit (Espiritu Santo) at all.[3] After he had crossed the North Sea mountains, he found that he was in Panuco, so that if he had not tried to go to the North sea, he would have come out in the

---

[1] Scattered through the papers of Dr J. Walter Fewkes on the Zuñi and Tusayan Indians will be found many descriptions of the páhos or prayer sticks and other forms used as offerings at the shrines, together with exact accounts of the manner of making the offerings.

[2] The northeastern province of New Spain.

[3] The conception of the great inland plain stretching between the great lakes at the head of the St Lawrence and the Gulf of Mexico came to cosmographers very slowly. Almost all of the early maps show a disposition to carry the mountains which follow the Atlantic coast along the Gulf coast as far as Texas, a result, doubtless, of the fact that all the expeditions which started inland from Florida found mountains. Coronado's journey to Quivira added but little to the detailed geographical knowl-edge of America. The name reached Europe, and it is found on the maps, along the fortieth parallel, almost everywhere from the Pacific coast to the neighborhood of a western tributary to the St Law-rence system. See the maps reproduced herein. Castañeda could have aided them considerably, but the map makers did not know of his book.

neighborhood of the border land, or the country of the Sacatecas,[1] of which we now have some knowledge.

This way would be somewhat better and more direct for anyone going back there in search of Quivira, since some of those who came with the Portuguese are still in New Spain to serve as guides. Nevertheless, I think it would be best to go through the country of the Guachichules,[2] keeping near the South Sea mountains all the time, for there are more settlements and a food supply, for it would be suicide to launch out on to the plains country, because it is so vast and is barren of anything to eat, although, it is true, there would not be much need of this after coming to the cows. This is only when one goes in search of Quivira, and of the villages which were described by the Indian called Turk, for the army of Francisco Vazquez Coronado went the very farthest way round to get there, since they started from Mexico and went 110 leagues to the west, and then 100 leagues to the northeast, and 250 to the north,[3] and all this brought them as far as the ravines where the cows were, and after traveling 850 leagues they were not more than 400 leagues distant from Mexico by a direct route. If one desires to go to the country of Tiguex, so as to turn from there toward the west in search of the country of India, he ought to follow the road taken by the army, for there is no other, even if one wished to go by a different way, because the arm of the sea which reaches into this coast toward the north does not leave room for any. But what might be done is to have a fleet and cross this gulf and disembark in the neighborhood of the Island of Negroes[4] and enter the country from there, crossing the mountain chains in search of the country from which the people at Tiguex came, or other peoples of the same sort. As for entering from the country of Florida and from the North sea, it has already been observed that the many expeditions which have been undertaken from that side have been unfortunate and not very successful, because that part of the country is full of bogs and poisonous fruits, barren, and the very worst country that is warmed by the sun. But they might disembark after passing the river of the Holy Spirit, as Don Hernando de Soto did. Nevertheless, despite the fact that I underwent much labor, I still think that the way I went to that country is the best. There ought to be river courses, because the necessary supplies can be carried on these more easily in

---

[1] Captain John Stevens' Dictionary says that this is "a northern province of North America, rich in silver mines, but ill provided with water, grain, and other substances; yet by reason of the mines there are seven or eight Spanish towns in it." Zacatecas is now one of the central states of the Mexican confederation, being south of Coahuila and southeast of Durango.

[2] Ternaux, p. 242, miscopied it Quachichiles.

[3] Ternaux, p. 243, reads: "puis pendant six cent cinquante vers le nord, . . . De sorte qu'après avoir fait plus de huit cent cinquante lieues." . . . . The substitution of six for two may possibly give a number which is nearer the actual distance traversed, but the fact is quite unimportant. The impression which the trip left on Castañeda is what should interest the historian or the reader.

[4] The dictionary of Dominguez says: "Isla de negros; ó isla del Almirantazgo, en el grande Océano equinoccial; grande isla de la América del Norte, sobre la costa oeste." Apparently the location of this island gradually drifted westward with the increase of geographical knowledge, until it was finally located in the Philippine group.

14 ETH——35

large quantities. Horses are the most necessary things in the new countries, and they frighten the enemy most. . . . Artillery is also much feared by those who do not know how to use it. A piece of heavy artillery would be very good for settlements like those which Francisco Vazquez Coronado discovered, in order to knock them down, because he had nothing but some small machines for slinging and nobody skillful enough to make a catapult or some other machine which would frighten them, which is very necessary.

I say, then, that with what we now know about the trend of the coast of the South sea, which has been followed by the ships which explored the western part, and what is known of the North sea toward Norway, the coast of which extends up from Florida, those who now go to discover the country which Francisco Vazquez entered, and reach the country of Cibola or of Tiguex, will know the direction in which they ought to go in order to discover the true direction of the country which the Marquis of the Valley, Don Hernando Cortes, tried to find, following the direction of the gulf of the Firebrand (Tizon) river. This will suffice for the conclusion of our narrative. Everything else rests on the powerful Lord of all things, God Omnipotent, who knows how and when these lands will be discovered and for whom He has guarded this good fortune.

Laus Deo.

Finished copying, Saturday the 26th of October, 1596, in Seville.

THE TEWA PUEBLO OF P'O-WHO-GI OR SAN ILDEFONSO

TRANSLATION OF THE LETTER FROM MENDOZA TO THE KING, APRIL 17, 1540.[1]

S. C. C. M.:

I wrote to Your Majesty from Compostela the last of February, giving you an account of my arrival there and of the departure of Francisco Vazquez with the force which I sent to pacify and settle in the newly discovered country, and of how the warden, Lope de Samaniego, was going as army-master, both because he was a responsible person and a very good Christian, and because he has had experience in matters of this sort; as Your Majesty had desired to know. And the news which I have received since then is to the effect that after they had passed the uninhabited region of Culuacan and were approaching Chiametla, the warden went off with some horsemen to find provisions, and one of the soldiers who was with him, who had strayed from the force, called out that they were killing him. The warden hastened to his assistance, and they wounded him in the eye with an arrow, from which he died. In regard to the fortress,[2] besides the fact that it is badly built and going to pieces, it seems to me that the cost of it is excessive, and that Your Majesty could do without the most of it, because there is one man who takes charge of the munitions and artillery, and an armorer to repair it, and a gunner, and as this is the way it was under the audiencia, before the fortresses were made conformable to what I have written to Your Majesty, we can get along without the rest, because that fortress was built on account of the brigantines, and not for any other purpose.[3] And as the lagoon is so dry that it can do no good in this way for the present, I think that, for this reason, the cost is superfluous. I believe that it will have fallen in before a reply can come from Your Majesty.

Some days ago I wrote to Your Majesty that I had ordered Melchior Diaz, who was in the town of San Miguel de Culuacan, to take some horsemen and see if the account given by the father, Friar Marcos, agreed with what he could discover. He set out from Culuacan with fifteen horsemen, the 17th of November last. The 20th of this present

---

[1] From the Spanish text in Pacheco y Cardenas, Documentos de Indias, vol. ii, p. 356. The letter mentioned in the opening sentence is not known to exist.

[2] Presumably the fortress of which Samaniego was warden.

[3] Buckingham Smith s Florida gives many documents relating to the damage done by French brigantines to the Spanish West Indies during 1540-41.

March I received a letter from him, which he sent me by Juan de Zal-
dyvar and three other horsemen. In this he says that after he left
Culuacan and crossed the river of Petatlan he was everywhere very
well received by the Indians. The way he did was to send a cross to
the place where he was going to stop, because this was a sign which the
Indians received with deep veneration, making a house out of mats in
which to place it, and somewhat away from this they made a lodging
for the Spaniards, and drove stakes where they could tie the horses,
and supplied fodder for them, and abundance of corn wherever they had
it. They say that they suffered from hunger in many places, because
it had been a bad year. After going 100 leagues from Culuacan, he
began to find the country cold, with severe frosts, and the farther he
went on the colder it became, until he reached a point where some
Indians whom he had with him were frozen, and two Spaniards were in
great danger. Seeing this, he decided not to go any farther until the
winter was over, and to send back, by those whom I mentioned, an
account of what he had learned concerning Cibola and the country
beyond, which is as follows, taken literally from his letter:

"I have given Your Lordship an account of what happened to me
along the way; and seeing that it is impossible to cross the uninhabited
region which stretches from here to Cibola, on account of the heavy
snows and the cold, I will give Your Lordship an account of what I have
learned about Cibola, which I have ascertained by asking many persons
who have been there fifteen and twenty years; and I have secured this
in many different ways, taking some Indians together and others separately, and on comparison they all seem to agree in what they say.
After crossing this large wilderness, there are seven places, being a
short day's march from one to another, all of which are together called
Cibola. The houses are of stone and mud, coarsely worked. They are
made in this way: One large wall, and at each end of this wall some
rooms are built, partitioned off 20 feet square, according to the description they give, which are planked with square beams. Most of the
houses are reached from the flat roofs, using their ladders to go to the
streets. The houses have three and four stories. They declare that
there are few having two stories. The stories are mostly half as high
again as a man, except the first one, which is low, and only a little
more than a man's height. One ladder is used to communicate with
ten or twelve houses together. They make use of the low ones and
live in the highest ones. In the lowest ones of all they have some
loopholes made sideways, as in the fortresses of Spain. The Indians
say that when these people are attacked, they station themselves in
their houses and fight from there; and that when they go to make
war, they carry shields and wear leather jackets, which are made of
cows' hide, colored, and that they fight with arrows and with a sort of
stone maul and with some other weapons made of sticks, which I have
not been able to make out. They eat human flesh, and they keep those
whom they capture in war as slaves. There are many fowls in the

country, tame.   They have much corn and beans and melons [squashes]. In their houses they keep some hairy animals, like the large Spanish hounds, which they shear, and they make long colored wigs from the hair, like this one which I send to Your Lordship, which they wear, and they also put this same stuff in the cloth which they make.[1]   The men are of small stature [plate LXII]; the women are light colored and of good appearance, and they wear shirts or chemises which reach down to their feet.   They wear their hair on each side done up in a sort of twist [plate LXIII], which leaves the ears outside, in which they hang many turquoises, as well as on their necks and on the wrists of their arms.   The clothing of the men is a cloak, and over this the skin of a cow, like the one which Cabeza de Vaca and Dorantes brought, which Your Lordship saw; they wear caps[2] on their heads; in summer they wear shoes made of painted or colored skin, and high buskins in winter.[3]

They were also unable to tell me of any metal, nor did they say that they had it.   They have turquoises in quantity, although not so many as the father provincial said.   They have some little stone crystals, like this which I send to Your Lordship, of which Your Lordship has seen many here in New Spain.   They cultivate the ground in the same way as in New Spain.   They carry things on their heads, as in Mexico.

[1] In his paper on the Human Bones of the Hemenway Collection (Memoirs of the National Academy of Sciences, VI, p. 156 et seq.), Dr Washington Matthews discusses the possible former existence of a variety of the llama in certain parts of the southwest.

[2] The headbands are doubtless here referred to.

[3] The Spanish text for the foregoing paragraph is as follows: "Salidos deste despoblado grande, están siete lugares y habrá una jornada pequeña del uno al otro, á los quales todos juntos llaman Civola; tienen las casas de piedra y barro, toscamente labradas. son desta manera hechas: una pared larga y desta pared á un cabo y á otro salen unas cámaras atajadas de veinte piés en cuadra, segund señalan, las cuales están maderadas de vigas por labrar; las más casas se mandan por las azoteas con sus escaleras á las calles; son las casas de tres y de cuatro altos; afirman haber pocas de dos altos, los altos son demás de estado y medio en alto, ecebto el primero ques bajo, que no terná sino algo más que un estado; mandánse diez ó doce casas juntas por una escalera, de los bajos se sirven y en los más altos habitan; en el más bajo de todos tienen unas saeteras hechas al soslayo como en fortalezas en España.   Dicen los indios que cuando les vienen á dar guerra, que se meten en sus casas todos y de allí pelean, y que cuando ellos van á hacer guerra, que llevan rodelas y unas cueras vestidas que son de vacas de colores, y que pelean con flechas y con unas macetas de piedra y con otras armas de palo que no he podido entender.   Comen carne humana y los que prenden en la guerra tiénenlos por esclavos.   Hay muchas gallinas en la tierra, mansas, tienen mucho maiz y frisoles y melones, tienen en sus casas unos animales bedijudos como grandes podencos de Castilla, los quales tresquilan, y del pelo hacen cabelleras de colores que se ponen, como esa que envio á V. S., y tambien en la ropa que hacen echan de lo mismo.   Los hombres son de pequeña estatura; las mujeres son blancas y de buenos gestos, andan vestidas con unas camisas que les llegan hasta los piés, y los cabellos parténselos á manera de lados con ciertas vueltas, que les quedan las orejas de fuera, en las cuales se cuelgan muchas turquesas y al cuello y en las muñecas de los brazos.   El vestido de los hombres son mantas y encima cueros de vaca, como el que V. S. veria que llevó Cabeza de Vaca y Dorantes; en las cabezas se ponen unas tocas; traen en verano zapatos de cuero pintados ó de color, y en el invierno borceguíes altos.

"De la misma manera, no me saben dar razon de metal ninguno, ni dicen que lo tengan; turquesas tienen en cantidad, aunque no tantas como el padre provincial dice; tienen unas pedrezuelas de christal como esa que envio á V. S., de las cuales V. S. habia visto hartas en esa Nueva España; labran las tierras á uso de la Nueva España; cárganse en la cabeza como en México; los hombres tejen la ropa ó hilan el algodon; comen sal de una laguna questá á dos jornadas de la provincia de Civola.   Los indios hacen sus bailes y cantos con unas flautas que tienen sus puntos do ponen los dedos, hacen muchos sones, cantan juntamente con los que tañen, y los que cantan dan palmas á nuestro modo. Aún indio de los que llevó Estéban el Negro, questuvo allá cautivo, le ví tañer, que selo mostraron allá, y otros cantaban como digo, aunque no muy desenvueltos; dicen que se juntan cinco ó seis á tañer, y que son las flautas unas mayores que otras."

The men weave cloth and spin cotton. They have salt from a marshy lake, which is two days from the province of Cibola.[1] The Indians have their dances and songs, with some flutes which have holes on which to put the fingers. They make much noise. They sing in unison with those who play, and those who sing clap their hands in our fashion. One of the Indians that accompanied the negro Esteban, who had been a captive there, saw the playing as they practiced it, and others singing as I have said, although not very vigorously. They say that five or six play together, and that some of the flutes are better than others.[2] They say the country is good for corn and beans, and that they do not have any fruit trees, nor do they know what such a thing is.[3] They have very good mountains. The country lacks water. They do not raise cotton, but bring it from Totonteac.[4] They eat out of flat bowls, like the Mexicans. They raise considerable corn and beans and other similar things.[5] They do not know what sea fish is, nor have they ever heard of it. I have not obtained any information about the cows, except that these are found beyond the province of Cibola. There is a great abundance of wild goats, of the color of bay horses; there are many of these here where I am, and although I have asked the Indians if those are like these, they tell me no. Of the seven settlements, they describe three of them as very large; four not so big. They describe them, as I understand, to be about three crossbow shots square for each place, and from what the Indians say, and their descriptions of the houses and their size, and as these are close together, and considering that there are people in each house, it ought to make a large multitude. Totonteac is declared to be seven short days from the province of Cibola, and of the same sort of houses and people, and they say that cotton grows there. I doubt this, because they tell me that it is a cold country. They say that there are twelve villages, every one of which is larger than the largest at Cibola. They also tell me that there is a village which is one day from Cibola, and that the two are at war.[6] They have the same sort of houses and people and customs. They declare this to be greater than any of those described; I take it that there is a great multitude of people there. They are very well known, on account of having these houses and abundance of food and turquoises. I have not been able to learn more than what I have

---

[1]The same salt lake from which the Zuñis obtain their salt supply today.

[2]Compare with this hearsay description of something almost unknown to the Spaniards, the thoroughly scientific descriptions of the Hopi dances and ceremonials recorded by Dr J. Walter Fewkes.

[3]The peaches, watermelons, cantaloupes, and grapes, now so extensively cultivated by the Pueblos, were introduced early in the seventeenth century by the Spanish missionaries.

[4]At first glance it seems somewhat strange that although Zuñi is considerably more than 100 miles south of Totonteac, or Tusayan, the people of the former villages did not cultivate cotton, but in this I am reminded by Mr Hodge that part of the Tusayan people are undoubtedly of southern origin and that in all probability they introduced cotton into that group of villages. The Pimas raised cotton as late as 1850. None of the Pueblos now cultivate the plant, the introduction of cheap fabrics by traders having doubtless brought the industry to an end. See page 574.

[5]"Y otras simillas como chia" is the Spanish text.

[6]Doubtless the pueblo of Marata (Makyata) mentioned by Marcos de Niza. This village was situated near the salt lake and had been destroyed by the Zuñis some years before Niza visited New Mexico.

PUEBLO OF JEMEZ

related, although, as I have said, I have had with me Indians who have lived there fifteen and twenty years.

"The death of Esteban the negro took place in the way the father, Friar Marcos, described it to your lordship, and so I do not make a report of it here, except that the people at Cibola sent word to those of this village and in its neighborhood that if any Christians should come, they ought not to consider them as anything peculiar, and ought to kill them, because they were mortal—saying that they had learned this because they kept the bones of the one who had come there; and that, if they did not dare to do this, they should send word so that those (at Cibola) could come and do it. I can very easily believe that all this has taken place, and that there has been some communication between these places, because of the coolness with which they received us and the sour faces they have shown us."

Melchior Diaz says that the people whom he found along the way do not have any settlements at all, except in one valley which is 150 leagues from Culuacan, which is well settled and has houses with lofts, and that there are many people along the way, but that they are not good for anything except to make them Christians, as if this was of small account. May Your Majesty remember to provide for the service of God, and keep in mind the deaths and the loss of life and of provinces which has taken place in these Indies. And, moreover, up to this present day none of the things Your Majesty has commanded, which have been very holy and good, have been attended to, nor priests provided, either for that country or for this. For I assure Your Majesty that there is no trace of Christianity where they have not yet arrived, neither little nor much, and that the poor people are ready to receive the priests and come to them even when they flee from us like deer in the mountains. And I state this because I am an eyewitness, and I have seen it clearly during this trip. I have importuned Your Majesty for friars, and yet again I can not cease doing it much more, because unless this be done I can not accomplish that which I am bound to do.

After I reach Mexico, I will give Your Majesty an account of everything concerning these provinces, for while I should like to do it today, I can not, because I am very weak from a slow fever which I caught in Colima, which attacked me very severely, although it did not last more than six days. It has pleased Our Lord to make me well already, and I have traveled here to Jacona, where I am.

May Our Lord protect the Holy Catholic Cæsarian person of Your Majesty and aggrandize it with increase of better kingdoms and lordships, as we your servants desire.

From Jacona, April 17, 1540.

S. C. C. M.

Your Holy Majesty's humble servant, who salutes your royal feet and hands,

D. ANTONIO DE MENDOZA.

TRANSLATION OF THE LETTER FROM CORONADO TO MENDOZA, AUGUST 3, 1540.[1]

THE ACCOUNT GIVEN BY FRANCISCO VAZQUEZ DE CORONADO, CAPTAIN-GENERAL OF THE FORCE WHICH WAS SENT IN THE NAME OF HIS MAJESTY TO THE NEWLY DISCOVERED COUNTRY, OF WHAT HAPPENED TO THE EXPEDITION AFTER APRIL 22 OF THE YEAR MDXL, WHEN HE STARTED FORWARD FROM CULIACAN, AND OF WHAT HE FOUND IN THE COUNTRY THROUGH WHICH HE PASSED.

Francisco Vazquez starts from Culiacan with his army, and after suffering various inconveniences on account of the badness of the way, reaches the Valley of Hearts, where he failed to find any corn, to procure which he sends to the valley called Señora. He receives an account of the important Valley of Hearts and of the people there, and of some lands lying along that coast.

On the 22d of the month of April last, I set out from the province of Culiacan with a part of the army, having made the arrangements of which I wrote to Your Lordship. Judging by the outcome, I feel sure that it was fortunate that I did not start the whole of the army on this undertaking, because the labors have been so very great and the lack of food such that I do not believe this undertaking could have been completed before the end of this year, and that there would be a great loss of life if it should be accomplished. For, as I wrote to Your Lordship, I spent eighty days in traveling to Culiacan,[2] during which time I and the gentlemen of my company, who were horsemen, carried on our backs and on our horses a little food, in such wise that after leaving this place none of us carried any necessary effects weighing more than a pound. For all this, and although we took all possible care and forethought of the small supply of provisions which we carried, it gave out. And this is not to be wondered at, because the road is rough and long, and what with our harquebuses, which had to be carried up the mountains and hills and in the passage of the rivers, the greater part of the

---

[1] Translated from the Italian version, in Ramusio's Viaggi, vol. iii, fol. 359 (ed. 1556). There is another English translation in Hakluyt's Voyages, vol. iii, p. 373 (ed. 1600). Hakluyt's translation is reprinted in Old South Leaflet, general series, No. 20. Mr Irving Babbitt, of the French department in Harvard University, has assisted in correcting some of the errors and omissions in Hakluyt's version. The proper names, excepting such as are properly translated, are spelled as in the Italian text.

[2] This statement is probably not correct. It may be due to a blunder by Ramusio in translating from the original text. See note on page 382. Eighty days (see pp. 564, 572) would be nearly the time which Coronado probably spent on the journey from Culiacan to Cibola, and this interpretation would render the rest of the sentence much more intelligible.

318

corn was lost.   And since I send Your Lordship a drawing of this route, I will say no more about it here.

Thirty leagues before reaching the place which the father provincial spoke so well of in his report,[1] I sent Melchior Diaz forward with fifteen horsemen, ordering him to make but one day's journey out of two, so that he could examine everything there before I arrived.   He traveled through some very rough mountains for four days, and did not find anything to live on, nor people, nor information about anything, except that he found two or three poor villages, with twenty or thirty huts apiece. From the people here he learned that there was nothing to be found in the country beyond except the mountains, which continued very rough, entirely uninhabited by people.   And, because this was labor lost, I did not want to send Your Lordship an account of it.   The whole company felt disturbed at this, that a thing so much praised, and about which the father had said so many things, should be found so very different; and they began to think that all the rest would be of the same sort. When I noticed this, I tried to encourage them as well as I could, telling them that Your Lordship had always thought that this part of the trip would be a waste of effort, and that we ought to devote our attention to those Seven Cities and the other provinces about which we had information—that these should be the end of our enterprise.   With this resolution and purpose, we all marched cheerfully along a very bad way, where it was impossible to pass without making a new road or repairing the one that was there, which troubled the soldiers not a little, considering that everything which the friar had said was found to be quite the reverse; because, among other things which the father had said and declared, he said that the way would be plain and good, and that there would be only one small hill of about half a league.   And the truth is, that there are mountains where, however well the path might be fixed, they could not be crossed without there being great danger of the horses falling over them.   And it was so bad that a large number of the animals which Your Lordship sent as provision for the army were lost along this part of the way, on account of the roughness of the rocks.   The lambs and wethers lost their hoofs along the way, and I left the greater part of those which I brought from Culiacan at the river of Lachimi,[2] because they were unable to travel, and so that they might proceed more slowly.   Four horsemen remained with them, who have just arrived. They have not brought more than 24 lambs and 4 wethers; the rest died from the toil, although they did not travel more than two leagues daily. I reached the Valley of Hearts at last, on the 26th day of the month of May, and rested there a number of days.   Between Culiacan and this place I could sustain myself only by means of a large supply of corn bread, because I had to leave all the corn, as it was not yet ripe.   In this Valley of Hearts we found more people than in any part of the country

---

[1] The valley into which Friar Marcos did not dare to enter.   See the Historical Introduction, p. 362.
[2] Doubtless the Yaquimi or Yaqui river.

which we had left behind, and a large extent of tilled ground. There was no corn for food among them, but as I heard that there was some in another valley called Señora, which I did not wish to disturb by force, I sent Melchior Diaz with goods to exchange for it, so as to give this to the friendly Indians whom we brought with us, and to some who had lost their animals along the way and had not been able to carry the food which they had taken from Culiacan. By the favor of Our Lord, some little corn was obtained by this trading, which relieved the friendly Indians and some Spaniards. Ten or twelve of the horses had died of overwork by the time that we reached this Valley of Hearts, because they were unable to stand the strain of carrying heavy burdens and eating little. Some of our negroes and some of the Indians also died here, which was not a slight loss for the rest of the expedition. They told me that the Valley of Hearts is a long five-days' journey from the western sea. I sent to summon Indians from the coast in order to learn about their condition, and while I was waiting for these the horses rested. I stayed there four days, during which the Indians came from the sea, who told me that there were seven or eight islands two days' journey from that seacoast, directly opposite, well populated with people, but poorly supplied with food, and the people were savages.[1] They told me they had seen a ship pass not very far from the land. I do not know whether to think that it was the one which was sent to discover the country, or perhaps some Portuguese.[2]

They come to Chichilticale; after having taken two days' rest, they enter a country containing very little food and hard to travel for 30 leagues, beyond which the country becomes pleasant, and there is a river called the River of the Flax (del Lino); they fight against the Indians, being attacked by these; and having by their victory secured the city, they relieve themselves of the pangs of their hunger.

I set out from the Hearts and kept near the seacoast as well as I could judge, but in fact I found myself continually farther off, so that when I reached Chichilticale I found that I was fifteen days' journey distant from the sea,[3] although the father provincial had said that it was only 5 leagues distant and that he had seen it. We all became very distrustful, and felt great anxiety and dismay to see that everything was the reverse of what he had told Your Lordship. The Indians of Chichilticale say that when they go to the sea for fish, or for anything else that they need, they go across the country, and that it takes them

---

[1] These were doubtless the Seri, of Yuman stock, who occupied a strip of the Gulf coast between latitude 28° and 29° and the islands Angel de la Guardia and Tiburon. The latter island, as well as the coast of the adjacent mainland, is still inhabited by this tribe.

[2] As Indian news goes, there is no reason why this may not have been one of Ulloa's ships, which sailed along this coast during the previous summer. It can hardly have been a ship of Alarcon's fleet.

[3] Ramusio: "mi ritrouauo lunge dal mare quindici giornate." Hakluyt (ed. 1600): "I found my selfe tenne dayes iourney from the Sea."

RUINS OF SPANISH CHURCH ABOVE JEMEZ

ten days; and this information which I have received from the Indians appears to me to be true. The sea turns toward the west directly opposite the Hearts for 10 or 12 leagues, where I learned that the ships of Your Lordship had been seen, which had gone in search of the port of Chichilticale, which the father said was on the thirty-fifth degree. God knows what I have suffered, because I fear that they may have met with some mishap. If they follow the coast, as they said they would, as long as the food lasts which they took with them, of which I left them a supply in Culiacan, and if they have not been overtaken by some misfortune, I maintain my trust in God that they have already discovered something good, for which the delay which they have made may be pardoned. I rested for two days at Chichilticale, and there was good reason for staying longer, because we found that the horses were becoming so tired; but there was no chance to rest longer, because the food was giving out. I entered the borders of the wilderness region on Saint John's eve, and, for a change from our past labors, we found no grass during the first days, but a worse way through mountains and more dangerous passages than we had experienced previously. The horses were so tired that they were not equal to it, so that in this last desert we lost more horses than before; and some Indian allies and a Spaniard called Spinosa, besides two negroes, died from eating some herbs because the food had given out. I sent the army-master, Don Garcia Lopez de Cardenas, with 15 horsemen, a day's march ahead of me, in order to explore the country and prepare the way, which he accomplished like the man that he is, and agreeably to the confidence which Your Lordship has had in him. I am the more certain that he did so, because, as I have said, the way is very bad for at least 30 leagues and more, through impassable mountains. But when we had passed these 30 leagues, we found fresh rivers and grass like that of Castile, and especially one sort like what we call *Scaramoio;* many nut and mulberry trees, but the leaves of the nut trees are different from those of Spain. There was a considerable amount of flax near the banks of one river, which was called on this account El Rio del Lino. No Indians were seen during the first day's march, after which four Indians came out with signs of peace, saying that they had been sent to that desert place to say that we were welcome, and that on the next day the tribe would provide the whole force with food. The army-master gave them a cross, telling them to say to the people in their city that they need not fear, and that they should have their people stay in their own houses, because I was coming in the name of His Majesty to defend and help them. After this was done, Ferrando Alvarado came back to tell me that some Indians had met him peaceably, and that two of them were with the army-master waiting for me. I went to them forthwith and gave them some paternosters and some little cloaks, telling them to return to their city and say to the people there that they could stay quietly in their houses and that they need not fear. After this I ordered the army-master to go and see if there were any bad passages which the Indians might be able to defend, and to seize and hold any such until the next day, when I would come up. He went, and found a very bad place in our way where we might have received much harm. He immediately established himself there with the force which he was conducting. The Indians came that very night to occupy that place so as to defend it, and finding it taken, they assaulted our men. According to what I have been told, they attacked like valiant men, although in the end they had to retreat in flight, because the army-master was on the watch and kept his men in good order. The Indians sounded a little trumpet as a sign of retreat, and did not do any injury to the Spaniards. The army-master sent me notice of this the same night, so that on the next day I started with as good order as I could, for we were in such great need of food that I thought we should all die of hunger if we continued to be without provisions for another day, especially the Indians, since altogether we did not have two bushels of corn, and so I was obliged to hasten forward without delay. The Indians lighted their fires from point to point, and these were answered from a distance with as good understanding as we could have shown. Thus notice was given concerning how we went and where we had arrived. As soon as I came within sight of this city, I sent the army-master, Don Garcia Lopez, Friar Daniel and Friar Luis, and Ferrando Vermizzo, with some horsemen, a little way ahead, so that they might find the Indians and tell them that we were not coming to do them any harm, but to defend them in the name of our lord the Emperor. The summons, in the form which His Majesty commanded in his instructions, was made intelligible to the people of the country by an interpreter. But they, being a proud people, were little affected, because it seemed to them that we were few in number, and that they would not have any difficulty in conquering us. They pierced the gown of Friar Luis with an arrow, which, blessed be God, did him no harm. Meanwhile I arrived with all the rest of the horse and the footmen, and found a large body of the Indians on the plain, who began to shoot with their arrows. In obedience to the orders of Your Lordship and of the marquis,[1] I did not wish my company, who were begging me for permission, to attack them, telling them that they ought not to offend them, and that what the enemy was doing was nothing, and that so few people ought not to be insulted. On the other hand, when the Indians saw that we did not move, they took greater courage, and grew so bold that they came up almost to the heels of our horses to shoot their arrows. On this account I saw that it was no longer time to hesitate, and as the priests approved the action, I charged them. There was little to do, because they suddenly took to flight, part running toward the city, which was near and well fortified, and others toward the plain, wherever chance led them. Some Indians

---

[1] It is possible that this is a blunder, in Ramusio's text, for "His Majesty." The Marquis, in New Spain, is always Cortes, for whom neither Mendoza nor Coronado had any especial regard.

were killed, and others might have been slain if I could have allowed them to be pursued. But I saw that there would be little advantage in this, because the Indians who were outside were few, and those who had retired to the city were numerous, besides many who had remained there in the first place. As that was where the food was, of which we stood in such great need, I assembled my whole force and divided them as seemed to me best for the attack on the city, and surrounded it. The hunger which we suffered would not permit of any delay, and so I dismounted with some of these gentlemen and soldiers. I ordered the musketeers and crossbowmen to begin the attack and drive back the enemy from the defenses, so that they could not do us any injury. I assaulted the wall on one side, where I was told that there was a scaling ladder and that there was also a gate. But the crossbowmen broke all the strings of their crossbows and the musketeers could do nothing, because they had arrived so weak and feeble that they could scarcely stand on their feet. On this account the people who were on top were not prevented at all from defending themselves and doing us whatever injury they were able. Thus, for myself, they knocked me down to the ground twice with countless great stones which they threw down from above, and if I had not been protected by the very good headpiece which I wore, I think that the outcome would have been bad for me. They picked me up from the ground, however, with two small wounds in my face and an arrow in my foot, and with many bruises on my arms and legs, and in this condition I retired from the battle, very weak. I think that if Don Garcia Lopez de Cardenas had not come to my help, like a good cavalier, the second time that they knocked me to the ground, by placing his own body above mine, I should have been in much greater danger than I was. But, by the pleasure of God, these Indians surrendered, and their city was taken with the help of Our Lord, and a sufficient supply of corn was found there to relieve our necessities. The army-master and Don Pedro de Tovar and Ferrando de Alvarado and Paulo de Melgosa, the infantry captain, sustained some bruises, although none of them were wounded. Agoniez Quarez was hit in the arm by an arrow, and one Torres, who lived in Panuco, in the face by another, and two other footmen received slight arrow wounds. They all directed their attack against me because my armor was gilded and glittered, and on this account I was hurt more than the rest, and not because I had done more or was farther in advance than the others; for all these gentlemen and soldiers bore themselves well, as was expected of them. I praise God that I am now well, although somewhat sore from the stones. Two or three other soldiers were hurt in the battle which we had on the plain, and three horses were killed—one that of Don Lopez and another that of Vigliega and the third that of Don Alfonso Manrich—and seven or eight other horses were wounded; but the men, as well as the horses, have now recovered and are well.

Of the situation and condition of the Seven Cities called the kingdom of
Cevola, and the sort of people and their customs, and of the animals
which are found there.

It now remains for me to tell about this city and kingdom and province, of which the Father Provincial gave Your Lordship an account.
In brief, I can assure you that in reality he has not told the truth in a
single thing that he said, but everything is the reverse of what he said,
except the name of the city and the large stone houses.   For, although
they are not decorated with turquoises, nor made of lime nor of good
bricks, nevertheless they are very good houses, with three and four
and five stories, where there are very good apartments and good rooms
with corridors,[1] and some very good rooms under ground and paved,
which are made for winter, and are something like a sort of hot baths.[2]
The ladders which they have for their houses are all movable and port-
able, which are taken up and placed wherever they please.   They are
made of two pieces of wood, with rounds like ours.   [See plates LVIII,
LVIX.]   The Seven Cities are seven little villages, all having the kind
of houses I have described.   They are all within a radius of 5 leagues.
They are all called the kingdom of Cevola, and each has its own name
and no single one is called Cevola, but all together are called Cevola.
This one which I have called a city I have named Granada, partly
because it has some similarity to it,[3] as well as out of regard for Your
Lordship.   In this place where I am now lodged there are perhaps 200
houses, all surrounded by a wall, and it seems to me that with the other
houses, which are not so surrounded, there might be altogether 500
families.   There is another town near by, which is one of the seven, but
somewhat larger than this, and another of the same size as this, and
the other four are somewhat smaller.   I send them all to Your Lordship, painted with the route.   The skin on which the painting is made
was found here with other skins.   The people of the towns seem to me
to be of ordinary size and intelligent, although I do not think that they
have the judgment and intelligence which they ought to have to
build these houses in the way in which they have, for most of them are
entirely naked except the covering of their privy parts, and they have
painted mantles like the one which I send to Your Lordship.   They do
not raise cotton, because the country is very cold, but they wear
mantles, as may be seen by the exhibit which I send.   It is also true
that some cotton thread was found in their houses.   They wear the
hair on their heads like the Mexicans.   They all have good figures,
and are well bred.   I think that they have a quantity of turquoises,
which they had removed with the rest of their goods, except the corn,
when I arrived, because I did not find any women here nor any men

---

[1]Hakluyt: .   .   .   "very excellent good houses of three or foure or fiue lofts high, wherein are
good lodgings and faire chambers with lathers in stead of staires."

[2]The kivas or ceremonial chambers.

[3]See the footnote on page 564 in regard to the similarity of names.   The note was written without
reference to the above passage.

under 15 years or over 60, except two or three old men who remained
in command of all the other men and the warriors. Two points of
emerald and some little broken stones which approach the color of
rather poor garnets[1] were found in a paper, besides other stone crystals,
which I gave to one of my servants to keep until they could be sent to
Your Lordship. He has lost them, as they tell me. We found fowls,
but only a few, and yet there are some. The Indians tell me that they
do not eat these in any of the seven villages, but that they keep them
merely for the sake of procuring the feathers.[2] I do not believe this,
because they are very good, and better than those of Mexico. The
climate of this country and the temperature of the air is almost like
that of Mexico, because it is sometimes hot and sometimes it rains. I
have not yet seen it rain, however, except once when there fell a little
shower with wind, such as often falls in Spain. The snow and the
cold are usually very great, according to what the natives of the country
all say. This may very probably be so, both because of the nature
of the country and the sort of houses they build and the skins and
other things which these people have to protect them from the cold.
There are no kinds of fruit or fruit trees. The country is all level, and
is nowhere shut in by high mountains, although there are some hills
and rough passages.[3] There are not many birds, probably because of
the cold, and because there are no mountains near. There are no trees
fit for firewood here, because they can bring enough for their needs from
a clump of very small cedars 4 leagues distant.[4] Very good grass is
found a quarter of a league away, where there is pasturage for our horses
as well as mowing for hay, of which we had great need, because our
horses were so weak and feeble when they arrived. The food which
they eat in this country is corn, of which they have a great abundance,
and beans and venison, which they probably eat (although they say
that they do not), because we found many skins of deer and hares and
rabbits. They make the best corn cakes I have ever seen anywhere,
and this is what everybody ordinarily eats. They have the very best
arrangement and machinery for grinding that was ever seen [plate LXIV].
One of these Indian women here will grind as much as four of the Mexicans. They have very good salt in crystals, which they bring from a
lake a day's journey distant from here. No information can be obtained
among them about the North sea or that on the west, nor do I know
how to tell Your Lordship which we are nearest to. I should judge that
it is nearer to the western, and 150 leagues is the nearest that it seems
to me it can be thither. The North sea ought to be much farther away.
Your Lordship may thus see how very wide the country is. They have

[1]Many garnets are found on the ant-hills throughout the region, especially in the Navajo country.
[2]The natives doubtless told the truth. Eagle and turkey feathers are still highly prized by them
for use in their ceremonies.
[3]It should be noted that Coronado clearly distinguishes between hills or mesas and mountains.
Zuñi valley is hemmed in by heights varying from 500 to 1,000 feet.
[4]This accords perfectly with the condition of the vegetation in Zuñi valley at the present time.

many animals—bears, tigers, lions, porcupines, and some sheep as big as a horse, with very large horns and little tails. I have seen some of their horns the size of which was something to marvel at.[1] There are also wild goats, whose heads I have seen, and the paws of the bears and the skins of the wild boars. For game they have deer, leopards, and very large deer,[2] and every one thinks that some of them are larger than that animal which Your Lordship favored me with, which belonged to Juan Melaz. They inhabit some plains eight days' journey toward the north. They have some of their skins here very well dressed, and they prepare and paint them where they kill the cows, according to what they tell me.

Of the nature and situation of the kingdoms of Totonteac, Marata, and Acus, wholly different from the account of Friar Marcos. The conference which they had with the Indians of the city of Granada, which they had captured, who had been forewarned of the coming of Christians into their country fifty years before. The account which was obtained from them concerning seven other cities, of which Tucano is the chief, and how he sent to discover them. A present sent to Mendoza of various things found in this country by Vazquez Coronado.

These Indians say that the kingdom of Totonteac, which the father provincial praised so much, saying that it was something marvelous, and of such a very great size, and that cloth was made there, is a hot lake, on the edge of which there are five or six houses.[3] There used to be some others, but these have been destroyed by war. The kingdom of Marata can not be found, nor do these Indians know anything about it. The kingdom of Acus is a single small city, where they raise cotton, and this is called Acucu.[4] I say that this is the country, because Acus, with or without the aspiration, is not a word in this region; and because it seems to me that Acucu may be derived from Acus, I say that it is this town which has been converted into 'the kingdom of Acus. They tell me that there are some other small ones not far from this settlement, which are situated on a river which I have seen and of which the Indians have told me. God knows that I wish I had better news to write to Your Lordship, but I must give you the truth, and, as I wrote you from Culiacan, I must advise you of the good as well as of the bad. But you may be assured that if there had been all the riches and treasures of the world, I could not have done more in His Majesty's service and in that of Your Lordship than I have done, in coming here where you commanded me to go, carrying, both my companions and myself, our food on our backs for 300 leagues, and

---

[1] See the translation of Castañeda's narrative, p. 487.

[2] Doubtless a slip of Ramusio's pen for cows, i. e., buffalos.

[3] Coronado doubtless misinterpreted what the natives intended to communicate. The "hot lake" was in all probability the salt lake alluded to on page 550, near which Marata was situated. Totonteac was of course Tusayan, or "Tucano."

[4] This is a form of the Zuñi name for Acoma—Hakukia.

THE KERES PUEBLO OF SIA

traveling on foot many days, making our way over hills and rough mountains, besides other labors which I refrain from mentioning. Nor do I think of stopping until my death, if it serves His Majesty or Your Lordship to have it so.

Three days after I captured this city, some of the Indians who lived here came to offer to make peace. They brought me some turquoises and poor mantles, and I received them in His Majesty's name with as good a speech as I could, making them understand the purpose of my coming to this country, which is, in the name of His Majesty and by the commands of Your Lordship, that they and all others in this province should become Christians and should know the true God for their Lord, and His Majesty for their king and earthly lord. After this they returned to their houses and suddenly, the next day, they packed up their goods and property, their women and children, and fled to the hills, leaving their towns deserted, with only some few remaining in them. Seeing this, I went to the town which I said was larger than this, eight or ten days later, when I had recovered from my wounds. I found a few of them there, whom I told that they ought not to feel any fear, and I asked them to summon their lord to me. By what I can find out or observe, however, none of these towns have any, since I have not seen any principal house by which any superiority over others could be shown.[1] Afterward, an old man, who said he was their lord, came with a mantle made of many pieces, with whom I argued as long as he stayed with me. He said that he would come to see me with the rest of the chiefs of the country, three days later, in order to arrange the relations which should exist between us. He did so, and they brought me some little ragged mantles and some turquoises. I said that they ought to come down from their strongholds and return to their houses with their wives and children, and that they should become Christians, and recognize His Majesty as their king and lord. But they still remain in their strongholds, with their wives and all their property. I commanded them to have a cloth painted for me, with all the animals that they know in that country, and although they are poor painters, they quickly painted two for me, one of the animals and the other of the birds and fishes. They say that they will bring their children so that our priests may instruct them, and that they desire to know our law. They declare that it was foretold among them more than fifty years ago that a people such as we are should come, and the direction they should come from, and that the whole country would be conquered. So far as I can find out, the water is what these Indians worship, because they say that it makes the corn grow and sustains their life, and that the only other reason they know is because their ancestors did so.[2] I have tried in every way to find out from the natives of these settlements whether they know of any other peoples

---

[1] As clear a description of the form of tribal government among the Pueblo Indians as is anywhere to be found is in Bandelier's story, The Delight Makers. Mr Bandelier has been most successful in his effort to picture the actions and spirit of Indian life.

[2] Dr J. Walter Fewkes has conclusively shown that the snake dance, probably the most dramatic of Indian ceremonials, is essentially a prayer for rain. Coming as it does just as the natural rainy season approaches, the prayer is almost invariably answered.

14 ETH——36

or provinces or cities. They tell me about seven cities which are at a considerable distance, which are like these, except that the houses there are not like these, but are made of earth [adobe], and small, and that they raise much cotton there. The first of these four places about which they know is called, they say, Tucano. They could not tell me much about the others. I do not believe that they tell me the truth, because they think that I shall soon have to depart from them and return home. But they will quickly find that they are deceived in this. I sent Don Pedro de Tobar there, with his company and some other horsemen, to see it. I would not have dispatched this packet to Your Lordship until I had learned what he found there, if I thought that I should have any news from him within twelve or fifteen days. However, as he will remain away at least thirty, and, considering that this information is of little importance and that the cold and the rains are approaching, it seemed to me that I ought to do as Your Lordship commanded me in your instructions, which is, that as soon as I arrived here, I should advise you thereof, and this I do, by sending you the plain narrative of what I have seen, which is bad enough, as you may perceive. I have determined to send throughout all the surrounding regions, in order to find out whether there is anything, and to suffer every extremity before I give up this enterprise, and to serve His Majesty, if I can find any way in which to do it, and not to lack in diligence until Your Lordship directs me as to what I ought to do. We have great need of pasture, and you should know, also, that among all those who are here there is not one pound of raisins, nor sugar, nor oil, nor wine, except barely half a quart, which is saved to say mass, since everything is consumed, and part was lost on the way. Now, you can provide us with what appears best; but if you are thinking of sending us cattle, you should know that it will be necessary for them to spend at least a year on the road, because they can not come in any other way, nor any quicker. I would have liked to send to Your Lordship, with this dispatch, many samples of the things which they have in this country, but the trip is so long and rough that it is difficult for me to do so. However, I send you twelve small mantles, such as the people of this country ordinarily wear, and a garment which seems to me to be very well made. I kept it because it seemed to me to be of very good workmanship, and because I do not think that anyone has ever seen in these Indies any work done with a needle, unless it were done since the Spaniards settled here. And I also send two cloths painted with the animals which they have in this country, although, as I said, the painting is very poorly done, because the artist did not spend more than one day in painting it. I have seen other paintings on the walls of these houses which have much better proportion and are done much better.

I send you a cow skin, some turquoises, and two earrings of the same, and fifteen of the Indian combs,[1] and some plates decorated with these turquoises, and two baskets made of wicker, of which the Indians have a large supply. I also send two rolls, such as the women usually wear on their heads when they bring water from the spring, the

---

[1] Possibly those used in weaving.

THE KERES PUEBLO OF COCHITÍ

same way that they do in Spain. One of these Indian women, with one of these rolls on her head, will carry a jar of water up a ladder without touching it with her hands. And, lastly, I send you samples of the weapons with which the natives of this country fight, a shield, a hammer, and a bow with some arrows, among which there are two with bone points, the like of which have never been seen, according to what these conquerors say. As far as I can judge, it does not appear to me that there is any hope of getting gold or silver, but I trust in God that, if there is any, we shall get our share of it, and it shall not escape us through any lack of diligence in the search.[1] I am unable to give Your Lordship any certain information about the dress of the women, because the Indians keep them guarded so carefully that I have not seen any, except two old women. These had on two long skirts reaching down to their feet and open in front, and a girdle, and they are tied together with some cotton strings. I asked the Indians to give me one of those which they wore, to send to you, since they were not willing to show me the women. They brought me two mantles, which are these that I send, almost painted over. They have two tassels, like the women of Spain, which hang somewhat over their shoulders. The death of the negro is perfectly certain, because many of the things which he wore have been found, and the Indians say that they killed him here because the Indians of Chichilticale said that he was a bad man, and not like the Christians, because the Christians never kill women, and he killed them, and because he assaulted their women, whom the Indians love better than themselves. Therefore they determined to kill him, but they did not do it in the way that was reported, because they did not kill any of the others who came with him, nor did they kill the lad from the province of Petatlan, who was with him, but they took him and kept him in safe custody until now. When I tried to secure him, they made excuses for not giving him to me, for two or three days, saying that he was dead, and at other times that the Indians of Acucu had taken him away. But when I finally told them that I should be very angry if they did not give him to me, they gave him to me. He is an interpreter; for although he can not talk much, he understands very well. Some gold and silver has been found in this place, which those who know about minerals say is not bad. I have not yet been able to learn from these people where they got it. I perceive that they refuse to tell me the truth in everything, because they think that I shall have to depart from here in a short time, as I have said. But I trust in God that they will not be able to avoid answering much longer. I beg Your Lordship to make a report of the success of this expedition to His Majesty, because there is nothing more than what I have already said. I shall not do so until it shall please God to grant that we find what we desire. Our Lord God protect and keep your most illustrious Lordship. From the province of Cevola, and this city of Granada, the 3d of August, 1540. Francisco Vazquez de Coronado kisses the hand of your most illustrious Lordship.

---

[1] This whole sentence is omitted by Hakluyt. The conquerors, in the literature of New Spain, are almost always those who shared with Cortes in the labors and the glory of the Spanish conquest of Mexico.

TRANSLATION OF THE TRASLADO DE LAS NUEVAS

COPY OF THE REPORTS AND DESCRIPTIONS THAT HAVE BEEN
RECEIVED REGARDING THE DISCOVERY OF A CITY WHICH IS
CALLED CIBOLA, SITUATED IN THE NEW COUNTRY.

His grace left the larger part of his army in the valley of Culiacan,
and with only 75 companions on horseback and 30 footmen, he set out
for here Thursday, April 22. The army which remained there was to
start about the end of the month of May, because they could not find
any sort of sustenance for the whole of the way that they had to go,
as far as this province of Cibola, which is 350 long leagues, and on
this account he did not dare to put the whole army on the road. As
for the men he took with him, he ordered them to make provision
for eighty days, which was carried on horses, each having one for himself and his followers. With very great danger of suffering hunger,
and not less labor, since they had to open the way, and every day discovered waterways and rivers with bad crossings, they stood it after a
fashion, and on the whole journey as far as this province there was not a
peck of corn.[2] He reached this province on Wednesday, the 7th of July
last, with all the men whom he led from the valley very well, praise be
to Our Lord, except one Spaniard who died of hunger four days from
here and some negroes and Indians who also died of hunger and thirst.
The Spaniard was one of those on foot, and was named Espinosa. In
this way his grace spent seventy-seven days on the road before reaching here, during which God knows in what sort of a way we lived, and
whether we could have eaten much more than we ate the day that his
grace reached this city of Granada, for so it has been named out of
regard for the viceroy, and because they say it resembles the Albaicin.[3]
The force he led was not received the way it should have been, because
they all arrived very tired from the great labor of the journey. This,
and the loading and unloading like so many muleteers, and not eating
as much as they should have, left them more in need of resting several
days than of fighting, although there was not a man in the army who
would not have done his best in everything if the horses, who suffered
the same as their masters, could have helped them.

The city was deserted by men over sixty years and under twenty,
and by women and children. All who were there were the fighting

---

[1]Translated from Pacheco y Cardenas, Documentos de Indias, vol. xix, p. 529. This document is
anonymous, but it is evidently a copy of a letter from some trusted companion, written from Granada-
Hawikuh, about the time of Coronado's letter of August 3, 1540. In the title to the document as
printed, the date is given as 1531, but there can be no doubt that it is an account of Coronado's journey.
[2]The printed Spanish text reads: "que como venian abriendo y descobriendo, cada dia, camino, los
arcabucos y rios, y malos pasos, se llevaban en parte." . . .
[3]A part of Granada, near the Alhambra. There is a curious similarity in the names Albaicin and
Hawikuh, the latter being the native name of Coronado's Granada.

336

THE TEWA PUEBLO OF NAMBE

men who remained to defend the city, and many of them came out, about a crossbow shot, uttering loud threats. The general himself went forward with two priests and the army-master, to urge them to surrender, as is the custom in new countries. The reply that he received was from many arrows which they let fly, and they wounded Hernando Bermejo's horse and pierced the loose flap of the frock of father Friar Luis, the former companion of the Lord Bishop of Mexico. When this was seen, taking as their advocate the Holy Saint James,[1] he rushed upon them with all his force, which he had kept in very good order, and although the Indians turned their backs and tried to reach the city, they were overtaken and many of them killed before they could reach it. They killed three horses and wounded seven or eight.

When my lord the general reached the city, he saw that it was surrounded by stone walls, and the houses very high, four and five and even six stories apiece, with their flat roofs and balconies. As the Indians had made themselves secure within it, and would not let anyone come near without shooting arrows at him, and as we could not obtain anything to eat unless we captured it, his grace decided to enter the city on foot and to surround it by men on horseback, so that the Indians who were inside could not get away. As he was distinguished among them all by his gilt arms and a plume on his headpiece, all the Indians aimed at him, because he was noticeable among all, and they knocked him down to the ground twice by chance stones thrown from the flat roofs, and stunned him in spite of his headpiece, and if this had not been so good, I doubt if he would have come out alive from that enterprise, and besides all this—praised be Our Lord that he came out on his own feet—they hit him many times with stones on his head and shoulders and legs, and he received two small wounds on his face and an arrow wound in the right foot; but despite all this his grace is as sound and well as the day he left that city. And you[2] may assure my lord of all this, and also that on the 19th of July last he went 4 leagues from this city to see a rock where they told him that the Indians of this province had fortified themselves,[3] and he returned the same day, so that he went 8 leagues in going and returning. I think I have given you an account of everything, for it is right that I should be the authority for you and his lordship, to assure you that everything is going well with the general my lord, and without any hesitation I can assure you that he is as well and sound as the day he left the city. He is located within the city, for when the Indians saw that his grace was determined to enter the city, then they abandoned it, since they let them go with their lives. We found in it what we needed more than gold and silver, and that was much corn and beans and fowls, better than those of New Spain, and salt, the best and whitest that I have seen in all my life.

---

[1] Uttering the war cry of Santiago.
[2] The printed manuscript is V. M., which signifies Your Majesty.
[3] Doubtless Thunder mountain.

RELACIÓN POSTRERA DE SIVOLA[1]

ESTA ES LA RELACIÓN POSTRERA DE SÍVOLA, Y DE MÁS DE CUATRO-
CIENTAS LEGUAS ADELANTE.

Desde Culhuacán á Sívola hay más de trescientas leguas; poco del camino poblado: hay muy poca gente: es tierra estéril: hay muy malos caminos: la gente anda del todo desnuda, salvo las mujeres, que de la cintura abajo traen cueros de venados adobados, blancos, á manera de faldíllas hasta los pies. Las casas que tienen son de petlatles hechos de cañas: son las casas redondas y pequeñas, que apenas cabe un hombre en pie dentro. Donde están congregados y donde siembran es tierra arenosa: cogen maiz, aunque poco, y frisoles y calabazas, y también se mantienen de caza, conejos, liebres y venados. No tienen sacrificios. Esto es desde Culhuacan á Síbola.

Sívola es un pueblo de hasta ducientas casas: son á dos y tres y cuatro y cinco sobrados: tienen las paredes de un palmo de ancho: los palos de la maderación son tan gruesos como por la muñeca, y redondos; por tablazón tienen cañas muy menudas con sus hojas, y encima tierra presada: las paredes son de tierra y barro: las puertas de las casas son de la manera de escotillones de navíos: están las casas juntas, asidas unas con otras: tienen delante de las casas unas estufas de barro de tierra donde se guarecen en el invierno del frio, porque le hace muy grande, que nieva seis meses del año. De esta gente algunos traen mantas de algodón y de maguey, y cueros de venados adobados, y traen zapatos de los mismos cueros, hasta encima de las rodillas. También hacen mantas de pellejos de liebres y de conejos, con que se cubren. Andan las mujeres vestidas de mantas de maguey hasta los pies: andan ceñidas: traen los cabellos cogidos encima de las orejas, como rodajas: cogen maíz y frisoles y calabazas, lo que les basta para su mantenimiento, porque es poca gente. La tierra donde siembran es toda arena; son las aguas salobres: es tierra muy seca: tienen algunas gallinas, aunque pocas; no saben qué cosa es pescado. Son siete pueblos en esta pro-vincia de Sivola en espacio de cinco leguas: el mayor será de ducientas casas, y otros dos, de á ducientas, y los otros á sesenta y á cincuenta y á treinta casas.

Desde Sívola al rio y provincia de Tibex hay sesenta leguas: el primer pueblo es cuarenta leguas de Sivola: llámase Acuco. Este pueblo está encima de un peñol muy fuerte: será de duzientas casas, asentado á la

---

[1]The source of this document is stated in the bibliographic note, p. 413. This appears to be a tran-script from letters written, probably at Tiguex on the Rio Grande, during the late summer or early fall of 1541.

manera de Sívola que es otra lengua.   Desde allí al rio de Tiguex hay
veinte leguas.   El rio es cuasi tan ancho como el de Sevilla, aunque no
es tan hondo: va por tierra llana: es buen agua: tiene algún pescado:
nace al norte.   El que esto dice vió doce pueblos en cierto compás del
río: otros vieron más: dicen el río arriba: abajo todos son pueblos
pequeños, salvo dos que ternán á ducientas casas: estas casas con las
paredes como á manera de tapías de tierra é arena, muy recias: son tan
anchas como un palmo de una mano.   Son las casas de á dos y tres terrados: tienen la maderación como en Sivola.   Es tierra muy fria: tiene
sus estufas como en Sivola; y hiélase tanto el río, que pasan bestias
cargadas por él, y pudieran pasar carretas.   Cogen maiz lo que han
menester, y frisoles y calabazas: tienen algunas gallinas, las cuales
guardan para hacer mantas de la pluma.   Cogen algodón, aunque poco:
traen mantas de ello, y zapatos de cuero como en Sívola.   Es gente que
defiende bien su capa, y desde sus casas, que no curan de salir fuera.
Es tierra toda arenosa.

Desde la provincia y río de Tiguex, á cuatro jornadas toparon cuatro
pueblos.   El primero terná treinta casas.   El segundo es pueblo grande
destruido de sus guerras: tenía hasta treinta y cinco casas pobladas:
el tercero [sic] hasta   Estos tres son de la manera de los del río en todo.
El cuarto es un pueblo grande, el cual está entre unos montes: llámase
Cicuic: tenía hasta cincuenta casas con tantos terrados como los de
Sívola: son las paredes de tierra y barro como las de Sívola.   Tienen
harto maiz y frisoles y calabazas y algunas gallinas. A cuatro jornadas de este pueblo toparon una tierra llana como la mar, en los cuales
llanos hay tanta multitud de vacas, que no tienen número.   Estas
vacas son como las de Castilla, y algunas mayores que tienen en la
cruz una corva pequeña, y son más bermejas, que tiran á negro: cuél-
gales una lana más larga que un palmo entre los cuernos y orejas y
barba, y por la papada abajo y por las espaldas, como crines, y de las
rodillas abajo todo lo más es de lana muy pequeñita, á manera de
merino: tienen muy buena carne y tierna, y mucho sebo.   Andando
muchos días por estos llanos, toparon con una ranchería de hasta
duzientas casas con gente: eran las casas de los cueros de las vacas
adobados, blancas, á manera de pabellones ó tiendas de campo.   El
mantenimiento ó sustentamiento de estos indios es todo de las vacas,
porque ni siembran ni cogen maiz: de los cueros hacen sus casas, de
los cueros visten y calzan, de los cueros hacen sogas y también de la
lana: de los niervos hacen hilo con que cosen sus vestiduras y también
las casas: de los huesos hacen alesnas: las boñigas les sirven de leña;
porque no hay otra en aquella tierra: los buches les sirven de jarros y
vasijas con que beben: de la carne se mantienen: cómenla medio asada
é un poco caliente encima de las boñigas, la otra cruda, y tomándola
con los dientes, tiran con la una mano, y en la otra tienen un navajon
de pedernal y cortan el bocado; ansí lo tragan como aves medio mas-
cado: comen el sebo crudo, sin calentallo: beben la sangre, ansí como

sale de las vacas, y otras veces despues de salida, fria y cruda: no tienen otro mantenimiento.   Esta gente tiene perros como los de esta tierra, salvo que son algo mayores, los cuales perros cargan como á bestias, y las hacen sus enjalmas como albardillas, y las cinchan con sus correas, y andan matados como bestias, en las cruces.   Cuando van á caza cárganlos de mantenimientos; y cuando se mueven estos indios, porque no están de asiento en una parte, que se andan donde andan las vacas para se mantener, estos perros les llevan las casas, y llevan los palos de las casas arrastrando, atados á las albardillas, allende de la carga que llevan encima: podrá ser la carga, según el perro, arroba y media y dos.   Hay de este Síbola á estos llanos adonde llegaron, treinta leguas, y aun más.   Los llanos proceden adelante, ni se sabe qué tanto. El capitán Francisco Vázquez fué por los llanos adelante con treinta de á caballo, y Fr. Juan de Padilla con él: toda la demás gente se volvieron á la población del río, para esperar á Francisco Vázquez, porque ansi se lo mandó: no se sabe sí es vuelto &c.

Es la tierra tan llana, que se pierden los hombres apartándose media legua, como se perdió uno á caballo, que nunca más pareció, y dos caballos ensillados y enfrenados que nunca más parecieron.   No queda rastro ninguno por donde van, y á esta causa tenían necesidad de amojonar el camino por donde iban, para volver, con boñigas de vacas, que no había piedras ni otra cosa.

Marco Polo, veneciano, en su tratado, en el cap. xv, trata y díce que [ha visto?] las mesmas vacas, y de la mesma manera en la corcova; y en el mesmo capitulo dice que también hay carneros tamaños como caballos.

Nicolás, veneciano, dió relación á Micer Pogio, florentino, en el libro segundo, cerca del fin, dice como en la Etiopia hay bueyes con corcova, como camellos, y tienen los cuernos largos de tres codos, y echan los cuernos encima sobre el espinazo, y hace un cuerno de estos un cántaro de vino.

Marco Polo, en el capítulo ciento y treinta y cuatro dice que en la tierra de los tártaros, hácia el norte, se hallan canes tan grandes ó poco menos que asnos; á los cuales echan uno como carro y entran con ellos en una tierra muy lodosa, toda cenagales, que otros animales no podrian entrar ni salir sin se anegar, y por eso llevan perros.

[*Scripsi et contuli, México, Marzo 11, 1893.*

Joaqⁿ. Garcia Icazbalceta.|

TRANSLATION

THIS IS THE LATEST ACCOUNT OF CIBOLA, AND OF MORE THAN FOUR HUNDRED LEAGUES BEYOND.

It is more than 300 leagues from Culiacan to Cibola, uninhabited most of the way.   There are very few people there; the country is sterile; the roads are very bad.   The people go around entirely naked,

A NAMBE INDIAN IN WAR COSTUME

except the women, who wear white tanned deer skins from the waist down, something like little skirts, reaching to the feet. Their houses are of mats made of reeds; the houses are round and small, so that there is hardly room inside for a man on his feet. The country is sandy where they live near together and where they plant. They raise corn, but not very much, and beans and melons, and they also live on game— rabbits, hares, and deer. They do not have sacrifices. This is between Culiacan and Cibola.

Cibola is a village of about 200 houses. They have two and three and four and five stories. The walls are about a handbreadth thick; the sticks of timber are as large as the wrist, and round; for boards, they have very small bushes, with their leaves on, covered with a sort of greenish-colored mud; the walls are of dirt and mud, the doors of the houses are like the hatchways of ships. The houses are close together, each joined to the others. Outside of the houses they have some hot-houses (or estufas) of dirt mud, where they take refuge from the cold in the winter—because this is very great, since it snows six months in the year. Some of these people wear cloaks of cotton and of the maguey (or Mexican aloe) and of tanned deer skin, and they wear shoes made of these skins, reaching up to the knees. They also make cloaks of the skins of hares and rabbits, with which they cover themselves. The women wear cloaks of the maguey, reaching down to the feet, with girdles; they wear their hair gathered about the ears like little wheels. They raise corn and beans and melons, which is all they need to live on, because it is a small tribe. The land where they plant is entirely sandy; the water is brackish; the country is very dry. They have some fowls, although not many. They do not know what sort of a thing fish is. There are seven villages in this province of Cibola within a space of 5 leagues; the largest may have about 200 houses and two others about 200, and the others somewhere between 60 or 50 and 30 houses.

It is 60 leagues from Cibola to the river and province of Tibex [Tiguex]. The first village is 40 leagues from Cibola, and is called Acuco. This village is on top of a very strong rock; it has about 200 houses, built in the same way as at Cibola, where they speak another language. It is 20 leagues from here to the river of Tiguex. The river is almost as wide as that of Seville, although not so deep; it flows through a level country; the water is good; it contains some fish; it rises in the north. He who relates this, saw twelve villages within a certain distance of the river; others saw more, they say, up the river. Below, all the villages are small, except two that have about 200 houses. The walls of these houses are something like mud walls of dirt and sand, very rough; they are as thick as the breadth of a hand. The houses have two and three stories; the construction is like those at Cibola. The country is very cold. They have hot-houses, as in Cibola, and the river freezes so thick that loaded animals cross it, and it would be possible for carts to do so. They raise as much corn as they need, and beans and melons. They have some fowls, which they keep so as to make cloaks of their feathers. They raise cotton, although not much; they wear cloaks made of this, and shoes of hide, as at Cibola. These people defend themselves very well, and from within their houses, since they do not care to come out. The country is all sandy.

Four days' journey from the province and river of Tiguex four villages are found. The first has 30 houses; the second is a large village destroyed in their wars, and has about 35 houses occupied; the third about   These three are like those at the river in every way. The fourth is a large village which is among some mountains. It is called Cicuic, and has about 50 houses, with as many stories as those at Cibola. The walls are of dirt and mud like those at Cibola. It has plenty of corn, beans and melons, and some fowls. Four days from this village they came to a country as level as the sea, and in these plains there was such a multitude of cows that they are numberless. These cows are like those of Castile, and somewhat larger, as they have a little hump on the withers, and they are more reddish, approaching black; their hair, more than a span long, hangs down around their horns and ears and chin, and along the neck and shoulders like manes, and down from the knees; all the rest is a very fine wool, like merino; they have very good, tender meat, and much fat. Having proceeded many days through these plains, they came to a settlement of about 200 inhabited houses. The houses were made of the skins of the cows, tanned white, like pavilions or army tents. The maintenance or sustenance of these Indians comes entirely from the cows, because they neither sow nor reap corn. With the skins they make their houses, with the skins they clothe and shoe themselves, of the skins they make rope, and also of the wool; from the sinews they make thread, with which they sew their clothes and also their houses; from the bones they make awls; the dung serves them for wood, because there is nothing else in that country; the stomachs serve them for pitchers and vessels from which they drink; they live on the flesh; they sometimes eat it half roasted and warmed over the dung, at other times raw; seizing it with their fingers, they pull it out with one hand and with a flint knife in the other they cut off mouthfuls, and thus swallow it half chewed; they eat the fat raw, without warming it; they drink the blood just as it leaves the cows, and at other times after it has run out, cold and raw; they have no other means of livelihood. These people have dogs like those in this country, except that they are somewhat larger, and they load these dogs like beasts of burden, and make saddles for them like our pack saddles, and they fasten them with their leather thongs, and these make their backs sore on the withers like pack animals. When they go hunting, they load these with their necessities, and when they move—for these Indians are not settled in one place, since they travel wherever the cows move, to support themselves—these dogs carry their houses, and they have the sticks of their houses dragging along tied on to the

A NAMBE WATER CARRIER

pack-saddles, besides the load which they carry on top, and the load may be, according to the dog, from 35 to 50 pounds. It is 30 leagues, or even more, from Cibola to these plains where they went. The plains stretch away beyond, nobody knows how far. The captain, Francisco Vazquez, went farther across the plains, with 30 horsemen, and Friar Juan de Padilla with him; all the rest of the force returned to the settlement at the river to wait for Francisco Vazquez, because this was his command. It is not known whether he has returned.

The country is so level that men became lost when they went off half a league. One horseman was lost, who never reappeared, and two horses, all saddled and bridled, which they never saw again. No track was left of where they went, and on this account it was necessary to mark the road by which they went with cow dung, so as to return, since there were no stones or anything else.

Marco Polo, the Venetian, in his treatise, in chapter 15, relates and says that (he saw) the same cows, with the same sort of hump; and in the same chapter he says that there are sheep as big as horses.

Nicholas, the Venetian, gave an account to Micer Pogio, the Florentine, in his second book, toward the end, which says that in Ethiopia there are oxen with a hump, like camels, and they have horns 3 cubits long, and they carry their horns up over their backs, and one of these horns makes a wine pitcher.

Marco Polo, in chapter 134, says that in the country of the Tartars, toward the north, they have dogs as large or little smaller than asses. They harness these into a sort of cart and with these enter a very miry country, all a quagmire, where other animals can not enter and come out without getting submerged, and on this account they take dogs.

TRANSLATION OF THE RELACION DEL SUCESO[1]

ACCOUNT OF WHAT HAPPENED ON THE JOURNEY WHICH FRANCISCO VAZQUEZ MADE TO DISCOVER CIBOLA.

When the army reached the valley of Culiacan, Francisco Vazquez divided the army on account of the bad news which was received regarding Cibola, and because the food supply along the way was small, according to the report of Melchor Diaz, who had just come back from seeing it. He himself took 80 horsemen and 25 foot soldiers, and a small part of the artillery, and set out from Culiacan, leaving Don Tristan de Arellano with the rest of the force, with orders to set out twenty days later, and when he reached the Valley of Hearts (Corazones) to wait there for a letter from him, which would be sent after he had reached Cibola, and had seen what was there; and this was done. The Valley of Hearts is 150 leagues from the valley of Culiacan, and the same distance from Cibola.[2]

This whole distance, up to about 50 leagues before reaching Cibola, is inhabited, although it is away from the road in some places. The population is all of the same sort of people, since the houses are all of palm mats, and some of them have low lofts. They all have corn, although not much, and in some places very little. They have melons and beans. The best settlement of all is a valley called Señora, which is 10 leagues beyond the Hearts, where a town was afterward settled. There is some cotton among these, but deer skins are what most of them use for clothes.

Francisco Vazquez passed by all these on account of the small crops. There was no corn the whole way, except at this valley of Señora, where they collected a little, and besides this he had what he took from Culiacan, where he provided himself for eighty days. In seventy-three days we reached Cibola, although after hard labor and the loss of many horses and the death of several Indians, and after we saw it these were all doubled, although we did find corn enough. We found the natives peaceful for the whole way.

[1] The Spanish text of this document is printed in Buckingham Smith's Florida, p. 147, from a copy made by Muñoz, and also in Pacheco y Cardenas, Documentos de Indias, vol. xiv, p. 318, from a copy found in the Archives of the Indies at Seville. The important variations in the texts are noted in the footnotes. See page 398 in regard to the value of this anonymous document. No date is given in the document, but there can be no doubt that it refers to Coronado's expedition. In the heading to the document in the Pacheco y Cardenas Coleccion, the date is given as 1531, and it is placed under that year in the chronologic index of the Coleccion. This translation, as well as that of the letter to Charles V, which follows, has already been printed in American History Leaflet, No. 13.

[2] The spelling of Cibola and Culiacan is that of the Pacheco y Cardenas copy. Buckingham Smith prints Civola and Culuacan.

The day we reached the first village part of them came out to fight us, and the rest stayed in the village and fortified themselves. It was not possible to make peace with these, although we tried hard enough, so it was necessary to attack them and kill some of them. The rest then drew back to the village, which was then surrounded and attacked. We had to withdraw, on account of the great damage they did us from the flat roofs, and we began to assault them from a distance with the artillery and muskets, and that afternoon they surrendered. Francisco Vazquez came out of it badly hurt by some stones, and I am certain, indeed, that he would have been there yet if it had not been for the army-master, D. Garcia Lopez de Cardenas, who rescued him. When the Indians surrendered, they abandoned the village and went to the other villages, and as they left the houses we made ourselves at home in them.

Father Friar Marcos understood, or gave to understand, that the region and neighborhood in which there are seven villages was a single village which he called Cibola, but the whole of this settled region is called Cibola. The villages have from 150 to 200 and 300 houses; some have the houses of the village all together, although in some villages they are divided into two or three sections, but for the most part they are all together, and their courtyards are within, and in these are their hot rooms for winter, and they have their summer ones outside the villages. The houses have two or three stories, the walls of stone and mud, and some have mud walls. The villages have for the most part the walls of the houses; the houses are too good for Indians, especially for these, since they are brutish and have no decency in anything except in their houses.

For food they have much corn and beans and melons, and some fowls, like those of Mexico, and they keep these more for their feathers than to eat, because they make long robes of them, since they do not have any cotton; and they wear cloaks of heniquen (a fibrous plant), and of the skins of deer, and sometimes of cows.

Their rites and sacrifices are somewhat idolatrous, but water is what they worship most, to which they offer small painted sticks and feathers and yellow powder made of flowers, and usually this offering is made to springs. Sometimes, also, they offer such turquoises as they have, although poor ones.

From the valley of Culiacan to Cibola it is 240 leagues in two directions. It is north to about the thirty-fourth-and-a-half degree, and from there to Cibola, which is nearly the thirty-seventh degree, toward the northeast.

Having talked with the natives of Cibola about what was beyond, they said that there were settlements toward the west. Francisco Vazquez then sent Don Pedro de Tobar to investigate, who found seven other villages, which were called the province of Tuzan;[1] this is 35

---

[1] Buckingham Smith prints Tovar and Tuçan.

leagues to the west. The villages are somewhat larger than those of Cibola, and in other respects, in food and everything, they are of the same sort, except that these raise cotton. While Don Pedro de Tobar had gone to see these, Francisco Vazquez dispatched messengers to the viceroy, with an account of what had happened up to this point.[1] He also prepared instructions for these to take to Don Tristan, who as I have said, was at Hearts, for him to proceed to Cibola, and to leave a town established in the valley of Señora, which he did, and in it he left 80 horsemen of the men who had but one horse and the weakest men, and Melchor Diaz with them as captain and leader, because Francisco Vazquez had so arranged for it. He ordered him to go from there with half the force to explore toward the west; and he did so, and traveled 150 leagues, to the river which Hernando de Alarcon entered from the sea, which he called the Buenaguia. The settlements and people that are in this direction are mostly like those at the Hearts, except at the river and around it, where the people have much better figures and have more corn, although the houses in which they live are hovels, like pig pens, almost under ground, with a covering of straw, and made without any skill whatever. This river is reported to be large. They reached it 30 leagues from the coast, where, and as far again above, Alarcon had come up with his boats two months before they reached it. This river runs north and south there. Melchor Diaz passed on toward the west five or six days, from which he returned for the reason that he did not find any water or vegetation, but only many stretches of sand; and he had some fighting on his return to the river and its vicinity, because they wanted to take advantage of him while crossing the river. While returning Melchor Diaz died from an accident, by which he killed himself, throwing a lance at a dog.

After Don Pedro de Tobar returned and had given an account of those villages, he then dispatched Don Garcia Lopez de Cardenas, the army-master, by the same road Don Pedro had followed, to go beyond that province of Tuzan to the west, and he allowed him eighty days in which to go and return, for the journey and to make the discoveries. He was conducted beyond Tuzan by native guides, who said there were settlements beyond, although at a distance. Having gone 50 leagues west of Tuzan, and 80 from Cibola, he found the edge of a river down which it was impossible to find a path for a horse in any direction, or even for a man on foot, except in one very difficult place, where there was a descent for almost 2 leagues. The sides were such a steep rocky precipice that it was scarcely possible to see the river, which looks like a brook from above, although it is half as large again as that of Seville, according to what they say, so that although they sought for a passage with great diligence, none was found for a long distance, during which they were for several days in great need of water, which could not be found, and they could not approach that of the river, although they

---

[1] See the letter of August 3, 1540, p. 562.

THE KERES PUEBLO OF KATISHTYA OR SAN FELIPE

could see it, and on this account Don Garcia Lopez was forced to return. This river comes from the northeast and turns toward the south-southwest at the place where they found it, so that it is without any doubt the one that Melchor Diaz reached.

Four days after Francisco Vazquez had dispatched Don Garcia Lopez to make this discovery, he dispatched Hernando de Alvarado to explore the route toward the east. He started off, and 30 leagues from Cibola found a rock with a village on top, the strongest position that ever was seen in the world, which was called Acuco[1] in their language, and father Friar Marcos called it the kingdom of Hacus. They came out to meet us peacefully, although it would have been easy to decline to do this and to have stayed on their rock, where we would not have been able to trouble them. They gave us cloaks of cotton, skins of deer and of cows, and turquoises, and fowls and other food which they had, which is the same as in Cibola.

Twenty leagues to the east of this rock we found a river which runs north and south,[2] well settled; there are in all, small and large, 70 villages near it, a few more or less, the same sort as those at Cibola, except that they are almost all of well-made mud walls. The food is neither more nor less. They raise cotton—I mean those who live near the river—the others not. There is much corn here. These people do not have markets. They are settled for 50 leagues along this river, north and south, and some villages are 15 or 20 leagues distant, in one direction and the other. This river rises where these settlements end at the north, on the slope of the mountains there, where there is a larger village different from the others, called Yuraba.[3] It is settled in this fashion: It has 18 divisions; each one has a situation as if for two ground plots;[4] the houses are very close together, and have five or six stories, three of them with mud walls and two or three with thin wooden walls, which become smaller as they go up, and each one has its little balcony outside of the mud walls, one above the other, all around, of wood. In this village, as it is in the mountains, they do not raise cotton nor breed fowls; they wear the skins of deer and cows entirely. It is the most populous village of all that country; we estimated there were 15,000 souls in it. There is one of the other kind of villages larger than all the rest, and very strong, which is called Cicuique.[5] It has four and five stories, has eight large courtyards, each one with its balcony, and there are fine houses in it. They do not raise cotton nor keep fowls, because it is 15 leagues away from the river to the east, toward the plains where the cows are. After Alvarado had sent an account of this

---

[1] The Acoma people call their pueblo Áko, while the name for themselves is Akómë, signifying "people of the white rock." The Zuñi name of Acoma, as previously stated, is Hákukia; of the Acoma people, Háku-kwe. Hacus was applied by Niza to Hawikuh, not to Acoma—*Hodge.*

[2] The Rio Grande.

[3] Evidently Taos, the native name of which is Tñatá, the Picuris name being Tuopá, according to Hodge.

[4] The Spanish text (p. 323) is: "Tiene diez é ocho barrios; cada uno tiene tanto sitio como dos solares, las casas muy juntas."

[5] Identical with Castañeda's Cicuyc or Cicuye—the pueblo of Pecos.

river to Francisco Vazquez, he proceeded forward to these plains, and at the borders of these he found a little river which flows to the southwest, and after four days' march he found the cows, which are the most monstrous thing in the way of animals which has ever been seen or read about. He followed this river for 100 leagues, finding more cows every day. We provided ourselves with some of these, although at first, until we had had experience, at the risk of the horses. There is such a quantity of them that I do not know what to compare them with, except with the fish in the sea, because on this journey, as also on that which the whole army afterward made when it was going to Quivira, there were so many that many times when we started to pass through the midst of them and wanted to go through to the other side of them, we were not able to, because the country was covered with them. The flesh of these is as good as that of Castile, and some said it was even better.

The bulls are large and brave, although they do not attack very much; but they have wicked horns, and in a fight use them well, attacking fiercely; they killed several of our horses and wounded many. We found the pike to be the best weapon to use against them, and the musket for use when this misses.

When Hernando de Alvarado returned from these plains to the river which was called Tiguex, he found the army-master Don Garcia Lopez de Cardenas getting ready for the whole army, which was coming there. When it arrived, although all these people had met Hernando de Alvarado peacefully, part of them rebelled when all the force came. There were 12 villages near together, and one night they killed 40 of our horses and mules which were loose in the camp. They fortified themselves in their villages, and war was then declared against them. Don Garcia Lopez went to the first and took it and executed justice on many of them. When the rest saw this, they abandoned all except two of the villages, one of these the strongest one of all, around which the army was kept for two months. And although after we invested it, we entered it one day and occupied a part of the flat roof, we were forced to abandon this on account of the many wounds that were received and because it was so dangerous to maintain ourselves there, and although we again entered it soon afterward, in the end it was not possible to get it all, and so it was surrounded all this time. We finally captured it because of their thirst, and they held out so long because it snowed twice when they were just about to give themselves up. In the end we captured it, and many of them were killed because they tried to get away at night.

Francisco Vazquez obtained an account from some Indians who were found in this village of Cicuique, which, if it had been true, was of the richest thing that has been found in the Indies. The Indian who gave the news and the account came from a village called Harale, 300 leagues east of this river. He gave such a clear account of what he told, as if it was true and he had seen it, that it seemed plain afterward that it was the devil who was speaking in him. Francisco Vazquez and all of

THE SOUTH TOWN OF THE TIWA PUEBLO OF TAOS

us placed much confidence in him, although he was advised by several gentlemen not to move the whole army, but rather to send a captain to find out what was there. He did not wish to do this, but wanted to take every one, and even to send Don Pedro de Tobar to the Hearts for half the men who were in that village. So he started with the whole army, and proceeded 150 leagues, 100 to the east and 50 to the south,[1] and the Indian failing to make good what he had said about there being a settlement there, and corn, with which to proceed farther, the other two guides were asked how that was, and one confessed that what the Indian said was a lie, except that there was a province which was called Quivira, and that there was corn and houses of straw there, but that they were very far off, because we had been led astray a distance from the road. Considering this, and the small supply of food that was left, Francisco Vazquez, after consulting with the captains, determined to proceed with 30 of the best men who were well equipped, and that the army should return to the river; and this was done at once. Two days before this, Don Garcia Lopez' horse had happened to fall with him, and he threw his arm out of joint, from which he suffered much, and so Don Tristan de Arellano returned to the river with the army. On this journey they had a very hard time, because almost all of them had nothing to eat except meat, and many suffered on this account. They killed a world of bulls and cows, for there were days when they brought 60 and 70 head into camp, and it was necessary to go hunting every day, and on this account, and from not eating any corn during all this time, the horses suffered much.

Francisco Vazquez set out across these plains in search of Quivira, more on account of the story which had been told us at the river than from the confidence which was placed in the guide here, and after proceeding many days by the needle (i. e., to the north) it pleased God that after thirty days' march we found the river Quivira, which is 30 leagues below the settlement. While going up the valley, we found people who were going hunting, who were natives of Quivira.

All that there is at Quivira is a very brutish people, without any decency whatever in their houses nor in anything. These are of straw, like the Tarascan settlements; in some villages there are as many as 200 houses; they have corn and beans and melons; they do not have cotton nor fowls, nor do they make bread which is cooked, except under the ashes. Francisco Vazquez went 25 leagues through these settlements, to where he obtained an account of what was beyond, and they said that the plains come to an end, and that down the river there are people who do not plant, but live wholly by hunting.

They also gave an account of two other large villages, one of which was called Tareque[2] and the other Arae, with straw houses at Tareque, and at Arae some of straw and some of skins. Copper was found here,

---

[1] Southeast, in Buckingham Smith's Muñoz copy.
[2] Tuxeque, in the Muñoz copy.

and they said it came from a distance.   From what the Indian had said, it is possible that this village of Arae contains more,[1] from the clear description of it which he gave.   We did not find any trace or news of it here.   Francisco Vazquez returned from here to the river of Tiguex, where he found the army.   We went back by a more direct route, because in going by the way we went we traveled 330 leagues, and it is not more than 200 by that by which we returned.   Quivira is in the fortieth degree and the river in the thirty-sixth.   It was so dangerous to travel or to go away from the camp in these plains, that it is as if one was traveling on the sea, since the only roads are those of the cows, and they are so level and have no mountain or prominent landmark, that if one went out of sight of it, he was lost, and in this way we lost one man, and others who went hunting wandered around two or three days, lost.   Two kinds of people travel around these plains with the cows; one is called Querechos and the others Teyas; they are very well built, and painted, and are enemies of each other.   They have no other settlement or location than comes from traveling around with the cows.   They kill all of these they wish, and tan the hides, with which they clothe themselves and make their tents, and they eat the flesh, sometimes even raw, and they also even drink the blood when thirsty.   The tents they make are like field tents, and they set them up over some poles they have made for this purpose, which come together and are tied at the top, and when they go from one place to another they carry them on some dogs they have, of which they have many, and they load them with the tents and poles and other things, for the country is so level, as I said, that they can make use of these, because they carry the poles dragging along on the ground.   The sun is what they worship most.   The skin for the tents is cured on both sides, without the hair, and they have the skins of deer and cows left over.[2] They exchange some cloaks with the natives of the river for corn.

After Francisco Vazquez reached the river, where he found the army, Don Pedro de Tobar came with half the people from the Hearts, and Don Garcia Lopez de Cardenas started off for Mexico, who, besides the fact that his arm was very bad, had permission from the viceroy on account of the death of his brother.   Ten or twelve who were sick went with him, and not a man among them all who could fight.   He reached the town of the Spaniards and found it burned and two Spaniards and many Indians and horses dead, and he returned to the river on this account, escaping from them by good fortune and great exertions.   The cause of this misfortune was that after Don Pedro started and left 40 men there, half of these raised a mutiny and fled, and the Indians, who remembered the bad treatment they had received, attacked them one night and overpowered them because of their carelessness and weakness, and they fled to Culiacan.   Francisco Vazquez fell while running

---

[1] Or mines, as Muñoz guesses.
[2] And jerked beef dried in the sun, in the Muñoz copy only.

THE TEWA PUEBLO OF K'HAPÓO OR SANTA CLARA

a horse about this time and was sick a long time, and after the winter was over he determined to come back, and although they may say something different, he did so, because he wanted to do this more than anything, and so we all came together as far as Culiacan, and each one went where he pleased from there, and Francisco Vazquez came here to Mexico to make his report to the viceroy, who was not at all pleased with his coming, although he pretended so at first. He was pleased that Father Friar Juan de Padilla had stayed there, who went to Quivira, and a Spaniard and a negro with him, and Friar Luis, a very holy lay brother, stayed in Cicuique. We spent two very cold winters at this river, with much snow and thick ice. The river froze one night and remained so for more than a month, so that loaded horses crossed on the ice. The reason these villages are settled in this fashion is supposed to be the great cold, although it is also partly the wars which they have with one another. And this is all that was seen and found out about all that country, which is very barren of fruits and groves. Quivira is a better country, having many huts and not being so cold, although it is more to the north.

TRANSLATION OF A LETTER FROM CORONADO TO THE KING, OCTOBER 20, 1541[1]

LETTER FROM FRANCISCO VAZQUEZ CORONADO TO HIS MAJESTY, IN WHICH HE GIVES AN ACCOUNT OF THE DISCOVERY OF THE PROVINCE OF TIGUEX.

HOLY CATHOLIC CÆSARIAN MAJESTY: On April 20 of this year I wrote to Your Majesty from this province of Tiguex, in reply to a letter from Your Majesty dated in Madrid, June 11 a year ago. I gave a detailed account of this expedition, which the viceroy of New Spain ordered me to undertake in Your Majesty's name to this country which was discovered by Friar Marcos of Nice, the provincial of the order of Holy Saint Francis. I described it all, and the sort of force I have, as Your Majesty had ordered me to relate in my letters; and stated that while I was engaged in the conquest and pacification of the natives of this province, some Indians who were natives of other provinces beyond these had told me that in their country there were much larger villages and better houses than those of the natives of this country, and that they had lords who ruled them, who were served with dishes of gold, and other very magnificent things; and although, as I wrote Your Majesty, I did not believe it before I had set eyes on it, because it was the report of Indians and given for the most part by means of signs, yet as the report appeared to me to be very fine and that it was important that it should be investigated for Your Majesty's service, I determined to go and see it with the men I have here. I started from this province on the 23d of last April, for the place where the Indians wanted to guide me. After nine days' march I reached some plains, so vast that I did not find their limit anywhere that I went, although I traveled over them for more than 300 leagues. And I found such a quantity of cows in these, of the kind that I wrote Your Majesty about, which they have in this country, that it is impossible to number them, for while I was journeying through these plains, until I returned to where I first found them, there was not a day that I lost sight of them. And after seventeen days' march I came to a settlement of Indians who are called Querechos, who travel around with these cows, who do not plant, and who eat the raw flesh and drink the blood of the cows they kill, and they tan the skins of the cows, with which all the people

---

[1] The text of this letter is printed in Pacheco y Cardenas, Documentos de Indias, vol. iii, p. 363, from a copy made by Muñoz, and also in the same collection, vol. xiii, p. 261, from a copy in the Archives of the Indies at Seville. There is a French translation in Ternaux, Cibola volume, p. 255. See the footnote to the preceding document.

THE TEWA PUEBLO OF OHKE OR SAN JUAN

of this country dress themselves here.   They have little field tents made
of the hides of the cows, tanned and greased, very well made, in which
they live while they travel around near the cows, moving with these.
They have dogs which they load, which carry their tents and poles and
belongings.   These people have the best figures of any that I have seen
in the Indies.   They could not give me any account of the country
where the guides were taking me.   I traveled five days more as the
guides wished to lead me, until I reached some plains, with no more
landmarks than as if we had been swallowed up in the sea, where they
strayed about, because there was not a stone, nor a bit of rising ground,
nor a tree, nor a shrub, nor anything to go by.   There is much very fine
pasture land, with good grass.   And while we were lost in these plains,
some horsemen who went off to hunt cows fell in with some Indians who
also were out hunting, who are enemies of those that I had seen in
the last settlement, and of another sort of people who are called Teyas;
they have their bodies and faces all painted, are a large people like the
others, of a very good build; they eat the raw flesh just like the Querechos, and live and travel round with the cows in the same way as these.
I obtained from these an account of the country where the guides were
taking me, which was not like what they had told me, because these made
out that the houses there were not built of stones, with stories, as my
guides had described it, but of straw and skins, and a small supply of
corn there.   This news troubled me greatly, to find myself on these lim-
itless plains, where I was in great need of water, and often had to drink
it so poor that it was more mud than water.   Here the guides confessed
to me that they had not told the truth in regard to the size of the houses,
because these were of straw, but that they had done so regarding the
large number of inhabitants and the other things about their habits.
The Teyas disagreed with this, and on account of this division between
some of the Indians and the others, and also because many of the men
I had with me had not eaten anything except meat for some days,
because we had reached the end of the corn which we carried from this
province, and because they made it out more than forty days' journey
from where I fell in with the Teyas to the country where the guides were
taking me, although I appreciated the trouble and danger there would
be in the journey owing to the lack of water and corn, it seemed to me
best, in order to see if there was anything there of service to Your Majesty, to go forward with only 30 horsemen until I should be able to see
the country, so as to give Your Majesty a true account of what was to
be found in it.   I sent all the rest of the force I had with me to this
province, with Don Tristan de Arellano in command, because it would
have been impossible to prevent the loss of many men, if all had gone
on, owing to the lack of water and because they also had to kill bulls
and cows on which to sustain themselves.   And with only the 30 horsemen whom I took for my escort, I traveled forty-two days after I left
the force, living all this while solely on the flesh of the bulls and cows
which we killed, at the cost of several of our horses which they killed,

because, as I wrote Your Majesty, they are very brave and fierce animals; and going many days without water, and cooking the food with
cow dung, because there is not any kind of wood in all these plains,
away from the gullies and rivers, which are very few.

It was the Lord's pleasure that, after having journeyed across these
deserts seventy-seven days, I arrived at the province they call Quivira,
to which the guides were conducting me, and where they had described
to me houses of stone, with many stories; and not only are they not of
stone, but of straw, but the people in them are as barbarous as all those
whom I have seen and passed before this; they do not have cloaks, nor
cotton of which to make these, but use the skins of the cattle they kill,
which they tan, because they are settled among these on a very large
river. They eat the raw flesh like the Querechos and Teyas; they are
enemies of one another, but are all of the same sort of people, and these
at Quivira have the advantage in the houses they build and in planting
corn. In this province of which the guides who brought me are natives,
they received me peaceably, and although they told me when I set out
for it that I could not succeed in seeing it all in two months, there are
not more than 25 villages of straw houses there and in all the rest of the
country that I saw and learned about, which gave their obedience to Your
Majesty and placed themselves under your royal overlordship. The people here are large. I had several Indians measured, and found that they
were 10 palms in height; the women are well proportioned and their features are more like Moorish women than Indians. The natives here gave
me a piece of copper which a chief Indian wore hung around his neck;
I sent it to the viceroy of New Spain, because I have not seen any other
metal in these parts except this and some little copper bells which I
sent him, and a bit of metal which looks like gold. I do not know
where this came from, although I believe that the Indians who gave it
to me obtained it from those whom I brought here in my service, because
I can not find any other origin for it nor where it came from. The
diversity of languages which exists in this country and my not having
anyone who understood them, because they speak their own language in
each village, has hindered me, because I have been forced to send captains and men in many directions to find out whether there was anything in this country which could be of service to Your Majesty. And
although I have searched with all diligence I have not found or heard
of anything, unless it be these provinces, which are a very small affair.
The province of Quivira is 950 leagues from Mexico. Where I reached
it, it is in the fortieth degree. The country itself is the best I have ever
seen for producing all the products of Spain, for besides the land itself
being very fat and black and being very well watered by the rivulets
and springs and rivers, I found prunes like those of Spain [or I found
everything they have in Spain] and nuts and very good sweet grapes
and mulberries. I have treated the natives of this province, and all
the others whom I found wherever I went, as well as was possible,

agreeably to what Your Majesty had commanded, and they have received no harm in any way from me or from those who went in my company.[1] I remained twenty-five days in this province of Quivira, so as to see and explore the country and also to find out whether there was anything beyond which could be of service to Your Majesty, because the guides who had brought me had given me an account of other provinces beyond this. And what I am sure of is that there is not any gold nor any other metal in all that country, and the other things of which they had told me are nothing but little villages, and in many of these they do not plant anything and do not have any houses except of skins and sticks, and they wander around with the cows; so that the account they gave me was false, because they wanted to persuade me to go there with the whole force, believing that as the way was through such uninhabited deserts, and from the lack of water, they would get us where we and our horses would die of hunger. And the guides confessed this, and said they had done it by the advice and orders of the natives of these provinces. At this, after having heard the account of what was beyond, which I have given above, I returned to these provinces to provide for the force I had sent back here and to give Your Majesty an account of what this country amounts to, because I wrote Your Majesty that I would do so when I went there. I have done all that I possibly could to serve Your Majesty and to discover a country where God Our Lord might be served and the royal patrimony of Your Majesty increased, as your loyal servant and vassal. For since I reached the province of Cibola, to which the viceroy of New Spain sent me in the name of Your Majesty, seeing that there were none of the things there of which Friar Marcos had told, I have managed to explore this country for 200 leagues and more around Cibola, and the best place I have found is this river of Tiguex where I am now, and the settlements here. It would not be possible to establish a settlement here, for besides being 400 leagues from the North sea and more than 200 from the South sea, with which it is impossible to have any sort of communication, the country is so cold, as I have written to Your Majesty, that apparently the winter could not possibly be spent here, because there is no wood, nor cloth with which to protect the men, except the skins which the natives wear and some small amount of cotton cloaks. I send the viceroy of New Spain an account of everything I have seen in the countries where I have been, and as Don Garcia Lopez de Cardenas is going to kiss Your Majesty's hands, who has done much and has served Your Majesty very well on this expedition, and he will give Your Majesty an account of everything here, as one who has seen it himself, I give way to him. And may Our Lord protect the Holy Imperial Catholic person of Your Majesty, with increase of greater kingdoms and powers, as your loyal servants and vassals desire.   From this province of Tiguex, October 20, in the year 1541. Your Majesty's humble servant and vassal, who would kiss the royal feet and hands:

FRANCISCO VAZQUEZ CORONADO.

---

[1] Coronado had apparently forgotten the atrocities committed by the Spaniards at Tiguex.

TRANSLATION OF THE NARRATIVE OF JARAMILLO

ACCOUNT GIVEN BY CAPTAIN JUAN JARAMILLO OF THE JOURNEY WHICH HE MADE TO THE NEW COUNTRY, ON WHICH FRANCISCO VAZQUEZ CORONADO WAS THE GENERAL.[1]

We started from Mexico, going directly to Compostela, the whole way populated and at peace, the direction being west, and the distance 112 leagues. From there we went to Culiacan, perhaps about 80 leagues; the road is well known and much used, because there is a town inhabited by Spaniards in the said valley of Culiacan, under the government of Compostela. The 70 horsemen who went with the general went in a northwesterly direction from this town. He left his army here, because information had been obtained that the way was uninhabited and almost the whole of it without food. He went with the said horsemen to explore the route and prepare the way for those who were to follow. He pursued this direction, though with some twisting, until we crossed a mountain chain, where they knew about New Spain, more than 300 leagues distant. To this pass we gave the name of Chichilte Calli, because we learned that this was what it was called, from some Indians whom we left behind.

Leaving the said valley of Culiacan, he crossed a river called Pateatlan (or Peteatlan), which was about four days distant. We found these Indians peaceful, and they gave us some few things to eat. From here we went to another river called Cinaloa, which was about three days from the other. From here the general ordered ten of us horsemen to make double marches, lightly equipped, until we reached the stream of the Cedars (arroyo de los Cedros), and from there we were to enter a break in the mountains on the right of the road and see what there was in and about this. If more time should be needed for this than we gained on him, he would wait for us at the said Cedros stream. This was done, and all that we saw there was a few poor Indians in some settled valleys like farms or estates, with sterile soil. It was about five more days from the river to this stream. From there we went to the river called Yaquemi, which took about three days. We proceeded along a dry stream, and after three days more of marching, although the dry stream lasted only for a league, we reached another stream where there were some settled Indians, who had straw huts and storehouses of corn and beans and melons. Leaving here, we went to

---

[1] The text of this narrative is found in Buckingham Smith's Florida, p. 154, from a copy made by Muñoz, and in Pacheco y Cardenas, Documentos de Indias, vol. xiv, p. 304, from the copy in the Archives of the Indies. A French translation is given in Ternaux-Compans' Cibola volume, p. 364.

A NATIVE OF SAN JUAN

the stream and village which is called Hearts (Corazones), the name which was given it by Dorantes and Cabeza de Vaca and Castillo and the negro Estebanillo, because they gave them a present of the hearts of animals and birds to eat.

About two days were spent in this village of the Hearts. There is an irrigation stream, and the country is warm. Their dwellings are huts made of a frame of poles, almost like an oven, only very much better, which they cover with mats. They have corn and beans and melons for food, which I believe never fail them. They dress in deerskins. This appeared to be a good place, and so orders were given the Spaniards who were behind to establish a village here, where they lived until almost the failure of the expedition. There was a poison here, the effect of which is, according to what was seen of it, the worst that could possibly be found; and from what we learned about it, it is the sap of a small tree like the mastick tree, or lentisk, and it grows in gravelly and sterile land.[1] We went on from here, passing through a sort of gateway, to another valley very near this stream, which opens off from this same stream, which is called Señora. It is also irrigated, and the Indians are like the others and have the same sort of settlements and food. This valley continues for 6 or 7 leagues, a little more or less. At first these Indians were peaceful; and afterward not, but instead they and those whom they were able to summon thither were our worst enemies. They have a poison with which they killed several Christians. There are mountains on both sides of them, which are not very fertile. From here we went along near this said stream, crossing it where it makes a bend, to another Indian settlement called Ispa.[2] It takes one day from the last of these others to this place. It is of the same sort as those we had passed. From here we went through deserted country for about four days to another river, which we heard called Nexpa, where some poor Indians came out to see the general, with presents of little value, with some stalks of roasted maguey and pitahayas. We went down this stream two days, and then left the stream, going toward the right to the foot of the mountain chain in two days' journey, where we heard news of what is called Chichiltic Calli. Crossing the mountains, we came to a deep and reedy river, where we found water and forage for the horses.

[1] The Spanish text reads: "Habrá como dos jornadas (;) en este pueblo de los Corazones. (es) Es un arroyo de riego y de tierra caliente, y tienen sus viviendas de unos ranchos que despues de armados los palos, casi á manera de hornos, aunque muy mayores, los cubren con unos petates. Tienen maiz y frisoles y calabazas para su comer, que creo que no le falta. Vístense de cueros de venados, y aquí por ser este puesto al parecer cosa decente, se mandó poblar aquí una villa de los españoles que iban traseros donde vivieron hasta casi que la jornada pereció. Aquí hay yerba y seguro (segund) lo que della se vió, y la operacion que hace es la más mala que se puede hallar, y de lo que tuvimos entendido ser, era de la leche de un árbol pequeño, á manera de lantisco en cuasci, (, E Nasce) en pizarrillas y tierra estéril.", This quotation follows the Pacheco y Cardenas text. The important variations of Buckingham Smith's copy are inclosed within parentheses. The spelling of the two, in such matters as the use of b and v, x and j, and the punctuation, differ greatly.

[2] See Bandelier's Gilded Man, p. 175. This is Castañeda's "Guagarispa" as mistakenly interpreted by Ternaux-Compans, the present Arispe, or, in the Indian dialect, Huc-aritz-pa. The words "Ispa, que" are not in the Pacheco y Cardenas copy.

From this river back at Nexpa, as I have said, it seems to me that the direction was nearly northeast. From here, I believe that we went in the same direction for three days to a river which we called Saint John (San Juan), because we reached it on his day. Leaving here, we went to another river, through a somewhat rough country, more toward the north, to a river which we called the Rafts (de las Balsas), because we had to cross on these, as it was rising. It seems to me that we spent two days between one river and the other, and I say this because it is so long since we went there that I may be wrong in some days, though not in the rest. From here we went to another river, which we called the Slough (de la Barranca.) It is two short days from one to the other, and the direction almost northeast. From here we went to another river, which we called the Cold river (el rio Frio), on account of its water being so, in one day's journey, and from here we went by a pine mountain, where we found, almost at the top of it, a cool spring and streamlet, which was another day's march. In the neighborhood of this stream a Spaniard, who was called Espinosa, died, besides two other persons, on account of poisonous plants which they ate, owing to the great need in which they were. From here we went to another river, which we called the Red river (Bermejo), two days' journey in the same direction, but less toward the northeast. Here we saw an Indian or two, who afterward appeared to belong to the first settlement of Cibola. From here we came in two days' journey to the said village, the first of Cibola. The houses have flat roofs and walls of stone and mud, and this was where they killed Steve (Estebanillo), the negro who had come with Dorantes from Florida and returned with Friar Marcos de Niza. In this province of Cibola there are five little villages besides this, all with flat roofs and of stone and mud, as I said. The country is cold, as is shown by their houses and hothouses (estufas). They have food enough for themselves, of corn and beans and melons. These villages are about a league or more apart from each other, within a circuit of perhaps 6 leagues. The country is somewhat sandy and not very salty (or barren of vegetation[1]), and on the mountains the trees are for the most part evergreen. The clothing of the Indians is of deerskins, very carefully tanned, and they also prepare some tanned cowhides, with which they cover themselves, which are like shawls, and a great protection. They have square cloaks of cotton, some larger than others, about a yard and a half long. The Indians wear them thrown over the shoulder like a gipsy, and fastened with one end over the other, with a girdle, also of cotton. From this first village of Cibola, looking toward the northeast and a little less, on the left hand, there is a province called Tucayan, about five days off, which has seven flat-roof villages, with a food supply as good as or better than these, and

---

[1] The Spanish text is either "ino mui salada de yerva" (B. Smith), or "y no muy solada de yerva" (Pacheco y Cardenas). Doubtless the reference is to the alkali soil and vegetation.

an even larger population; and they also have the skins of cows and of deer, and cloaks of cotton, as I described.[1]

All the waterways we found as far as this one at Cibola— and I do not know but what for a day or two beyond—the rivers and streams run into the South sea, and those from here on into the North sea.

From this first village of Cibola, as I have said, we went to another in the same province, which was about a short day's journey off, on the way to Tihuex. It is nine days, of such marches as we made, from this settlement of Cibola to the river of Tihuex. Halfway between, I do not know but it may be a day more or less, there is a village of earth and dressed stone, in a very strong position, which is called Tutahaco.[2] All these Indians, except the first in the first village of Cibola, received us well. At the river of Tihuex there are 15 villages within a distance of about 20 leagues, all with flat-roof houses of earth, instead of stone, after the fashion of mud walls. There are other villages besides these on other streams which flow into this, and three of these are, for Indians, well worth seeing, especially one that is called Chia,[3] and another Uraba,[4] and another Cicuique.[5] Uraba and Cicuique have many houses two stories high. All the rest, and these also, have corn and beans and melons, skins, and some long robes of feathers which they braid, joining the feathers with a sort of thread; and they also make them of a sort of plain weaving with which they make the cloaks with which they protect themselves. They all have hot rooms underground, which, although not very clean, are very warm.[6] They raise and have a very little cotton, of which they make the cloaks which I have spoken of above. This river comes from the northwest and flows about southeast, which shows that it certainly flows into the North sea. Leaving this settlement[7] and the said river, we passed two other villages whose names I do not know,[8] and in four days came to Cicuique, which I have already mentioned. The direction of this is toward the northeast. From there we came to another river, which the Spaniards named after Cicuique, in three days; if I remember rightly, it seems to me that we went rather toward the northeast to reach this river where we crossed it, and after crossing this, we turned more to

---

[1]The Spanish text (p. 308) is: "el vestido de los indios es de cueros de venados, estremadísimo el adobo, alcanzan ya algunos cueros de vacas adobado con que se cobijan, que son á manera de bernias y de mucho abrigo; tienen mantas de algodon cuadradas; unas mayores que otras, como de vara y media en largo; las indias las traen puestas por el hombro á manera de gitanas y ceñidas una vuelta sobre otra por su cintura con una cinta del mismo algodon; estando en este pueblo primero de Cibola, el rostro el Nordeste; un poquito ménos está á la mano izquierda de él, cinco jornadas, una provincia que se dice Tucayan."

[2]Acoma. See note on page 492.

[3]Sia.

[4]Identical with Taos—the Braba of Castañeda and the Yuraba of the Relacion del Suceso.

[5]Pecos. In Pacheco y Cardenas this is spelled Tienique.

[6]All references to hot rooms or estufas are of course to be construed to mean the kivas or ceremonial chambers.

[7]Tiguex is here doubtless referred to.

[8]One of the villages whose names Jaramillo did not know was probably the Ximena (Galisteo) of Castañeda.

the left hand, which would be more to the northeast, and began to enter the plains where the cows are, although we did not find them for some four or five days, after which we began to come across bulls, of which there are great numbers, and after going on in the same direction and meeting the bulls for two or three days, we began to find ourselves in the midst of very great numbers of cows, yearlings and bulls all in together. We found Indians among these first cows, who were, on this account, called Querechos by those in the flat-roof houses. They do not live in houses, but have some sets of poles which they carry with them to make some huts at the places where they stop, which serve them for houses. They tie these poles together at the top and stick the bottoms into the ground, covering them with some cowskins which they carry around, and which, as I have said, serve them for houses. From what was learned of these Indians, all their human needs are supplied by these cows, for they are fed and clothed and shod from these. They are a people who wander around here and there, wherever seems to them best. We went on for eight or ten days in the same direction, along those streams which are among the cows. The Indian who guided us from here was the one that had given us the news about Quevira and Arache (*or* Arahei) and about its being a very rich country with much gold and other things, and he and the other one were from that country I mentioned, to which we were going, and we found these two Indians in the flat-roof villages. It seems that, as the said Indian wanted to go to his own country, he proceeded to tell us what we found was not true, and I do not know whether it was on this account or because he was counseled to take us into other regions by confusing us on the road, although there are none in all this region except those of the cows. We understood, however, that he was leading us away from the route we ought to follow and that he wanted to lead us on to those plains where he had led us, so that we would eat up the food, and both ourselves and our horses would become weak from the lack of this, because if we should go either backward or forward in this condition we could not make any resistance to whatever they might wish to do to us. From the time when, as I said, we entered the plains and from this settlement of Querechos, he led us off more to the east, until we came to be in extreme need from the lack of food, and as the other Indian, who was his companion and also from his country, saw that he was not taking us where we ought to go, since we had always followed the guidance of the Turk, for so he was called, instead of his, he threw himself down in the way, making a sign that although we cut off his head he ought not to go that way, nor was that our direction. I believe we had been traveling twenty days or more in this direction, at the end of which we found another settlement of Indians of the same sort and way of living as those behind, among whom there was an old blind man with a beard, who gave us to understand, by signs which he made,

A NATIVE OF PECOS

that he had seen four others like us many days before, whom he had seen near there and rather more toward New Spain, and we so understood him, and presumed that it was Dorantes and Cabeza de Vaca and those whom I have mentioned. At this settlement the general, seeing our difficulties, ordered the captains, and the persons whose advice he was accustomed to take, to assemble, so that we might discuss with him what was best for all. It seemed to us that all the force should go back to the region we had come from, in search of food, so that they could regain their strength, and that 30 picked horsemen should go in search of what the Indian had told about; and we decided to do this. We all went forward one day to a stream which was down in a ravine in the midst of good meadows, to agree on who should go ahead and how the rest should return. Here the Indian Isopete, as we had called the companion of the said Turk, was asked to tell us the truth, and to lead us to that country which we had come in search of. He said he would do it, and that it was not as the Turk had said, because those were certainly fine things which he had said and had given us to understand at Tihuex, about gold and how it was obtained, and the buildings, and the style of them, and their trade, and many other things told for the sake of prolixity, which had led us to go in search of them, with the advice of all who gave it and of the priests. He asked us to leave him afterward in that country, because it was his native country, as a reward for guiding us, and also, that the Turk might not go along with him, because he would quarrel and try to restrain him in everything that he wanted to do for our advantage; and the general promised him this, and said he would be with one of the thirty, and he went in this way. And when everything was ready for us to set out and for the others to remain, we pursued our way, the direction all the time after this being toward the north, for more than thirty days' march, although not long marches, not having to go without water on any one of them, and among cows all the time, some days in larger numbers than others, according to the water which we came across, so that on Saint Peter and Paul's day we reached a river which we found to be there below Quibira. When we reached the said river, the Indian recognized it and said that was it, and that it was below the settlements. We crossed it there and went up the other side on the north, the direction turning toward the northeast, and after marching three days we found some Indians who were going hunting, killing the cows to take the meat to their village, which was about three or four days still farther away from us. Here where we found the Indians and they saw us, they began to utter yells and appeared to fly, and some even had their wives there with them. The Indian Isopete began to call them in his language, and so they came to us without any signs of fear. When we and these Indians had halted here, the general made an example of the Indian Turk, whom we had brought along, keeping him all the time out of sight among the rear guard, and having arrived where the place was prepared, it was done in such a way that the other Indian, who was called Isopete, should not see it, so as to give him the satisfaction he had asked. Some satisfaction was experienced here on seeing the good appearance of the earth, and it is certainly such among the cows, and from there on. The general wrote a letter here to the governor of Harahey and Quibira, having understood that he was a Christian from the lost army of Florida, because what the Indian had said of their manner of government and their general character had made us believe this. So the Indians went to their houses, which were at the distance mentioned, and we also proceeded at our rate of marching until we reached the settlements, which we found along good river bottoms, although without much water, and good streams which flow into another, larger than the one I have mentioned. There were, if I recall correctly, six or seven settlements, at quite a distance from one another, among which we traveled for four or five days, since it was understood to be uninhabited between one stream and the other. We reached what they said was the end of Quibira, to which they took us, saying that the things there were of great importance.[1] Here there was a river, with more water and more inhabitants than the others. Being asked if there was anything beyond, they said that there was nothing more of Quibira, but that there was Harahey, and that it was the same sort of a place, with settlements like these, and of about the same size. The general sent to summon the lord of those parts and the other Indians who they said resided in Harahey, and he came with about 200 men—all naked—with bows, and some sort of things on their heads, and their privy parts slightly covered. He was a big Indian, with a large body and limbs, and well proportioned. After he had heard the opinion of one and another about it, the general asked them what we ought to do, reminding us of how the army had been left and that the rest of us were there, so that it seemed to all of us that as it was already almost the opening of winter, for, if I remember rightly, it was after the middle of August, and because there was little to winter there for, and we were but very little prepared for it, and the uncertainty as to the success of the army that had been left, and because the winter might close the roads with snow and rivers which we could not cross, and also in order to see what had happened to the rest of the force left behind, it seemed to us all that his grace ought to go back in search of them, and when he had found out for certain how they were, to winter there and return to that country at the opening of spring, to conquer and cultivate it. Since, as I said, this was the last point which we reached, here the Turk saw that he had lied to us, and one night he called on all these people to attack us and kill us. We learned of it, and put him under guard and strangled him that night so that he never waked up. With the plan

---

[1] In Buckingham Smith's copy occurs the phrase, "que decian ellos para significarnoslo Teucarea." This is not in Pacheco y Cardenas.

mentioned, we turned back it may have been two or three days, where we provided ourselves with picked fruit and dried corn for our return. The general raised a cross at this place, at the foot of which he made some letters with a chisel, which said that Francisco Vazquez de Coronado, general of that army, had arrived here.

This country presents a very fine appearance, than which I have not seen a better in all our Spain nor Italy nor a part of France, nor, indeed, in the other countries where I have traveled in His Majesty's service, for it is not a very rough country, but is made up of hillocks and plains, and very fine appearing rivers and streams, which certainly satisfied me and made me sure that it will be very fruitful in all sorts of products. Indeed, there is profit in the cattle ready to the hand, from the quantity of them, which is as great as one could imagine. We found a variety of Castilian prunes which are not all red, but some of them black and green; the tree and fruit is certainly like that of Castile, with a very excellent flavor. Among the cows we found flax, which springs up from the earth in clumps apart from one another, which are noticeable, as the cattle do not eat it, with their tops and blue flowers, and very perfect although small, resembling that of our own Spain (*or* and sumach like ours in Spain). There are grapes along some streams, of a fair flavor, not to be improved upon. The houses which these Indians have were of straw, and most of them round, and the straw reached down to the ground like a wall, so that they did not have the symmetry or the style of these here; they have something like a chapel or sentry box outside and around these, with an entry, where the Indians appear seated or reclining.[1] The Indian Isopete was left here where the cross was erected, and we took five or six of the Indians from these villages to lead and guide us to the flat-roof houses.[2] Thus they brought us back by the same road as far as where I said before that we came to a river called Saint Peter and Paul's, and here we left that by which we had come, and, taking the right hand, they led us along by watering places and among cows and by a good road, although there are none either one way or the other except those of the cows, as I have said. At last we came to where we recognized the country, where I said we found the first settlement,

---

[1] The Spanish text (p. 315) of this description of the Kansas-Nebraska plains is: "Esta tierra tiene muy linda la apariencia, tal que no la he visto yo mejor . . . porque no es tierra muy doblada sino de lo más (de lomas) y llanos, y rios de muy linda apariencia y aguas, que cierto me contento y tengo presuncion que será muy fructífera y de todos frutos. En los ganados ya está la esperencia (inspiriencia) en la mano por la muchedumbre que hay, que es tanta cuanto quieran pensar: jallamos cirguelas de Castilla, un género dellas que ni son del todo coloradas, sino entre coloradas y algo negras y verdes. (,) El árbol y el fruto es cierto de Castilla, de muy gentil sabor; jallamos entre las vacas, lino, que produce la tierra, é brecitas (hebrecitas) arredradas unas de otras, que como el ganado no las come se quedan por allí con sus cabezuelas y flor azul, y aunque pequeño muy perfecto, natural del de nuestra España (perfecto; zumaque natural . . .). En algunos arroyos, uvas de razonable sabor para no beneficiadas: las casas que estos indios tenian, eran de paxa y muchas dellas redondas, y la paxa llegaba hasta el suelo como pared que no tenia la proporcion y manera de las de acá; por de fuera y encima desto, tenian una manera como capilla ó garita, con una entrada donde se asomaban los indios sentados ó echados."

[2] The pueblos of the Rio Grande.

where the Turk led us astray from the route we should have followed. Thus, leaving the rest aside, we reached Tiguex, where we found the rest of the army, and here the general fell while running his horse, by which he received a wound on his head which gave symptoms of turning out badly, and he conceived the idea of returning, which ten or twelve of us were unable to prevent by dissuading him from it. When this return had been ordered, the Franciscan friars who were with us—one of them a regular and the other a lay brother—who were called, the regular one Friar Juan de Padilla and the lay one Friar Luis de Escalona, were told to get ready, although they had permission from their provincial so that they could remain. Friar Luis wished to remain in these flat-roof houses, saying that he would raise crosses for those villagers with a chisel and adze they left him, and would baptize several poor creatures who could be led, on the point of death, so as to send them to heaven, for which he did not desire any other company than a little slave of mine who was called Christopher, to be his consolation, and who he said would learn the language there quickly so as to help him; and he brought up so many things in favor of this that he could not be denied, and so nothing more has been heard from him. The knowledge that this friar would remain there was the reason that many Indians from hereabouts stayed there, and also two negroes, one of them mine, who was called Sebastian, and the other one of Melchor Perez, the son of the licentiate La Torre. This negro was married and had his wife and children. I also recall that several Indians remained behind in the Quivira region, besides a Tarascan belonging to my company, who was named Andrew. Friar Juan de Padilla preferred to return to Quivira, and persuaded them to give him those Indians whom I said we had brought as guides. They gave him these, and he also took a Portuguese and a free Spanish-speaking Indian, who was the interpreter, and who passed as a Franciscan friar, and a half-blood and two Indians from Capottan (or Capotean) or thereabouts, I believe. He had brought these up and took them in the habits of friars, and he took some sheep and mules and a horse and ornaments and other trifles. I do not know whether it was for the sake of these or for what reason, but it seems that they killed him, and those who did it were the lay servants, or these same Indians whom he took back from Tiguex, in return for the good deeds which he had done. When he was dead, the Portuguese whom I mentioned fled, and also one of the Indians that I said he took in the habits of friars, or both of them, I believe. I mention this because they came back to this country of New Spain by another way and a shorter route than the one of which I have told, and they came out in the valley of Panico.[1] I have given Gonzalo Solis de Meras and Isidoro de Solis an account of this, because it seemed to me important, according to what I say I have understood, that

---

[1] This is the spelling of Panuco in both texts.

His Majesty ordered Your Lordship to find or discover a way so as to unite that land to this. It is perhaps also very likely that this Indian Sebastian, during the time he was in Quivira, learned about its territory and the country round about it, and also of the sea, and the road by which he came, and what there is to it, and how many days' journey before arriving there. So that I am sure that if Your Lordship acquires this Quivira on this account, I am certain that he can confidently bring many people from Spain to settle it according to the appearance and the character of the land.

14 ETH——38

TRANSLATION OF THE REPORT OF HERNANDO DE ALVARADO

ACCOUNT OF WHAT HERNANDO DE ALVARADO AND FRIAR JUAN DE PADILLA DISCOVERED GOING IN SEARCH OF THE SOUTH SEA.[1]

We set out from Granada on Sunday, the day of the beheading of Saint John the Baptist, the 29th of August, in the year 1540, on the way to Coco.[2] After we had gone 2 leagues, we came to an ancient building like a fortress, and a league beyond this we found another, and yet another a little farther on, and beyond these we found an ancient city, very large, entirely destroyed, although a large part of the wall was standing, which was six times as tall as a man, the wall well made of good worked stone, with gates and gutters like a city in Castile. Half a league or more beyond this, we found another ruined city, the walls of which must have been very fine, built of very large granite blocks, as high as a man and from there up of very good quarried stone. Here two roads separate, one to Chia and the other to Coco; we took this latter, and reached that place, which is one of the strongest places that we have seen, because the city is on a very high rock, with such a rough ascent that we repented having gone up to the place. The houses have three or four stories; the people are the same sort as those of the province of Cibola; they have plenty of food, of corn and beans and fowls like those of New Spain. From here we went to a very good lake or marsh, where there are trees like those of Castile, and from there we went to a river, which we named Our Lady (Nuestra Señora), because we reached it the evening before her day in the month of September.[3] We sent the cross by a guide to the villages in advance, and the next day people came from twelve villages, the chief men and the people in order, those of one village behind those of another, and they approached the tent to the sound of a pipe, and with an old man for spokesman. In this fashion they came into the tent and gave me the food and clothes and skins they had brought, and I gave them some trinkets, and with this they went off.

This river of Our Lady flows through a very wide open plain sowed with corn plants; there are several groves, and there are twelve vil-

---

[1] The text of this report is printed in Buckingham Smith's Florida, p. 65, from the Muñoz copy, and in Pacheco y Cardenas, Documentos de Indias, vol. iii, p. 511. See note on page 391. A translation of this document was printed in the Boston Transcript for October 14, 1893.

[2] Acuco or Acoma. The route taken by Alvarado was not the same as that followed by Coronado, who went by way of Matsaki. Alvarado's course was the old Acoma trail which led directly eastward from Hawikuh or Ojo Caliente.

[3] Day of the nativity of the Blessed Virgin, September 8. This was the Tiguex or present Rio Grande.

384

lages. The houses are of earth, two stories high; the people have a good appearance, more like laborers than a warlike race; they have a large food supply of corn, beans, melons, and fowl in great plenty; they clothe themselves with cotton and the skins of cows and dresses of the feathers of the fowls; they wear their hair short. Those who have the most authority among them are the old men; we regarded them as witches, because they say that they go up into the sky and other things of the same sort. In this province there are seven other villages, depopulated and destroyed by those Indians who paint their eyes, of whom the guides will tell Your Grace; they say that these live in the same region as the cows, and that they have corn and houses of straw.

Here the people from the outlying provinces came to make peace with me, and as Your Grace may see in this memorandum, there are 80 villages there of the same sort as I have described, and among them one which is located on some streams; it is divided into twenty divisions, which is something remarkable; the houses have three stories of mud walls and three others made of small wooden boards, and on the outside of the three stories with the mud wall they have three balconies; it seemed to us that there were nearly 15,000 persons in this village. The country is very cold; they do not raise fowls nor cotton; they worship the sun and water. We found mounds of dirt outside of the place, where they are buried.

In the places where crosses were raised, we saw them worship these. They made offerings to these of their powder and feathers, and some left the blankets they had on. They showed so much zeal that some climbed up on the others to grasp the arms of the cross, to place feathers and flowers there; and others bringing ladders, while some held them, went up to tie strings, so as to fasten the flowers and the feathers.

TESTIMONY CONCERNING THOSE WHO WENT ON THE EXPEDITION WITH FRANCISCO VAZQUEZ CORONADO[1]

At Compostela, on February 21, 1540, Coronado presented a petition to the viceroy Mendoza, declaring that he had observed that certain persons who were not well disposed toward the expedition which was about to start for the newly discovered country had said that many of the inhabitants of the City of Mexico and of the other cities and towns of New Spain, and also of Compostela and other places in this province of New Galicia were going on the expedition at his request or because of inducements offered by him, as a result of which the City of Mexico and New Spain were left deserted, or almost so. Therefore, he asked the viceroy to order that information be obtained, in order that the truth might be known about the citizens of New Spain and of this province who were going to accompany him. He declared that there were very few of these, and that they were not going on account of any attraction or inducement offered by him, but of their own free will, and as there were few of them, there would not be any lack of people in New Spain. And as Gonzalo de Salazar, the factor or royal agent, and Pero Almidez Cherino, the veedor or royal inspector of His Majesty for New Spain, and other citizens of Mexico who knew all the facts and had the necessary information, were present there, Coronado asked His Grace to provide and order that which would best serve His Majesty's interests and the welfare and security of New Spain.

The viceroy instructed the licenciate Maldonado, oidor of the royal audiencia,[2] to procure this information. To facilitate the hearing he provided that the said factor and veedor and the regidores, and others who were there, should attend the review of the army, which was to be held on the following day. Nine of the desired witnesses were also commanded by Maldonado to attend the review and observe those whom they knew in the army.

On February 26[3] the licentiate Maldonado took the oaths of the witnesses in proper form, and they testified to the following effect:

Hernand Perez de Bocanegra, a citizen of Mexico, stated that he had been present on the preceding Sunday, at the review of the force which the viceroy was sending for the pacification of the country recently discovered by the father provincial, Fray Marcos de Niza, and that he

---

[1]Translated freely and abridged from the depositions as printed in Pacheco y Cardenas, Documentos de Indias, vol. xiv, p. 373. See note on page 377. The statements of the preceding witnesses are usually repeated, in effect, in the testimony of those who follow.

[2]Judge of the highest court of the province.

[3]Thursday.

386

had taken note of the force as the men passed before him; and at his request he had also been allowed to see the list of names of those who were enrolled in the army; and he declared that in all the said force he did not recognize any other citizens of Mexico who were going except Domingo Martin, a married man, whom he had sometimes seen living in Mexico, and provided him with messengers; and one Alonso Sanchez, who was going with his wife and a son, and who was formerly a shoe-maker; and a young man, son of the *bachiller* Alonso Perez, who had come only a few days before from Salamanca, and who had been sent to the war by his father on account of his restlessness; and two or three other workmen or tradespeople whom he had seen at work in Mexico, although he did not know whether they were citizens there; and on his oath he did not see in the whole army anyone else who was a citizen of Mexico, although for about fourteen years he had been a citizen and inhabitant of that city, unless it was the captain-general, Francisco Vazquez de Coronado, and Lopez de Samaniego the army-master; and, moreover, he declared that he felt certain that those above mentioned were going of their own free will, like all the rest.

Antonio Serrano de Cardona, one of the magistrates of Mexico, who was present from beginning to end of the review of the preceding Sunday, testified in similar form. He said that Alonso Sanchez had formerly been a citizen of Mexico, but that for a long time his house had been empty and he had traveled as a trader, and that he was going in search of something to live on; and one Domingo Martin was also going, who formerly lived in Mexico, and whose residence he had not known likewise for a long time, nor did he think that he had one, because he had not seen him living in Mexico. He did not think it would have been possible for any citizens of Mexico to have been there whom he did not know, because he had lived in Mexico during the twenty years since he came to Mexico, and ever since the city was established by Christians, and besides, he had been a magistrate for fifteen years. And besides, all those whom he did see who were going, were the most contented of any men he had ever seen in this country starting off for conquests. After the force left the City of Mexico, he had been there, and had noticed that it was full of people and that there did not seem to be any scarcity on account of those who had started on this expedition.

Gonzalo de Salazar, His Majesty's factor for New Spain, and also a magistrate of the City of Mexico, declared that the only person on the expedition who possessed a repartimiento or estate in New Spain was the captain-general, Vazquez de Coronado, and that he had noticed one other citizen who did not have a repartimiento. He had not seen any other citizen of Mexico, nor of New Spain, although one of the greatest benefits that could have been done New Spain would have been to draw off the young and vicious people who were in that city and all over New Spain.

Pedro Almidez Cherino, His Majesty's veedor in New Spain, had, among other things, noted the horses and arms of those who were going, during the review. He had noticed Coronado and Samaniego, and Alonso Sanchez and his wife, whom he did not know to be a citizen, and Domingo Martin, who was away from Mexico during most of the year. All the rest of the force were people without settled residences, who had recently come to the country in search of a living. It seemed to him that it was a very fortunate thing for Mexico that the people who were going were about to do so because they had been injuring the citizens there. They had been for the most part vicious young gentlemen, who did not have anything to do in the city nor in the country. They were all going of their own free will, and were very ready to help pacify the new country, and it seemed to him that if the said country had not been discovered, almost all of these people would have gone back to Castile, or would have gone to Peru or other places in search of a living.

Servan Bejarano, who had been in business among the inhabitants of Mexico ever since he came to that city, added the information that he knew Alonso Sanchez to be a provision dealer, buying at wholesale and selling at retail, and that he was in very great need, having nothing on which to live, and that he was going to that country in search of a living. He was also very sure that it was a great advantage to Mexico and to its citizens to have many of the unmarried men go away, because they had no occupation there and were bad characters, and were for the most part gentlemen and persons who did not hold any property, nor any repartimientos of Indians, without any income, and lazy, and who would have been obliged to go to Peru or some other region.

Cristobal de Oñate had been in the country about sixteen years, a trifle more or less, and was now His Majesty's veedor for New Galicia. He knew the citizens of Mexico, and also declared that not a citizen of Compostela was going on the expedition. Two citizens of Guadalajara were going, one of whom was married to an Indian, and the other was single. As for the many young gentlemen and the others who were going, who lived in Mexico and in other parts of New Spain, it seemed to him that their departure was a benefit rather than a disadvantage, because they were leading vicious lives and had nothing with which to support themselves.

When these statements and depositions had all been duly received, signed, and attested, and had been shown to his most illustrious lord-ship, the viceroy, he ordered an authorized copy to be taken, which was made by Joan de Leon, clerk of Their Majesties' court and of the royal audiencia of New Spain, the 27th of February, 1540, witnessed by the secretary, Antonio de Almaguer, and sent to His Majesty, to be laid before the lords of the council, that they might provide and order that which should be most serviceable to their interests.

A LIST OF WORKS

USEFUL TO THE STUDENT OF THE CORONADO EXPEDITION

The following list contains the titles of the books and documents which have been found useful during the preparation of the preceding memoir on the Coronado expedition of 1540–1542. The works cited have helped, in one way or another, toward the formation of the opinions expressed in the Historical Introduction, and in them may be found the authority for the statements made in the introduction and in the notes to the translations of the Spanish narratives. It is hoped that no source of information of prime importance has been overlooked. The comments on the various books, essays, and documents are such as suggested themselves in the course of the examination of the works in question.

References are given to the location of the more important documents, so far as these are available in the various collections of printed documents. The value of these sources has been discussed in the preceding pages, and these opinions are not repeated in this list. The titles of the printed books are quoted from the editions which came nearest to the authors' manuscripts, so far as these editions could be consulted. Reference is made also to the most available later editions, and to the English and French translations of Spanish, Italian, and Latin works. With hardly an exception, the titles are quoted from the volumes themselves, as they were found in the Harvard College Library or in the John Carter Brown Library of Providence. The Lenox Library of New York supplied such volumes as were not to be found in Cambridge, Boston, or Providence.

Dr Justin Winsor and Mr F. W. Hodge have rendered very material assistance in giving this list such completeness as it possesses. To Mr Hodge especially are due many of the titles which relate to the ethnological and archeological aspects of the subject.

Abelin, Johann Phillip; *pseud.* Johann Ludwig Gottfriedt.
Newe Welt vnd Americanische Historien.—Franckfurt, M. DC. LV.
Page 560. Beschreibung der grossen Landschafft Cibola.

Alarcon, Hernando.
De lo que hizo por la mar Hernando de Alarcon, que con dos nauios andaua por la costa por orden del Visorrey don Antonio de Mendoça.
Herrera, Dec. VI, lib. ix, cap. xlii.

— Relatione della Navigatione & scoperta che fece il Capitano Fernando Alarcone per ordine dello Illustrissimo Signor Don Antonio di Mendozza Vice Re della nuoua Spagna.
Ramusio, III, fol. 363–370, edition of 1556; III, fol. 303 verso, edition of 1606.

— The relation of the nauigation and discouery which Captaine Fernando Alarchon made by the order of the right honourable Lord Don Antonio de Mendoça vizeroy of New Spaine.
Hakluyt, III, 425–439, edition of 1600. This translation is made from Ramusio's text.

— Relation de la navigation et de la découverte faite par le capitaine Fernando Alarcon. Par l'ordre de . . . don Antonio de Mendoza.
Ternaux, IX (Cibola volume), 299–348. From Ramusio's text.

Alarcon, Hernando—Continued.
— Relacion del armada del Marqués del Valle, capitaneada de Francisco de Ulloa . . . y de la que el virey de Nueva España envió con un Alarcon.
Doc. de España, IV, 218–219. A very brief, probably contemporary, mention of the discovery of Colorado river.

Alvarado, Hernando de.
Relacion de lo que Hernando de Alvarado y Fray Joan de Padilla descubrieron en demanda de la mar del Sur.—Agosto de 1540.
Doc. de Indias, III, 511–513. B. Smith's *Florida*, 65–66. Translated in the *Boston Transcript*, 14 Oct., 1893, and on page 594 *ante*.

Alvarado, Pedro de.
Asiento y capitulaciones, entre el virey de Nueva España, D. Antonio de Mendoza, y el adelantado, D. Pedro de Alvarado, para la prosecucion del descubrimiento de tierra nueva, hecho por Fr. Márcos de Niza.—Pueblo de Tiripitio de la Nueva España, 29 Noviembre, 1540.
Doc. de Indias, III, 351–362. Also in the same collection, XVI, 342–355. See page 353 *ante*.

— Proceso de residencia contra Pedro de Alvarado, . . . sacadas de los antiguos codices mexicanos, y notas y noticias . . . por D. Jose Fernando

Alvarado, Pedro de—Continued.

Ramirez. Lo publica paleografiado del MS. original el Lic. Ignacío L. Rayon.—Mexico, 1847.

A collection of documents of considerable interest; with facsimile illustrations and portrait.

— *See* Carta del Obispo de Guatemala.

Ardoino, Antonio.

Examen apologetico de la historica narracion de los naufragios, peregrinaciones, i milagros de Alvar Nuñez Cabeza de Baca, en las tierras de la Florida, i del Nuevo Mexico.—Madrid, 1736.

Barcia, *Historiadores Primitivos*. I (VI), pp. 50. See note under Cabeza de Vaca *Relacion*.

Ayllon, Lucas Vazquez de.

Testimonio de la capitulacion que hizo con el Rey, el Licenciado Lucas Vazquez de Ayllon, para descubrir la tierra que está á la parte del Norte Sur, de la Isla Española, 35 á 37 grados.—Valladolid, 12 Junio, 1523.—Presentó en Madrid, 31 Marzo, 1541.

Doc. de Indias, XIV, 503-515.

Bancroft, George.

History of the United States. Author's latest revision.—New York, 1883.

For *Coronado* see Vol. I, 32-37. Written from the documents translated in Ternaux, *Cibola*.

Bancroft, Hubert Howe.

History of the Pacific states of North America.—San Francisco, 1882-1890.

34 volumes. Vol. V, Mexico, II, 1521-1600. Vol. X, North Mexican States, 1531-1800. Vol. XII, Arizona and New Mexico, 1530-1888; pages 1-73 are devoted to Cabeza de Vaca and Coronado. The range of Mr H. H. Bancroft's extensive literary labors has seriously interfered with the accuracy in statement and the soundness of judgment which are so essential to satisfactory historical writing. His volumes, however, contain an immense number of references, often mentioning documentary sources and manuscript materials which are as yet practically beyond the reach of other students.

Bandelier, Adolph Francis (Alphonse).

Historical introduction to studies among the sedentary Indians of New Mexico.—Santa Fé, N. M., Sept. 19, 1880.

Papers of the Archæological Institute of America, American series, I, Boston, 1881. 2d edition, 1883, pp. 1-33. Relates especially to the Coronado expedition. Cited in the preceding pages as Bandelier's *Introduction*.

— A visit to the aboriginal ruins in the valley of the Rio Pecos.

Papers of the Archæological Institute of America, American series, I, 1881, pp. 37-133. In the same volume as the preceding entry.

— Ein Brief über Akoma.

Das Ausland, 1884, No. XIII, pp. 241-243.

— Report of an archæological tour in Mexico in 1881.

Papers of the Archæological Institute of America, American series, II, Boston, 1884.

— Report by A. F. Bandelier on his investigations in New Mexico in the

Bandelier, Adolph Francis (Alphonse)—Continued.

spring and summer of 1882.—Highland, Ill., Aug. 15, 1882.

Bulletin of the Archæological Institute of America, I, Boston, Jan., 1883, pp. 13-33.

— The historical archives of the Hemenway southwestern archæological expedition.

Congrès International des Américanistes, 1888, pp. 450-459.—Berlin, 1890.

— Contributions to the history of the southwestern portion of the United States.

Papers of the Archæological Institute of America, Am. series, V, and *The Hemenway Southwestern Archæological Expedition*, Cambridge, 1890. Cited in the preceding pages as Bandelier's *Contributions*. An invaluable work, the result of careful documentary study and of much experience in field work in the southwest. It will always serve as the foundation of all satisfactory study of the history of the Spaniards in that portion of the United States.

— Quivira.

Nation, N. Y., 31 Oct. and 7 Nov., 1889. (Nos. 1270, 1271.) Letters dated Santa Fé, October 15, 1889.

— The ruins of Casas Grandes.

Nation, N. Y., 28 Aug. and 4 Sept., 1890 (Nos. 1313, 1314.) Letters dated Santa Fé, Aug. 1, 11, 1890.

— The Delight Makers.—New York, 1890.

A story, in which Mr Bandelier has portrayed, with considerable success, the ways of life and of thinking among the Indians of the New Mexican pueblos, before the advent of Europeans.

— Fray Juan de Padilla, the first Catholic missionary and martyr in eastern Kansas. 1542.

American Catholic Quarterly Review, Philadelphia, July, 1890, XV, 551-565.

— An outline of the documentary history of the Zuñi tribe.

Journal American Ethnology and Archæology, III, Boston, 1892, pp. 1-115. This work remained in manuscript for some years before it was printed. It contains many extracts from the contemporary narratives, in translation; that of Castañeda being taken from Ternaux's version. See note on page 389.

— Final report of investigations among the Indians of the southwestern United States, carried on mainly in the years from 1880 to 1885.

Papers of the Archæological Institute of America. Cambridge; Part I, 1890; Part II, 1892.

The most valuable of all of Bandelier's memoirs on southwestern history and ethnology. It bears the same relation to the work of the American ethnologist as his *Contributions* do to that of the historical student.

— The "Montezuma" of the pueblo Indians.

American Anthropologist, Washington, Oct., 1892, V, 319.

— The Gilded Man.—New York, 1893.

This work contains much valuable material concerning the early history of the southwest, but should be used with care, as it was edited and published during the author's absence in Peru.

Bandelier, Adolph Francis (Alphonse)—
Continued.

— La découverte du Nouveau-Mexique par le moine franciscain frère Marcos de Nice en 1539.
    Revue d'Ethnographie, v (1886), 31, 117, 193 (50 pages).

— The discovery of New Mexico by Fray Marcos of Nizza.
    Magazine of Western History, IV, Cleveland, Sept., 1886, pp. 659–670. The same material was used in the articles in the *Revue d'Ethnographie*.

— Alvar Nuñez Cabeza de Vaca, the first overland traveler of European descent, and his journey from Florida to the Pacific coast—1528–1536.
    Magazine of Western History, IV, Cleveland, July, 1886, pp. 327–336.

Barcia, Andres Gonzales.
Historiadores primitivos de las Indias Occidentales, que juntó, traduxo en parte, y sacó á luz, ilustrados con erudítas notas, y copiosos indices, el ilustrissimo Señor D. Andres Gonzalez Barcia, del Consejo, y Camara de S. M. Divididos en tres tomos.—Madrid, año MDCCXLIX.
    These three folio volumes are made up of very satisfactory reprints of a number of the narratives of the early Spanish conquerors of America. The *Naufragios* and *Comentarios* of Cabeza de Vaca are in the first volume.

— Ensayo cronologico, para la historia general de la Florida . . . desde 1512 hasta 1722, escrito por Don Gabriel de Cardenas z Cano.—Madrid, CIƆIƆCCXXIII.
    The name on the title page is an anagram for that of Sʳ Gonzalez Barcia. Florida, in this work, comprises all of America north of Mexico. The Ensayo was published with the *Florida del Ynca* of 1723.

Baxter, Sylvester.
The father of the pueblos.
    Harper's Magazine, LXV, June, 1882, pp. 72–91.

— An aboriginal pilgrimage.
    Century Magazine, II (XXIV), August, 1882, pp. 526–536.

— The old new world. An account of the explorations of the Hemenway southwestern archæological expedition.—Salem, Mass., 1888.
    Reprinted from the *Boston Herald*, April 15, 1888.

Begert, or Baegert, Jacob.
Nachrichten von der Amerikanischen Halbinsel Californien: mit einem zweyfachen Anhang falscher Nachrichten. Geschrieben von einem Priester der Gesellschaft Jesu, welcher lang darinn diese letztere Jahr gelebet hat. Mit' Erlaubnuss der Oberen.—Mannheim, 1773.
    Translated and arranged for the Smithsonian Institution by Charles Rau, of New York City, in the *Smithsonian Reports*, 1863, pp. 352–369; 1864, pp. 378–399. Reprinted by Rau in *Papers on Anthropological Subjects*, pp. 1–40.

Benavides, Alonso de.
Memorial qve Fray Ivan de Santander de la Orden de san Francisco, presenta á Felipe Qvarto, hecho por el Padre Fray Alonso de Benauides, Custodio qve ha sido de las prouincias, y conuersiones del Nueuo-Mexico.—Madrid, M. DC. XXX.
    Translations of this valuable work were published in French at Bruxelles, 1631, in Latin at Salzburg, 1634, and in German at Salzburg, probably also in 1634.

Benzoni, Girolamo.
La historia del Mondo Nvovo.—(Colophon) Venetia, MDLXV.
    Besides early Latin, Dutch, and German translations of Benzoni, there is an old French edition (Geneva, 1579). An English translation was published by the Hakluyt Society in 1857.

Blackmar, Frank Wilson.
Spanish institutions of the southwest.—Baltimore, 1891.
    Johns Hopkins University Studies in Historical and Political Science, extra volume, x.

— Spanish colonization in the southwest.
    Johns Hopkins University Studies, VIII, April, 1890, pp. 121–193.

— The conquest of New Spain.
    Agora, Lawrence, Kans., beginning Jan., 1896. This series of papers is not yet completed.

Botero, Giovanni.
La prima parte delle relationi vniversali di Giovanni Botero Benese.—Bergamo, MDXCIIII.
    For *Ceuola* and *Quiuira*, libro quarto (p. 277). The text was considerably altered and amplified in the successive early editions. In the 1603 Spanish edition, fol. 141.

Bourke, John Gregory.
Snake dance of the Moquis of Arizona.—New York and London, 1884.

Cabeza de Vaca, Alvar Nuñez.
La relacion que dio Aluar nuñez cabeça de vaca de lo acaescido . . en la armada donde yua por gouernador Pãphilo de narbaez.—(Colophon) Zamora, 6 Octubre, 1542.
    This was reprinted, with the addition of the *Comentarios* . . . *del Rio dela Plata*, at Valladolid in 1555. It was translated by Ramusio, III, fol. 310–330 (ed. 1556). and was paraphrased into English, from Ramusio, by Purchas, *Pilgrimes*, Part IV, lib. VIII, chap. I, pp. 1499–1528. There is a useful note regarding the first edition of the *Naufragios* and its author, in Harrisse, *Bibliotheca Americana Vetustissima*, p. 382. The *Naufragios* and *Comentarios* were reprinted at Madrid in 1736, preceded by the *Examen Apologetico* of Ardoino (see entry under his name), and it is this edition which was included in Barcia's collection of 1749, the 1736 title pages being preserved.

— Relacion del viaje de Pánfilo de Narvaez al Rio de las Palmas hasta la punta de la Florida, hecha por el tesorero Cabeza de Vaca.
    Doc. de Indias, XIV, 265–279. Instruccion para el factor, por el Rey, pp. 265–269. Apparently an early copy of a fragment of the *Naufragios*.

Cabeza de Vaca, Alvar Nuñez—Cont'd.

— Relation et naufrages d'Alvar Nuñez Cabeça de Vaca—Paris, 1837.

This French translation of the *Naufragios* forms volume VII of Ternaux's *Voyages*. The *Commentaires* are contained in volume VI. The translation is from the 1555 edition.

— Relation of Alvar Nuñez Cabeça de Vaca, translated from the Spanish by Buckingham Smith.—New York, 1871.

This English translation was printed at Washington in 1851, and was reprinted at New York, with considerable additions and a short sketch of the translator, shortly after Mr Smith's death. Chapters XXX-XXXVI were reprinted in an *Old South Leaflet*, general series, No. 39, Boston.

— Relation of what befel the persons who escaped from the disasters that attended the armament of Captain Pamphilo de Narvaez on the shores and in the countries of the North.

Historical Mag. (Sept.–Dec., 1867), XII, 141, 204, 267, 347. Translated and condensed from an account printed in Oviedo's *Historia General*, Lib. XXXV, cap. i-vi, which was sent to the Real Audiencia of Sancto Domingo by the four survivors of the expedition. See Introduction, p. 349 *ante*.

— Capitulacion que se tomó con Alvar Nuñez Cabeza de Vaca.—Madrid, 18 Marzo, 1540.

Doc. de Indias, XXIII, 8-33.

Cabrillo, Juan Rodriguez. *See* Paez, Juan.

Camus, Armand Gaston.

Mémoire sur la collection des grands et petits voyages (de Théodore de Bry).—Paris, Frimaire an XI (1802).

For "Cornado," see p. 176.

Cartas de Indias. Publícalas por primera vez el Ministerio de Fomento.—Madrid, 1877.

This splendid volume contains 108 letters, 29 of which are reproduced in facsimile, written from various portions of Spanish America during the XVI century. The indices contain a large amount of information concerning the people and places mentioned.

Cartas de Religiosos de Nueva España. 1539-1594.—México, 1886.

Volume I of Icazbalceta's *Nueva Colección*. The 26 letters which make up this volume throw much light on the early civil and economical as well as on the ecclesiastical history of New Spain. The second volume of the *Nueva Colección*, entitled *Códice Franciscano Siglo XVI*, contains 14 additional letters.

Castañeda, Pedro de.

Relacion de la jornada de Cibola conpuesta por Pedro de Castañeda de Naçera donde se trata de todos aquellos poblados y ritos, y costumbres, la cual fue el año de 1540.

Printed for the first time in the *Fourteenth Annual Report of the Bureau of Ethnology*, pp. 414-469, from the manuscript in the Lenox Library in New York. This narrative has been known chiefly through the French translation printed in 1838 by Henri Ternaux-Compans, the title of which follows.

Castañeda, Pedro de—Continued.

— Relation du voyage de Cibola entrepris en 1540; ou l'on traite de toutes les peuplades qui habitent cette contrée, de leurs mœurs et coutumes, par Pédro de Castañeda de Nagera.

Ternaux, *Cibola*, 1-246.

Castaño de Sosa, Gaspar.

Memoria del descubrimiento que Gaspar Castaño de Sosa, hizo en el Nuevo México, siendo teniente de gobernador y capitan general del Nuevo Reino de Leon.

Doc. de Indias, vol. XV. pp. 191-261. The exploring party started 27th July, 1590, and this report was presented to the Council 10th November, 1592.

Cervántes Salazar, Francisco.

México en 1554: Tres diálogos latinos que Francisco Cervántes Salazar escribió ó imprimió en México en dicho año. Los reimprime, con traduccion castellana y notas, Joaquin Garcia Icazbalceta—México, 1875.

Invaluable for anyone who wishes to understand the early social and economic conditions of Spanish America. The bibliography at the end of the volume is not only of great value as a guide to the study of this history, but it is of interest as a partial catalog of the library of Sr Garcia Icazbalceta.

Chapin, Frederick Hastings.

The land of the cliff-dwellers.—Boston, 1892.

Congrès International des Américanistes.

Compte-rendu de la première session.—Nancy, 1875; . . . Actas de la Novena Reunión, Huelva, 1892–Madrid, 1894.

Many of the papers presented at the meetings of the *Congrès des Américanistes*, have been of the very greatest interest to the American ethnologist and to the historian of early Spanish America. Several of the papers presented at Berlin in 1888 are entered under the authors' names in the present list.

Coronado, Francisco Vazquez.

Svmmario di lettere del Capitano Francesco Vazquez di coronado, scritte ad vn Secretario del Illustriss. Don Antonio di Mendozza Vicere della nuoua Spagna, Date à Culnacan, MDXXXIX, alli otto di Marzo.

Ramusio, III, fol. 354, ed. 1556. Translated in Ternaux, *Cibola*, app. V, pp. 349-351. The special value of these Italian translations of Spanish documents, to which reference is made in the present list, is due to the fact that in very many cases where Ramusio used original documents for his work later students have been unable to discover any trace of the manuscript sources.

— Copia delle lettere di Francesco Vazquez di Coronado, gouernatore della nuoua Galitia, al Signor Antonio di Mendozza, Vicere della nuoua Spagna, date in san Michiel di Culnacan, alli otto di Marzo, MDXXXIX.

Ramusio, III, fol. 354 verso, ed. 1556. Translated in Ternaux, *Cibola*, app. V, pp. 352-354.

Coronado, Francisco Vazquez—Cont'd.

— Relatione che mandò Francesco Vazquez di Coronado, Capitano Generale della gente che fu mandata in nome di Sua Maesta al paese nouamente scoperto, quel che successe nel viaggio dalli ventidua d' Aprile di questo anno MDXL, che parti da Culiacan per innanzi, & di quel che trouò nel paese doue andaua.—Dalla prouincia di Ceuola & da questa città di Granata il terzo di Agosto, 1540.

> *Ramusio*, III, fol. 359 (verso)–363, ed. 1556. This letter is translated on pages 552–563 of the present volume. See note on page 386. An earlier English translation by Hakluyt has the following title:

— The relation of Francis Vazquez de Coronado, Captaine generall of the people which were sent to the Countrey of Cibola newly discouered, which he sent to Don Antonio de Mendoça viceroy of Mexico, of . . . his voyage from the 22. of Aprill in the yeere 1540. which departed from Culiacan forward, and of such things as hee found in the Countrey which he passed. (August 3, 1540.)

> *Hakluyt*, III, 373–380 (ed. 1600), or III. 446 (ed. 1800). Reprinted in *Old South Leaflet*, gen. series, No. 20. Boston.

— Carta de Francisco Vazquez Coronado al Emperador, dándole cuenta de la espedicion á la provincia de Quivira, y de la inexactitud de lo referido á Fr. Márcos de Niza, acerca de aquel pais.—Desta provincia de Tiguex, 20 Octubre, 1541.

> *Doc. de Indias*, III, 363–369, and also XIII, 261–268. Translated on pages 580–583 of the present volume, and also in *American History Leaflet*, No. 13. There is a French translation in Ternaux, *Cibola*, app. v, p. 355–363. See note on page 580 *ante*.

— Traslado de las nuevas y noticias que dieron sobre el descobrimiento de una cibdad, que llamaron de Cibola, situada en la tierra nueva.—Año de 1531 [1541].

> *Doc. de Indias*, XIX, pp. 529–532. Translated on pages 564–565 of the present volume.

— Relacion del suceso de la jornada que Francisco Vazquez hizo en el descubrimiento de Cibola.—Año de 1531 [1541].

> B. Smith, *Florida*, 147–154; *Doc. de Indias*, XIV, 318–329. Translated on pages 572–579 of the present volume. See the notes to that translation. Also translated in *American History Leaflet*, No. 13.

Cortés, Hernan.

Copia y relacion de los gastos y espensas que . . . Fernando Cortés hizo en el armada de que fué por capitan Cristóbal Dolid al Cabo de las Higueras . . . Se hizo á primero de Agosto de 1523.—Fecho en México, 9 Hebrero 1529.

> *Doc. de Indias*, XII, 386–403. This document is printed again in the same volume, pp. 497–510.

Cortés, Hernan—Continued.

— Título de capitan general de la Nueva-España y Costa del Sur, expedido á favor de Hernan-Cortés por el Emperador Cárlos V.—Dada en Barcelona, á 6 Julio, 1529.

> *Doc. de Indias*, IV, 572–574, and also XII, 384–386.

— Título de marqués del Valle (de Guaxaca) otorgado á Hernando Cortés.—Barcelona, 6 Julio, 1529.

> *Doc. de Indias*, XII, 381–383.

— Merced de ciertas tierras y solares en la Nueva España, hecha á Fernan Cortés, marqués del Valle, por el Emperador.—Barcelona, 27 Julio, 1529.

> *Doc. de Indias*, XII, 376–378. It is printed also in Icazbalceta's *Mexico*, II, 28–29.

— Testimonio de una informacion hecha en México por el presidente y oydores de aquella audiencia, sobre el modo de contar los 23.000 indios, vasallos del Marqués del Valle, de que el Rey le habia hecho merced.—Temixtitan, 23 Febrero, 1531.

> *Doc. de Indias*, XVI, 548–555.

— Real provision sobre descubrimientos en el mar del Sur, y respuesta de Cortés á la notificacion que se le hizo de ella.—México, 19 Agosto, 1534; y respuesta, México, 26 Setiembre, 1534.

> Icazbalceta's *Mexico*, II, 31–40.

— Traslado de una provision de la Audiencia de México, dirigida á Hernan-Cortés, mandándole que no vaya á pacificar y poblar cierta isla del mar del Sur, insertando otra provision que con igual fecha se envió á Nuño de Guzman, gobernador de la Nueva Galicia, para el mismo efecto, y diligencias hechas en apelacion de la misma.—Fecho en México, 2–26 Setiembre, 1534.

> *Doc. de Indias*, XII, 417–429.

— Carta de Hernan Cortés al emperador, enviando un hijo suyo para servicio del príncipe.—Desta Nueva Spaña, diez de Hebrero, 1537.

> *Doc. de Indias*, II, 568–569.

— Carta de Hernan Cortés, al Consejo de Indias, pidiendo ayuda para continuar sus armadas, y recompensa para sus servicios, y dando algunas noticias sobre la constitucion de la propiedad de las tierras entre los indios.—México, 20 Setiembre, 1538.

> *Doc. de Indias*, III, 535–543.

— Carta de Hernan Cortés al Emperador.—De Madrid á xxvi de Junio de 1540.

> *Doc. Inéd. España*, CIV, 491–492.

— Memorial que dió al Rey el Marqués del Valle en Madrid á 25 de junio de 1540 sobre agravios que le habia hecho el Virey de Nueva España D. Antonio de Mendoza, estorbándole la prosecucion del descubrimiento de las costas é islas del mar del Sur que le pertene-

Cortés, Hernan—Continued.

cia al mismo Marqués segun la capitulacion hecha con S. M. el año de 1529, á cuyo efecto habia despachado ya cuatro armadas, y descubierto con ellas por sí y por sus capitanes muchas tierras é islas, de cuyos viajes y el suceso que tuvo hace una relacion sucinta.

Doc. Inéd. España, IV, 209–217.

— Memorial dado á la Magestad del Cesar D. Cárlos Quinto, Primero de España, por el Sr. D. Hernando Cortés, Marqués del Valle, hallándose en estos reinos, en que hace presentes sus dilatados servicios en la conquista de Nueva España por los que pide las mercedes que contiene el mismo.

Doc. Inéd. España, IV, 219–232. "No tiene fecha. . . . despues de 1541."

— Peticion que dió Don Hernando Cortés contra Don Antonio de Mendoza, Virey, pidiendo residencia contre él.

Icazbalceta, *Mexico*, II, 62–71. About 1542–43.

— Historia de Nueva-España, escrita por Hernan Cortés, aumentada con otros documentos, y notas, por Don Francisco Antonio Lorenzana.—México, 1770.

See page 325 and the map; "Domingo del Castillo Piloto me Fecit en Mexico año . . . M. D. XLI." This volume contains the letters of Cortes to the Spanish King, for a bibliographic account of which see Sabin's *Dictionary of American Books*. These dispatches may also be conveniently consulted in volume I of Barcia, *Historiadores*.

The above entries are chiefly such as are of interest for their bearing on the troubles between Cortes and Mendoza, which were very closely connected with the history of the Coronado expedition. The best guide to the study of the personal history and the conquests of Cortes is found in Winsor's *America*, II, pages 397–430.

Cushing, Frank Hamilton.

Zuñi fetiches.

Second Annual Report of the Bureau of Ethnology, 1880–81, pp. 9–45.

— A study of pueblo pottery as illustrative of Zuñi culture growth.

Fourth Annual Report of the Bureau of Ethnology, 1882–83, pp. 467–521.

— Preliminary notes on the origin, working hypothesis and primary researches of the Hemenway southwestern archæological expedition.

Congrès International des Américanistes, 7me session, 1888, pp. 151–194. Berlin, 1890.

— Zuñi breadstuff.

The *Millstone*, Indianapolis, Jan., 1884, to Aug., 1885.

— Outlines of Zuñi creation myths.

Thirteenth Annual Report of the Bureau of Ethnology, 1891–92, pp. 321–447.

Davila, Gil Gonzalez.

Teatro eclesiastico de la primitiva iglesia de las Indias Occidentales, vidas de svs arzobispos, obispos, y cosas

Davila, Gil Gonzalez—Continued.

memorables de svs sedes.—Madrid, M.DC.XLIX.

These two volumes are a valuable source of biographical and other ecclesiastical information, for much of which this is perhaps the only authority.

Davis, William Watts Hart.

The Spanish conquest of New Mexico.—Doylestown, Pa., 1869.

The first 230 pages of this volume contain a very good outline of the narratives of the explorations of Cabeza de Vaca, Fray Marcos, and Coronado.

— The Spaniard in New Mexico.

Papers of the *American Historical Association*, III, 1889, pp. 164–176. A paper read before the association, at Boston, May 24, 1887.

De Bry, Theodore. *See* Abelin.

Diaz del Castillo, Bernal.

Historia verdadera de la conqvista de la Nveva España, escrita por . . . vno de sus conquistadores.—Madrid, 1632.

This interesting work, which counteracts many of the impressions given by the dispatcher of Cortes, was reprinted in 1632 and again in 1795, 1837, 1854, and in volume XXVI (Madrid, 1853) of the *Bibl. de Autores Españoles*. It was translated into English by Keating, London, 1800, reprinted at Salem, Mass., 1803; and by Lockhart, London, 1844.

Discurso y proposicion que se hace á Vuestra Magestad de lo tocante á los descubrimientos del Nuevo México por sus capítulos de puntos diferentes.

Doc. de Indias, XVI, 38–66.

Documentos de España.

Coleccion de documentos inéditos para la historia de España.—Madrid, 1842 (–1895).

There are now (1895) 112 volumes in this series, and two or three volumes are usually added each year. A finding list of the titles relating to America, in volumes I–CX, prepared by G. P. Winship, was printed in the *Bulletin of the Boston Public Library* for October, 1894. A similar list of titles in the Pacheco y Cardenas Coleccion is in preparation. Cited as *Doc. Inéd. España*.

Documentos de Indias. *See* Pacheco-Cardenas.

Donaldson, Thomas.

Moqui Pueblo Indians of Arizona and Pueblo Indians of New Mexico.

Extra Census Bulletin, Washington, 1893. This "special expert" report on the numbers and the life of the southwestern village Indians contains a large number of reproductions from photographs showing the people and their homes, which render it of very considerable interest and usefulness. The text is not reliable.

Drake, Francis. *See* Fletcher, Francis.

Emory, William Hemsley.

Notes of a military reconnoissance from Fort Leavenworth, in Missouri, to San Diego, in California.—Washington, 1848.

Ex. Doc. 41, Thirtieth Congress, first session.

Espejo, Antonio de.
Expediente y relacion del viaje que hizo Antonio de Espejo con catorce soldados y un religioso de la órden de San Francisco, llamado Fray Au gustin Rodriguez; el cual debía de entender en la predicacion de aquella gente.
Doc. de Indias, XV, 151–191. See also page 101 of the same volume.

— El viaie qve hizo Antonio de Espeio en el anno de ochenta y tres: el qual con sus companneros descubrieron vna tierra en que hallaron quinze Prouincias todas llenas de pueblos, y de casas de quatro y cinco altos, a quien pusieron por nombre El nueuo Mexico.
Hakluyt, III, 383–389 (ed. 1600). The Spanish text is followed by an English translation, pp. 390–396. A satisfactory monograph on the expedition of Espejo, with annotated translations of the original narratives, would be a most desirable addition to the literature of the southwest.

Evans, S. B.
Observations on the Aztecs and their probable relations to the Pueblo Indians of New Mexico.
Congrès International des Américanistes, 7me session, 1888, pp. 226–230. Berlin, 1890.

Fernández Duro, Cesáreo.
Don Diego de Peñalosa y su descubrimiento del reino de Quivira. Informe presentado á la Real Academia de la Historia.—Madrid, 1882.
On page 123 the author accepts the date 1531 as that of an expedition under Coronado, from the title of the *Relacion del Suceso*, misprinted in volume XIV, 318, of the *Doc. de Indias*.

Ferrelo, Bartolome. *See* **Paez, Juan.**

Fewkes, Jesse Walter.
A few summer ceremonials at Zuñi pueblo.
Journal American Ethnology and Archæology, I, Boston, 1891, pp. 1–61.

— A few summer ceremonials at the Tusayan pueblos.
Ibid., II, Boston, 1892, pp. 1–159.

— Reconnoissance of ruins in or near the Zuñi reservation.
Ibid., I, pp. 95–132; with map and plan.

— A report on the present condition of a ruin in Arizona called Casa Grande.
Ibid, II, pp. 179–193.

— The snake ceremonials at Walpi.
Journal American Ethnology and Archæology, IV, 1894.
With map, illustrations, and an excellent bibliography of this peculiar ceremonial, which Dr Fewkes has studied with much care, under most favorable circumstances.

The four volumes of the *Journal of American Ethnology and Archæology* represent the main results of Dr Fewkes' studies at Zuñi and Tusayan, under the auspices of the Hemenway Southwestern Archæological Expedition, of which he was the head from 1889 to 1895. Besides the *Journal*, the Hemenway expedition resulted in a large collection of Pueblo pottery and ceremonial

Fewkes, Jesse Walter—Continued.
articles, which are, in part, now displayed in the Peabody Museum at Cambridge, Massachusetts.

— The Wa-wac-ka-tci-na. A Tusayan foot race.
Bulletin Essex Institute, XXIV, Nos. 7–9, Salem, July–Sept., 1892, pp. 113–133.

— A-wá-to-bi: An archæological verification of a Tusayan legend.
American Anthropologist, Oct., 1893.

— The prehistoric culture of Tusayan.
American Anthropologist, May, 1896.

— A study of summer ceremonials at Zuñi and Moqui pueblos.
Bulletin Essex Institute, XXII, Nos. 7–9, Salem, July–Sept., 1890, pp. 89–113.
Consult, also, many other papers by this authority on all that pertains to the ceremonial life of the Pueblo Indians, in the *American Anthropologist*, Washington, and *Journal of American Folk-Lore*, Boston.

Fiske, John.
The discovery of America, with some account of ancient America and the Spanish conquest.—Cambridge, 1892.
Coronado and *Cibola*, II, 500-510.

Fletcher, Francis.
The world encompassed by Sir Francis Drake. . . . Carefully collected out of the notes of Master Francis Fletcher preacher in this imployment.—London, 1628.
Reprinted in 1635 and 1652, and in 1854 by the *Hakluyt Society*, edited by W. S. W. Vaux.

Gallatin, Albert.
Ancient semi-civilization of New Mexico, Rio Gila, and its vicinity.
Transactions American Ethnological Society, II, New York, 1848, pp. liii-xcvii.

Galvano, Antonio.
Tratado . . dos diuersos & desuayrados caminhos, . . . & assi de todos os descobrimentos antigos & modernos, que são feitos ate a era de mil & quinhentos & cincoenta.—(Colophon, 1563.)
This work was reprinted at Lisboa in 1731. An English translation was published by Hakluyt, London, 1601. The Portuguese and English texts were reprinted by the *Hakluyt Society*, edited by vice-admiral Bethune, London, 1862. For Coronado's expedition, see pages 226–229 of the 1862 edition.

Garcilaso de la Vega, el Ynca.
La Florida del Ynca. Historia del Adelantado de Soto . . . y de otros heroicos caualleros Españoles è Indios.—Lisboa, 1605.
For an English version, see Barnard Shipp's *History of Hernando de Soto and Florida*, Philadelphia, 1881. There were several early French editions. The Spanish was reprinted at Madrid in 1723, and again in 1803

— Primera parte de los commentarios reales, qve tratan del origen de los Yncas, reyes qve fveron del Perv, de sv idolatria, leyes, y gouierno en paz

Garcilaso de la Vega, el Ynca—Cont'd.
y en guerra: de sus vidas y conquistas, y de todo lo que fue aquel Impe-
rio y su Republica, antes que los
Españoles passaran a el.—Lisboa,
M. DCIX.

— Historia general del Perv. Trata
el desevbrimiento del, y como lo
ganaron los Españoles. Las guerras
ciuiles que huuo entre Piçarros, y
Almagros, sobre la partija de la
tierra. Castigo y leuantamiento de
tiranos: y otros sucessos particulares
que en la historia se contienen.—Cor-
doua, 1616.

　　La II parte de los commentarios reales del
　　Perú. Segunda impresion; Madrid, 1721-
　　23. The two parts were "rendred into Eng-
　　lish, by Sir Pavl Rycavt, Kt." London,
　　1688. A new translation, with notes by
　　Clements R. Markham, was published by
　　the *Hakluyt Society*, London, 1869 and 1871.

Gatschet, Albert Samuel.
Classification into seven linguistic
stocks of western Indian dialects contained in forty vocabularies.

　　U. S. Geol. Survey West of the 100th Me-
　　ridian, VII, 399-485, Washington, 1879.

— Zwölf sprachen aus dem südwesten
Nordamerikas.—Weimar, 1876.

Girava, Hieronymo.
Dos libros de cosmographia compuestos
nueuamente por Hieronymo Giraua
Tarragones, —en Milan, M. D. LVI.

　　See p. 230 for *Ciuola*.

Gomara, Francisco Lopez de.
Primera y segunda parte de la historia
general de las Indias con todo el descubrimiento y cosas notables que han
acaecido dende que se ganaron ata el
año de 1551. Con la cõquista de México y de la nueua España.—En Cara-
goça, 1553 (1552).

　　There were at least fifteen editions of Go-
　　mara's three works printed during the years
　　1552 to 1555. Before the end of the century
　　translations into French and Italian had
　　been reprinted a score of times. English
　　translations of the *Conquest of the Indies*
　　were printed in 1578 and 1596. For *Coro-*
　　nado, see cap. CCXII-CCXV of the *Historia de*
　　las Indias. Chapters 214-215 were trans-
　　lated by *Hakluyt*, III, 380-382 (ed. 1600), or
　　III, 454 (ed. 1810).

Gottfriedt, Johann Ludwig. *See* **Abelin,**
Johann Phillip.

Guatemala, Obispo de.
Carta del Obispo de Guatemala á Su
Magestad, en que se refiere á lo que
de México escribirán sobre la muerte
del adelantado Alvarado, y habla de
la gobernacion que se le encomendó
y de los cargos de su mitra.—De Santiago de Guatemala 20 Febrero, 1542.

　　Doc. de Indias, XIII, 268-280.

Guzman, Diego.
Relacion de lo que yo Diego de Guzman
he descobierto en la costa de la mar
del Sur, por Su Magestad y por el ilus-
tre señor Nuño de Guzman, goberna-

Guzman, Diego—Continued.
dor de la Nueva Galicia.—Presentó
en el Consejo de Indias, 16 Marzo 1540.

　　Doc. de Indias, XV, 325-340. This expedi-
　　tion was made during the autumn of 1533.

Guzman, Nuño de.
Provanza ad perpetuan, sobre lo de la
villa de la Purificacion, de la gente
que alli vino con mano armada.—En
Madrid á 16 de Marzo de 1540 la presentó en el Consejo de las Indias de Su
Magestad, Nuño de Guzman.

　　Doc. de Indias, XVI, 539-547.

— Fragmentos del proceso de residencia instruido contra Nuño de Guzman,
en averiguacion del tormento y muerte que mandó dar á Caltzontzin, rey
de Mechoacan.

　　In Proceso. . .Alvarado (ed. Ramirez y
　　Rayon) pp. 185-276. The full title is entered
　　under **Alvarado**.

Hakluyt, Richard.
The principal navigations, voiages,
traffiqves and discoueries of the
English nation . . . Deuided into
three seuerall volumes.—London,
1598.

　　The third volume (1600) contains the narra-
　　tives which relate to Cibola, as well as those
　　which refer to other portions of New Spain.
　　There was an excellent reprint. London,
　　1809-1812, which contained all the pieces
　　which were omitted in some of the earlier
　　editions, with a fifth volume containing a
　　number of rare pieces not easily available
　　elsewhere. The changes made by the editor
　　of the 1890 edition render it almost a new
　　work. The title is as follows:

— The principal navigations, voyages,
traffiques, and discoveries of the
English nation. Collected by Richard Hakluyt, preacher, and edited by
Edmund Goldsmid.—Edinburg, 1885-
1890.

　　Sixteen volumes. Vol. XIV; America,
　　part iii, pp. 59-137, contains the Cibola nar-
　　ratives.

Hakluyt Society, London.
　　This most useful society began in 1847 the
　　publication of a series of volumes contain-
　　ing careful, annotated translations or re-
　　prints of works relating to the "naviga-
　　tions, voyages, traffics, and discoveries" of
　　Europeans during the period of colonial
　　expansion. The work has been continued
　　without serious interruption since that
　　date. Ninety-seven volumes have been
　　issued with the society's imprint, includ-
　　ing the issues for 1895. Several of these
　　are entered in the present list under the
　　names of the respective authors.

Hale, Edward Everett.
Coronado's discovery of the seven cities.

　　Proceedings American Antiquarian So-
　　ciety, Worcester, new series I, 236-245.
　　(April, 1881.) Includes a letter from Lieut.
　　John G. Bourke, arguing that the Cibola
　　pueblos were the Moki villages of Tusayan,
　　in Arizona.

Haynes, Henry Williamson.
Early explorations of New Mexico.

　　Winsor's *Narrative and Critical History*
　　of America, II, 473-503.

Haynes, Henry Williamson—Continued.
-- What is the true site of "the seven cities of Cibola" visited by Coronado in 1540?

Proceedings American Antiquarian Society, Worcester, new series, I, 421-435 (Oct., 1881).

The revival of interest in the early history of the southwestern United States has been, in no slight measure, due to the impetus given by Professor Haynes of Boston. He was most active in furthering the researches of Mr Bandelier, under the auspices of the Archæological Institute of America, and to his careful editorial supervision a large part of the accuracy and the value of Mr Bandelier's printed reports and communications are due.

Herrera, Antonio de.
Historia general de los hechos de los Castellanos en las islas y tierra firme del mar oceano.—Madrid, 1601–1615.

There is a French translation of three Decades of Herrera, printed between 1659 and 1671, and an English translation of the same three decades, by Captain John Stevens, London, 1725-26, and reissued in 1740, in which the arrangement of the work is altered. The most available and also the best edition of the Spanish is the admirable reprint issued at Madrid by Barcia, in 1730. Some titles are dated as early as 1726, being altered as successive delays hindered the completion of the work. For *Coronado*, see decada VI, libro V, cap. ix, and dec. VI, lib. ix, cap. xi–xv.

Hodge, Frederick Webb.
A Zuñi foot race.

Am. Anthropologist, III, Washington, July, 1890.

— Prehistoric irrigation in Arizona.
Ibid., VI, July, 1893.

— The first discovered city of Cibola.
Ibid., VIII, April, 1895.

— The early Navajo and Apache.
Ibid., VIII, July, 1895.

— Pueblo snake ceremonials.
Ibid., IX, April, 1896.

Holmes, William Henry.
Report on the ancient ruins of southwestern Colorado.

Tenth Annual Report of the (Hayden) U. S. Geol. Survey. Washington, 1876.

— Illustrated catalogue of a portion of the collections made . . . during the field season of 1881.

Third Annual Report of the Bureau of Ethnology, 1881-82, pp. 427-510.

— Pottery of the ancient Pueblos.
Fourth Annual Report of the Bureau of Ethnology, 1882-83, pp. 265-360.

Icazbalceta, Joaquin Garcia.
Coleccion de documentos para la historia de México. (2 tomos).—México, 1858–1866.

Cited in the preceding pages as *Icazbalceta's Mexico.*

— Nueva colección de documentos para la historia de México. (5 tomos).— México, 1886–1892.

Cited as *Icazbalceta's Nueva coleccion.*

Icazbalceta, Joaquin Garcia—Continued.
— Don Fray Juan de Zumárraga primer obispo y arzobispo de México. Estudio biográfico y bibligráfico. Con un apéndice de documentos inéditos ó raros.—México, 1881.

See also the entries under Cervantes de Salazar, Mendieta, Mota Padilla, for works edited by Señor Icazbalceta. Possessed of ample means and scholarly tastes, untiring industry and great historical and literary ability, Señor Garcia Icazbalceta will always be one of the masters of Spanish-American history. The extent of his researches, the accuracy and care which characterize all of his work, and the breadth and insight with which he treated whatever subject attracted him, leave little for future students to desire. The more intimate the student becomes with the first century of the history of New Spain, the greater is his appreciation of the loss caused by the death of Señor Garcia Icazbalceta.

Informacion del virrey de Nueva España, D. Antonio de Mendoza, de la gente que va á poblar la Nueva Galicia con Francisco Vazquez Coronado, Gobernador de ella.— Compostella, 21–26 Febrero 1540.

Doc. de Indias, XIV, 373–384. Partly translated on pp. 596–597 *ante.*

Informacion habida ante la justicia de la villa de San Cristóbal de la Habana, por do consta, el visorey (Mendoza) haber mandado ó personado que navíos algunos de los quél embíaba [no] tocasen en la dicha villa, á fin ó causa que no diesen noticia del nuevo descobrimiento al Adelantado (de Soto).—12 Noviembre, 1539 en Habana. Presentó en Madrid, 23 Diciembre, 1540.

Doc. de Indias, XV, 392–398. See page 370 *ante.*

Jaramillo, Juan.
Relacion hecha por el capitan Juan Jaramillo, de la jornada que habia hecho á la tierra nueva en Nueva España y al descubrimiento de Cibola, yendo por general Francisco Vazquez Coronado.

Doc. de Indias, XIV, 304–317. B. Smith's *Florida*, 154-163. Translated on pages 584–593 *ante.* There is a French translation in Ternaux, *Cibola*, app. vi, 364-382.

King, Edward; Viscount Lord Kingsborough.
Antiquities of Mexico: comprising facsimiles of ancient Mexican paintings and hieroglyphics . . . illustrated by many valuable inedited manuscripts.—Mexico and London, 1830–1848.

Nine vols. Besides the reproductions of Mexican hieroglyphic writings, for which this magnificent work is best known, the later volumes contain a number of works printed from Spanish manuscripts. Despite the statement on the last page of many copies, the work was never completed, Motolinia's *Historia* breaking off abruptly in the midst of the text. See the note under *King*, in Sabin's *Dictionary of American Books.*

Kretschmer, Konrad.

Die Entdeckung Amerika's in ihrer Be-
deutung für die Geschichte des Welt-
bildes.—Berlin, 1892.

Festschrift der Gesellschaft für Erdkunde
zu Berlin zur vierhundertjährigen Feier
der Entdeckung Amerika's. The atlas
which accompanies this valuable study is
made up of a large number of admirable facsimiles and copies of early maps, some of
which are reproduced in the present memoir. It is certainly the best single book
for the student of early American carto-
graphy.

Ladd, Horatio Oliver.

The story of New Mexico.—Boston,
(1892).

For *Niça* and *Coronado*, see pp. 19-72.

Leyes y ordenanças nueuamēte hechas
por su magestad pa la gouernacion de
las Indias y buen tratamiento y con-
seruacion de los Indios: que se
han de guardar en el consejo y au-
diēcias reales q̃ en ellas residen: y por
todos los otros gouernadores, juezes
y personas particulares dellas.—
(Colophon) Alcala de Henares, M. D.
XLIII.

These "New Laws" were reprinted in
1585 and again in 1603. A new edition, with
English translation and an introduction by
Henry Stevens and F. W. Lucas, was issued
in London, 1893. The Laws are printed in
Icazbalceta, *Mexico*, II, 204-227.

—*See* Recopilacion.

Lummis, Charles F.

— Some strange corners of our country.
—New York, 1892.

— The land of poco tiempo.—New York,
1893.

— The Spanish pioneers.—Chicago,
1893.

— The man who married the moon and
other Pueblo Indian folk-stories.—
New York, 1894.

Mallery, Garrick.

Sign language among North American
Indians compared with that among
other peoples and deaf mutes.

*First Annual Report Bureau of Ethnol-
ogy*, 1879-80, pp. 263-552. Fully illustrated.

Matthews, Washington.

Human bones of the Hemenway collection in the United States Army Med-
ical Museum.

Memoirs National Academy of Sciences,
vol. VI, pp. 139-286, LIX plates. Washington, 1893.

Mendieta, Fray Gerónimo de.

Historia eclesiástica Indiana; obra escrita á fines del siglo XVI, . . . la
publica por primera vez Joaquin
Garcia Icazbalceta.—México, 1870.

Mendoza, Antonio de.

— Lo que D. Antonio de Mendoza, virey y gobernador de la Nueva Spaña
y presidente en la nueva audiencia
y chancillería real que en ella resi-
de, demas de lo que por otra instruc-

Mendoza, Antonio de—Continued.

cion se le ha mandado hacer por
mandado de S. M.—Barcelona, 17
Abril, 1535.

Doc. de Indias, XXIII, 423-425.

— Lo que D. Antonio de Mendoza visorey y gobernador de la provincia
de la Nueva Spaña, ha de hacer en
servicio de Dios y de esta república,
demas de lo contenido en sus poderes
y comisiones, por mandado de S. M.—
Barcelona, 25 Abril, 1535.

Doc. de Indias, XXIII, 426-445.

— Lo que don Antonio de Mendoza
virey ó gobernador de la Nueva
Spaña y presidente de la real audiencia, ha de hacer en la dicha tierra,
por mandado de S. M.—Madrid, 14
Julio, 1536.

Doc. de Indias, XXIII, 454-467.

—Carta de D. Antonio de Mendoza á la
emperatriz, participando que vienen
a España Cabeza de Vaca y Francisco
Dorantes, que se escaparon de la armada de Pánfilo de Narvaez, á hacer
relacion de lo que en ella sucedió.—
Méjico, 11 Hebrero 1537.

Doc. de Indias, XIV, 235-236.

— Provision dada por el virey don Antonio de Mendoza al reverendo y
magnífico señor Don Vasco de Quiro-
ga, obispo electo de Mechoacan y
oidor de Méjico, para contar los
vasallos del marqués del Valle, Don
Hernando Cortés.—Méjico, á 30 Noviembre, 1537.

Doc. de Indias, XII, 314-318.

—Carta de D. Antonio de Mendoza,
virey de Nueva España, al Emperador, dándole cuenta de varios asuntos de su gobierno.—De México, 10
Diciembre, 1537.

Doc. de Indias, II, 179-211. B. Smith, *Florida*, 119-139, with facsimile of Mendoza's sig-
nature.

— Instruccion de don Antonio de Mendoza, visorey de Nueva España, (al
Fray Marcos de Niza).

Doc. de Indias, III, 325-328, written previous to December, 1538. There is a French
translation in Ternaux, *Cibola*, 249-253. A
modern English translation is in Bandelier,
Contributions, 109-112.

— Lettere scritte dal illvstrissimo signor don Antonio di Mendozza, vice re
della nuoua Spagna, alla maesta dell'
Imperadore. Delli cauallieri quali
con lor gran danno si sono affaticati
per scoprire il capo della terra ferma
della nuoua Spagna verso tramontana,
il gionger del Vazquez con fra Marco
à san Michiel di Culnacan con com-
missione à quelli regenti di assicurare
& non far piu schiaui gli Indiani.

Ramusio, III, fol. 355 (1556 ed.). There is
a French translation in Ternaux, *Cibola*,
285-290. This appears to be the letter which
Mendoza sent to the king to accompany the
report of Fray Marcos de Niza.

Mendoza, Antonio de—Continued.

— Carta del virey Don Antonio de Mendoza al Emperador.—De Jacona, 17 Abril, 1540.

　Doc. de Indias, II, 356-362. A French translation is in Ternaux, *Cibola*, 290-298. For an English translation, see pp. 547-551 *ante*.

— Instruccion que debia observar el capitan Hernando de Alarcon en la expedicion á la California que iba á emprender de órden del virey D. Antonio de Mendoza.—México, postrero dia del mes de mayo de myll y quinientos y quarenta ó uno.

　B. Smith, *Florida*, 1-6.

— Carta de D. Antonio de Mendoza á Juan de Aguilar, pidiendo se la autorizase para avenirse con los portugueses, sobre la posesion de territorios conquistados . . . para que dello haga relacion á S. A. y á los señores de su consejo.

　Doc. de Indias, III, 506-511. B. Smith, *Florida*, 7-10. "Acerca del descubrimiento de las siete ciudades de Poniente." Circa 1543.

— Carta de Don Antonio de Mendoza virey de la Nueva España, al comendador mayor de Leon, participándole la muerte del adelantado de Guatemala y Honduras, y el estado de otros varios asuntos.—Mexico, 10 marzo, 1542.

　Cartas de Indias, pp. 253-255, and in facsimile.

— Carta del virey Don Antonio de Mendoza, dando cuenta al príncipe Don Felipe de haber hecho el reparto de la tierra de Nueva España, y exponiendo la necesidad que tenia de pasar á Castilla, para tratar verbalmente con S. M. de ciertos negocios de gobernacion y hacienda.—Mexico, 30 octubre, 1548.

　Cartas de Indias, pp. 256-257.

— Carta del virey Don Antonio de Mendoza al Emperador Don Carlos, contestando á un mandato de S. M. relativo al repartimiento de los servicios personales en la Nueva España.—Guastepeque, 10 junio, 1549.

　Cartas de Indies, pp. 258-259.

— Fragmento de la visita hecha á don Antonio de Mendoza. Interrogatorio por el cual han de ser examinados los testigos que presente por su parte don Antonio de Mendoza.—8 Enero, 1547.

　XLIV cargos, 303 paragrafos. Icazbalceta's *Mexico*, II, 72-140.

— See the *Asiento y Capitulaciones con Alvarado* above.

Mindeleff, Cosmos.

Casa grande ruin.

　Thirteenth Annual Report of the Bureau of Ethnology, 1891-92, pp. 295-319.

— Aboriginal remains in Verde valley, Arizona.

　Ibid, pp. 179-261.

14 ETH——39

Mindeleff, Victor.

A study of pueblo architecture: Tusayan and Cibola.

　Eighth Annual Report of the Bureau of Ethnology, 1886-87, pp. 1-228, CXI plates. The text and illustrations of this admirable paper convey a very clear idea of the pueblo dwellings of New Mexico and Arizona, and make it, on this account, of great value to students who have never visited these regions.

Molina, Alonso de.

Aqui comiença vn vocabulario en la lengua Castellana y Mexicana—(Colophon) Mexico, 1555.

　Father Molina prepared a *Vocabulario*, *Arte*, and *Confessionario* in the Mexican languages, which are very valuable as a means of interpreting the native words adopted by the conquistadores. The originals, and the later editions as well, of all three works are of very considerable rarity.

Morgan, Lewis Henry.

Houses and house life of the American aborigines.—Washington, 1881.

　Contributions to North American Ethnology, vol. IV. Houses of the Sedentary Indians of New Mexico, cap. VI-VIII, pp. 132-197.

— On the ruins of a stone pueblo on the Animas river, in New Mexico; with a ground plan.

　Report of the Peabody Museum, XII, Cambridge, 1880, pp. 536-556.

— The seven cities of Cibola.

　North American Review, April, 1869, CVIII, 457-498.

Moses, Bernard.

The Casa de Contratacion of Seville.

　Report of the American Historical Association for 1894, Washington, 1895, pp. 93-123. This paper is a very useful outline of the legal constitution and functions of the Casa de Contratacion, derived for the most part from Capt. John Stevens' English version (London, 1702) of Don Joseph de Veitia Linage's *Norte de la Contratacion de las Indias Occidentales*. (Seville, 1672.)

　There is an admirable account of the form of government adopted by the Spaniards for New Spain, by Professor Moses, in the *Yale Review*, vol. iv, numbers 3 and 4 (November, 1895, and Febuary, 1896).

Mota Padilla, Matias de la.

Historia de la conquista de la provincia de la Nueva-Galicia, escrita en 1742.—Mexico, 1870.

　Published in the *Boletin* of the Sociedad Mexicana de Geografia y Estadistica, and also issued separately with *Noticias Biograficas* by Señor Garcia Icazbalceta, dated Marzo 12 de 1872. It is an extensive work of the greatest value, although there are reasons for fearing that the printed text is not an accurate copy of the original manuscript. Cited as *Mota Padilla*.

Motolinia, Fray Toribio de Benavente ó.

Historia de los Indios de la Nueva España.

　Icazbalceta's *Mexico*, I, pp. 249, with an introduction of 100 pp. by Sr José Fernando Ramirez; in *Doc. de España*, LIII, 297-574; and also printed in Lord Kingsborough's *Antiquities of Mexico*, vol. IX. See note under King.

Motolinia, Fray Toribio de Benavente ó—
Continued.
— Esta es la relación postrera de Sívola,
y de más de cuatrocientas leguas adelante.
A manuscript found among the "Memo-
riales" de Motolinia, now in the archives
of the late Sr Icazbalceta. Printed for the
first time in the present volume. See pages
566-571 *ante*.

Muriel, Domingo.
Fasti Novi Orbis et ordinationum apos-
tolicarum, . . . opera D. Cyriaci
Morelli.—Venetiis, MDCCLXXVI.
See page 23 for a mention of events in 1539-
1542.

Niza, Fray Marcos de.
Relacion del descubrimiento de las siete
ciudades, por el P. Fr. Márcos de
Niza.—2 Setiembre 1539.
Doc. de Indias, III, 325-351. Translated
into Italian by *Ramusio*, III, fol. 356-359
(1556 ed.), and thence into English by *Hakluyt*, III, 366-373 (1600 ed.). A French translation is in Ternaux, *Cibola*, app. I and II,
249-284.

Nordenskiöld, Gustav.
The cliff dwellers of the Mesa Verde,
southwestern Colorado, their pottery
and implements. Translated by D.
Lloyd Morgan.—Stockholm, 1894.
Chapter XIV, "The Pueblo tribes in the
sixteenth century," pp. 144-166, contains a
translation of portions of Castañeda, from
the French version.

Oviedo y Valdés, Gonzalo Fernandez de.
La historia general de las Indias.—
(Colophon) Seuilla, 1535.
Reprinted at Salamanca in 1547, and at
Madrid in 1851, as follows:

—Historia general y natural de las Indias, por el Capitan Gonzalo Fernandez de Oviedo y Valdés, primer cro-
nista del Nuevo Mundo. Publícala la
Real Academia de la Historia, con
las enmiendas y adiciones del autor,
é ilustrada . . por D. José Amador
de los Rios.—Madrid, 1851-1855.
These four volumes form the definitive
edition of Oviedo. They were printed from
the author's manuscript, and include the
fourth volume, which had not hitherto
been printed.

Owens, John G.
Natal ceremonies of the Hopi Indians.
Journal Am. Ethnology and Archæology
(Boston, 1893), II, 163-175.

Pacheco-Cardenas Coleccion.
Coleccion de documentos inéditos rela-
tivos al descubrimiento, conquista, y
colonizacion de las posesiones espa-
ñolas en América y Occeanía, sacados
. . bajo la direccion de D. Joaquin
F. Pacheco y D. Francisco de Cár-
denas.—Madrid, 1864-1884.
In 42 volumes. The title-page varies
much from year to year. There is as yet
no useful index in print. Cited as *Doc. de
Indias*.

Paez, Juan.
Relacion del descubrimiento que hizo
Juan Rodriguez [Cabrillo] navegan-

Paez, Juan—Continued.
do por la contracosta del mar del Sur
al Norte, hecha por Juan Paez.
Doc. de Indias, XIV, 165-191; B. Smith,
Florida, 173-189. Partió 27 Junio 1542.
This report, which was probably written
by the pilot Bartolome Ferrel or Ferrelo,
has been translated in the *Report of the U.
S. Geol. Survey West of the 100th Meridian*,
VII, 293-314. See note on page 412 *ante*.

Peralta. *See* Suarez de Peralta.

Prince, Le Baron Bradford.
Historical sketches of New Mexico from
the earliest records to the American
occupation.—New York and Kansas
City, 1883.
For *Cabeza de Baca, Marcos de Niza*, and
Coronado, see pp. 40-148.

Proceso del Marqués del Valle y Nuño de
Guzman y los adelantados Soto y
Alvarado, sobre el descubrimiento de
la tierra nueva—en Madrid, 3 Marzo,
1540; 10 Junio, 1541.
Doc. de Indias, XV, 300-408. See page 380
ante.

Proctor, Edna Dean.
The song of the ancient people.—Boston 1893.
Contains preface and note by John Fiske
and commentary by F. H. Cushing.

Ptolemy, C.
La Geografia di Clavdio Ptolemeo, con
alcuni comenti & aggiunti fatteui da
Sebastiano munstero, con le tauole
non solamente antiche & moderne
solite di stäparsi, ma altre nuoue.—
In Venetia, M. D. XLVIII.
The maps in this edition of Ptolemy's
Geography for the first time present the
results of Coronado's explorations. See
plate XLI *ante*. The bibliography of Ptolemy has been set forth with great clearness
and in most convenient form by Dr Justin
Winsor in the *Bibliographical Contributions*
of the Harvard College Library, No. 18;
and with greater detail by Mr Wilberforce
Eames, in volume XVI of Sabin's *Dictionary
of American Books*.

Purchas, Samuel.
Pvrchas his pilgrimage. Or relations of
the world and the religions observed
and places discouered . . .—London, 1613.
The eighth book, America, chap. VIII, *Of
Cibola, Tiguez, Quivira, and Noua Albion*,
pp. 648-653. There were two editions of this
work in 1614, one in 1617, and one, the best,
in 1626, forming the fifth volume of the *Pilgrimes*.

— Haklvytvs posthumus or Purchas,
his pilgrimes. Contayning a history
of the world, in sea voyages, &
lande-trauells, by Englishmen &
others . . . In fower parts, each
containing fiue bookes. By Samvel
Pvrchas.—London, 1625.
Part (volume) IV, pp. 1560-1562, gives a
sketch of the discovery of Cibola and Quivira, abridged from Ramusio. The best
guide to the confused bibliography of Purchas is that of Mr Wilberforce Eames, in
vol. XVI of Sabin's *Dictionary of American
Books*.

Putnam, Frederick Ward.
The pueblo ruins and the interior tribes.
Edited by Frederick W. Putnam.
U. S. Geog. Survey West 100th Meridian, VII, Archæology pt. ii, p. 315, Washington, 1879. Appendix (p. 399) contains Albert S. Gatschet's classification into seven linguistic stocks, etc.

Ramusio, Giovanni Battista.
Terzo volvme delle navigationi et viaggi.—In Venetia, MDLVI.
In this, the first edition of the third volume of Ramusio's collection, folios 354–370 contain the narratives which relate to the discoveries in the territory of the present southwestern United States. The volumes of Ramusio have an especial value, because in many cases the editor and translator used the originals of documents which have not since been found by investigators. Ramusio's Italian text furnished one chief reliance of Hakluyt, and of nearly all the collectors and translators who followed him, including, in the present century, Henri Ternaux-Compans. The best guide to the various issues and editions of Ramusio is that of Mr Wilberforce Eames, in Sabin's *Dictionary of American Books.* The most complete single edition of the three volumes is that of 1606.

Recopilacion de leyes de los reynos de las Indias. Mandadas imprimir, y pvblicar por la magestad catolica del rey don Carlos II. Tomo I (–IV).—Madrid, 1681.
New editions were issued in 1756, 1774, and 1791.

Ribas, Andres Perez de.
Historia de los trivmphos de nvestra Santa Fee entre gentes del nueuo Orbe: refierense assimismo las costvmbres, ritos, y supersticiones que vsauan estas gentes; sus puestos, y temples: . . .—Madrid, 1645.
The mass of facts collected into this heavy volume throw much light on the civil as well as the ecclesiastical history of New Spain.

Rudo Ensayo, tentativa de una prevencional descripcion geografica de la provincia de Sonora, . . . compilada así de noticias adquiridas por el colector en sus viajes por casi toda ella, como subministradas por los padres missioneros y practicos de la tierra.—San Augustin de la Florida, 1863.
Edited by Buckingham Smith. An English translation by Eusebio Guitéras is in the *Records of the American Catholic Historical Society,* Philadelphia, June, 1894.

Ruge, Sophus.
Geschichte des Zeitalters der Entdeckungen.—Berlin, 1881.
In *Allgemeine Geschichte,* von Wilhelm Oncken. *Coronado's Feldzug nach Cibola und Quivira,* pp. 415–423. The map on page 417 is one of the best suggestions of Coronado's probable route.

— Die Entdeckungs-Geschichte der Neuen Welt.
In *Hamburgische Festschrift zur Erinnerung an die Entdeckung Amerika's,* Hamburg, 1892. I Band. *Coronado's Zug nach Cibola und Quivira,* pp. 87–89.

Ruge, Sophus—Continued.
— Die Entwickelung der Kartographie von America bis 1570.—Gotha, 1892.
Festschrift zur 400jährigen Feier der Entdeckung Amerikas. Ergänzungsheft no. 106 zu "Petermann's Mitteilungen." An admirable outline of the early history of the geographical unfolding of America.

Salazar, Francisco Cervantes. *See* Cervantes Salazar.

Santisteban, Fray Gerónimo de.
Carta escrita por Fr. Gerónimo de Santisteban á don Antonio Mendoza, virey de Nueva España, relacionando la pérdida de la armada que salió en 1542 para las islas del poniente, al cargo de Ruy Lopez de Villalobos.—De Cochin, de la India del Rey de Portugal. 22 Henero 1547.
Doc. de Indias, XIV, 151–165. See page 412 ante.

Savage, James Woodruff.
The discovery of Nebraska.
Nebraska Historical Society Transactions, I, 180–202. Read before the Society, April 16, 1880. In this paper Judge Savage accepts the statements that Quivira was situated in latitude 40 degrees north as convincing evidence that Coronado's Spaniards explored the territory of the present State of Nebraska. This paper, together with one by the same author on "A visit to Nebraska in 1662" (by Peñalosa), was reprinted by the Government Printing Office (Washington, 1893) for the use of the United States Senate, for what purpose the resolution ordering the reprint does not state. It forms Senate Mis. Doc. No. 14, 53d Congress, 2d session.

Schmidt, Emil.
Vorgeschichte Nordamerikas im Gebiet der Vereinigten Staaten.—Braunschweig, 1894.
Die vorgeschichtlichen Indianer im Südwesten der Vereinigten Staaten, pp. 177–216. Compiled in large part from Nordenskiöld and V. Mindeleff.

Schoolcraft, Henry Rowe.
Historical and statistical information respecting the history, condition, and prospects of the Indian tribes of the United States.—Philadelphia, 1851–1855.
For *Coronado's expedition* see vol. IV, pp. 21–40. Schoolcraft's map of Coronado's route is opposite p. 38.

Shipp, Barnard.
The history of Hernando de Soto and Florida; or, record of the events of fifty-six years, from 1512 to 1568.—Philadelphia, 1881.
For *Coronado,* see pp. 121–132.

Simpson, James Hervey.
Journal of a military reconnaissance from Santa Fé, New Mexico, to the Navajo country.
Senate Ex. Doc. 64, 31st Congress, 1st sess., Washington, 1850, pp. 56–168.

—Coronado's march in search of the "Seven Cities of Cibola," and discussion of their probable location.
Smithsonian Report for 1869, pp. 309–340. Reprinted by the Smithsonian Institution, Washington, 1884. Contains an excellent map of Coronado's route.

Smith, (Thomas) Buckingham.

Coleccion de varios documentos para la historia de la Florida y tierras adyacentes. Tomo I [1516–1794].—Londres (Madrid, 1857).

Only one volume was ever published. Cited as B. Smith's *Florida*. These documents are printed, for the most part, from copies made by Muñoz or by Navarrete. See note to the English translation of Cabeza de Vaca's *Naufragios*, and see also Rudo Ensayo and Soto.

Sosa, Gaspar Castaño de. *See* **Castaño de Sosa.**

Soto, Hernando de.

Asiento y capitulacion hechos por el capitan Hernando de Soto con el Emperador Carlos V para la conquista y poblacion de la provincia de la Florida, y encomienda de la gobernacion de la isla de Cuba.—Valladolid, 20 Abril, 1537.

Doc. de Indias, XV, 354–363. B. Smith, *Florida*, 140–146.

— Narratives of the career of Hernando de Soto in the conquest of Florida, as told by a Knight of Elvas and in a relation by Luys Hernandez de Biedma, factor of the expedition. Translated by Buckingham Smith.—New York, 1866.

Bradford Club series, V.

— Letter of Hernando de Soto [in Florida, to the Justice and Board of Magistrates in Santiago de Cuba. July 9, 1539] and memoir of Hernando de Escalante Fontaneda. Translated from the Spanish by Buckingham Smith.—Washington, 1854.

This is not the place for an extensive list of the sources for the history of de Soto's expedition, and no effort has been made to do more than mention two volumes which have proved useful during the study of the Coronado expedition. The best guide for the student of the travels of de Soto and Narvaez is the critical portions of John Gilmary Shea's chapter in Winsor's *Narrative and Critical History of America*, vol. II, pp. 283–298.

Squier, Ephraim George.

New Mexico and California. The ancient monuments, and the aboriginal, semicivilized nations, . . . with an abstract of the early Spanish explorations and conquests.

American Review, VIII, Nov., 1848, pp. 503–528. Also issued separately.

Stevens, John.

A new dictionary, Spanish and English. . . . Much more copious than any hitherto extant, with . . . proper names, the surnames of families, the geography of Spain and the West Indies.—London, 1726.

Captain John Stevens was especially well read in the literature of the Spanish conquest of America, and his dictionary is often of the utmost value in getting at the older meaning of terms which were employed by the conquistadores in a sense very different from their present use. Captain Stevens translated Herrera and Veitia Linage (see note under Moses), taking very great liberties with the texts.

Stevenson, James,

(Illustrated catalogues of collections obtained from the Indians of New Mexico in 1879, 1880, and 1881.)

Second Annual Report of the Bureau of Ethnology, 1880–81, pp. 307–465; *Third Annual Report*, 1881–82, pp. 511–594.

Stevenson, Matilda Coxe.

The religious life of the Zuñi child.

Fifth Annual Report of the Bureau of Ethnology, 1883–84, pp 539–555.

— The Sia.

Eleventh Annual Report of the Bureau of Ethnology, 1889–90, pp. 9–157.

Suarez de Peralta, Joan.

Tratado del descubrimiento de las Yndias y su conquista, y los ritos . . . de los yndios; y de los virreyes y gobernadores, . . . y del principio que tuvo Françisco Draque para ser declarado enemigo.—Madrid, 1878.

See entry under Zaragoza and note on page 377 *ante*. This very valuable historical treatise was written in the last third of the XVI century.

Tello, Fray Antonio.

Fragmentos de una historia de la Nueva Galicia, escrita hácia 1650, por el Padre Fray Antonio Tello, de la órden de San Francisco.

Icazbalceta's *Mexico*, II, 343–438. Chapters viii–xxxix are all that are known to have survived.

Ternaux-Compans, Henri.

Voyages, relations et mémoires originaux pour servir a l'histoire de la découverte de l'Amérique publiés pour la première fois, en français.—Paris, 1837–1841.

Twenty volumes. Volume IX contains the translation of *Castañeda* and of various other narratives relating to the Coronado expedition. These narratives are referred to under the authors' names in the present list. It is cited as Ternaux's *Cibola*.

Thomas, Cyrus.

Quivira: A suggestion.

Magazine of American History X, New York, Dec., 1883, pp. 490–496.

Tomson, Robert.

The voyage of Robert Tomson marchant, into Noua Hispania in the yeere 1555, with diuers obseruations concerning the state of the countrey: And certaine accidents touching himselfe.

Hakluyt, III, 447–454 (ed. 1600). See note on page 375 *ante*.

Torquemada, Juan de.

Los veynte i vn libros rituales y monarchia Yndiana, con el origen y guerras de los Yndios Occidentales. Compvesto por Fray Ivan de Torquemada, Ministro Prouincial de la orden de S. Françisco en Mexico, en la Nueba España.—Seuilla, 1615.

This work was reprinted at Madrid in 1723 by Barcia. This, the second, is the better edition. The first two volumes contain an invaluable mass of facts concerning

Torquemada, Juan de—Continued.
the natives of New Spain. The comments by the author are, of course, of less significance.

Ulloa, Francisco de.
A relation of the discouery, which in the name of God the fleete of the right noble Fernando Cortez Marques of the Vally, made with three ships; the one called Santa Agueda of 120. tunnes, the other the Trinitie of 35. tunnes, and the thirde S. Thomas of the burthen of 20. tunnes. Of which fleete was captaine the right worshipfull knight Francis de Vlloa borne in the citie of Merida.
Hakluyt, III, 397–424 (ed. 1600). Translated from Ramusio, III, fol. 339–354 (ed. 1556).

— *See* **Alarcon.**

Vetancurt, Augustin de.
Teatro Mexicano descripcion breve de los svcessos exemplares, historicos, politicos, militares y religiosos del nuevo mundo Occidental de las Indias.—México, 1698.

— Menologio Franciscano de los Varones mas señalados, que con sus vidas exemplares . . . ilustraron la Provincia de el Santo Evangelio de Mexico.
This work forms a part of the second volume of the Teatro Mexicano.

Villagra, Gaspar de.
Historia de la Nveva Mexico.—Alcala, 1610.

Villalobos, Ruy Lopez de. *See* **Santisteban, Fray Gerónimo de.**

Ware, Eugene F.
Coronado's march.
Agora, Lawrence, Kansas, Nov., 1895 [not completed.] A translation of Castañeda's narrative from the French of Ternaux.

Whipple, A. W., *et al.*
Report upon the Indian tribes [of Arizona and New Mexico].
Pacific Railroad Reports, vol. III, pt. 3, Washington, 1856.

Winship, George Parker.
A list of titles of documents relating to America, in volumes I–CX of the Coleccion de documentos inéditos para la historia de España.
Bulletin of the Boston Public Library, October, 1894. Reprinted, 60 copies.

— The Coronado Expedition, 1540–1542.
Fourteenth Annual Report Bureau of Ethnology, Washington, 1896. Contains the Spanish text of Castañeda, and translations of the original narratives.

Winship, George Parker—Continued.
— Why Coronado went to New Mexico in 1540.
Papers of American Historical Association, 1894, Washington, 1895, pp. 83–92.

— New Mexico in 1540.
Boston Transcript. Oct. 14, 1893. A translation of the *Relacion de lo que* . . . *Alvarado y Padilla descubrieron.*

— Coronado's journey to New Mexico and the great plains. 1540–1542.
American History Leaflet, No. 13, New York, 1894. Contains a translation of the *Relacion del Suceso*, and of Coronado's *Letter to Mendoza*, 20 October, 1541.

Winsor, Justin.
Narrative and critical history of America, edited by Justin Winsor (8 volumes).—Boston, 1889.
Besides Professor Haynes' chapter in volume II, pp. 473–503 (see entry under Haynes), the same volume contains chapters by Dr Winsor on *Discoveries on the Pacific Coast of North America*, pp. 431–472; by Clements R. Markham on *Pizarro and the Conquest and Settlement of Peru and Chile*, pp. 505–573, and by John G. Shea on *Ancient Florida*, pp. 231–298. The fact that special investigators in minute fields of historical study have found omissions and errors in this encyclopedic work only serves to emphasize the value of the labors of Dr Winsor. There is hardly a subject of study in American history in which the student will not, of necessity, begin his work by consulting the critical and bibliographical portions of Winsor's *America*.

Wytfliet, Cornelius.
Descriptionis Ptolemaicæ Avgmentvm, siue Occidentis Notitia Breui commentario illustrata Studio et opera Cornely Wytfliet Louaniensis.—Lovanii, M.D.XCVII.
For *Coronado*, see p. 170, or p. 91 of the French translation of 1611. Qvivira et Anian. See plates LI–LIII *ante*.

Zamacois, Niceto de.
Historia de Méjico desde sus tiempos mas remotos.—Méjico, 1878–1888.
Nineteen volumes. For the chronicl of events in New Spain during the years 1 35–1546, see vol. IV, 592–715.

Zaragoza, Justo.
Noticias históricas de la Nueva España.—Madrid, 1878.
In this volume Señor Zaragoza has added much to the inherent value of the Tratado of Suarez de Peralta (see entry above) by his ample and scholarly notes, and by a very useful "Indice geográfico, biográfico, y de palabras Americanas." These indices, within their inevitable limitations, contain a great deal of information for which the student would hardly know where else to look. This is equally true of the indices to the *Cartas de Indias*, for the excellence of which Señor Zaragoza was largely responsible.